Paul S. Goodman
and Associates

Change in Organizations

□ □ □ □ □ □ □ □ □ □ □ □ □ □ □ □ □

New Perspectives on Theory,
Research, and Practice

Jossey-Bass Publishers
San Francisco • Washington • London • 1982

CHANGE IN ORGANIZATIONS
New Perspectives on Theory, Research, and Practice
    by Paul S. Goodman and Associates

Copyright © 1982 by: Jossey-Bass Inc., Publishers
                     433 California Street
                     San Francisco, California 94104

                    &

                    Jossey-Bass Limited
                    28 Banner Street
                    London EC1Y 8QE

Library of Congress Cataloging in Publication Data

Goodman, Paul S.
    Change in organizations.

    Includes bibliographries and index.
        1. Organization—Addresses, essays, lectures.
    2. Organizational change—Addresses, essays, lectures.
    I. Title.
    HM131.G585   1982   302.3'5   82-48069
    ISBN 0-87589-547-6

Manufactured in the United States of America

The paper in this book meets the guidelines for
permanence and durability of the Committee on
Production Guidelines for Book Longevity of the
Council on Library Resources.

JACKET DESIGN BY WILLI BAUM

FIRST EDITION

The Jossey-Bass
Social and Behavioral Science Series

Preface

Creating effective change in organizations is one of the most difficult and challenging problems faced by organizational theorists,
organization development or change specialists, and managers. The
need to understand more about the process of change will continue
to increase. Organizations are constantly challenged by new technologies, new government policies, international competition, and
new demands to improve productivity. To meet these challenges
organizations must adapt and change.

This book presents an array of new theoretical insights regarding change by some of the top scholars in the organizational
field. The goal of the book is to change our thinking about change.
It is hoped that readers will be captured by some of the chapters in
this volume and that new perspectives on change will be generated.

The book opens with a status report on the literature on
planned organizational change and the literature on organizational

adaptation. This review identifies major themes and gaps in the literature on change and sets the stage for the chapters that follow. Chapter Two is an extension of Argyris's work on single- and double-loop learning. The chapter focuses on why organizations have difficulty in moving toward double-loop learning and includes some strategies for change. Staw, in the third chapter, examines change or adaptability by examining counterforces to change. Specifically, Staw examines escalation and commitment as processes that inhibit change. Chapter Four, by Alderfer, moves the discussion on change from the individual level to the intergroup level. Alderfer examines problems in changing white males' attitudes and beliefs regarding race relations. His chapter closes with a series of propositions about creating change in race relations.

Cole, in Chapter Five, focuses on diffusion. He provides an exciting analysis of the differential diffusion of various forms of participatory work structures in Japan, Sweden, and the United States. Chapter Six concerns the process of institutionalization, or why some programs for change persist while others do not. In this chapter, Goodman and Dean identify the critical factors for maintaining change over time. In Chapter Seven, Lawler presents a framework for creating high involvement work systems. His analysis examines the relationships among different design options, motivation, individual performance capability, coordination, control, and organizational effectiveness.

Smith, in Chapter Eight, and Weick, in Chapter Nine, focus on some of the basic theoretical issues about change. Smith argues that we are not ready to develop a theory on change until we tackle some of the unresolved epistemological problems latent in most discussions of change. Weick examines the meaning of change in the context of loosely coupled systems. The final chapter, by Robert Kahn, identifies the major themes in this volume. His integrative discussion closes by identifying some new directions for change.

As this brief description indicates, this book is interdisciplinary in nature and should be of interest to psychologists, sociologists, political scientists, and others concerned with creating change in organizations. While topics such as institutionalization and diffusion should be of interest to most social scientists, the book as a whole was not developed with any particular organization or discipline in mind. Our focus was to develop concepts of change that would be important to people in the private sector, in the public sector, in production organizations, health care organizations, educational institutions, and so on. Topics such as changing race relations or developing high involvement systems are relevant in any type of organization. In addition, while the book is a collection of new theoretical approaches to change, many of the chapters (especially those on race relations, developing high involvement systems, making change programs last, and diffusion) are written to be useful for practitioners.

The unique feature of the book is the caliber of the contributors. Clayton Alderfer, Chris Argyris, Robert Cole, Robert Kahn, Edward Lawler, Kenwyn Smith, Barry Staw, and Karl Weick have produced chapters that will make significant contributions to the field. Their effort and cooperation in producing and revising their contributions made this book possible.

It is important for the reader to understand the process by which the book was created. The "contract" with the contributors called for them to generate original chapters on change. Some negotiations took place to identify acceptable topics. After the initial draft was completed, all the contributors met at Carnegie-Mellon for an intensive workshop. The purpose of the workshop was to generate new ideas on each chapter. A tape of the workshop discussion was given to each contributor to use in revising his chapter.

The intellectual effectiveness of the workshop format in generating new ideas was based on the work of the major contributors and a group of Carnegie-Mellon faculty who served as "provocateurs" for the discussion of the chapters. The CMU faculty included Linda Argote, Robert Atkin, Pat Crecine, Richard Cyert, Mark Fichman, Charles Kiesler, Lance Kurke, and Lee Sproull. They made a significant contribution to this book. I also want to acknowledge the important work by Lance Kurke and James Dean, who coauthored, respectively, Chapters One and Six with me.

The major support for this endeavor came from the Office of Naval Research (ONR contract #N000 14-79-C-0167). I greatly appreciate the interest and support of David Stonner, our project officer. Additional funds were provided by Dean Kaplan of the

Graduate School of Industrial Administration, Carnegie-Mellon University.

Virginia Jones, who helped arrange the workshop, and Jennifer Gray, who helped with the typing and coordination of the final chapters, also made important contributions to the book.

The book is dedicated to my parents and family.

Pittsburgh, Pennsylvania   Paul S. Goodman
September 1982

Contents

The Authors

□ □ □ □ □ □ □ □ □ □ □ □ □ □ □ □ □ □

PAUL S. GOODMAN is a professor of industrial administration and psychology at the Graduate School of Industrial Administration, Carnegie-Mellon University, Pittsburgh. Previously he was on the faculty at the Graduate School of Business at the University of Chicago and was a visiting professor at Cornell University. He received his bachelor's degree in economics from Trinity College, Hartford, Connecticut (1959), his master's degree from Dartmouth College (1961), and his Ph.D. degree in organizational psychology from Cornell University (1966).

Goodman's main professional interests are in research on work motivation and attitudes, organizational design, productivity, and organizational effectiveness. Some of this research has concerned the effects of pay inequity on performance, motivation of scientists and engineers, designing organizations to retain disadvantaged workers, and the effects of new forms of work organizations on organizational effectiveness. His research has been published in many professional journals and books, including the *Journal of Applied Psychology, Organizational Behavior and Human Performance*, and *Human Relations.*

Goodman is on the editorial board of *Organizational Behavior and Human Performance* and also serves in a consulting capacity for private industry and the government. His current research includes a large-scale study on group productivity and absenteeism, new forms of work organization, the impact of robotics on the work force, and organizational effectiveness.

CLAYTON P. ALDERFER is professor of organizational behavior and associate dean for professional studies, School of Organization and Management, Yale University.

CHRIS ARGYRIS is James Bryant Conant Professor of Education and Organizational Behavior, Graduate School of Education, Harvard University.

ROBERT E. COLE is professor of sociology and director of the Center for Japanese Studies, University of Michigan.

JAMES W. DEAN JR., is assistant professor of organizational behavior, College of Business Administration, Pennsylvania State University.

ROBERT L. KAHN is professor of psychology and medical care organization, and program director of the Institute for Social Research, University of Michigan.

LANCE B. KURKE is assistant professor of industrial administration, Graduate School of industrial administration, Carnegie-Mellon University.

EDWARD E. LAWLER III is professor and director for the Center for Effective Organizations, Graduate School of Business Administration, University of Southern California.

KENWYN K. SMITH is assistant professor of psychology, Department of Psychology, University of Maryland.

BARRY M. STAW is professor of organizational behavior and industrial relations, School of Business Administration, University of California, Berkeley.

KARL E. WEICK is Nicholas H. Noyes Professor of Organizational Behavior, Graduate School of Business and Public Administration, Cornell University.

Change in Organizations

New Perspectives on Theory,
Research, and Practice

◨ ◨ ◨ ◨ ◨ ◨ ◨ 1

Studies of Change in Organizations: A Status Report

◨ ◨ ◨ ◨ ◨ ◨ ◨ ◨ ◨ ◨ ◨ ◨ ◨ ◨ ◨ ◨ ◨ ◨

Paul S. Goodman
Lance B. Kurke

This book is a collection of essays on change. Its purpose is to sharpen our conceptualizations of change. The audience is anyone concerned with developing his or her theoretical view of change. At the conclusion there is no neatly drawn theory of change. We do not see that the current state of knowledge as represented in the literature supports such an endeavor. Nor is it clear that such a theory could be constructed in the near future. Neither is the book a comprehensive statement about change. Although this first chapter provides a brief status report on the change literature, the principal essays only sample certain domains of change. A casual reflection on change should indicate that it encompasses almost all our concepts in the organizational behavior literature. Think about leadership motivation, organizational environment, and roles. It is impossible to think about these and other concepts without inquiring about change. Our strategy is not to be comprehensive but to focus on some central concepts or processes about change that may be generalizable over different topic areas.

We selected the book title because it focuses attention on change in organizations rather than solely on changing organizations. We are interested in change at the individual, group, organization, or organizational-environment interface, but not in particular organizations such as schools, businesses, or governments. Indeed, most of the essays are not specific to any type of organization.

The rationale for this venture is straightforward. First, we have already argued that the concept of change pervades all our intellectual endeavors. Second, the state of the literature does not provide some clear theoretical perspectives that might help us organize our thinking on change. Third, in the last eight to ten years there has been a proliferation of attempts to bring about large-scale system changes, and these activities are likely to continue.

We thus need to think about change and to change our thinking about change. It is hoped that readers will be sufficiently intrigued by the ideas presented in this volume to generate new perspectives on change.

This chapter sets the stage. First we present a brief status report on the literature on change in organizations. We discuss a way to think about the literature and highlight a set of themes. The chapter concludes with an introduction to the essays.

A Status Report

A brief review of the literature about change in organizations should prepare you for the major essays. Let us start with a definition of change. There are many meanings for the word: to make change, to put on fresh clothes, to shift (from one side to another), to exchange, to replace, to transfer, to transform. The meaning common to all these definitions is to make different. So in the context of change in organizations, the object of the change process—that is, what is to be made different—could be attitudes, beliefs and behaviors of individuals, interaction patterns of roles or groups, organizations, and so on. Change is the alteration of one state to another.

The source, type, or level of change is not, and should not be, part of the definition. The notion of change as making something different does not imply the source, type, or level of that change. The source could be internal (to the individual) or external. The reason for keeping the definition general is that many people write about changing in organizations as planned change. Change, they imagine, comes about when an agent introduces techniques in some intentional manner to modify or alter the organization or its members or both. The view of change is limiting because it does not reflect that changes in an organizational context occur randomly, through evolutionary processes, via adaptation and other mechanisms. We want a general definition of change—change as making something different—and we want to focus that definition in an organizational context. Our attention may be on the individual, group, organization, or organizational-environmental interfaces.

Few people talk about the meanings of change (for an exception, see Zaltman and Duncan, 1977). Writers on change assume that we understand the concept, at least at some definitional level. That assumption may not be true and should be explored.

To review the vast area of change in organizations is a complicated task. We have therefore adopted a set of conventions in order to make some sense of the literature.

1. A method of organizing. We need to find some way to organize the literature. At the most general level we sorted the literature into *planned organizational change* and *adaptation*. Some initial sort was necessary for our own search and writing activities. At the same time we wanted the distinctions general enough to cast a broad net.

   There are precedents for organizing literatures in such broad ways. In the economic and political science literatures are the metaphors of state as manager and state as reactor (Padgett, 1981). In the life sciences is a dichotomy between nature and nurture. In organization theory there is a debate over the significance of environmental forces as opposed to managerial action. Our method of organizing the change literature parallels this general distinction.

Planned organizational change refers to a set of activities and processes designed to change individuals, groups, and organization structure and processes. The key word is "planned." There is some a priori theory and methods that are brought to bear on some target (individual attitudes, organizational processes) in order to reach some goal (humanization of the work place, organizational efficiency). The term "organizational development" is often used instead of planned organizational change. Planned organizational change emphasizes managerial choice.

Adaptation concerns modification of an organization or its parts to fit or to be adjusted with its environment. Adaptive process may include "selecting environments, monitoring and predicting change . . . learning and buffering fluctuation in the flow of resources across organizational boundaries" (Hedberg, Nystrom, and Starbuck, 1976, p. 46). "Adaptational" emphasizes externally induced changes.

The distinction between planned organizational change and adaptation is arbitrary. The two concepts are not independent. Planned organizational change can increase adaptability, and adaptability can lead to planned organizational change.

Planned organizational change deals with the basis of change; adaptation deals with the conditions or sources of change. Planned organizational change focuses primarily on change within the organization, but the adaptation literature focuses primarily on populations of organizations and on organization-environment interfaces, and on changes within an organization that are environmentally dictated. The planned organizational literature emphasizes the process of actually creating change rather than writing about the processes of change (adaptation literature). The planned organizational change literature is devoted to methods and techniques, but the adaptation literature is devoted to theorizing about the change processes or outcomes.

2.   Themes. The second convention for our review was to organize the literature by themes, that is, to highlight the basic issues and problems about change and how people think about them. Where appropriate, we will reference some of the empirical findings relevant to the basic themes. Unfortunately, the empir-

ical studies on change are not cumulative or of sufficient quality to provide some nice summary of what we know. Rather, our focus will be on the basic themes in the literatures on planned organizational change and adaptation. When possible, changes or new emphases on themes will be noted.

3. Time frame. Our review focuses mainly on materials published since 1977. Prior review pieces (Alderfer, 1976; Friedlander and Brown, 1974) were examined to provide continuity to our analysis.

Planned Organizational Change

A Review of Reviews. Friedlander and Brown (1974) provide a useful review of the organizational development literature through the 1973-74 period. Organizational development (OD) for these writers refers to a method for facilitating change and development in people, in technology, and in organizational processes and structure (Friedlander and Brown, p. 314). They focus primarily on technostructural approaches (job design, job enlargement, and so on) and human process approaches (survey feedback, group development, interventions). The value of the review is that Friedlander and Brown focus on a set of OD methods and provide the reader with a summary of the empirical knowledge about these methods. For example, they note that "human process approaches have a number of positive effects on attitudes. . . . There is little evidence, however, that organizational processes actually change or that performance or effectiveness is increased" (p. 334). They also identify two other emerging themes in the literature: what characterizes successful versus unsuccessful interventions and how multiple interventions of a total system are different from single interventions. At the time of the review there was only scattered evidence on these two themes. There is more attention given to these topics in the current literature (that published in the last five years).

Alderfer (1977) provides an update of the Friedlander-Brown review. His review is organized around trends in OD practice and OD research. In the area of practice, Alderfer indicates the following: (1) The practice of OD is no longer focused solely on business organizations—schools, governments, health organizations were more involved in OD. (2) New types of survey feedback techniques and new structural approaches, such as the collateral organization, have emerged. (3) There is a greater focus on organizational-environmental interfaces. (Much of the literature in the Friedlander-Brown review focuses on within-organizational change.) (4) In terms of research, Alderfer sees more sophistication in the designs used to evaluate organizational interventions. Also, new instruments designed to capture some of the changing process and outcome variables have been developed. (5) Alderfer also notes the emergence of more sophisticated theories on change. Argyris and Schön (1978) and Alderfer (1976) illustrate some new theoretical developments occurring during this period.

White and Mitchell completed another review in 1976. Their strategy was first to develop a classification system for coding OD-type studies and then to analyze the literature following this system. They used three facets: (1) the recipient of change (individual, group), (2) the level of expected change (conceptual, structural), and (3) relationships involved in change (intrapersonal, interpersonal). Applying this facet scheme to the literature from 1964 to 1974, they report that most OD programs attempt to change attitudes or behavior of either the individual or his or her immediate subgroup and focus the change on factors concerning self-relationships or relationships to peers (White and Mitchell, 1976, p. 65). White and Mitchell also review the quality of OD research. Their basic findings are that most of it takes place in the field. Most of the changes are represented in percentages without statistical comparisons. The majority of data is collected from reports by participation of researchers who were committed to the success of the intervention.

This review of reviews is intended to give the reader a picture of the literature on planned organizational change in the early and mid 1970s. There are some obvious central themes—methods or techniques of change and empirical assessment of change. Other themes, such as the role of values in OD interventions, also appear. In the Alderfer (1976) review we get some feeling about movements in these themes. That is, methods become more elaborate. The target population moves to include nonbusiness organizations, and some greater sophistication on the level of theory and measurement is underway.

Five Major Current Themes. As noted, our review of planned organizational change focused mainly on the literature since 1977. We have tried to draw a fairly representative sample of journal articles and books. Although our search was not exhaustive, it includes enough materials to enable us to trace the major themes.

One major theme is *intervention methods.* Interest in thinking about organizational change in terms of intervention methods and strategies still persists. In one of the most significant review books in our field (Katz and Kahn, 1978), organizational change is discussed in terms of alternative approaches (methods) to change at different levels of analysis—individual, group, and organizational. We thought it would be interesting to review some good "textbooks" on organizational change (Beer, 1980; Huse, 1980) to see what people are learning about changes. Again, intervention methods represent the primary way to organize the current state of knowledge. Common to all these accounts are concern with how to categorize methods and a discussion of method characteristics. Also, a similar set of methods (or approaches)—counseling, survey feedback, sociotechnical—reappears in most of these discussions. Peters (1978) also examines methods of change, but differs by arguing that managers have a set of mundane tools that are proposed as alternatives to more traditional OD methods. The mundane tools are symbols, patterns, and settings that are part of the daily work activities. Peters examines how the manipulation of these daily activities as symbols can create change in organizations.

Within the focus on methods of change, we found a set of studies that reports on the effectiveness of these methods. Porras and Berg (1978) examine the impact of a set of OD methods that includes laboratory training, the managerial grid, and survey feedback. Their strategy was to review the literature from 1959 to 1975 and determine the impact of these approaches on outcome variables. They report that overall satisfaction changed 38 percent of the time, with greater changes appearing in satisfaction with the company, security, and pay than with the job itself. OD methods appear to affect both process variables (decision making) and outcome variables (performance).

When examining the effectiveness of different OD approaches, Porras and Berg indicate that focusing on process *and* on outcome variables (rather than on one of them) may be more effective, but the differences they report across methods are probably not significantly different. In other findings they report that the number of interventions and the length of exposure are related to the degree of positive change. Although there are some interesting ideas in this paper, it is based on a review of studies that were not tightly controlled empirical investigations. Also, the authors use bivariate design to examine a multivariate problem. (For other studies in this area see Quinn, 1978.)

Another class of empirical studies examines the impact of a particular intervention method. In most cases we did not find a coherent set of good empirical studies that provides a cumulative body of knowledge about these intervention methods. We were more apt to find isolated studies.

Nadler, Mirvis, and Cammann (1976) examine the impact of an elaborate *survey feedback* system on the attitudes and performance of employees in branches of a bank. After describing the feedback system and its implementation, they report that the degree of involvement of the different branches in the use of survey feedback differently influenced the effects of that method on attitudes and performance. Employees in branches involved in a high use of feedback show more positive changes in some satisfaction and performance indicators, although the differences are small.

Rosen and Primps (1981) provide the best review of research concerning the effects of a *compressed workweek* (such as four days and forty hours). They identify a framework for tracing through the effect of compressed workweeks and then carefully examine fourteen studies. They report that attitudes toward the compressed workweek are favorable, with some generalizations to job attitudes (p. 61). The effect of the compressed workweek on performance is ambiguous. Schein (1969) examines the impact on productivity of a four-month flexible working-hour experiment on five production units. The results are mixed across the different groups, with no clear trend supporting evidence of a productivity increase. This finding is not surprising in that flextime programs will probably affect the decision to participate more than the decision to produce.

The literature on *job redesign* and worker attitudes has been more comprehensive and cumulative. Hackman and Oldham (1977) have provided much of the direction. Many of the studies point to a positive relationship between increasing job variety, autonomy, and work satisfaction and involvement. Hackman, Pearce, and Wolfe (1978) examine the effect of changes in clerical jobs on employee attitudes and work behaviors. The results indicate that job changes affect general satisfaction, growth satisfaction, and internal motivation. Results on absenteeism and performance are less clear, but seem to be moderated by individual differences. The effects of individual differences on job design have been discussed by White (1978) and O'Connor, Rudolf, and Peters (1980). Other studies (Hackman and Frank, 1977; Hall and others, 1978) point to the complexities of achieving positive work outcomes from job redesign.

Walton (1977) and Goodman (1979) report on the introduction of *autonomous work groups* in two organizational settings. Both reports indicate that the initial impact of this intervention technology was to increase positive worker attitudes and performance. For example, Goodman (1979) reports on the introduction of autonomous work groups in coal mining crews. A longitudinal design indicates more positive attitudes about work and a slight positive increase in performance over a three-year period.

To summarize, first, cataloguing intervention methods is still a dominant way of thinking about planned change. Second, both in the empirical and nonempirical writings, there is a movement toward structural interventions and away from process interventions, such as laboratory training. Third, the empirical literature is still wanting. Friedlander and Brown (1974) provide a nice status report on what we know about certain methods. We tried to search the literature since 1977 to provide an update. Our rule was to focus on studies that had some reasonable empirical controls. In general we did not find a coherent, cumulative literature.

A second major theme is *large-scale multiple system interventions*. Here a combination of intervention methods is introduced, often on a total-system basis. Although the idea of multiple system interventions appears in some of our earlier reviews (Friedlander and Brown, 1974), the emphasis has clearly changed since 1977. There is much more attention given to the introduction of coherent sets of intervention methods on a total-system basis.

The interest in quality of working life (QWL) probably has had the greatest influence on this theme or trend. Since the mid 1970s, there has been a series of large-scale experimental programs designed to increase QWL. These have occurred in union and non-union situations, in new plant and old plant situations, and in the private and public sectors. The strong interest in QWL provided a legitimating force for experimenting with new organizational forms. Although it is not within the scope of this chapter to detail QWL activities, a modal effort would have begun with some union management agreement to improve QWL. An outside consultant would have been hired. In a series of QWL projects, an independent evaluation team would have been put in place. Funding may or may not have come from government or foundation sources. The changes introduced would have included labor-management problem-solving groups, greater delegation of authority of work force, more communication channels between labor and management, new evaluation systems, job redesign, and new pay systems.

Although it is difficult to summarize the results of these projects, there seem to be positive effects on work attitudes, lower absenteeism, positive effects of safety, some mixed results on productivity (some improvements, some no change, none with declines), and positive effects on job skills (Goodman, 1979; Goodman and Lawler, 1977; Macy, Ledford, and Lawler, 1982; Macy and Nurick, 1982). There also has been a set of persistent problems across all these interventions. There has been fairly common reporting of increased stress for foremen and middle management, problems of managing individual differences, and problems in maintaining these interventions over time (Goodman and Lawler, 1977).

The focus on QWL change activities has not been limited to the organization as a unit of analysis. Community or labor-management area QWL programs have been initiated. The Jamestown area labor-management project is probably the best example. In these projects it would be common to find area labor-management committees concerned with the economic and QWL issues of the community and corollary labor-management committees at the firm level. The emergence of statewide QWL organizations (for example, in Michigan) illustrates an attempt to create change by diffusion. In a larger social unit, the state, as well as the area organizations, provides a communication mechanism among those already possessing and those planning to initiate QWL activities. This linking of firm, area, and state into a common effort provides an important method for legitimation, diffusion, and maintaining change.

There were other large-scale multiple system interventions that did not emanate from the QWL tradition. One of the best documented is a study by Beyer and Trice (1978) on the introduction of EEO and alcoholism programs in government agencies. These researchers begin with a general framework of change built around (1) implementation process—diffusion, receptivity, and use; (2) actors—supervisors, facilitators, directors; and (3) constraints—community, union, and organizational structure. The empirical work then examines characteristics of the actors with respect to the processes. For example, supervisors who implemented the two policies were older, had longer length of service, were more receptive to change in general, and had greater familiarity with the policies (Beyer and Trice, 1978, p. 260). Directors who implemented both policies had higher job involvement, longer length of service, higher job status, and believed that performance was important for career advancement. Concerning constraints, Beyer and Trice (1978) discuss how the community and the role of the union also influence implementation. These results are only isolated findings from a complex network of relationships. We cite this book because it examines the introduction of two different but related policies using multiple intervention in a very complex system. The empirical documentation is good and the book deserves a close reading. There is a related and broader literature on large-scale implementation of social programs in public organizations (Scheirer, 1981; Williams and others, 1982).

To summarize, the idea of large-scale multiple system intervention has been an important trend in planned organizational change efforts. The idea of multiple interventions is not new, but the scale on which it has been implemented over the last five to eight years *is* new. This theme is important because (1) it represents a set of activities in which there is a strong emphasis on devising innovative forms of work organization, (2) it generated a set of well-documented analyses of planned organizational changes with sufficient similarity to permit identification of uniformities as to strategies and results, and (3) it highlighted the role of linking firm, community, state, and national systems in diffusing and sustaining change.

A third major theme is *assessment of change.* One consequence of large-scale multiple system interventions has been a noticeable development in the technology for assessing planned organizational change. Since about 1976, there has been funding to develop technology for organizational assessment. Researchers at the Institute for Social Research and their associates have been prime movers in this development. Lawler, Nadler, and Cammann (1980), Seashore, Lawler, Mirvis, and Cammann (1982), and Goodman (1979) summarize this work.

A number of different types of output can be categorized from this research:

1. Models of assessment. There have been some more refined frameworks for assessment (Nadler and Tushman, 1980; Van de Ven and Morgan, 1980). There has also been more concern with sharpening our understanding of the concept of effectiveness in change efforts (Carnall, 1980; Goodman and Pennings, 1980). The Goodman-Pennings paper identifies some approaches for defining the domain of effectiveness, selecting constituencies, identifying boundaries, and identifying the appropriate time frames.

2. Instrumentation. New standardized measures have been developed to assess organizational instrumentation. The Michigan Organizational Assessment package is probably the most extensive. It contains a list that covers a wide range of traditional attitude items (for example, boss and work group) and a newer set of items to describe the organization (for example, technology and structure) and the union. This package could be used in a survey or interview format. Other instrument procedures have been developed for observing group behavior (Goodman and Conlon, 1982), networks (Tichy, Tuchman, and Fombrun, 1980), measuring job characteristics (Seashore, Lawler, Mirvis, and Cammann, 1982), organizational episodes (Seashore, Lawler, Mirvis, and Cammann, 1982), and so on.

3. Designs. The use of more complicated time series designs characterizes the current assessment work. Also, more attention has been given to the use of control groups to better estimate internal validity (Goodman, 1979). This is in contrast to the earlier empirical work on planned organizational change, which used single observations after the experimental change (White and Mitchell, 1976).

4. Analytical procedures. There has been increasing and more sophisticated use of analytical and statistical procedures. Much of the earlier work analyzed percentage changes without any statistical procedures (White and Mitchell, 1976). Now we find better model specification and testing in attitude areas (Goodman, 1979). Analytical and statistical models for assessing productivity are presented by Epple, Goodman, and Fidler (1982). Cost-benefit analysis procedures can be found in Macy and Mirvis (1976) and Goodman (1979).

5. Other. There are other evaluation issues that we have not enumerated. Golembiewski, Billingsley, and Yeager (1976) propose that there are three types of change—Alpha, Beta, and Gamma—and that different designs and methodologies fit these different types of changes. Alpha change, for example, refers to changes in degree within a state. Beta change is similar, except that measurement continuum associated with a state has been recalibrated. Gamma change refers to changes of the state. Some controversies about measuring change that have been raised by these distinctions are found in Lindell and Drexler (1979) and Golembiewski and Billingsley (1980).

A much different perspective on assessing organizational change is found in Staw (1977). He proposes some innovative ideas on how the assessment methods can become an integral part of the changing organization.

To summarize, the key idea in this theme is that a large set of evaluation technologies has been developed. Although we do not have a complete package, there are enough models, procedures, and methods to document most change processes.

A fourth major theme is *failure,* specifically, the documentation of failures of planned organizational change. Mirvis and Berg's

Failures in Organization Development and Change (1977) is a compilation of cases and essays. (Researchers mentioned in this paragraph are contributors to this work.) Some of the cases point to problems in initial entry that lead to failure. D. N. Berg reports that the perceived importance of the change effort, the degree to which the organization is loosely coupled, and the perceptions that the change agent supports one of the conflicting groups all bear on the success of change. R. Lewicki and C. Alderfer explore a change agent's entry problem in a situation of labor-management conflict and how this affects change. W. Crockett's chapter outlines the problems in introducing and maintaining the multiple intervention change program in the State Department. The role of sponsorship, conflicting values, and lack of commitment are critical issues in this change activity. L. Frank and R. Hackman examine the failure of a job enrichment program. Our intent is not to summarize each chapter of this book but rather to indicate that the book is a valuable resource for the examination of failures in organizational change. The reader can abstract from each case a list of factors that are related to failure.

Other published work on the lack of significant changes in planned organizational programs is available. Billings, Klimoski, and Breaugh (1977) examine the change in technology from batch to mass production in a hospital dietary department. The paper is very good both in theoretically identifying potential effects and in carefully analyzing the results using a time series design. An analysis of the major dependent variables, such as job importance, task variety, task interdependence, and closeness of supervision, did not support the hypothesized effects of technological change. One of the explanations for the lack of effects after the change was in place was that employees anticipated many of the changes before the new technology was introduced.

Hall and others (1978) examine the effect of top-down departmental and job change on employee behavior and attitude using a longitudinal design. They report that "contrary to the findings of a sizeable number of correlational studies, but in agreement with four other longitudinal studies, changes in job characteristics were not related to changes in perceived effort, performance, or satisfaction. Job changes were . . . related to job involvement" (p. 62).

Other findings indicate negative outcomes associated with departmental changes. For example, feelings of psychological success were lower in departments that initiated "positive" (job design) or "negative" changes (greater controls) than in departments that experienced no change. Hall and his associates attribute the departmental effects to their top-down (versus participatory) nature.

Walton's (1978) report on the famous Topeka pet food experiment is another example of research in this area. His historical analysis ends with that organizational change in decline. A number of factors explain the decline. There was an "absence of potent corrective devices, of a capacity for self-renewal" (p. 46). Some of the initial sponsors of the project had left the plant. No new challenges existed that might have stimulated renewal activities. A nearby plant went on line without many of the new work structures introduced in the original Topeka plant. Because of this failure to diffuse the new work structure to the new plant, a mechanism that might have legitimated and supported the activities in the original plant was lost. Other accounts of problems in introducing change can be found in Blumberg (1977) and Firestone (1977).

To summarize, the documentation of failures is an important theme in planned change. It focuses our attention on the problem of maintaining change and requires some sharpening of our theoretical understanding of change process. That is, it forces us to account in some theoretical way for failure to bring out planned organizational change.

A fifth major theme in the literature is the *level of theorizing*. We see three trends. The first is that general frameworks have always characterized the literature on change (Lewin, 1951; Schein, 1969). Current work on change continues this broad-systems theoretical orientation (Beer, 1980; Huse, 1980). Nadler (1981) proposes a congruence model of change organized around inputs, transformation processes, and outputs. Inputs are the environmental resources and history; transformation refers to the tasks, informal organization, and individual and formal organization components; and outputs can be at the individual, group, or organizational level. "Organizations will be most effective when their major components are congruent" (Nadler, 1981, p. 194). The problem of implementing change becomes one of managing the inputs, transformation, and outputs in a way to maintain congruence. The main value of this and other general models of change is that they identify a broad set of variables that should be considered. The disadvantage of this type of theorizing is its imprecision. The critical variables are not identified. Functional relationships among variables are ignored. It is impossible to generate testable hypotheses.

A second trend is the development of propositional inventories. Hage (1980) divides change processes into evaluation, initiation, implementation, and routinization and then generates a list of propositions for each part of the process. For example, in the routinization subprocess, Hage (1980, pp. 227–228) offers hypotheses such as:

- The greater the consensus about the performance gap, the less the extent of conflict, and the extent of costs and the more the extent of benefits perceived, the more likely the decision to institutionalize the innovation.
- The greater the consensus about the performance gap, the greater the duration of the time span for experimentation.
- The greater the measurability of benefits and of costs, the greater the number of benefits and of costs perceived, and the more likely the decision to institutionalize the innovation.

Kochan and Dyer (1976) develop an inventory about organizational change in the context of union-management relations. This is an important piece because it attempts to develop a theoretically coherent inventory in an area where little work has been done. Their change propositions are organized around stimuli for union-management change, the decision to participate in a joint program, and maintaining a commitment over time. Some selected propositions for maintaining commitment include (Kochan and Dyer, 1976, p. 72):

- The less the union leaders are seen as being coopted into performing roles and indistinguishable from management, the more likely the union will be to continue its commitment to the program over time.
- The more the program is buffered from the strategic maneuvers of the formal contract negotiations process (that is, the distributive tactics of the union and manage-

ment organizations), the more likely the parties are to
maintain their commitment to the program over time.

- The more union leaders continue to aggressively pursue
  their constituents' goals on distributive issues through
  the formal bargaining process, the more likely the union
  will be to continue its commitment to the joint program
  over time.

Walton's (1980, p. 279) chapter on establishing and maintaining high-commitment work systems is another example of thoughtful theoretical work on change. His propositions are organized
around facilitating conditions in the prehistory period, effectiveness
of work systems, the fit among structure technology and human
resources, commitment generated by the structure, and meanings of
incentives and maturation, adaptation, and survival. Some sample
propositions from the maturation, adaptation, and survival area
include:

- The greater the differences between the inventory of
  human resources at the time of forming the structure and
  the human resources required to support the work structure planned for steady-state conditions, the longer it will
  take for the work structure to mature. Relatively large
  differences can be the result of any of several factors: a
  planned structure that is highly organic, inherently difficult task technologies, low skill levels possessed by
  workers at the time they are hired, and predispositions to
  lower-level involvement.
- The more changes that occur in the character of the task
  technology during the period of formation, the longer
  the time required to establish a work structure.

Dunn and Swierczek (1977) examine a set of hypotheses or
propositions generated by other researchers on change. These propositions range from whether change efforts in economic (versus
noneconomic) organizations will be more successful to the role of
internal versus external change agents in successfully introducing
change. In reviewing the literature, the authors found support for
propositions indicating the positive effect of collaboration and the
participation in change and less support for propositions concerning organizational types, origin of the change agent, and so on. This
study's value is in the enumeration of propositions, not in the em-

pirical findings. Like other studies we have reviewed (for example, Porras and Berg, 1978), it portrays aspects of change (such as origin of change agents) and success in a bivariate fashion; the world, unfortunately, is multivariate.

Although it is difficult to sense any movement away from general frameworks of change to propositional inventory on change, we feel the inventory approach can be more productive in sharpening our thinking about change and in stimulating empirical research.

A third trend is elaborating a particular change process. There is a growing literature on implementation processes (Elmore, 1978; Scheirer, 1981; Williams and others, 1982). Many of the researchers in this domain come from a political science, policy, or educational administration tradition and focus on problems of implementation in public organizations. Scheirer (1981) provides a nice review of some of the empirical work in this area and then develops a set of propositions on how: macrolevel components (decision processes, control processes, and so on), intermediate processes (supervisory expectations, standard operating procedures, and so on), and individual variables (behavior skills, incentives, and cognitive processes) bear on the implementation of new programs.

Institutionalization, which concerns the persistence of change over time, is another process that has been examined recently. Levine (1980) examines the process of institutionalization of fourteen innovations in a university. Two major concepts are used in this analysis—compatibility and profitability. Compatibility is defined as the degree of congruence between the personality, norms, values, and goals of an innovation and its host. Profitability is defined as the degree to which an innovation satisfies the host's organizational, group, and personal needs.

Goodman, Conlon, and Bazerman (1978) provide another approach to institutionalization. They identify a two-stage model that underlies the process of institutionalization and, via literature review, relate factors such as rewards systems and commitment to the two-stage model. Other recent important pieces on institutionalization have been done by Zucker (1977), Meyer and Rowan (1978), and Kimberly (1979).

Walton (1977) initiated some of the earlier analyses of diffusion processes at the firm or company level. He examines several cases where diffusion failed and identifies a set of factors explaining the lack of diffusion. Some of these include confusion over what is to be diffused, inappropriateness of the concepts employed, and lack of top management commitment.

A much different approach to elaborating one of the processes in organizational change comes from the work of Biggart (1977). She analyzes the destructive processes in organizational change. Destruction includes any action that abolishes, discredits, suppresses, or otherwise renders useless an organizational structure (p. 410). The basic argument is that these destructive processes are a necessary part of the reorganizing activity. The empirical material for this analysis is derived from a major change in organization of the United States Post Office. The destructive processes include eliminating former ideologies, power alliances, and leadership in order to permit the development of new ones congruent with the new organizational structure.

To summarize, there are no clear trends in the theoretical elaboration of change. The tendency of the past literature to represent broad systems like flowcharts of change processes still persists. Although this approach has some heuristic value, it is not really a coherent theory about change and it probably impedes theoretical development. The work on propositional inventories or on conceptualizing one of the change processes seems more fruitful. These latter two approaches provide a more coherent set of concepts through which to understand change and improve our chances of developing and testing theories about change processes.

Adaptation

Adaptation concerns the modification of the organization or its components to fit or to be adjusted to its environment. In this section we follow the strategy of identifying the major themes in the current literature on organizational adaptation. We open with a brief review of reviews and then consider three themes on adaptation: the population ecology perspective, the organizational-environmental perspective, and adaptation within an organization.

A Review of Reviews. Organization theorists only recently began writing about the adaptation of organizations to their environments. The earliest piece that can be considered a review is Child (1972). His is an advocacy review. Although others have proposed that the environment, the technology, or the size of the organization dictate the structure or how the organization adapts, Child argues that the strategic choices made by decision makers in the dominant coalition are essential to understanding how organizations adapt to their environments. Specifically, Child argues that the dominant coalition has autonomy over many variables that enable organizations to adapt proactively, rather than merely to accommodate to uncontrollable changes. For example, organizations can choose which environment or market to operate in; they can manipulate and control their environment; they can choose technologies that grant them subsequent control; they can employ control systems to deal with their large size; and they may perceive and reevaluate their environments in ways that enable them to adapt creatively to contingencies.

Aldrich and Pfeffer (1976) review the organization literature that considers the relationship between organizations and environments. They consider two models, which they called the natural selection model and the resource dependence model. Both models allow for the importance of environmental influences on organizational decisions and structures. They differ in the emphasis placed on environmental selection and on managerial decision making.

The resource dependence perspective has also been called the political economy model and the dependence exchange model. This perspective portrays managers as making choices to adapt their organizations to their environments. It begins with the premise that all organizations must enter into transactions with certain elements of their environments, which creates an interdependence. In analyzing these interdependencies, this model fleshes out how and why decisions are made in organizations. Most decisions originate from interdependencies and transactions. Organizations are seen as active agents able to respond to, as well as change, their environments. Because many organizational configurations enable the organization to survive, strategic choices are recognized as central to the understanding of organization-environment interfaces and changes in organizations.

The natural selection model is essentially a model of organizational evolution. It contrasts sharply with both Child's (1972) view of the world and the resource dependence model. The natural selection model applies to populations of organizations. In it the environment differentially selects organizations, basing its selection on the ability of the organization structure to exploit environmental resources. This model, in downplaying the importance of managerial decision making, primarily provides a post hoc or historical explanation for organizational change and adaptation. Adaptation takes on a different meaning in an evolutionary model. Campbell (1969) proposes a three-step evolutionary model that Aldrich and Pfeffer (1976) elaborate. First, variations in structure occur. From an evolutionary perspective, the source of these variations (random, borrowed, or created by decision makers) is irrelevant. People may adapt to an environment, but all they have done collectively is provide a pool of variations in the populations of organizations. In the second step, selection, the environment differentially selects one or some of these variations. Other organizations fail, which removes their variations from the pool. In the third step, retention, variations that were selected are retained. This model ascribes little importance to people's ability to adapt.

To summarize, these reviews span a continuum of the attributed importance of managerial decision making in the role of adaptation. Child (1972) anchors one end of the continuum—managers can and do strongly influence how their organizations adapt to the environment. The resource dependence model is more balanced in its viewpoint—managers can influence their environments and organizations, but there are real contingencies that must be adapted to. The natural selection perspective anchors the other end of this continuum—managers have little significant effect on the population of surviving (adapting) organizations.

Most of the important works on adaptation since Aldrich and Pfeffer's (1976) review have taken strong advocacy stands. Because they are not really reviews, we will consider them under their respective themes (Aldrich, 1979; Hannan and Freeman, 1977; Pfeffer and Salancik, 1978). We shall sample what is potentially a huge litera-

ture on adaptation. But that literature is without form, and there are
few guides to it. We impose some form by proposing a list of themes,
which fundamentally parallels the level of analysis of the authors'
works. We discuss three themes: populations of organizations, adaptation at the level of the organization-environment interface, and
adaptations within organizations.

   Populations of Organizations. We consider the population
ecology perspective and systematics in this section. Neither of these
approaches to adaptation concedes much importance to strategic
choices; indeed, these were written in part to provide alternatives to
models of managerial choice. The population level perspectives
share certain basic premises about adaptation. First, adaptation has
meaning only when viewed in terms of a population of organizations being differentially selected by the environment—after the selection has occurred, we can say that the organization was adapted.
Second, managerial choice is viewed as an unnecessary or misleading explanation for adaptation. It is considered more parsimonious
to explain change and adaptation by examining when the organization was founded, what historical events occurred at key transition
points, or how frequently changes in the environment occurred.

   From the *population ecology perspective,* Hannan and
Freeman (1977, p. 930) try to present an alternative to the dominant
mode of modeling, which presumes that "subunits of the organization, usually managers or dominant coalitions, scan the relevant
environment for opportunities and threats, formulate strategic responses, and adjust organizational structure appropriately."* Their
alternative rests upon two broad issues: the appropriate unit of
analysis for studying organizations and the general applicability of
the population ecology to studying social organization. They are
clear on both points. They argue explicitly for a focus on populations of organizations. We have therefore featured them in this section. They also argue that structural inertias so proscribe managerial
choices that the study of social organization is fundamentally (it

   *Hannan and Freeman (1977) introduced the phrase "adaptation perspec-
tive" to refer to models that stress managerial decision making. What we call "adaptation" is significantly more inclusive than what Hannan and Freeman refer to. Indeed,
adaptation for us includes both the population ecology perspective and models of
choice that Hannan and Freeman eschew.

cannot be reduced to a lower level of analysis) a study of population ecologies. At this level of analysis, we see an adaptation perspective that does not rely heavily on managerial choice. The following hypothesis, which represents a simplified version of Hannan and Freeman's argument, exemplifies the reification typical of this level of analysis and the lack of managerial choice. "Faced with unstable environments, organizations ought to develop a generalist structure that is not optimally adapted to any single environmental configuration but is optimal over the entire set of configurations. In other words, we ought to find specialized organizations in stable and certain environments and generalist organizations in unstable and uncertain environments" (Hannan and Freeman, 1977, p. 946).

Aldrich (1979) greatly elaborates the population ecology perspective by using the variation—selection—retention model of natural selection. His book integrates a huge array of literature in such a way that he presents the population ecology model as a powerful and researchable alternative to those models that draw primarily on managerial choice. Besides exploring the implications of this perspective on adaptation, he directly challenges Child's (1972) arguments on strategic choice. Specifically, Aldrich argues that there are severe constraints on managers' choices of new environments and on their abilities to influence their environments. Also, managers' perceptions of reality are so homogeneous as to make truly novel strategic choices improbable. These and other limits on managerial choice suggest that we must look elsewhere for explanations of the differential adaptation and survival of organizations.

A number of other researchers have empirically tested and extended the population ecology model or employed it in their modeling. Notable among them are Nielsen and Hannan (1977), Brittain and Freeman (1980), Carroll (1981), Aldrich and Fish (1981), Padgett (1981), and Rundall and McClain (1982).

McKelvey (1978; 1982) argues persuasively that *systematics*, which is the science of classification, is a prerequisite to understanding general organization functions and processes. That is, we cannot develop an understanding of how organizations adapt until we can discriminate among different kinds of organizations, trace the lineages of these organizational differences, and develop procedures to identify and categorize organizational forms into classes. These three tasks are the three tasks of systematics—taxonomy, evolution, and classification. Of these, evolution bears most heavily on our understanding of adaptation and change.

McKelvey's (1982) exposition of the evolutionary perspective is axiomatic and propositional. We can convey how McKelvey views organizational change by paraphrasing a few of his succinct axioms and propositions. Environments of organizations change. Organizations respond to environmental forces. Thus, organizations respond or adapt to changing environments. This adaptation to changing environments accounts for the evolution of organizations—the differences and slow changes in structures, processes, and competencies over successive generations. The specific course of organizational evolution and change is ultimately determined by characteristics of environments. In essence, adaptation to a changing environment explains organizational differences and thus change and evolution. To understand change, study the differences of the environment.

To summarize, we have used three works to exemplify different population level approaches to adaptation and change. Hannan and Freeman's (1977) work is a relatively abstract piece that predicts the occurrence and change of structures based on changes in environmental niches. Aldrich's (1979) book greatly elaborates the three-stage natural selection model. Change derives from variations in organizational forms, one source of which is managerial choices, which are selected and retained. McKelvey (1982) presents an axiomatic model of evolution that explains change in terms of organizations adapting to changing environments. All these works aggregate organizations into populations; all of them downplay or eschew the importance of managerial choice; and all of them view the source of adaptation as an inconsequential artifact of evolution.

Organizations Interfacing with Environments. We turn now to a theme whose level of analysis is less aggregated than a population. The authors using this level of analysis focus on how organizations interface with environments. Specifically, we review works that share the theme that managers, in their attempts to adapt to their environments, make choices about their interactions with their environments. These choices, not the environment itself, are the most important explanation for change. This basic theme has been approached several ways: through a resource dependence model, in terms of how strategy and structure affect adaptation, and phenomenologically. All these approaches share the explanation that adaptation and change come about through the accommodation of organizational decision makers to their environments.

Resource dependence model. Pfeffer and Salancik (1978) attempt to shift the focus of organizational research from a strictly internal perspective (that of focusing on managerial behavior) to an external one (that of focusing on the context of managerial behavior). This shift in focus is revealed in their approach to organizational change. There are two broadly defined contingent-adaptive responses—"the organization can adapt and change to fit environmental requirements, or the organization can attempt to alter the environment so that it fits the organization's capabilities" (Pfeffer and Salancik, 1978, p. 106). Their primary contribution to our thinking about change lies in their focus on the latter approach to change. They argue that organizations adapt their environments to them by such tactics as merging with other organizations, diversifying, co-opting important others through interlocking directorates, and engaging in political activities to influence matters such as regulation.

We will use the example of mergers to show how organizations change their environments in order to adapt better. We draw heavily on Pfeffer and Salancik (1978) and on Pfeffer (1972). Mergers, and growth in general, stabilize organization-environment relations. There are three types of mergers: vertical integration, horizontal expansion, and diversification. Each type helps manage a specific kind of interdependence. For example, vertical mergers manage symbiotic interdependence and horizontal mergers reduce competitive interdependence. Pfeffer and Salancik (1978, pp. 115–116) argue that "if organizations merge to control interdependence" rather than to increase profits or to achieve economies of scale, "then they should acquire organizations in areas in which they exchange resources." Pfeffer (1972) examines mergers between companies that manufacture different products and between petroleum producers and refiners. He interprets this finding as support for his hypothesis that organizations adapt by merging to absorb interdependence.

The resource dependence approach shares neither of the extreme explanations for adaptation, that is, that change is explained predominantly by the environment or predominantly by choices. Another balanced approach that relates organizational change to choices and the environment comes from the study of strategy and structure.

Strategy and structure. Many researchers have investigated how choices about strategy and structure enable organizations to adapt to environments. We have subdivided this group of research into those studies dealing primarily with strategy, with structure, or with their interaction. Strategy is a very general term denoting a general plan for meeting some objective. In this discussion, we will consider planning and organizational structure as two components of strategy, that is, as tactics for achieving a strategic objective.

Several studies have addressed the ways choice of strategy enables organizations to adapt. Hall (1980) investigates how a turbulent and hostile environment (low growth, inflation, regulation, and competition) would affect the survival strategies used by top management. Using published data and field interviews, he found that success in eight major domestic industries depended upon achieving either the lowest cost or the greatest differentiation. Planning is another important part of strategies of change. Lindsay and Rue (1980) use a two-stage survey to explore how long-range planning processes are affected by the complexity and instability of the environment. Khandwalla's (1976) findings are similar to those of Lindsay and Rue (1980): Complex uncertain environments elicit comprehensive and elaborate planning strategies.

Kurke (1981) examines how strategies themselves change or persist over time. He uses a quasi-longitudinal laboratory design to test how uncertainty of the environment and frequency of the change in it affect the choice of and perpetuation of decision-making strategies. Kurke (1981) finds that the frequency of change and uncertainty interact to produce a tradition of change among decision makers. This tradition of change enables decision makers to adapt their organization quickly by rapidly changing their strategy.

Organizational structure is another component that people change in an effort to adapt to environmental changes. Most people accept the idea that the environment somehow affects structure: Burns and Stalker (1961), Woodward (1965), and Lawrence and Lorsch (1967) convincingly demonstrate this relationship. Investigators have studied many different variables that may explain how and why the environment affects structure (DuBick, 1978; Marks, 1977; Segal, 1974). Explanations range from (Lincoln, Olson, and Hanada, 1978) how cultural presence (of Japanese in this example) affects functional specialization (it varies inversely) to how public bureaucracies respond to environmental changes (Meyer, 1979). Specifically, Meyer (1979, p. 205) finds that, "despite the openness and variability of bureaucratic structures, there is also evidence that organizational change does not occur as rapidly as do shifts in the environment. As a result, the fit between organizations and environments is greatest at the time of formation and declines gradually thereafter until reorganization or replacement of existing units becomes necessary. Structure, which is initially an accommodation to the environment, eventually becomes an impediment to change and must be altered fundamentally." In these and other examples, various facets of the environment are found strongly to influence structure.

While most discussions focus on one or the other, some writers, whose work we review in this section, explicitly combine strategy and structure, usually typologically. Miles and Snow (1978; Miles, Snow, Meyer, and Coleman, 1978) propose an adaptive cycle model of the adaptive process, using a strategic-choice perspective. In this model, managers had three problems to resolve. The problems were entrepreneurial, engineering, and administrative. In solving them, managers became one of four kinds of strategists: defenders, analyzers, prospectors, and reactors. Defenders create stability (solution to the entrepreneurial problem), produce and distribute goods as efficiently as possible (solution to the engineering problem), and tightly control the organization to ensure efficiency (solution to the administrative problem). Prospectors actively locate and develop new opportunities with engineering and administrative solutions supportive of this entrepreneurial thrust. The analyzer strategy is a combination of these two. The reactor strategy, as the name implies, is a strategy of failure—an inconsistent and unstable set of solutions to the three problems. These authors argue that if the predominant market orientation or strategy is known, there will be a particular structure predictably associated with it. Each combination of strategy and structure, except the reactor, is the ideal form of adaptation.

Snow and Hrebiniak (1980) elaborate upon this work by showing that managers perceive themselves to have distinctive competence that enables them to adapt their organization effectively. "Specifically, the Defender's strong emphasis on manufacturing efficiency typically resulted in an organization that showed strengths in general management, production, applied engineering, and financial management. At the other extreme, the Prospector's emphasis on product and market effectiveness developed an organization whose distinctive competencies lay in general management, product research and development, market research, and basic engineerings." Exploiting distinctive competence is an effective adaptive tactic.

Miller and Friesen (1980a) propose another typology to categorize the various forms, or archetypes, that organizations use during periods of change or adaptation. They argue (Miller and Friesen, 1980b) that, in general, organizations are usually sluggish in adapting to environmental changes; there is tremendous "momentum" built into organizational structures that precludes rapid change. However, the authors find that when organizations do change, there are "revolutionary" reversals in many structural variables simultaneously. Although organizations normally are resistant to change due to momentum, when they do change and adapt, they change in a revolutionary rather than an evolutionary fashion. The archetypes they propose are the most typical configurations found during these revolutionary transitions. For instance, the archetype called consolidation "is usually triggered by a perceived need to retrench and consolidate. For example, the firm may have diversified too quickly and into some unprofitable areas, or resources may have been taxed due to overexpansion. The decline in profits and the sense that the firm is out of control cause the realization that some sort of change is necessary" (Miller and Friesen, 1980a, p. 282). These strategic archetypes do not necessarily imply improved adaptation—they may be dysfunctional.

Phenomenological approaches. Several conceptual articles appeared recently that begin to explain, from a more phenomenological perspective, why structures appear, endure, and change. Most of the authors of these articles draw upon Weick's (1979) work on enactment. Like the explanation for enactment, phenomenological explanations for change rely on introspection, description, and interpretation to understand how social actors construct their life-worlds and come to share them as if they were real. Change and adaptation, for phenomenologists, would be effected by altering actors' constructed realities (Meyer and Rowan, 1978; Zucker, 1977). We will review two representative pieces.

Ranson, Hinings, and Greenwood (1980) propose an integrative framework—a unified theoretical and methodological framework—that draws on three abstract conceptual categories. The first, provinces of meaning, embodies an interpretive scheme for organizational members that enables them to understand their worlds as meaningful and that provides values for implementing structures. The second, dependencies of power, enables different factions to resolve their alternative interpretive schemes and value preferences. The third category is contextual constraints. These constraints are "inherent in characteristics of the organization and the environment, with organizational members differentially responding to and enacting their contextual conditions according to the opportunities provided by infrastructure and time" (Ranson, Hinings, and Greenwood, 1980, p. 4). Their framework would imply that organizational change comes about by changing members' provinces of meaning, the dependencies of power, or the contextual constraints.

Pfeffer (1981) argues that managers have two basic tasks: to manage interdependencies (a notion that we reviewed under the resource dependence model) and to manage on the symbolic level, internal to the organization. For Pfeffer (1981, p. 1) the symbolic level is where "the use of political language and symbolic action serves to legitimate and rationalize organizational decisions and policies. Organizations are viewed as systems of shared meanings and beliefs, in which a critical administrative activity involves the construction and maintenance of belief systems which assume continued compliance, commitment and positive affect on the part of participants." Management creates and maintains these "paradigms" through language, symbolism, and ritual. In Pfeffer's symbolic world, change and adaptation would come about by managers applying different languages, rituals, and so on to modify participants' shared meanings. How managers enact the environment will strongly affect how well they are able to adapt their organizations. Peters (1978), reviewed previously, gives us the best cookbook approach on how to modify paradigms that would permit managers to adapt.

To summarize, the resource dependence model, studies of strategy and structure, and phenomenological approaches to changes are parts of a theme that relates organizational adaptation to both the environments and to managerial choices. The studies portrayed in this theme represent a diverse set of approaches, methods, and styles of theorizing. This diversity is a healthy development from the 1960s and early 1970s in the study of organizational change.

Adaptation Within Organizations. Research that focuses on adaptation within an organization is the least aggregated and most compatible with a strategic choice perspective. Authors of this research take environmental change or perturbation for granted—and concentrate on the adaptations that go on inside the organization.

Our search for papers on change reaffirmed our belief that *innovation* can be an important component of organizational changes. However, we have not attempted thoroughly to review the innovation literature. We might have included innovation under planned organizational change, and indeed we have previously cited innovation references. However, we have included several studies on innovation here because innovation fits well, because innovations may not be planned, and because not all planned changes are innovative. Furthermore, the works included here help us understand adaptation ex post, whereas the works included under planned organizational change help us ex ante.

There have been many approaches to innovation. They range from the study of personality attributes of people who are or are not innovative, to methods for measuring perceptions of innovation, to studies of different phases of innovation.

Kirton (1980) continues to develop and elaborate his theory of adaptation and innovation. He "posits that individuals have characteristically different styles of creativity, problem solving, and decision making. In brief, adaptors tend to operate cognitively within the confines of the appropriately conceptually accepted paradigm . . . within which a problem (novel stimulus) is generally initially perceived. Innovators, by contrast, are more liable to treat (formally or intuitively) the enveloping paradigm as part of the problem" (Kirton, 1980, pp. 213–214). He predicts how the proportions of adaptors and innovators will vary by organizational structure. Presumably, the proportion of innovators will affect how quickly organizations can adapt.

Siegel and Kaemmerer (1978) have tried to measure how organizational members perceive innovation in their organization. They propose that five dimensions would be characteristic of innovative organizations: the kind of leadership, the feeling of ownership of ideas, norms for diversity, continuous development or experimentation with alternative conceptions, and consistency. They then develop a scale, test it, and refine it. From their five dimensions, they find that one major factor (support for creativity) and two lesser factors (diversity and ownership) are reliable indicators of the perceptions of innovativeness in traditional and alternative schools. This work suggests that support for creativity may be crucial to the adaptability of organizations.

The remainder of the authors we will review here write about specific stages or phases (such as conception, proposal, adoption, and implementation) of innovation.

Daft (1978), in an attempt to understand the source of innovation, examines its proposal stage. In his study of school systems, his basic finding is that teachers are the main source of technical innovations, but principals and superintendents provide most administrative innovations. This finding was influenced by the degree of professionalism (for example, highly professional teachers propose more innovations than less professional teachers; the less the professionalism of the teachers, though, the more administrators propose technical innovations). Size has little or no effect. He proposes a dual-core model of innovation that accounts for the innovations originating both with leaders and with lower-level employees. That is, innovations come both top-down and bottom-up.

Dickson (1976) concentrates on the adoption phase (rather than on the proposal phase). His concern is with why or when people will adopt an innovative proposal that is variably probable of achieving an outcome, that has an expected value, and that has a range of variance of that value. Using this expected value approach, he derives a simple model and tests it. Rewards and penalties are independent variables and influence decision makers' choices. Expectancy dominates these choices.

Kimberly and Evanisko (1981) studied the effects of individual, organizational, and contextual variables on medical and managerial innovations. Their basic findings are that all three sets of variables affect both medical and managerial innovations, but that organizational variables have a much larger influence on innovations, especially medical innovations. Moch (1976) also has studied how organizational factors—specifically, structural attributes—affect the adoption of innovation. His data show that increases in size, specialization, functional differentiation, and decentralization all increase the adoption of innovations.

Self-design, or designing into the organization a flexibility that facilitates continuous redesign, is another approach to change in organizations. Transient structures, an ideology of change, and an ability to redesign structure repeatedly and regularly are characteristics of self-designing organizations. Two papers represent this approach.

Hedberg, Nystrom, and Starbuck (1976) argue that organizational environments are not static, placid, and benign. They change, present turmoil, and become nasty. To design organizations that can adapt to these environments requires unorthodox thinking and prescriptions. We will review two prescriptions of the many they propose. First, they suggest that designing organizations should be more like erecting tents than palaces. "An organizational tent places greater emphasis on flexibility, creativity, immediacy, and initiative than on authority, clarity, decisiveness, or responsiveness" (Hedberg, Nystrom, and Starbuck, 1976, p. 45). Second, they prescribe that adapting through self-design means that one must "unlearn yesterday. . . . The first step toward new behaviors is unlearning old behaviors. The effectiveness of existing activity programs and traditional strategies is disconfirmed, and the process binding the organization to today's behavioral patterns are disengaged" (p. 51). By erecting tents and unlearning yesterday, the organization will achieve a state of ongoing self-design that will permit it to survive the more turbulent times.

Weick (1977) takes a similar approach to self-design. He considers the strike by the Skylab 3 crew an example of a problem in self-design and of the need to be able to alter design as the organization evolves. He characterizes organizations that are incapable of self-design, including Skylab, as follows: "They value forecasts more than improvisation, they dwell on constraints rather than opportunities, they borrow solutions rather than invent them, they defend past actions rather than devise new ones, they cultivate permanence rather than impermanence, they value serenity more highly than argument, they rely on accounting systems as their sole means to assess performance rather than use more diverse measures, they remove doubt rather than encourage it, they search for final solutions rather than continuously experimenting, and they discourage contradictions rather than seek them" (Weick, 1977, p. 37). That list implies how Weick would construct organizations so that they are ongoing self-designers and therefore remain adaptable.

Ambiguity and choice constitute yet another focus for researchers looking at adaptation within organizations. March and Olsen's (1976) work on ambiguity and choice has had a significant impact on organizational theory and hence on perspectives on change. They argue that choice situations are extremely complex and ambiguous. During the choice process, activities besides making choices are introduced; for example, standard operating procedures are executed, truth is defined, history is interpreted, glory and blame are distributed, self-interests are discovered, and people enjoy themselves. These complexities and the ambiguities of intention, understanding, history, and organization together place severe limitations on the complete rational cycle of choice; each connection in the cycle of choice is at times severed by the extreme ambiguity present in organizational settings.

Having set forth a very different set of assumptions, March and Olsen (1976) provide a major departure from the organization and change literatures. They propose a number of alternative theories, formulations, and observations. For example, they propose that we view organizations as garbage cans (Cohen, March, and Olsen, 1972) wherein streams of problems, solutions, participants, and choice opportunities intermingle. A fortuitous confluence of these streams may indeed produce a "decision," but the production is not the certain, unambiguous, and rational process portrayed in the organizational literature. Decisions to adapt or to change an organization are subject to major properties of the garbage can decision process. One of these properties is that, although "important problems are more likely to be solved than unimportant ones . . . important choices are much *less* likely to resolve problems than are unimportant ones. Important choices are made by oversight and flight." Furthermore, "the few choice failures that do occur are concentrated among the most important and least important choices" (March and Olsen, 1976, p. 37). There are several implications of their findings. Assuming a problem in adaptation is important, it will probably be solved, though it may not be. If it is solved, it will probably be solved by oversight (ignoring the choice) or flight (escaping the choice). This model of choice is extremely different from rational models.

Another formulation of March and his associates is that of an organized anarchy. Without reviewing them in detail, we refer the reader to the two key works on organized anarchies: Cohen and March (1974), who studied college presidents, and Sproull, Weiner, and Wolf (1978), who studied the formation and early development of the National Institute of Education. In both of these settings, the key impediment to change is that the members' preferences are often problematic, the technology is unclear, and participation is fluid. Organized anarchies are very loosely coupled (Weick, 1976), which makes the management of change a problematic enterprise.

March (1981) directs his attention and perspective specifically toward organizational change. He argues that basic organizational processes are stable—they derive from the mundane, day-to-day activities of managers and leaders; they slowly adapt the organization; and they may involve the interplay of rationality and foolishness. March (1981, pp. 574–575) argues that:

> These stable processes of change, however, produce a
> great variety of action and their outcomes are sometimes sur-

prisingly sensitive to the details of the context in which they occur.

A view of change as resulting from stable processes realized in a highly contextual and sometimes confusing world emphasizes the idea that things happen in organizations because most of the time organizational participants respond in elementary ways to the environment, including that part of the environment that might be called management or leadership. Managers and leaders propose changes, including foolish ones; they try to cope with the environment and to control it; they respond to other members of the organization; they issue orders and manipulate incentives. Since they play conventional roles, organizational leaders are not likely to behave in strikingly unusual ways. And if a leader tries to march toward strange destinations, an organization is likely to deflect the effort. Simply to describe leadership as conventional and constrained by organizational realities, however, is to risk misunderstanding its importance. Neither success nor change requires dramatic action. The conventional, routine activities that produce most organizational change require ordinary people to do ordinary things in a competent way.

Social movements in organizations can constitute an important source of change. Zald and Berger (1978) describe organizational coups, bureaucratic insurgency, and mass movements as three types of social movements that enable organizations to adapt through major changes in top managers, in goals, or in linkages to external elements, to name just a few dimensions of their discussion.

To summarize, at the level of aggregation corresponding to our theme of change within individual organizations, we see an acceptance of strategic choice and managerial decision making as influencing adaptation. Choices are inherent in the adaptive activity, whether of innovation, self-design, social movement, or ambiguity. As this section has demonstrated, there is considerable latitude in theorizing about how choices affect adaptation and change.

Plan and Organization of the Book

The purpose of the status report is to give the reader a sketch of the basic themes in the current literature on change. Although the division we make between planned change and adaptation is arbitrary, it is useful for cataloguing the literature.

The chapters on change that follow build from this review of the literature. They are intended to provide the conceptual apparatus for understanding change. The topics are not comprehensive in the sense that they take off from all the themes we have identified. Some do—such as the Lawler, Cole, and Goodman and Dean chapters, which follow in the tradition of planned organizational change. Cole and Goodman and Dean extend our conceptualization of diffusion and institutionalization processes. Other chapters, such as those of Staw and Weick, can be placed in the adaptation literature. Still others, such as Smith's encounter with some epistemological issues of change, cut across both planned organizational change and adaptation. The strategy in selecting the contributors was to identify provocative researchers rather than to cover all the contemporary issues on change.

To assist the reader in moving through this book, a brief discussion of each chapter follows.

In Chapter Two, Argyris builds on his earlier theoretical work on single- and double-loop learning. Particular consideration is given to problems both individuals and organizations have in double-loop learning. The focus is on change at the individual level. Argyris argues that change at this level must precede changes at other levels of analysis. Some ideas for moving toward double-loop learning are examined.

Staw, in Chapter Three, examines change as a potential mechanism for organizational adaptation. His approach is to examine counterforces to change. That is, by examining why it is difficult for organizations to change or to adapt, one can learn more about the process of change. Escalation and commitment are two counterforces to change that are examined in detail and models describing these processes are presented. These models are thoughtful and extend previous work. The analysis is primarily at the individual level, but extensions to the organization are also discussed.

Chapter Four, by Alderfer, focuses on the group level of analysis, particularly on intergroup theory and how it bears on changing race relations. The chapter is different from the other chapters in style and form. It concludes with a set of propositions for changing white men's attitudes and beliefs about race relations.

Chapter Five, by Cole, provides an interesting analysis of one process of change—diffusion. His comparative analysis takes the reader to Japan, Sweden, and the United States to explore why organizations in these countries have differentially adopted participative structures. His examination generates a set of institutional, structural, and strategic factors that affect diffusion of new forms of work organizations.

Goodman and Dean, in Chapter Six, focus on another process of change—institutionalization. The chapter develops a framework for explaining the persistence of change, an operational procedure for representing institutionalization, and some data relevant to the framework. This chapter focuses on the organizational levels and draws from the planned organizational change perspective.

Lawler (Chapter Seven) presents a framework for developing high-involvement work systems. Motivation, individual performance capability, and communication coordination and control are the three critical elements in his framework. The chapter outlines organizational design features that affect these three elements. The congruence of the design features is central to enhancing organizational effectiveness. The focus of analysis in this chapter is on changing the organization and its structure.

Smith (Chapter Eight) argues that we are not ready to develop a theory of change or to advance our conceptualization of change until we tackle some unresolved epistemological problems latent in most discussions of change. He organizes his analysis around issues: metaphor and metonymy, the boundary "not" condition, sense making of collectivities, and morphostasis and morphogenesis. Although this is probably the most abstract of the chapters, Smith tries to root these themes into a common organizational example with the other papers in this book and to "hint" for change.

In Chapter Nine, Weick examines the meaning of change in the context of loosely coupled systems. He begins with a detailed description of loosely coupled systems, contrasts change in this type of system versus a rational system, and then explores targets for change in a loosely coupled system. The chapter is provocative.

The final chapter, by Kahn, is integrative in nature; it builds from discussion about the chapters and from Kahn's own views. This concluding chapter is not meant to be comprehensive. Rather, it attempts to identify critical themes on change in organizations.

References

Alderfer, C. P. "Change Processes in Organizations." In M. D. Dunnette (Ed.), *Handbook of Industrial and Organizational Psychology.* Chicago: Rand McNally, 1976.

Alderfer, C. P. "Organization Development." *Annual Review of Psychology,* 1977, *28,* 197–223.

Aldrich, H. E. *Organizations and Environments.* Englewood Cliffs, N.J.: Prentice-Hall, 1979.

Aldrich, H. E., and Fish, D. "Origins of Organizational Forms: Births, Deaths, and Transformations." Working paper, Dept. of Sociology, Cornell University, 1981.

Aldrich, H. E., and Pfeffer, J. "Environments of Organizations." *Annual Review of Sociology,* 1976, *2,* 79–105.

Argyris, C., and Schön, D. A. *Organizational Learning: A Theory of Action Perspective.* Reading, Mass.: Addison-Wesley, 1978.

Beer, M. *Organization Change and Development.* Santa Monica, Calif.: Goodyear, 1980.

Beyer, J. M., and Trice, H. M. *Implementing Change.* New York: Macmillan, 1978.

Biggart, N. W. "The Creative-Destructive Process of Organizational Change: The Case of the Post Office." *Administrative Science Quarterly,* 1977, *22*(3), 410–426.

Billings, R. S., Klimoski, R. J., and Breaugh, J. A. "The Impact of a Change in Technology on Job Characteristics: A Quasi-Experiment." *Administrative Science Quarterly,* 1977, *22,* 318–339.

Blumberg, A. "A Complex Problem—An Overly Simple Diagnosis." *The Journal of Applied Behavioral Science,* 1977, *13,* 184–191.

Brittain, J. W., and Freeman, J. H. "Organizational Proliferation and Density." In J. R. Kimberly, R. H. Miles, and Associates, *The Organizational Life Cycle: Issues in the Creation, Transforma-*

tion, and Decline of Organizations. San Francisco: Jossey-Bass, 1980.

Burns, T., and Stalker, G. M. *The Management of Innovation.* London: Tavistock, 1961.

Campbell, D. T. "Variation and Selective Retention in Socio-Cultural Evolution." *General Systems,* 1969, *16,* 69–85.

Carnall, C. A. "The Evaluation of Work Organization Change." *Human Relations,* 1980, *33,* 885–916.

Carroll, G. R. "Dynamics of Organizational Expansion in National Systems of Education." *American Sociological Review,* 1981, *46,* 585–599.

Child, J. "Organizational Structure, Environment, and Performance: The Role of Strategic Choice." *Sociology,* 1972, *6,* 1–22.

Cohen, M. D., and March, J. G. *Leadership and Ambiguity: The American College President.* New York: McGraw-Hill, 1974.

Cohen, M. D., March, J. G., and Olsen, J. P. "A Garbage Can Model of Organizational Choice." *Administrative Science Quarterly,* 1972, *17,* 1–25.

Daft, R. L. "A Dual-Core Model of Organizational Innovation." *Academy of Management Journal,* 1978, *21,* 193–210.

Dickson, J. W. "The Adoption of Innovative Proposals as Risky Choice: A Model and Some Results." *Academy of Management Journal,* 1976, *19,* 291–303.

DuBick, M. A. "The Organizational Structure of Newspapers in Relation to Their Metropolitan Environments." *Administrative Science Quarterly,* 1978, *23,* 418–433.

Dunn, W. N., and Swierczek, F. W. "Planned Organizational Change: Toward Grounded Theory." *Journal of Applied Behavioral Science,* 1977, *13*(2), 135–157.

Elmore, R. F. "Organizational Models of Social Program Implementation." *Public Policy,* 1978, *26,* 185–228.

Epple, D., Goodman, P. S., and Fidler, E. "Assessing the Economic Consequences of Organizational Change." In S. Seashore and others (Eds.), *Assessing Organizational Change: A Guide to Methods, Measures and Practices.* New York: Wiley-Interscience, 1982.

Firestone, W. A. "Participation and Influence in the Planning of Educational Change." *Journal of Applied Behavioral Science,* 1977, *13,* 167–183.

Friedlander, F., and Brown, L. D. "Organization Development." *Annual Review of Psychology*, 1974, *25*, 313–341.

Golembiewski, R. T., and Billingsley, K. "Measuring Change in OD Panel Designs: A Response to Critics." *Academy of Management Review*, 1980, *5*, 97–103.

Golembiewski, R. T., Billingsley, K., and Yeager, S. "Measuring Change and Persistence in Human Affairs: Types of Change Generated by OD Designs." *Journal of Applied Behavioral Science*, 1976, *12*, 133–157.

Goodman, P. S. *Assessing Organizational Change: The Rushton Quality of Work Experiment*. New York: Wiley-Interscience, 1979.

Goodman, P. S., and Conlon, E. "Observation of Meetings." In S. Seashore, E. Lawler, P. Mirvis, and C. Cammann (Eds.), *Assessing Organizational Change: A Guide to Methods, Measures and Practices*. New York: Wiley-Interscience, 1982.

Goodman, P. S., Conlon, E., and Bazerman, M. "Institutionalization of Planned Organizational Change." In B. M. Staw and L. L. Cummings (Eds.), *Research in Organizational Behavior*. Vol. 2. Greenwich, Conn.: JAI Press, 1978.

Goodman, P. S., and Lawler, E. E. "New Forms of Work Organization in the United States." Monograph prepared for the International Labor Organization, Geneva, Switzerland, 1977.

Goodman, P. S., and Pennings, J. "Critical Issues in Assessing Organizational Effectiveness." In E. Lawler, D. Nadler, and C. Cammann (Eds.), *Organizational Behavior and the Quality of Working Life*. New York: Wiley-Interscience, 1980.

Hackman, J., and Frank, L., "A Failure of Job Enrichment: The Case of the Change that Wasn't." In P. H. Mirvis and D. N. Berg (Eds.), *Failures in Organization: Development and Change*. New York: Wiley-Interscience, 1977.

Hackman, J., and Oldham, G. R. "Motivation Through the Design of Work: Test of a Theory." *Organizational Behavior and Human Performance*, 1977, *16*(2), 250–279.

Hackman, J., Pearce, J. L., and Wolfe, J. C. "Effects of Changes in Job Characteristics on Work Attitudes and Behaviors: A Naturally Occurring Quasi-Experiment." *Organizational Behavior and Human Performance*, 1978, *21*, 289–304.

Hage, J. *Theories of Organizations: Form, Process, and Transformation*. New York: Wiley-Interscience, 1980.

Hall, D. T., and others. "Effects of Top-Down Departmental and Job Change Upon Perceived Employee Behavior and Attitudes: A Natural Field Experiment." *Journal of Applied Psychology,* 1978, *63,* 62–72.

Hall, W. K. "Survival Strategies in a Hostile Environment." *Harvard Business Review,* 1980, *58,* 75–85.

Hannan, M. T., and Freeman, J. "The Population Ecology of Organizations." *American Journal of Sociology,* 1977, *82,* 929–965.

Hedberg, B. L., Nystrom, P. C., and Starbuck, W. H. "Camping on Seesaws: Prescription for a Self-Designing Organization." *Administrative Science Quarterly,* 1976, *21,* 41–65.

Huse, E. F. *Organization Development and Change.* St. Paul, Minn.: West, 1980.

Katz, D., and Kahn, R. L. *The Social Psychology of Organizations.* (2nd ed.) New York: Wiley-Interscience, 1978.

Khandwalla, P. N. "The Techno-Economic Ecology of Corporate Strategy." *Journal of Management Studies,* 1976, *13,* 62–75.

Kimberly, J. R. "Issues in the Creation of Organizations: Initiation, Innovation and Institutionalization." *Academy of Management Journal,* 1979, *22,* 437–457.

Kimberly, J. R., and Evanisko, M. J. "Organizational Innovation: The Influence of Individual Organizational and Contextual Factors on Hospital Adoption of Technological and Administrative Innovations." *Academy of Management Journal,* 1981, *24,* 689–713.

Kirton, M. "Adaptors and Innovators in Organizations." *Human Relations,* 1980, *33,* 213–224.

Kochan, T. A., and Dyer, L. "A Model of Organizational Change in the Context of Union-Management Relations." *Journal of Applied Behavioral Science,* 1976, *12,* 59–78.

Kuhn, T. S. *The Structure of Scientific Revolutions.* (2nd ed.) Chicago: University of Chicago Press, 1980.

Kurke, L. B. "Adaptability in Organizations: The Role of Environmental Change and Uncertainty in the Perpetuation of Decision Making Strategies." Unpublished doctoral dissertation, Graduate School of Business and Public Administration, Cornell University, 1981.

Lawler, E. E. III, Nadler, D. A., and Cammann, C. *Organizational Assessment.* New York: Wiley-Interscience, 1980.

Lawrence, P. R., and Lorsch, J. W. *Organization and Environment.* Homewood, Ill.: Irwin, 1967.

Levine, A. *Why Innovation Fails.* Albany: State University of New York Press, 1980.

Lewin, K. *Field Theory in Social Science.* (D. Cartwright, Ed.) New York: Harper & Row, 1951.

Lincoln, J. R., Olson, J., and Hanada, M. "Cultural Effects on Organizational Structure: The Case of Japanese Firms in the United States." *American Sociological Review,* 1978, *43*, 829–847.

Lindell, M. K., and Drexler, J. A., Jr. "Issues in Using Survey Methods for Measuring Organizational Change." *Academy of Management Review,* 1979, *4*(1), 13–19.

Lindsay, W. M., and Rue, L. W. "Impact of the Organization Environment on the Long-Range Planning Process: A Contingency View." *Academy of Management Journal,* 1980, *23*, 385–404.

McKelvey, W. "Organizational Systematics: Taxonomic Lessons from Biology." *Management Science,* 1978, *24*, 1428–1440.

McKelvey, W. *Organizational Systematics: Taxonomy, Evolution, Classification.* Berkeley: University of California Press, 1982.

Macy, B. A., Ledford, G. E., and Lawler, E. E. III. *An Assessment of the Bolivar Quality of Work Experiment: 1972–1979.* New York: Wiley-Interscience, 1982.

Macy, B. A., and Mirvis, P. H. "A Methodology for Assessment of Quality of Work Life and Organizational Effectiveness in Behavioral-Economic Terms." *Administrative Science Quarterly,* 1976, *21*(2), 212–226.

Macy, B. A., and Nurick, A. J. *Assessing Organization Change and Participation: The TVA Quality of Work Experiment.* New York: Wiley-Interscience, 1982.

March, J. G. "Footnotes to Organizational Change." *Administrative Science Quarterly,* 1981, *26*, 563–577.

March, J. G., and Olsen, J. P. *Ambiguity and Choice in Organizations.* Bergen, Norway: Universitetsforlaget, 1976.

Marks, M. "Organizational Adjustment to Uncertainty." *Journal of Management Studies,* 1977, *14*, 1–15.

Meyer, J. W., and Rowan, B. "Institutionalized Organizations: Formal Structure as Myth and Ceremony." *American Journal of Sociology,* 1978, *83*, 340–363.

Meyer, M. W. *Change in Public Bureaucracies.* Cambridge, Mass.: Harvard University Press, 1979.

Miles, R. E., and Snow, C. C. *Organizational Strategy, Structure, and Process.* New York: McGraw-Hill, 1978.

Miles, R. E., Snow, C. C., Meyer, A. O., and Coleman, H. J., Jr. "Organizational Strategy, Structure, and Process." *Academy of Management Review,* 1978, *3,* 546–562.

Miller, D., and Friesen, P. H. "Archetypes of Organizational Transition." *Administrative Science Quarterly,* 1980a, *25,* 268–299.

Miller, D., and Friesen, P. H. "Momentum and Revolution in Organizational Adaptation." *Academy of Management Journal,* 1980b, *23,* 591–694.

Mirvis, P. H., and Berg, D. N. (Eds.). *Failures in Organization Development and Change.* New York: Wiley-Interscience, 1977.

Moch, M. K. "Structure and Organizational Resource Allocation." *Administrative Science Quarterly,* 1976, *21,* 661–674.

Nadler, D. A. "Managing Organizational Change: An Integrative Perspective." *Journal of Applied Behavioral Science,* 1981, *17,* 191–211.

Nadler, D. A., Mirvis, P., and Cammann, C. "The Ongoing Feedback System—Experimenting with a New Managerial Tool." *Organizational Dynamics,* 1976, *4,* 63–80.

Nadler, D. A., and Tushman, M. L. "A Model for Diagnosing Organizational Behavior." *Organizational Dynamics,* 1980, *9,* 35–51.

Nielsen, F., and Hannan, M. T. "The Expansion of National Education Systems: Tests of a Population Ecology Model." *American Sociological Review,* 1977, *42,* 479–490.

O'Connor, E. J., Rudolf, C. J., and Peters, L. H. "Individual Differences and Job Design Reconsidered: Where Do We Go From Here?" *Academy of Management Review,* 1980, *5,* 249–254.

Padgett, J. F. "Hierarchy and Ecological Control in Federal Budgetary Decision Making." *American Journal of Sociology,* 1981, *87,* 75–129.

Peters, T. J. "Symbols, Patterns, and Settings: An Optimistic Case for Getting Things Done." *Organizational Dynamics,* 1978, *7,* 3–23.

Pfeffer, J. "Merger as a Response to Organizational Interdependence." *Administrative Science Quarterly,* 1972, *17,* 382–394.

Pfeffer, J. "Management as Symbolic Action: The Creation and Maintenance of Organizational Paradigms." In L. L. Cummings and B. M. Staw (Eds.), *Research in Organizational Behavior.* Vol. 3. Greenwich, Conn.: JAI Press, 1981.

Pfeffer, J., and Salancik, G. R. *The External Control of Organizations: A Resource Dependence Perspective.* New York: Harper & Row, 1978.

Porras, J. I., and Berg, P. O. "The Impact of Organization Development." *Academy of Management Review,* 1978, *3,* 249-266.

Quinn, R. E. "Towards a Theory of Changing: A Means-Ends Model of the Organizational Improvement Process." *Human Relations,* 1978, *31,* 395-416.

Ranson, S., Hinings, B., and Greenwood, R. "The Structure of Organizational Structures." *Administrative Science Quarterly,* 1980, *25,* 1-17.

Rosen, S., and Primps, S. B. "The Compressed Work Week as Organizational Change: Behavioral and Attitudinal Outcomes." *Academy of Management Review,* 1981, *6,* 61-74.

Rundall, T. G., and McClain, J. O. "Environmental Selection and Physician Supply." *American Journal of Sociology,* 1982, *87,* 1090-1112.

Schein, E. H. "The Mechanisms of Change." In W. Bennis, K. Benne, and R. Chin (Eds.), *The Planning of Change.* (2nd ed.) New York: Holt, Rinehart and Winston, 1969.

Scheirer, M. A. *Program Implementation: The Organizational Context.* Contemporary Evaluation Series, edited by H. E. Freeman and R. A. Berg, Vol. 5. Beverly Hills, Calif.: Sage, 1981.

Seashore, S., Lawler, E., Mirvis, P., and Cammann, C. (Eds.). *Assessing Organizational Change: A Guide to Methods, Measures and Practices.* New York: Wiley-Interscience, 1982.

Segal, M. "Organization and Environment: A Typology of Adaptability and Structure." *Public Administration Review,* 1974, *34,* 212-220.

Siegel, S. M., and Kaemmerer, W. F. "Measuring the Perceived Support for Innovation in Organizations." *Journal of Applied Psychology,* 1978, *63,* 553-562.

Snow, C. C., and Hrebiniak, L. G. "Strategy, Distinctive Competence, and Organizational Performance." *Administrative Science Quarterly,* 1980, *25,* 317-336.

Sproull, L., Weiner, S., and Wolf, D. *Organizing an Anarchy: Belief, Bureaucracy, and Politics in the National Institute of Education.* Chicago: University of Chicago Press, 1978.

Staw, B. M. "The Experimenting Organization." *Organizational Dynamics,* 1977, *6,* 3–18.

Tichy, N. M., Tushman, M. L., and Fombrun, C. "Network Analysis in Organizations." In E. E. Lawler, D. A. Nadler, and C. Cammann (Eds.), *Organizational Assessment.* New York: Wiley-Interscience, 1980.

Van de Ven, A. H., and Morgan, M. A. "A Revised Framework for Organizational Assessment." In E. E. Lawler, D. A. Nadler, and C. Cammann (Eds.), *Organizational Assessment.* New York: Wiley-Interscience, 1980.

Walton, R. "The Diffusion of New Work Structures: Explaining Why Success Didn't Take." In P. H. Mirvis and D. N. Berg (Eds.), *Failures in Organization Development and Change.* New York: Wiley-Interscience, 1977.

Walton, R. "Teaching an Old Dog Food New Tricks." *Wharton Magazine,* Winter 1978, pp. 38–46.

Walton, R. "Establishing and Maintaining High Commitment Work Systems." In J. R. Kimberly, R. H. Miles, and Associates, *The Organizational Life Cycle: Issues in the Creation, Transformation, and Decline of Organizations.* San Francisco: Jossey-Bass, 1980.

Weick, K. E. "Educational Organizations as Loosely-Coupled Systems." *Administrative Science Quarterly,* 1976, *21,* 1–19.

Weick, K. E. "Organization Design: Organizations as Self-Designing Systems." *Organizational Dynamics,* 1977, *6,* 31–46.

Weick, K. E. *The Social Psychology of Organizing.* (2nd ed.) Reading, Mass.: Addison-Wesley, 1979.

White, J. K. "Individual Differences and the Job Quality-Worker Response Relationship: Review, Integration, and Comments." *Academy of Management Review,* 1978, *2,* 267–280.

White, S. E., and Mitchell, T. R. "Organization Development: A Review of Research Content and Research Design." *Academy of Management Review,* 1976, *1*(2), 57–73.

Williams, W., and others. *Studying Implementation.* (A. Wildavsky, Ed.) Chatham, N.J.: Chatham House, 1982.

Woodward, J. *Industrial Organization: Theory and Practice.* Oxford: Oxford University Press, 1965.

Zald, M., and Berger, M. "Social Movements in Organizations: Coup d'etat, Insurgency and Mass Movements." *American Journal of Sociology*, 1978, *83*, 823–861.

Zaltman, G., and Duncan, R. *Strategies for Planned Change.* New York: Wiley-Interscience, 1977.

Zucker, L. G. "The Role of Institutionalization in Cultural Persistence." *American Sociological Review*, 1977, *42*, 726–743.

□ □ □ □ □ □ □   2

How Learning and Reasoning Processes Affect Organizational Change

□ □ □ □ □ □ □ □ □ □ □ □ □ □ □ □ □ □

Chris Argyris

Change in behavior is considered a primary criterion for effectiveness by organizational development researchers and practitioners. One way to alter behavior is through direct behavior modification. Learning theorists have been especially vocal in this approach. Another way is to understand the meanings people create when they deal with each other. Cognitive psychologists and sociologists, many ethnomethodologists, and existentialists have been primary contributors to this line of inquiry.*

The experientially oriented theorists have tended to be biased in the second approach, one that might be called the individual and

I should like to thank Donald Schön, Viviane Robinson, and Lee Bolman for their helpful comments.

*For reviews of the relevant literature, see Argyris, 1980b; Argyris and Schön, 1974, 1978.

47

social construction of reality. Donald Schön and I have attempted to build on this approach in several ways. We have suggested that there are important differences in the meanings created when people espouse their views versus acting them out. Moreover, individuals are often unaware of these differences. They can best be discovered by observing people in action and inferring the meanings embedded in their actions. Finally, we have suggested that the source of meanings is in the theories of action people use (not those they espouse) and that the learning systems of society reinforce these theories. Hence, behavior change that is more than a "gimmick" requires changes in the theories that people use and in the learning systems of the organization.

In this chapter, I describe some recent research results. They suggest that equally, if not more, fundamental to the theories of action that people use are their reasoning processes. Reasoning processes are those activities by which we create premises that are assumed or proven to be valid and from which we draw conclusions about how to act. Popper (1969) has suggested these reasoning processes are at the core of how individuals construe reality.

Organizational Learning: Single- and Double Loop

Learning is defined as occurring under two conditions. First, learning occurs when an organization achieves what it intended; that is, there is a *match* between its design for action and the actuality or outcome. Second, learning occurs when a *mismatch* between intentions and outcomes is identified and it is corrected; that is, a mismatch is turned into a match.

Organizations do not perform the behavior that produces the learning. It is individuals acting as agents of organizations who produce the behavior that leads to learning. Organizations can create conditions that may significantly influence what individuals frame as the problem, design as a solution, and produce as action to solve a problem. Individuals may also bring to the learning situation biases and constraints that are relatively independent of the organization's requirements. An example of constraint is the human mind's limited capability for information processing. An example of bias is the theories of action with which people are socialized and which they necessarily bring to the organization. These theories significantly influence how individuals and groups solve problems and make choices.

Whenever an error is detected and corrected without questioning or altering the underlying values of the system (be it individual, group, intergroup, organizational, or interorganizational), the learning is single-loop. The term is borrowed from electrical engineering or cybernetics, where, for example, a thermostat is defined as a single-loop learner. The thermostat is programmed to detect states of "too cold" or "too hot" and to correct the situation by turning the heat on or off. If the thermostat asked itself such questions as why it was set at 68 degrees or why it was programmed as it was, it would be a double-loop learner.

Single-loop learning and double-loop learning are diagrammed in Figure 1. Single-loop learning occurs when matches are created or when mismatches are corrected by changing actions. Double-loop learning occurs when mismatches are corrected by examining and altering first the governing variables and then the actions. Governing variables are the preferred states that individuals strive to satisfice when they are acting. These governing variables are *not* the underlying beliefs or values people espouse; they are the variables that can be inferred, by observing individuals acting as agents for the organization, to drive and guide their actions.

Figure 1 indicates that learning has not occurred until a match or a mismatch is produced. Learning may *not* be said to occur if someone (acting for the organization) discovers a new problem or invents a solution to a problem. Learning occurs when the invented solution is actually produced. This distinction is important because it implies that discovering problems and inventing solutions are necessary, but not sufficient, conditions for organizational learning. Organizations exist in order to act and to accomplish their intended consequences. Another reason this distinction is important is related to my recent research, which suggests that significantly different designs, heuristics for action, and criteria for success are used when individuals discover and invent concerning an issue than when they discover and invent in order to produce an outcome about the issue (Argyris, 1980b; Argyris & Schön, 1978).

Figure 1. Single- and Double-Loop Learning.

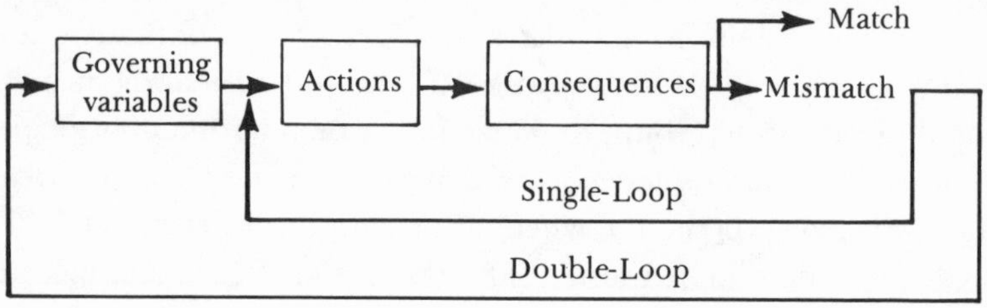

All organizations require single- and double-loop learning. One might say that one of the features of organizations as a social technology is to decompose double-loop issues into single-loop issues because they are then more easily programmable and manageable. Single-loop learning is appropriate for the routine, repetitive issue—it helps get the everyday job done. Double-loop learning is more relevant for the complex, nonprogrammable issues—it assures that there will be another day in the future of the organization. (There are times, however, when single-loop learning may be relevant to long-range survival. For example, one of Europe's leading organizational research institutes was having difficulties with certain important clients because some of its interventionists failed to meet deadlines, to be on time for meetings, and so forth.)

This chapter examines the reasoning processes people use when they are attempting to double-loop learn for themselves or for the organization. I will show that the reasoning processes people use for double-loop learning are actually counterproductive to such learning, that people are unaware of the counterproductive features of their own actions but usually aware of such features in others, and that the unawareness exists in all subjects and hence may be due to a program in people's heads of which they must necessarily be unaware.

The Importance of Double-Loop Learning to Science and Practice

The overwhelming number of organizational changes reported in organizational development, political science, management information systems, and organizational sociology represent single-loop changes (Argyris, 1972, 1973, 1976a; Argyris & Schön, 1978). Recent reviews by Hage (1980) and Lammers (1980) appear to arrive at similar conclusions. The emphasis on organizational single-loop learning may be at least partially due to the fact that most organizational activities are single-loop, that is, decomposing complex tasks into simpler tasks that produce the intended result when correctly carried out.

But several unintended consequences result when social scientists study primarily single-loop change. First, although single-loop actions are the most numerous, they are not necessarily the most powerful. Double-loop actions—the master programs—control the long-range effectiveness and hence the ultimate destiny of the system.

Some Gaps in Current Change Models

Lewin, many years ago, developed a model of change that has been used for single- and double-loop organizational learning. The model suggested three stages: unfreezing, introducing the new values and behavior, and then refreezing. This model has been developed further by several writers (for example, Schein and Bennis, 1965).

Essentially, most of these models assume that unfreezing is produced by showing that actions lead to unintended inconsistencies (the impact is not what is intended). They also assume that human beings abhor such inconsistency and hence seek to learn new actions and values so that they do not repeat such errors. Practice or experimentation with the new actions is assumed to lead to attitude and value change, as well as behavioral change.

At the outset, Donald Schön and I used essentially the same model to describe our views on change (Argyris and Schön, 1974), but we soon learned that the model was useful primarily at an abstract level of discourse and for single-loop learning. When we attempted to help individuals unfreeze the old in order to produce double-loop learning, we found that there were several crucial gaps in the model.

The first gap was that the old model assumed that individuals had the skills to learn the new behavior, or at least the skills to learn the new skills. It now appears that this is not necessarily the case for double-loop learning. For example, we believed that if individuals were able to experience an inconsistency in their actions, they would correct it. This belief proved valid only when the individuals could alter their actions without examining their governing variables (for example, listen more or ask specific questions). But if the error was of a magnitude to produce mistrust rather than trust, correcting it was not simple. In order to produce trust, individuals must act in ways that entrust themselves to others; they make themselves vulnerable. Before they are willing to take such action, they must examine their fears about what others may do to them or their fears about designing their own vulnerability. Such an inquiry will lead to the underlying assumptions and values they hold, which, in our language, are part of the governing variables of their theory of action. It is important for social scientists to study double-loop change because, if they focus only on single-loop change, they may unwittingly become servants of the status quo (Argyris, 1972, 1980b; Moscovici, 1976).

This consequence holds negative outcomes for social science as a science. It is becoming evident that there may be a paradox embedded in the goal that social science should be descriptive of the world as it is. If social scientists aspire to study individuals and systems as they are, they will inevitably fall short of this goal because a complete description of what they are would have to include a valid description of their capacity to make significant changes and of the mechanisms by which these changes will occur. Knowledge of these mechanisms will also produce valid generalizations about constraints to double-loop organizational change. Such significant changes require changes in the organizational governing variables and master programs, that is, double-loop changes. But double-loop changes cannot occur without unfreezing the models of organizational structures and processes now in good currency. These models, in turn, cannot be unfrozen without a model of a significantly different organizational state of affairs. Otherwise toward what is the organization to change? If these models are genuinely new, then they do not now exist. If they do not now exist, then their invention and their use is an act of proscription, a normative stance. Yet if the logic is correct, the normative stance is needed to get at the inner nature of the present double-loop features and potentials of organization. Hence, a full description of the world as is requires the stimulation of the world as is with stimuli from a world that presently is a rare event.

This leads to the second gap, namely, the pervasiveness with which individuals are unaware that they do not have the skills that they may value. The gap is compounded by the fact that the unawareness may not be due simply to some void or lack of knowledge. The unawareness may actually be tacitly designed, highly automatic, and hence, a highly skilled action.

The third gap is related to the belief held by many of us dealing with experiential learning that unawareness is primarily related to some form of suppression, especially of feelings. We assumed that if individuals could learn to get in touch with, and to express, their relevant feelings, their scope of unawareness would decrease and the probability of producing competent actions would increase. Again, as in the case of the other assumptions, this is partially valid but incomplete. It appears now that the basis for individuals not being in touch with their feelings, or being reluctant to express them, is not simply some kind of defensiveness or resistance. It appears that human beings may use reasoning processes that unknowingly distort the necessity to be in touch with and express their feelings. In other words, in order to express feelings, we must first alter reasoning processes.

A fourth gap is the assumption that one can understand individuals' values by asking them to state them. If individuals do not behave consistently with the values that they espouse, then that is usually seen as an error to be corrected. It now appears that a somewhat more complex interpretation is more valid. If an error is a mismatch between intentions and actual consequences, if individual actions are designed, and if they are free of situational constraints on their design and implementation, it is not possible for individuals knowingly to design and execute an error. If A decides to act in a way that will produce dysfunctional consequences, then such "errors" are intended, and hence there is a match, not an error.

If such errors are not errors, they must be the consequence of some design. If this is so, then individuals must have some sort of map, schemata, or microtheory that they use to inform their design.

Because this design or theory is different from the one they espouse, a differentiation must be made between espoused values and theory and the theory-in-use. Social scientists have focused for many years on the inconsistencies between espoused values and actual behavior. What has hardly been discussed are the values, or the theory-in-use, that explain the inconsistencies, that is, that show how the inconsistent is consistent.

These gaps suggest that the differences in complexity between single- and double-loop learning may be more profound than previously anticipated. If so, the programs for organizational double-loop learning may require more effort than those designed for single-loop learning.

Some recent data may help illustrate the points I have made and set the foundation for my view of designing organizational double-loop learning.

The Case of X and Y: Getting at the Underlying Reasoning Processes. Fifty-three local and state government officials (25 percent women and 19 percent other minorities, ranging in age from early thirties to late fifties) were given an excerpt from a transcript between Y and X. Y, the superior, had been asked to "help X change his attitudes and behavior so that he could improve his performance." Although the organization was genuinely interested in keeping X, he would probably have to be dismissed if his attitudes and performance did not improve. Y made the following comments to X:

1. X, your performance is not up to standard (and moreover. . .).
2. You seem to be carrying a chip on your shoulder.
3. It appears to me that this has affected your performance in a number of ways. I have heard words like "lethargy," "uncommitted," and "disinterested" used by others in describing your recent performance.
4. Our senior professionals cannot have those characteristics.
5. Let's discuss your feelings about your performance.
6. X, I know you want to talk about the injustices that you believe have been perpetrated on you in the past. The problem is that I am not familiar with the specifics of those problems. I do not want to spend a lot of time discussing something that happened

several years ago. Nothing constructive will come from it. It's behind us.

7. I want to talk about you today, and about your future in our system.

Each official was asked to answer three questions:

1. What is your reaction or diagnosis of the way Y helped X?
2. What advice, if any, would you give Y to improve his performance when helping individuals like X?
3. Assume that Y met you in the hall and asked, "What did you think of the way I handled X?" How would you respond? Please write up your response in the form of a scenario, using the righthand side of the page.

   On the lefthand side of the page, write any thoughts or feelings that you might have during the conversation that you would not, for whatever reason, communicate to Y.

All but two (96 percent) of the respondents diagnosed Y's actions as largely counterproductive to helping X. Two believed that Y behaved only partially effectively because he did make a few errors "in the manner that he talked with X." Hence, the first feature of the diagnosis was that there was near consensus that Y's actions were not effective. If consensus is an indication of valid information, then the respondents were getting at what they believed to be the truth.

The second feature was that the reasoning processes used to construct the diagnosis involved inferences that were at varying degrees of distance from the relatively directly observable data (that is, the sentences in the first list). Comments that appeared to be easily inferable from the transcript were "Y cut off X," "Y criticized X's attitudes," and "Y quoted others to illustrate his points."

Next there were such statements as "Y was too blunt," "Y did not give X an opportunity to defend self," and "Y prejudged X." These sentences may well be correct inferences, but their validity is not self-evident. For example, Y may believe that he was not too blunt, that he did give X an opportunity to defend himself, and that he did not prejudge X. Y could maintain he was appropriately blunt

in order to be honest, that he did not give X an opportunity to
defend himself because he did not wish to open up the past, or that
he expressed a judgment made by top management about X's performance, a judgment of which X was aware.

In the sentences in the previous paragraph, the respondents
were making inferences about the meanings Y was producing when
"helping" X. A third and higher level of inference is evidenced in
the respondents' sentences that went beyond meanings and attributed motives to Y, presumably to explain his actions. For example,
"Y was not interested in getting at the truth," "Y was aggressive,
cold, detached," and "Y was unwilling and not interested in understanding X."

Examining some simple quantitative data, we find that in
every individual diagnosis, the largest number of comments was at
Level III on a ladder of inference; the second largest number of
comments was at Level II; and there was a significant drop-off to
Level I. For example, of 114 scorable sentences in the respondents'
written diagnoses, 60 percent were Level III, 36 percent were Level
II, and 4 percent were Level I. The important point is that the
diagnoses with which the respondents framed the answer contained
primarily attributions and evaluations that required complex levels
of reasoning about the sentences spoken by Y. Less than 15 percent
of the respondents illustrated these inferences.

The different levels of inference individuals made became
their premises. They then generated their conclusions from these
premises. For example, if Y was described as "blunt" or "not interested in getting at the truth," then it followed (given a tacit theory of
defense) that he would probably upset X and hence little learning
would occur. The inferences from the premises appear valid. The
problem is that the premise is subject to question. It is doubtful, for
example, that Y would agree with it. If so, it is also doubtful that
they can help Y by using premises whose validity he may doubt. In
other words, the premises should be subject to test.

When we examine the scenarios they wrote as to how they
would communicate with Y, we see they did not attempt to test their
premises. The participants assumed that their premises were valid,
and obviously so. "Anyone reading this conversation can see that Y
was insensitive and blunt" is a representative comment. The near-

perfect consensus of views previously described appears to support this claim.

Some readers may wonder if the words "reaction" and "diagnosis" may not trigger different responses. I have tried each word separately, jointly, and in combination with other words (for example, "Give us your views of Y's effectiveness" or "How effective do you believe Y was with X?"). To date, the different combinations have not led to different results. In the early studies, when we interviewed respondents about the instrument, the overwhelming number of them interpreted our intent as learning their evaluation of Y's effectiveness with X. In this connection, our difficulty is not that Y made evaluations or attributions; indeed, we asked for such reactions. My point is that all the respondents assumed that their evaluations and attributions were obvious, concrete, and required no testing.

The fourth feature is that embedded in the diagnoses was a microcausal theory of what happened between Y and X. For example:

> If Y is blunt and negative, judgmental and offensive, threatening and lacking in sensitivity, not interested in understanding X, dominating X
> *Then* X will feel rejected, prejudged, unfairly treated, and defensive.
> If the above is true, *then* there will be little learning going on between Y and X so that X is helped.

Another way to describe what the respondents did is as follows. When asked to give their reactions to the sentences, the respondents organized the meanings inferred from the sentences into a causal sequence to explain the probable effectiveness of Y with X. In so doing, they enacted, or constructed, reality; that is, the diagnoses represented their view of what happened. All appeared to enact reality by creating a causal view that contained Levels II and III (attribution and evaluation) from which conclusions were drawn (X would feel defensive). Thus, little learning would occur.

Embedded in this causal analysis is the fact that, if the respondents communicated their diagnostic frames to Y, they would be creating the same conditions for Y that they condemn Y for creating with X. For example, to tell someone that he is "blunt," "cold," and "insensitive" could be experienced by the receiver as blunt, cold, and insensitive. In other words, the respondents (all of them, including the two who had expressed some ambivalence) used reasoning processes (that is, premises and conclusions) that produced a causal analysis of Y's impact on X. There was a high degree of agreement that, if the analysis were told to Y, it would create the very conditions that they deplored.

When this puzzle was pointed out, the participants reacted in two ways. The initial reaction of the majority was to deny that this was the case and to try to prove that the logic used by the instructor was incorrect.* But the further the discussion progressed, the greater the number of respondents who agreed with the faculty member. Moreover, an increasing number pointed out that their reactions to the faculty member's comments, and each other's, contained the same type of reasoning (attributions and evaluations that were neither illustrated nor tested) they had used with Y. They pointed out that the faculty member was also making attributions and evaluations about their actions. He was, however, illustrating them and testing them publicly.

When the faculty member asked the class what they were now thinking and feeling, all those who replied (about 50 percent) used such words as "surprised," "shocked," and "disbelief." When asked if anyone had a different set of reactions, no one described any.

The sixth feature of the diagnosis was that the respondents were unaware of the inconsistencies. Otherwise why were they surprised and shocked? This attribution by the faculty member appeared to help some of the participants formulate a new reaction. They reported that, although the attribution might be true, many of them had no intention of telling Y what was in their diagnostic frame. They intended to censor the ideas in their frame. A few did say that they did not expect to censor the content. They believed that someone had to be direct and forthright with Y, just as they believed that Y had to be direct with X. I call this group the "direct" or

*Transcripts of such discussions will be available in a forthcoming book by Argyris tentatively titled *Reasoning and Learning: Individual and Organizational.*

"forthright" group. They represented about 11 percent of the respondents.

An overwhelming number of the respondents (89 percent) took what may be described as an "easing-in" approach. Primarily through questions and what some described as "neutral" statements, they would get Y to realize his errors. The easing-in approach meant that Y would be asked questions by which—if correctly answered—he would discover what the "helpers" had been keeping secret in their diagnostic frames. If Y could answer these questions in the manner considered appropriate by the framers, he might not have acted toward X as he did.

The reasoning behind the easing-in approach appears to be as follows. The respondents hold a microtheory of defensiveness (Y's) that they use to design their actions. The theory of defense suggests do not prejudge, do not evaluate, do not upset, do not appear negative. There are four troublesome characteristics of this microtheory: (1) It does not tell an actor what to do; it informs him what not to do. (2) It advises the actor not to do what he is already doing or has already done. In this case, the participants have already prejudged, have evaluated negatively, and so on, hence the advice to hide what they have done. (3) The advice is at such a high level of inference that the recipients can violate it without being aware of the violation. (4) The organizational reality was that Y had to be evaluated and judged.

Table 1 gives an example of the easing-in approach. Keep in mind that the scenario and the thoughts and feelings were written by the same person.

From the material on the lefthand side, we infer the writer was always "in control." She had diagnosed Y as ineffective, and her task was to get Y to gain this insight without telling him directly. She did not suspend her diagnostic frame but used it covertly to judge and evaluate Y's responses. Note her unexpressed thoughts are not nondirective, do not ease in. The easing-in feature is primarily related to the questions she asked and the comments she made. However, these comments may not have had the impact intended.

Table 2 analyzes Table 1. It includes other reasonable interpretations. The first column contains the lefthand, unexpressed thoughts. The next column contains my inference of the meaning

Table 1. An Example of the Easing-In Approach.

Unexpressed Thoughts and Feelings	Conversation
	Y: Did you read my memo on the X meeting?
Let him commit himself first so I can see what he thinks happened.	*Me:* Yeah, looks like it was quite a meeting.
"A guy like X" . . . there's my cue.	*Y:* So how do you ever know if you got through to a guy like X?
	Me: You didn't write much about what he was like.
	Y: He didn't talk a lot. Wouldn't look directly at me when he was talking.
How much planning did Y do?	*Me:* What were you thinking he'd say? You know, before the meeting.
Apparent from your memo.	*Y:* I expected he'd complain a lot but I cut him off when he started in on it.
	Me: If he didn't talk much, how come he opened up with you to complain?
	Y: I asked him what he felt about his past.
Let's see if he catches on by himself.	*Me:* (pause)
	Y: Then I turned right around and cut him off. That wasn't very smart.
Agree with him a little before you lead him into the big question.	*Me:* It's hard to know how much of the past to listen to. But you must have some idea where he went wrong.
	Y: Everybody tells me he has a terrible attitude. I kept trying not to pay attention to how defensive he was. But he sat back kind of smug and. . . .

Table 1. An Example of the Easing-In Approach, Cont'd.

Unexpressed Thoughts and Feelings	Conversation
Get his attention back on his own problem of dealing with X.	*Me:* (breaking in) What do you think of this assignment anyway?
	Y: Almost hopeless.
Should I take him into the "what if fire" or the "what if succeed"? I'll go this way first, come back again.	*Me:* You could be right. But what would happen if you did succeed?
	Y: Management—and old Z— would pat me on the back and then forget it. And I'd still have X.
Give him a little sympathy. Then let's see if he knows what he's got here.	*Me:* Sounds like the boys have been razzing you about X. But really, if you do turn him around, won't he be of some value? He must have been at one time.
You've got it. I won't rub it in. However, there's another one to mention.	*Y:* Yes, I suppose if he wasn't, management wouldn't keep him around. I should have told him that, too.
	Me: I don't know, Y. It sounds to me like you didn't do enough homework. How can you work on this guy if you don't know what made him so good up until three years ago?
Now he's getting enthusiastic. That's better.	*Y:* That's for sure.

embedded in the first column material. The third column is what the writer of the case actually said. The fourth column contains my inference of Y's possible interpretation of what was said to him in the third column. The fifth column contains near quotes of how Y responded to the conversation in the third column.

Table 2. An Analysis of an Easing-In Case.

Thoughts on the Lefthand Side of the Case	Meaning Inferred by the Writer	What the Respondent Said	Possible Meaning to Y as Inferred by the Writer	Y Said
Let him commit himself first so I can see what he thinks happened.	I would like to get Y's view without telling Y that this is my intent.	"Yeah, looks like it was getting a meeting."	I wonder what she means by that. Can I get her to commit herself without telling her my intent?	"So how do you ever know if you got through to a guy like X?"
"A guy like X"—there's my cue.	I'll use Y's unillustrated evaluation of X to get him to commit himself about what he thinks happened.	"You didn't write much about what he was like."	"You have not communicated to me your view of X." I wonder why she says that? What is she trying to find out?	"He didn't talk a lot. Wouldn't look directly at me when he was talking."
How much planning did Y do?	I'll try another way of discovering his view of the situation. I wonder if he thought through the approach.	"What were you thinking he'd say? You know, before the meeting."	What is she getting at? Doesn't anyone expect a guy in trouble to complain and find fault with others?	"I expected he'd complain a lot but I cut him off when he started in on it."
Apparent from your memo.	I know you cut him off. I have to get you to see your errors.	"If he didn't talk much, why did he open up with you to complain?"	What is she getting at? I initiated that by asking him about the past.	"I asked him what he felt about his past."

Let's see if he catches on by himself.	(meaning is covert) His inconsistencies are so obvious that perhaps a pause with a pause he will reflect on them.	Pause	I guess she wants me to say that I cut him off and that was not effective. I'll admit that so maybe I can learn what she's driving at.	"Then I turned right around and cut him off. That wasn't very smart."
Agree with him a little before you lead him into the big question.	Softsoap Y a bit to prepare him for what is a threatening question.	"It's hard to know how much of the past to listen to. but you must have some idea where he went wrong."	I'm glad she sees my dilemma, but if she does, why has she asked me all those questions? Of course I have an idea of where he went wrong. It was his attitude. What is she driving at?	"Everybody tells me he has a terrible attitude. I kept trying not to pay attention to how defensive he was. But he sat back kind of smug and. . . ."
Get his attention back on his own problems of dealing with X.	I've got to get him back to what I think is the problem, namely, the way he dealt with X.	(breaking in) "What do you think of this assignment anyway?"	She must know this is almost a hopeless case. Why is she asking me such obvious questions? What does she *really* have in mind?	"Almost hopeless."
Should I take him into the "what if fire" or the "what if succeed"? I'll go this way first, come back again.	Maybe I can get him to see the possible payoff if he is able to succeed with X.	"You could be right. But what would happen if you did succeed?"	She doesn't think I'm right. I believe it is hopeless and hence believe that the best that can come of this is that Z will feel good and I'll be stuck with X. She is trying to get me to either see something or say something.	"Management—and old Z—would pat me on the back and then forget it. And I'd still have X."

Table 2. (Continued)

Thoughts on the Lefthand Side of the Case	Meaning Inferred by the Writer	What the Respondent Said	Possible Meaning to Y as Inferred by the Writer	Y Said
Give him a little sympathy. Then let's see if he knows what he's got here.	Sympathize with him in order to get him ready for my confrontation.	"Sounds like the group has been razzing you about X. But really, if you do turn him around, won't he be of some value? He must have been at one time."	No one is razzing me. Z and others are depending on me. She does not understand me. Of course if you turn X around it would be of value—but I think that it is hopeless. I'm feeling that it is hopeless to understand her or to get her to understand my views.	"I suppose. If he wasn't, management wouldn't keep him around. I should have told him that, too."
You've got it. I won't rub it in. However, there's another one to mention.	Finally you see it. I'll lay off that problem and go to another.	"I don't know, Y. Sounds to me like you didn't do enough homework. How can you work on this guy if you don't know what made him so good up until three years ago?"	Finally! She believes that I did not do a good job. I know what made him so good up until three years ago. The trouble is that he doesn't have it and he refuses to see it. Not much sense in arguing with her.	"That's for sure."
Now he's getting enthusiastic—that's better	He finally sees what I have seen all the			

It is important to keep in mind that gaps between what the helper intended and the meanings Y could have inferred were found in all the cases. The content of the gap may have varied, but the existence of the gap, and unawareness of it, did not vary. Table 3 shows two more examples.

To summarize, although the respondents appeared to hold tacitly a microtheory of client defensiveness that led them to con-

Table 3. Two More Examples of the Easing-In Approach.

Respondent Asked	*Y Could Have Thought*
1. What kind of reaction did you get from X?	1. She knows that he resisted. I wonder what she is driving at.
2. Did you discuss specific examples of poor performance that X could undertake to correct?	2. Of course I discussed his poor attitude. What is she driving at?
3. Did you talk about any specifics, such as his lateness in meeting deadlines?	3. I had to keep it general, lest we get into his rehashing old alibis. I wonder why she does not see that.
4. Do you think it would have been helpful to him to know exactly what it is he is doing that fails to meet the standards we expect?	4. She should know that. Besides, I wish that I knew what specifics she is driving at.
1. Well, I'm not sure. What were you trying to accomplish in the meeting?	1. I'll bet he knows and is not saying.
2. Do you think he left with that understanding?	2. Of course I do. I wonder if he thinks so. What is he driving at?
3. I wonder if X isn't concerned about whether he'll really have a fair chance this time.	3. Of course that is the way X will feel. Whose side is he on? What is he driving at?
4. It's probably difficult for X to understand your genuine interest in understanding his problems and providing him with a fresh start. I think you could have emphasized this a little more.	4. Of course that's X's trouble. He is blind to those who wish to help him. Now I'm beginning to see what he is driving at.

clude that unilateral control, prejudging, and unilateral attributions were counterproductive, they acted in ways to produce these conditions *and* simultaneously advised Y not to produce these conditions; yet they were unaware of this inconsistency.

If one criterion of incompetence is to act in a way that one advises others not to act, then the actions of the respondents may be judged as incompetent. But there is an additional, and perhaps more troublesome, inference. Whenever individuals state propositions about how all should act under given conditions, *and* when they themselves do not act in accordance with that proposition yet appear to believe that they are, they are creating conditions of injustice. It is not just to say that, under condition *A*, all individuals should behave *B*, when the person who states this proposition acts "not B" (opposite of B) when in condition *A* and acts as if that is correct.

Advice the Respondents Gave to Y. The advice that the respondents gave in their papers may be categorized as advice about processes that are internal and external to the actual interview. Advice about the internal processes was primarily advice about how Y should behave toward X in order to help X improve his performance. Advice about processes that are external to the actual interview included advice that Y should have studied X's file more thoroughly, made it clear that management wanted to keep X, and jointly defined with X specific assignments, measurable goals, and a timetable.

There was a high degree of consensus about the advice the respondents wrote they would give Y. For example, the comments listed illustrate advice given by all the respondents. No advice is excluded that might have contradicted the following comments.

The following are examples of advice about how Y should have behaved toward X:

1. Encouraged X to discuss his view of his successes and failures candidly
2. Found out from X what he feels are his strong points and where he needs improvement
3. Helped X express his prior problems (without getting into personality issues)

4.   Given him the feeling that he was wanted, that the senior staff saw good potential in him
5.   Ended the conference on a positive, upbeat note
6.   Expressed a genuine concern for X's future in the organization
7.   Listened genuinely to X's version of the problem
8.   Showed that he (Y) had an open mind
9.   Been more tactful to indicate the hope for a more cordial relationship
10. Helped X vent his feelings in order to release his frustrations
11. Been more specific and constructive in feedback concerning X's performance
12. Motivated X toward improved performance
13. Drawn out from X his ideas as to what he (X) perceived as his needs on the job and needs of supervision
14. Avoided making subjective statements

These are examples of advice about what Y should have brought to the session. Y should have done the following:

1.   Given X an indication that all were behind him to succeed, that they wished to give him a genuine fresh start
2.   Reviewed X's history and performance in detail in order to discover when and why X's performance deteriorated
3.   Developed jointly with X specific assignments, measurable goals, and a timetable for completion
4.   Developed jointly with X regularly scheduled reviews
5.   Established jointly with X a system that would monitor improvement and, if essential, prepare for an ultimate dismissal
6.   Welcomed X to his department and explained to X how important his job was and how important it would be for him to succeed at it

The gap between the advice and producing the action is not large in the second or "external" category. Most respondents would know how (have the required skills) to study X's performance, to inform X that the company is behind him, and to define specific tasks, goals, and timetables.

The gap in the first category of advice is large. That is, the respondents who recommended this advice had difficulty applying it themselves and were unaware that this was the case.

It is not clear why most individuals completing these cases are able to produce advice easily, yet are unable to follow their own advice when they write their scenarios, and why they appear unaware that this is the case. We think that part of the answer is the way they frame their advice. They may be unaware that their advice involves a very high level of inference.

Generalizability of These Results. Some readers may find the lack of variance troublesome. Everyone seems to create diagnostic frames that contain the same features he advises others not to use, and when acting, everyone seems to get into difficulties of inconsistency, incompetence, and injustice. I, too, was troubled by these consistencies because I assumed variance is a necessary feature of the universe. Indeed, such consistent data could illustrate a poor theory or flawed empirical work.

Every time a new experiment was attempted, we tried to be aware of, and deal with, ways that our instruments and methods might be creating these results. We had enthusiastic support from the subjects because they did not like the inconsistencies they were producing or their apparent inability to correct them. If they could show that the results were somehow forced by the methods (including the behavior of the faculty), then they would feel greatly relieved.

To date, we have collected data using the X and Y case from seventeen groups, with nearly six hundred respondents (including respondents from Europe, South America, Africa, the Near East [Israel and Egypt] and India). The results are highly consistent. Indeed, if we include the results obtained from the three thousand individuals using different cases, the results are still the same. Why the high degree of consistency in the data?

Treating High Levels of Inference as Concrete Reality

A possible answer to the question of why there is so little variance in the reasoning processes and actions of the respondents is that all individuals must distance themselves from the relatively directly observable data in order to design and manage their actions. It is not possible to react in an organized manner without first extracting from, and organizing from, what occurs. This is what is meant by "constructing or enacting reality." High levels of inference are necessary because they make possible on-line management of reality. In this connection, one is reminded of Simon's (1969) view that the environment is more complex than the human mind can deal with directly, and of Miller's (1956) work, which states that the human mind at a given moment may be able to process seven (plus or minus two) units of information. Beyond this number, new and more abstract concepts that subsume the lower level units of information are needed. The work of both men suggests that there is a hierarchy of concepts that makes it possible to organize, make sense out of, and enact reality.

However, there is nothing in their work that requires this hierarchy of concepts be attributions or evaluations that are not illustrated or tested. That is, perhaps the human mind must use concepts requiring high levels of inference from the raw data. But why must individuals use concepts that contain such a high probability for miscommunication? And why do individuals use such concepts when they advise others not to do so? And why, in many cases, do they do so when they are simultaneously advising others not to do so (for example, "The trouble with you is that you are putting the other person down")? Scholars working with attribution theory have frequently documented that individuals act like naive scientists. They create causal explanations to explain what they observe. More often than not, they tend to blame others for errors, and they tend to attribute any positive consequences to themselves (Kelley, 1979; Kruglanski, 1980). But again, the question is why.

Model I Theory-in-Use

A second cause of the consistency in results is related to the fact that the focus is not on predicting the actual words or behavior individuals will use. These factors may vary widely, as do the values that people espouse. The focus is on understanding the master programs in individuals' heads so that we can predict the kind of meanings and behavioral strategies they will or will not produce.

Donald Schön and I have proposed a theory of action perspective that assumes human beings design their actions (Argyris and Schön, 1974, 1978). Because it is not likely they can design complex actions de novo in every situation, individuals must hold theories about effective action that they bring to bear on any given situation. We suggest that there are two kinds of theories of action. The first is espoused theories. The advice that the respondents gave to Y were aspects of espoused theories of effective action. But few respondents acted congruently with those espoused theories. Most seemed to be unaware of the gap between their espoused theory and their actions. Such discrepancies are not new in social science.

The theory of action perspective does not stop there. It suggests that the unawareness is designed. It suggests that the incongruence is designed. It suggests, in other words, that human beings must have a theory of action that they use to produce all these difficulties. We call this type of theory their theory-in-use. If we can make explicit the theory-in-use, then we can explain, predict, and have the basis for changing these findings.

One of the difficulties with the attribution theorist's view is that it implies that individuals act as they do (make attributions that are untested) because they have to; it is "human nature." We could agree that it is human nature if we call it theory-in-use. We have been able to devise other theories-in-use that, once learned, allow individuals to behave other than according to the prediction of attribution theory (Argyris, 1976a, 1976b). This work suggests, therefore, that the cause is not a static human nature but rather that human nature is significantly alterable.

We have created a model of theory-in-use that most individuals appear to us to use. A Model I theory-in-use has four governing variables or values for the actor to satisfice: (1) strive to be in unilateral control, (2) minimize losing and maximize winning, (3) minimize the expression of negative feelings, and (4) be rational. Along with the governing variables are a set of behavioral strategies such as (1) advocate your views without encouraging inquiry (hence, remain in unilateral control and, it is hoped, win) and (2) unilaterally save face—your own and other people's (hence, minimize upsetting others or making them defensive).

These governing variables and behavioral strategies form a master program that influences the diagnostic and action frames that individuals produce. Hence, when Y behaved as he did, he violated the governing variable of not eliciting negative feelings and the behavioral strategy of unilaterally protecting others and one's self. Such actions would not assist Y to win because winning, in this case, was defined as helping X change his attitude.

This theory-in-use, which we call Model I, is held by all the individuals studied so far (Argyris, 1976a, 1976b, 1980b; Argyris & Schön, 1974, 1978). Model I individuals are able to behave according to Model I, the opposite to Model I, or an oscillating Model I (that is, *A* unilaterally controls *B*, and then *B* does the same to *A*, and so on). The behavioral strategies, once learned, are highly skilled, meaning that the action achieves its objectives. Although complex, it is performed effortlessly; actions are produced so fast that they appear automatic.

At the moment, our hypothesis is that Model I has been learned through socialization. This hypothesis, which has yet to be proven directly, is inferred from the following types of experiences. We observe many different individuals in many different settings using Model I. When we ask them when they learned to act as they do, they reply, in effect, that they have been acting so ever since they can remember. When we ask them to try another model of action in their organization, they quickly point out that no one would understand them, that they might be seen as deviants, or that such an attempt might be held against them. When they decide they do want to learn to act according to a different model, and after they understand that model, they are still unable to behave according to it because automatic responses learned early in life get in their way. In order to overcome their automatic responses, they must go through experiences where they identify the rules—the theories—behind their responses. When they identify the rules, they can frequently identify that they learned them early in life.

We may now hypothesize that the respondents enacted the diagnostic frames that they did because they were being consistent with Model I, and being so made it possible for them to make recommendations and take action. But being programmed with Model I theory-in-use, they also made unillustrated attributions and evaluations; they saw no reason to test their attributions and evaluations because they believed they were true. They were unaware of the many inferences embedded in their reasoning processes because, according to their Model I theory-in-use, everything they thought and said was not only true, it was obvious and concrete. But it was obvious and concrete because they had learned throughout life (in socialization) that most people would agree with them. This expectation was confirmed by the data in "the case of X and Y." Recall that 95 percent of the respondents had a similar diagnosis, and the remaining 5 percent were in partial agreement.

To summarize, the respondents made inferences that were at high levels of abstraction, whose validity was problematic. They acted as if their inferences were not abstract but concrete and as if the validity of their views was obvious.

These actions and thoughts are congruent with Model I theory-in-use. What is also predictable from, and congruent with, Model I is that such thoughts and actions will lead to unrecognized inconsistencies, self-fulfilling prophecies, self-sealing processes, and hence, escalating error. This, in turn, will lead to a world that may be said to be unjust. Unaware of what many of these consequences are, most individuals have no hesitation in advising others how to deal with Y; yet they will not be able to produce the actions that they themselves recommend. Injustice is a double-loop problem, precisely the learning domain in which human beings are programmed to be less than effective.

The thrust of the preceding analysis is that human beings have theories-in-use that make it likely that they will inhibit their own and others' double-loop learning, that they are largely unaware of these theories-in-use, and that both the unawareness and the counterproductive actions are due to highly skilled, internalized, and hence tacit, automatic reactions. If individuals reflected on their actions correctly (which is unlikely because of their theories-in-use), they would become aware of the counterproductive aspects of their action.

Human beings are said to be programmed to act automatically and tacitly in ways that are counterproductive to their espoused theories and to the advice they give others. They are not unaware of the inconsistencies in others' behavior, but they are programmed to withhold feedback on this lest they be held responsible for upsetting others.

Factors that Inhibit Organizational Double-Loop Learning

If it is true that all these consequences are due to highly skilled and programmed, and hence automatic, reactions, then it follows that individuals will carry these skills into *any* social system, be it a private or public organization, family, school, union, or hospital. If it is also true that individuals who act as agents for systems do the learning, then they will necessarily create conditions within the systems that inhibit double-loop learning. This prediction should not be disconfirmed, even if individuals are placed in systems where the internal environmental conditions encourage double-loop learning and the external environmental conditions are at least benign.

Such conditions may be said to exist in the temporary systems created in the semester classes or week-long seminars designed specifically to facilitate double-loop learning. To date, the hypothesis has not been disconfirmed. All individuals who have entered such new learning environments, who have become aware of their Model I theories-in-use, who have learned about a theory of action that can facilitate double-loop learning, who have chosen to learn to act according to it, and who try to do so under supportive conditions, are unable to do so when left to their own devices.

For example, a group of six executives kept producing Model I actions after nearly thirty hours of attempts to alter their actions by themselves (Argyris, 1976a). In five different classrooms (ranging in size from forty to one hundred advanced graduate students) students were unable to produce actions that facilitated their own double-loop learning (Argyris, 1976a). A group of twelve executives were similarly thwarted after twelve hours of learning over a period of two days, each day separated by several months (Heller, 1982).

In all cases the participants diagnosed their own failures, and in all cases the faculty member was able to produce actions that satisfied most students (to date, more than 95 percent in any group) that it was possible to produce actions that facilitated double-loop learning. These results suggest that the students had learned a new theory of action they could use to identify facilitative actions and that facilitative actions were producible.

If it is unlikely that double-loop learning will occur in organizations specifically designed for double-loop learning, it is plausible that double-loop learning will not occur naturally in organizations whose structure is congruent with Model I. For example, the three underlying assumptions of formal pyramidal structure are specialization of work, unity of command, and centralization of power, with information flow following the structure of power. These conditions are congruent with the Model I theory-in-use of unilateral control, win-lose competitive dynamics, and a focus on rationality of ideas to the exclusion of rationality of feelings (Argyris, 1970).

Does this mean we are predicting that organizations should not be observed to produce double-loop learning? The answer is yes. Does this mean organizations should not be observed changing their underlying values and norms? The answer is yes for values related to how human beings deal with each other. The answer is not necessarily for organizational policies. Double-loop changes in substantive areas may occur, but *not* because the present participants detected and corrected errors (which is our definition of learning). The changes could occur by fiat or unilateral imposition. For example, the Pentagon Papers may be viewed as a beginning act of double-loop learning about organizational policies and practices. Those chosen to write them had the technical skills and access to the relevant information required to accomplish the task. But these inquiries were ordered by the top. Indeed, the case could be made that there were participants who held the views eventually described in the documents, but those views, previous to McNamara's edict, were undiscussable, and their undiscussability was undiscussable. Did the Defense Department learn how to deal with undiscussables and their undiscussability? I would venture the answer is no.

But at the core of this management information system were several interpersonal values, such as "valid information is a good idea." The difficulty was that (as is the case in most organizations) the theory-in-use about valid information tends to be that valid information is a good idea when it is not threatening. The moment any substantive or technical information is threatening, our Model I theories-in-use are automatically engaged.

When the requirements of our Model I theories-in-use are contrary to the technical requirements, a conflict occurs. Participants' predisposition is to hide the clash, yet play the Model I political games that they have learned to "cover themselves." They will, in effect, violate the formal technical requirements and conceal the fact that they are fighting them. If successful, they will create a situation where the executives on top and the staff in charge of the management information systems will not know about the games, the camouflage of the games, or the camouflage of the camouflage.*

Elsewhere I have tried to show how these features will necessarily have to occur in any organization whose participants are programmed with Model I (Argyris and Schön, 1978). I suggest that human beings programmed with Model I theory-in-use will create and impose an O-I learning system on any organization in which they participate.

Briefly, Argyris and Schön attempt to identify the cognitive features of information that would tend to facilitate and inhibit the production of error. They hypothesize the continua shown in Figure 2. They then suggest that when individuals programmed with a Model I theory-in-use strive to solve difficult and threatening problems for which available information nears the left end of these continua, they will create conditions of undiscussability, self-fulfilling prophecies, self-sealing processes, and escalating error. These conditions reinforce vagueness, lack of clarity, inconsistency, and incongruity, which in turn reinforce the use of Model I (people strive harder to be in unilateral control, to minimize losing and maximize winning, and so forth).

Argyris and Schön (1978) suggest these conditions tend to create win-lose groups and intergroup dynamics with competitiveness dominating over cooperation, mistrust overcoming trust, and unquestioned obedience replacing informed dissent. They also lead to the coalition groups and the organizational politicking that have

---

*It may also be possible for individuals to fight the management information system by going outside the organization. An example is the federal law that greatly reduced the requirement of PPBS.

Figure 2. Conditions for Error and Error Correction.

Conditions that Enhance the Probability of Error	*Conditions that Enhance the Probability of Learning*

Information is	Information is
vague	concrete
unclear	clear
inconsistent	consistent
incongruent	congruent
scattered	available

been described by Allison (1971), Bacharach and Lawler (1980), Baldridge (1971), Cyert and March (1963), and Pettigrew (1973).

Under these conditions, it is difficult to see how structural and policy changes will lead to double-loop learning. In order for this to occur, individuals must be able to alter their theories-in-use and to neutralize the O-I learning system while simultaneously, and probably under stress, acting according to a new theory-in-use (such as Model II) and creating an O-II learning system. Unless they alter the Model I features, they will use their automatic, highly skilled Model I responses. This may be an explanation for the findings previously described—that individuals who value Model II and wish to learn it and who are economically autonomous and powerful are unable to produce Model II actions during the early phases of learning even though they are in an environment that approximates Model II.

These findings also imply that structural changes congruent with Models II and O-II will not work until they become part of the theory-in-use of individuals and until people act in ways to create conditions congruent with O-II learning systems. This is one reason interventions should begin at the highest levels of power in the organization. If the top people do not implement the new actions and learning system, it is doubtful that those below can do so.

I hypothesize, therefore, that the automatic reasoning processes that lead to the inconsistency and the escalating error will be triggered off, whether the problem being discussed is about long-range investments, internal resource allocation, or marketing strategy and whether the unit involved is groups, intergroups, or organizations. The major conditions that should exist are (1) individuals are programmed only with Model I, (2) they are embedded in an O-I learning system, and (3) the subject matter is individually or systematically threatening.

The hypothesis should not hold if the error in question is easily and objectively identifiable and/or the cost of hiding it is greater than the cost of violating the Model I values and behavioral strategies. Also, to the extent the error is easily illustrated and the illustration difficult to disconfirm, individuals may violate the hypothesis. Indeed, one reason management information systems (in the broadest sense) are becoming popular is that management hopes they will make it easier to surface error and more difficult to hide it and hence will lower the cost to individuals for surfacing it and raise the cost for not doing so.

The coverage of the hypothesis is broad, intendedly so. Simultaneously, it is easily falsifiable. All one has to do is present a case where individuals programmed with Model I theories-in-use and embedded in O-I learning systems (in any social organization) deal with a double-loop threatening issue (excluding the exceptions previously noted) in such a way that errors do not escalate. The empirical illustrations contrary to this hypothesis are presently more easily obtained from organizations that deal with double-loop issues and whose problem-solving processes are more likely to be subject to inquiry, for example, governmental decision making (Argyris, 1976c) and schools (Argyris, 1974). Illustrations from industry do exist (the Firestone tire, the Ford Pinto), but to date they are more difficult to document.

I am presently observing and tape recording problem-solving and decision-making meetings in several organizations. I have developed a model of how the reasoning processes and the inconsistencies found in cases like X and Y also are found when individuals are trying to solve investment problems or new product problems or to alter marketing strategies. The model is based on the assumption that it is possible to raise the level of abstraction of the X and Y case to a point where:

1. The individuals involved have different views regarding the problem and its causes. The differences are directly related to basic values and underlying assumptions.

2. The different views imply that if one side is correct, the other side is incorrect. Hence, the differences imply faulty reasoning and inadequate competence on someone's part.
3. The implication of inadequate competence and faulty reasoning is experienced as threatening.
4. The parties involved must continue to work with each other in order to achieve specified goals.

In the substantive problems studied so far, there are five that approximate the listed conditions, where the differences are based on different views of the world and they involve questioning and threatening the governing values of the organization and coalition groups. A pattern is beginning to emerge as to the dynamics of problem solving and decision making under these conditions.

First, after individuals frame the nature of the technical problem (let us say, a new investment policy), they explore it with others in order to learn the reactions of relevant participants. Assume they find strong opposition to the investment policy because it implies changes in the organization's existing policies and governing values. As these differences become explicit, coalition groups are formed. Each side views its approach as the correct one, and depending on the position, views the other side as liberal or conservative, forward-looking or backward-looking. These attributions become symbols around which intergroup rivalries are formed and maintained. They also serve in an individual's diagnostic frame as guides of how one will deal with, and interpret, the actions of others (as in the case of Y). For example, the forward-looking members tend to see the status quo members as well-meaning individuals who are blind to the future. The status quo members see the forward-looking group as alarmists and fuzzy thinkers.

Whenever each side meets by itself and produces a new set of recommendations that it believes the other side will disagree with, it generates an action frame for its members to use when they meet with the opposing group:

1. Do not do or say anything that will make the other side defensive. Do not discuss and do not test the attributions made by the other side's incompetence and counterproductive reasoning.

2.   Focus on the negative consequences of the present (or projected) policies.
3.   Do not polarize or overstate the case. Present the case, as much as possible, as one based on present governing values and one that does not represent a major change.

During the meeting, the liberal members present their views by continually emphasizing that their plan (1) is not a panacea, (2) will help the organization do better what it is already doing—the plan is building on existing practice, (3) is experimental, and (4) should be monitored by a group representing a wide range of views.

The group representing the conservative or status quo faction appears to take advantage of this action frame by continually pointing out how glad they are that the liberals realize their plan is not a panacea; that they conceive of it as an extension of, and hence consistent with, present organizational values; that it should be experimental; and that it should be monitored by a group with a variance of views. The double-loop features are, in effect, translated as much as possible into single-loop features. The other side emphasizes, and whenever possible magnifies, the single-loop features.

Finally, the agreement is written up, with much wrangling over language to protect whatever gains each side believes it has achieved. The words eventually agreed on tend to be at a high enough level of inference that each side can use them to protect its respective position if it is attacked.

The precise way in which the implementation of each decision is monitored varies in specifics but not in underlying strategy. Each side appears to hold the other to the commitments made in writing. But as in the case of Y, there comes a time when the high level of inference language no longer hides the actions. Whenever, for example, the actions indicate that the forward-looking group is violating the agreed upon limits by going beyond them, or that the status group is preventing implementation, the offended group complains of a misunderstanding, "unfair," "betrayal and dishonesty." When the reactions are intense, the problem is typically bucked up to the next higher level, where a superior is asked to make the final judgment. Most superiors attempt to take an easing-in approach that induces the warring factions to cooperate. It may be this type of action and consequence that leads to the coalitions and intergroup dynamics that create the basis of the political approach described by Allison (1971), Bacharach and Lawler (1980), Baldridge (1971), Cyert and March (1963), and Pettigrew (1973) and the intergroup approach described by Alderfer (1977).

Recently, Asplund and Asplund (1980) have presented cases where the interpersonal issues are intimately related to marketing issues. For example, in order to correct major marketing errors, it is important to discuss them. Yet major errors were a taboo subject. In order to examine the marketing errors, the Asplunds had to help the clients explore such questions as (1) What is it about failure that makes this client unable to discuss it? (2) How and why did failure become a forbidden topic? (3) What is the cover-up process doing to the client's capacities to double-loop learn about major marketing issues?

Organizations will be unlikely to learn because the participants are programmed with a Model I theory-in-use and therefore create and/or are embedded in an O-I learning system, which, in turn, requires or sanctions a Model I theory-in-use. A circular, self-reinforcing system that leads to self-fulfilling, self-sealing, escalating error is created whenever double-loop issues are involved.

My analysis may seem pessimistic, but I am optimistic for several reasons. Many people espouse actions and values related to Model II. Hence, they would prefer such a world if it could be created. Second, none of the multilevel, self-sealing, error-escalating processes identified appear to be due to unconscious or "deep" personality factors. They are related to skills and people can learn new skills. Third, although any given actor is unaware of his or her counterproductive action, his or her fellow actors are not. Hence, cooperation is a necessary condition for learning. Fourth, as people learn Model II, they necessarily create an O-II learning system that feeds back to reinforce the new theory-in-use. Fifth, change cannot occur without putting one's premises to test and that can lead to an increasing sense of trust. Sixth, after the first few days of trying to learn quickly, most participants relaxed and slowed down. They realized that learning Model II was going to be at least as difficult as learning to play, moderately well, a musical instrument or a sport. Moreover, the very requirement for extended practice provides everyone with an opportunity to test each other's sincerity. So far, the few who have tried to learn Model II action strategies in order to use them with Model I governing variables have been confronted on the inconsistency. It is hard to fool individuals about a theory-in-use they can implement well.

Possibility of Organizations Being Helped to Double-Loop Learn

Argyris and Schön (1978) and Argyris (1976a, 1976b) illustrate attempts to help organizations become double-loop learners. I will briefly outline the process. The first step is to help individuals become aware of their Model I theories-in-use and automatic reasoning processes that lead to counterproductive skilled responses.

The second step is to help them see how they create and/or maintain features of O-I learning systems that, in turn, feed back to sanction Model I theories-in-use. The second step will necessarily begin to occur as the first one is taken. For example, we have asked top management groups to write cases (in the format of the X and Y case) on issues that are currently important in their organization. Some wrote about problems of evaluating marginal performers, others about limiting the power of financial personnel (power obtained through design and control of the financial system), others about the difficulty in making certain investment or marketing decisions. They met for several days to discuss their cases. The discussions typically began by examining the way individuals dealt with these difficult issues. As the cases were discussed, the executives began to identify patterns in the way that they solved problems. They began to see how issues became undiscussable and how the undiscussability was covered up with games or even new policies. In short, they began to infer the features of the learning system that existed in their organization. Whenever there were differences of opinion, new cases were generated to illustrate the respective views, and this led to a richer map of the O-I learning system. Whenever differences in view persisted, executives designed ways to test the competing views.

The third step is to help individuals learn a new theory of action (in our case, called Model II) in such a way that they could use it in an on-line manner under zero to moderate stress, thereby providing evidence that their new theory of action has become not only an espoused theory but also a theory-in-use. Incidentally, this does not mean that individuals learn to discard Model I. Quite the contrary, they develop rules that state under what conditions Model I and Model II theories-in-use would be preferable.

The fourth step is to introduce their new actions into the organization and simultaneously help others learn them also. They may have staff individuals create learning environments to provide others with the same learning opportunities that they had. But in the final analysis, the subordinates' learning will be reinforced or extinguished by their superiors' actions.

As both levels learn a new theory-in-use and hence can produce new actions, they necessarily also produce new learning systems, making it more likely that individuals can alter organizational features such as reward and penalty systems, evaluation, and control procedures. Simultaneously, the reeducation of the next lower level will begin, and learning will spread throughout the organization. (An operational definition of "gimmick" from this perspective is any change in behavioral strategies without concomitant change in governing values. For example, if individuals combine advocacy with inquiry in order to win and not lose, they will soon be manipulating others and close themselves off from inquiry.)

There are two implicit assumptions in this stage theory of organizational double-loop learning that should be made explicit. The first is that intervention should begin at the highest levels of the organization, that is, at a level that has the required autonomy to implement the learning. The key criterion is that the individuals have enough power and autonomy to assure themselves and others that they are not kidding themselves or others when they strive to learn new theories-in-use and create new learning systems.

The second assumption is that organizational double-loop learning must begin at the individual level and then spread to the organizational level. This assumption implies another, namely, that it should not be possible to alter Model I theories-in-use and O-I learning systems by intervening at the organizational level with a new structure or policy. This is predicted to be the case because even if a world that encourages Model II actions is created, individuals should not be able to produce such actions even if they wish to do so.

This is what has happened so far in every Model II learning environment. The participants persevered in Model I until the faculty member intervened. This does not prove, however, that individuals can never learn Model II by themselves. It only illustrates that they have not been able to do so within the seminar time restrictions.

Our approach, which begins—and I should like to emphasize *begins*—with individuals, must begin so because ironically we are dealing with one of the most successful and powerful socializing processes identified to date. We have found variance in espoused theories (for example, many individuals espoused Model II); we have found variance in behavioral strategies (for example, a Patton and a domineering mother have different strategies of unilateral control); but we have found almost no variance in theories-in-use. We find, therefore, that even across cultures individuals hold a Model I theory-in-use (although the Africans, South Americans, Indians, and others who have participated were all highly educated, many in Western school systems).

Individuals are walking social structures. The socialization is so extensive and efficient that individuals will normally not act in ways to undermine it. They can be left alone because they are programmed with automatic responses that, as we have seen, are highly skilled. The irony is that successful socialization probably cannot be altered without beginning at the individual level. Those who suggest that it is possible to conceive of organizations as individual, group, or organizational phenomena (Bidwell and Abernathy, 1980) probably are correct if they limit their propositions to steady states or self-maintaining patterns. The moment one focuses on double-loop learning, the individual becomes the basic social structure, and suprastructures cannot be changed without beginning with the individual.

Conclusion

Individuals appear to be programmed with Model I theories-in-use that make it unlikely that they will produce double-loop learning and highly likely that they will create O-I learning environments within organizations that will inhibit double-loop learning. The theories-in-use and learning systems interact not only to maintain and reinforce these consequences, but also to keep individuals unaware of the degree to which they are causally responsible for contributing to and reinforcing these consequences.

The individual-level phenomenon of almost no variance in theories-in-use is probably evidence of effective socialization processes. Yet to change such extensive socialization processes, one must paradoxically begin by altering the individual automatic skilled reactions of socialization.

Individuals are walking social structures who cannot undergo double-loop learning without reflecting on their actions. As we have seen, this includes reflecting on their diagnostic and action frames. Such reflection requires examining the validity of the reasoning processes they use. But to test for such validity requires a commonly accepted view of a process and criteria for testing and falsification. Moving from Model I toward Model II therefore requires the existence of a way to test that the move is occurring effectively. We thus depend on another successful socialization result, namely, that individuals can agree on the logic of falsifiability.

Double-loop learning at the individual and organizational levels also involves the important issues of competence and justice. It is not just for individuals to define certain actions as incompetent and unjust and then act as if the incompetence and injustice do not occur when they behave in the same way. Double-loop learning must also deal with undiscussability, the undiscussability of the undiscussable, and the puzzling fact that most individuals are unaware of their own causal contribution to these organizational features yet are aware of others' causal contributions.

Research on intervention suggests that it is possible to help individuals learn new theories-in-use and to create new learning systems. The intervention requires the creation of a dialectical learning process where the participants can continually compare their theories-in-use and the learning system in which they are embedded with alternative models. Interventionists must thus make available alternative models with significantly different governing values and behavioral strategies. To the extent that social scientists remain rigorously descriptive of the world as is, they will unintentionally reinforce the status quo and add yet another set of factors to the difficulty individuals and organizations have in double-loop learning.

References

Alderfer, C. P. "Group and Intergroup Relations." In J. R. Hackman and J. L. Suttle (Eds.), *Improving Life at Work*. Santa Monica, Calif.: Goodyear, 1977.

Allison, G. T. *Essence of Decision: Explaining the Cuban Missile Crisis*. Boston: Little, Brown, 1971.

Argyris, C. *Intervention Theory and Method*. Reading, Mass.: Addison-Wesley, 1970.

Argyris, C. *The Applicability of Organizational Sociology*. Cambridge, England: Cambridge University Press, 1972.

Argyris, C. "Some Limits on Rational Man Organizational Theory." *Public Administration Review*, June 1973, *33*, 253–267.

Argyris, C. "Alternative Schools: A Behavioral Analysis." *Teachers College Record*, 1974, *75*(4), 429–452.

Argyris, C. *Increasing Leadership Effectiveness*. New York: Wiley-Interscience, 1976a.

Argyris, C. "Single- and Double-Loop Models in Research on Decision-Making." *Administrative Science Quarterly*, 1976b, *21*, 363–375.

Argyris, C. "Theories of Action That Inhibit Individual Learning." *American Psychologist*, 1976c, *31*(9), 638–654.

Argyris, C. "Is Capitalism the Culprit?" *Organizational Dynamics*, Spring, 1978, *3*, 36.

Argyris, C. "Educating Administrators and Professionals." In C. Argyris and R. M. Cyert (Eds.), *Leadership in the Eighties: Essays on Higher Education*. Cambridge, Mass.: Institute for Educational Management, Harvard University, 1980a.

Argyris, C. *Inner Contradictions of Rigorous Research*. New York: Academic Press, 1980b.

Argyris, C., and Schön, D. *Theory in Practice: Increasing Professional Effectiveness*. San Francisco: Jossey-Bass, 1974.

Argyris, C., and Schön, D. *Organizational Learning*. Reading, Mass.: Addison-Wesley, 1978.

Asplund, G., and Asplund, G. "The IDS: An Integrated Developmental Strategy for Effective Organizational Adaptation." Stockholm, Sweden, 1980. (Mimeographed.)

Bacharach, S. B., and Lawler, E. J. *Power and Politics in Organizations: The Social Psychology of Conflict, Coalitions, and Bargaining.* San Francisco: Jossey-Bass, 1980.

Baldridge, J. V. *Power and Conflict in the University: Research in the Sociology of Organizations.* New York: Wiley-Interscience, 1971.

Bidwell, C., and Abernathy, D. "Structural and Behavioral Theories of Organizations: A Bibliographic Review." School of Education, University of Chicago, 1980. (Mimeographed.).

Campbell, D. T., and Stanley, J. C. *Experimental and Quasi-Experimental Designs for Research.* Chicago: Rand McNally, 1966.

Cyert, R. M., and March, J. G. *A Behavioral Theory of the Firm.* Englewood Cliffs, N.J.: Prentice-Hall, 1963.

Hage, J. *Theories of Organization: Form, Process, and Transformation.* New York: Wiley-Interscience, 1980.

Heller, J. *Increasing Effectiveness in Colleges and Universities: Theory and Practice.* San Francisco: Jossey-Bass, 1982.

Kelley, H. H. *Personal Relationships: Their Structures and Process.* Hillsdale, N.J.: Erlbaum, 1979.

Kruglanski, A. W. "Lay Epistemologic Process and Contents: Another Look at Attribution Theory." *Psychological Review*, 1980, *87*(1), 70–87.

Lammers, C. J. "Comparative Sociology of Organizations." *Annual Review of Sociology*, 1980, *4*, 485–510.

Miller, G. A. "The Magical Number Seven, Plus or Minus Two: Some Limits on Our Capacity for Processing Information." *Psychological Review*, 1956, *63*, 81–97.

Moscovici, S. *Social Influence and Social Change.* (C. Sherrard and G. Heinz, Trans.) London: Academic Press, 1976.

Pettigrew, A. S. *The Politics of Organizational Decision Making.* London: Tavistock, 1973.

Popper, K. R. *Conjectures and Refutations: The Growth of Scientific Knowledge.* (3rd ed., rev.) London: Routledge & Kegan Paul, 1969.

Schein, E. H., and Bennis, W. *Personal and Organizational Change Through Group Methods.* New York: Wiley-Interscience, 1965.

Simon, H. A. *The Sciences of the Artificial.* Cambridge, Mass.: M.I.T. Press, 1969.

□ □ □ □ □ □ □ 3

Counterforces
to Change

□ □ □ □ □ □ □ □ □ □ □ □ □ □ □ □

Barry M. Staw

Terrible consequences suffered by an organization are not often the result of a single foolhardy decision or of a failure to choose the one course of action that best fits environmental conditions. Instead, when disasters are discovered, what frequently lie beneath the rubble are failures to adapt to new circumstances or refusals to change behaviors that had worked well under conditions that no longer apply. Thus, methods to increase adaptability rather than additional heuristics to find *that* form of organization, policy, or decision precisely suited to a given set of circumstances may be crucial to improving organizations.

I treat change as a potential adaptation mechanism. Rather than relying upon variety and the fortuitous match between organizational and environmental characteristics (Weick, 1977), I view organizations as having adaptive potential through the change of products, policies, and procedures. The difficulty is in making timely and appropriate changes. From the ecologists' perspective (for example, Aldrich, 1979; Hannan and Freeman, 1977) the differential ability of organizations to make correct changes would be one factor determining the shape and variety of surviving entities. Although ecologists are less concerned with the struggles of individual organizations than the longer-run evolution of the larger set of entities, change is certainly important from a policy perspective. Though difficult to achieve, change can make an organization more adaptive and extend its life cycle appreciably.

I address the topic of change in this chapter by considering its opposite or counterforce. If we are to understand why it is so difficult for organizations to change or adapt, we must first explore what holds individuals and collectivities to their old sets of behaviors. Studying behavioral persistence may enable us to design organizations and structure situations so that greater flexibility is achieved.

There are numerous approaches one can make in addressing the question of behavioral persistence. Platt (1973), for example, has examined situations in which sliding reinforcement schedules can maintain behavior even when change would seem desirable; Nisbett and Ross (1980) have studied the resilience of beliefs in the face of discrediting data; and Staw, Sandelands, and Dutton (1981) have shown how outside threats can lead to behavioral rigidities. Although each of these approaches isolates variables that may lead to behavioral persistence, the question of what binds individuals and organizations to a course of action is still unanswered. Because we need to know more about the counterforces to change, I examine forces that are strong enough to maintain behavior in the face of increasing costs and indications of the necessity for change. I emphasize individual sources of inflexibility because an understanding of individual-level effects would seem to be a prerequisite to a more complex and global theory of organizational change.

In the first half of this chapter, I describe a set of conditions in which individuals often become locked in to a course of action. I refer to these as "escalation situations" because they are settings where administrators can and do commit increasing resources to a line of behavior, even in the face of negative outcomes. After examining some determinants of escalation decisions, I broaden the discussion to include factors that may make any behavior resistant to change. I propose a framework that includes forces that bind individuals to their actions and reexamine escalation situations in light of these commitment variables. Finally, I draw implications from the study of escalation and commitment to the ability of organizational administrators to adapt to changing environmental conditions.

Persistence in Escalation Situations

From both learning theory and common experience we would expect change to result from failure. When individuals and organizations receive negative consequences, their behavior should be altered or at least deflected from its prior trajectory. However, there does appear to be a set of instances in which behavior not only persists in the face of failure but can become intensified precisely because of the negative consequences received. These escalation situations can be especially dangerous to the welfare of individuals and collectivities because errors can be compounded or behaviors cumulated until a major disaster strikes. Consider the following examples:*

1. An individual has spent three years working on an advanced degree in a field with minimal job prospects (for example, the humanities or social science Ph.D.). The individual chooses to invest further time and effort to finish the degree rather than switching to an entirely new field of study. Having attained the degree, the individual is faced with the options of unemployment, working under dissatisfying conditions such as part-time or temporary status, or starting anew in a completely unrelated field.
2. An individual purchased a stock at $50 a share, but the price has gone down to $20. Because the individual is still convinced of the merit of the stock, he buys more shares at this lower price. Soon the price declines further and the individual is again faced with the decision to buy more, hold what he already has, or sell out entirely (case taken from personal experience).
3. A city spends a large amount of money to improve the area's sewer and drainage system. The project is the largest public

---

*These examples and some of the discussion of the escalation effect are based on an earlier article, "The Escalation of Commitment to a Course of Action," *Academy of Management Review,* 1981, *6*(4), 577–587.

works project in the nation and involves digging 131 miles of tunnel shafts, reservoirs, and pumping stations. The excavation is only 10 percent completed and is useless until it is totally finished. The project will take the next twenty years to complete and will cost $11 billion. Unfortunately, the deeper the tunnels go, the more money they cost and the greater are the questions about the wisdom of the entire venture (see "Money Down the Drain," 1979).

4. A company overestimates its capability to build an airplane brake that will meet certain technical specifications at a given cost. Because it wins the government contract, it is forced to invest greater and greater effort into meeting the contract terms. As a result of increasing pressure to meet specifications and deadlines, records and tests of the brake are misrepresented to government officials. Corporate careers and company credibility are increasingly staked to the airbrake contract, although many in the firm know the brake will not work effectively. At the conclusion of the construction period, a government test pilot flies the plane; it skids off the runway and narrowly averts injuring the pilot (see Vandiver, 1972).

5. At an early stage of the U.S. involvement in the Vietnam War, George Ball, then undersecretary of state, wrote the following statement in a memo to Lyndon Johnson: "The decision you face now is crucial. Once large numbers of U.S. troops are committed to direct combat, they will begin to take heavy casualties in a war they are ill-equipped to fight in a noncooperative if not downright hostile countryside. Once we suffer large casualties, we will have started a well-nigh irreversible process. Our involvement will be so great that we cannot—without national humiliation—stop short of achieving our complete objectives. Of the two possibilities I think humiliation would be more likely than the achievement of our objectives—even after we have paid terrible costs" (Sheehan and Kenworthy, 1971).

Each of the examples describes a situation in which an individual or organization did not withdraw from an ill-fated course of action. In each, negative consequences were received, but behavior persisted or was intensified to reach the original goal. Such escalation situations are common, most frequently appearing in marriage, career, investment, and conflict decisions. Despite the variety of escalation situations, they seem to possess some common properties. Each involves a series of behaviors linked within a course of action. Each contains some feedback that the course of action is not working. Each includes the opportunity to commit further energy or resources toward the original goal-state. An initial hypothesis is that there is a tendency to become overly committed in escalation situations—to throw good money after bad or to stake fresh resources to the losing course of action. I call this behavior pattern the escalation effect.

Understanding Escalation Decisions. If we posit an economically rational model of escalation decisions (for example, Edwards, 1954; Vroom, 1964), resources should be allocated when future benefits exceed future costs. Such a rational perspective assumes that decision makers function as good economists and that they make choices that maximize their own welfare. As many researchers have noted (March and Olsen, 1976; Simon, 1957), individuals fall far short of the rational model in terms of information processing and choice. Errors in data perception and summarization are flagrant, as are mistakes in weighing and evaluating evidence when making decisions (see Nisbett and Ross, 1980, for a review).

Besides the shortcomings of information processing that accompany most decisions, choices about whether to persist in a course of action have some special properties that may lead to departures from rationality. In terms of economic rationality, losses or costs experienced in the past but that are not expected to recur should not enter into decision calculations. But perhaps the crucial feature of escalation decisions is that an entire series of outcomes is determined by a given choice, the consequences of any single decision having implications for past as well as future outcomes. Thus, the sunk costs that economists exclude from decision calculations may not be sunk psychologically. To date, much of the research on persistence of escalation situations has attempted to show how sunk costs can affect resource allocation decisions and to specify a theoretical mechanism for their effect.

Entrapment. In an early study on what the authors called "entrapment" (Rubin and Brockner, 1975), it was demonstrated that most individuals will wait for a valued resource beyond the point where benefits exceed costs. In performing an anagram task, subjects had to wait in line for a needed dictionary, but the longer they waited, the lower was their overall reward. Results showed a generally high level of entrapment and also a heightening of entrapment when the value of the reward decreased slowly over time, when decline in the reward was not salient, and when subjects were led to believe they were soon to receive the resource (the dictionary) necessary to attain the valued goal. Rubin and Brockner (1975) posited that escalation or entrapment decisions are the result of a field of forces that includes the approach of goal accomplishment as well as the avoidance of past losses or wasted investment.

Tegar (1980) devised a related demonstration of the escalation effect using the Dollar Auction Game. This game (Shubik, 1971) involves bidding for a dollar sold at auction in which the highest bidder receives the dollar. The game proceeds as would a normal auction except for the rule that the second highest bidder must also pay his or her last bid, even if no prize is forthcoming. Thus, final bids are similar to irretrievable investments or sunk costs present in escalation situations. Tegar found that subjects frequently bid more than a dollar for a dollar, thereby demonstrating the basic escalation effect. As bidding escalated, individuals reported their motives as shifting from a desire to make money, to a desire to recoup prior losses, and finally to a competitive urge to defeat their opponents. Unfortunately, these reasons for escalation in the Dollar Auction Game are difficult to interpret because the game is structured as a situation of *both* individual investment and interpersonal conflict.

In an investment simulation that more directly parallels administrative decision making, Staw (1976) also demonstrated the escalation effect. In this study, business school students were asked to play the role of a corporate financial officer in allocating research and development funds. Half the subjects allocated R&D funds to one of two operating divisions of a company, were given feedback on their decisions, and then were asked to make a second allocation of R&D funds. The other half did not make the initial investment decision themselves, but were told that it was made by another financial officer of the firm. The results showed that subjects allocated significantly more money to the initially chosen division when they, rather than another financial officer, were responsible for the initial decision. These findings suggest that administrators seek to justify an ineffective course of action by escalating their commitment of resources to it.

Subsequent studies have replicated the effect of responsibility for negative consequences upon the escalation of commitment (Bazerman, Schoorman, and Goodman, 1981; Fox, 1980; Staw and Fox, 1977). Escalation is also associated with the perceived importance of the decision and disappointment with initial losses (Bazerman, Schoorman, and Goodman, 1981). These results support the proposition that at least some of the tendency to escalate may be explained by self-justification motives (Aronson, 1976; Festinger, 1957). By committing new resources, an individual may be attempting to turn the situation around so as to demonstrate the rationality of an original course of action. In short, when individuals escalate their commitment, they may be as motivated to rectify past losses as to seek future gain.

External Versus Internal Justification. Although much research on the escalation effect has emphasized the role of justification, what has been tapped by these studies could be labeled an *internal justification* process. When justification is considered primarily an intraindividual process, individuals are posited to attend to events and to act in ways that protect their own self-images (Aronson, 1968, 1976). But within many social settings justification may also be directed externally. When faced with an external threat or evaluation, individuals may be motivated to prove to others that they were not wrong in an earlier decision and the force for such *external justification* could well be stronger than the protection of individual self-esteem.

An empirical demonstration of the effect of external justification was conducted by Fox and Staw (1979). They hypothesized that administrators who have a strong need for external justification would be most likely to attempt to save a policy failure by committing more resources to it. To test this idea, they conducted an experimental simulation in which business students were asked to play the role of administrators under various conditions of job insecurity and policy resistance. Results showed that, when a course of action led to negative results, the administrators who were both insecure in their jobs and who faced stiff policy resistance were most likely to escalate their commitment of resources and become locked in to a losing course of action.

Also providing support for the external form of justification is a study by Caldwell and O'Reilly (1982). They showed that individuals can be made accountable for negative results even though they were not responsible for an original decision that went sour. They also showed that individuals will construct rationalizations of events if they are forced to present an accounting of events to external parties. Like companies that must explain poor results in their annual reports, individuals are highly selective in the information they pass to others, and this biasing is significantly affected by responsibility for negative consequences.

Objective Forces. Cutting across these justification-predicted findings are studies that have shown more *objective* variables to affect escalation decisions. Some antecedents that have been explored are whether the cause of a setback is perceived to be endogenous or exogenous to a course of action (Staw and Ross, 1978), whether resources allocated are perceived to be capable of turning the situation around (Staw and Fox, 1977), and how escalation varies over time as repeated negative consequences are received (McCain, 1981; Staw and Ross, 1978). These studies generally show that escalation can be increased or decreased by beliefs about a course of action and its likelihood of success. However, as Conlon and Wolf (1980) have shown, individuals who follow a "calculating" decision strategy can still fall into the trap of escalation. Individuals can use calculations of expected value to justify a commitment decision as well as to see more clearly how withdrawal is the rational path. They can also mold the information used to reach a decision. As Fox (1980) showed, individuals have a strong preference for exonerating over implicating information, even when they may be sacrificing relevant data. Thus, although objective forces do affect escalation decisions, they are not so powerful as to reduce the escalation effect to a simple, rational calculus.

Norms for Consistency. In addition to justification and objective forces, a third factor has been identified as a possible contributor to the escalation effect. A number of popular press articles have argued that *consistency* is an essential aspect of political leadership, and national surveys on reactions to the presidency have shown that the perception of "indecisiveness" can be a major political liability (Gallup, 1978). Thus, it is possible that a lay theory may exist in our society, or at least within many organizational settings, that administrators who are consistent in their actions are better leaders than those who switch from one line of behavior to another.

In order to test the preference for consistency empirically, Staw and Ross (1980) conducted an experiment on the reactions of individuals to selected forms of administrative behavior. Subjects included practicing managers, business school students, and undergraduates in psychology. Each subject was asked to study a case description of an administrator's behavior. Manipulated in these case descriptions was consistency versus experimentation in the administrator's course of action as well as the ultimate success versus failure of the administrator's efforts. In the consistency conditions, the administrator was portrayed as sticking to a single course of action through a series of negative results. In the experimenting conditions, the administrator was portrayed as trying one course of action and, when positive results did not appear, moving to a second and finally a third alternative (as an administrator might behave within Campbell's, 1969, "experimenting society"). Ultimate success or failure of the administrator's actions was manipulated after two sets of negative results had been received by either the consistent or experimenting administrator.

Results showed that the administrator was rated highest when he followed a consistent course of action and was ultimately successful. There was also a significant interaction of consistency and success such that the consistent-successful administrator was rated more highly than would be predicted by the two main effects of these variables. This interaction supported a predicted "hero effect" for the administrator who remained committed through two apparent failures of a course of action, *only to succeed in the end*. Finally, the effect of consistency upon the administrator's ratings varied by subject group, being strongest among practicing administrators, next strongest among business students, and weakest among psychology undergraduates. These results suggest not only that consistency in action is perceived as part of effective leadership, but that

this perception may be acquired through socialization for administrative roles.

Toward a Summary Model

Reviewing the research conducted to date shows that the escalation effect is a complex product, subject to multiple and sometimes conflicting processes. Therefore, it may be helpful to
consolidate in a single theoretical model the shape of forces now
thought to affect persistence in escalation situations.

Figure 1 depicts four major determinants of persistence to a
course of action: motivation to justify previous decisions, norms for
consistency, probability of future outcomes, and value of future outcomes. Escalation research has concentrated upon the first two of
these determinants; the latter are obviously the two accepted determinants of economic and behavioral decision making.

In examining Figure 1, motivation to justify decisions can be
seen as a function of responsibility for negative consequences as well
as both internal and external demands for competence. As depicted
in the model, responsibility for negative consequences leads to a
motivation to justify previous decisions if there is a need to demonstrate competence to oneself or others. The traditional literature on
dissonance and self-justification considers only individuals' internal
desire to be correct or accurate in decision making, but the need to
demonstrate competence to external parties may also be a potent
force. Such predictions may be culture bound, but emphases on
individual rationality and competence are so strong in Western societies that they are likely to foster concomitant needs of rationaliz-
ing one's actions (Wicklund and Brehm, 1976). Likewise, because
norms for rationality are so dominant in business and government
organizations (Thompson, 1967), role occupants in these settings
may also find it necessary to justify their actions to constituents
within and outside the organization.

Figure 1 also shows probabilities and value to be determinants of persistence in escalation situations. What adds to the complexity, however, is the possibility that individual perceptions of the
likelihood and value of various outcomes can themselves be influenced by justification motives. Having been responsible for negative

Figure 1. Determinants of Persistence in an Escalation Situation.

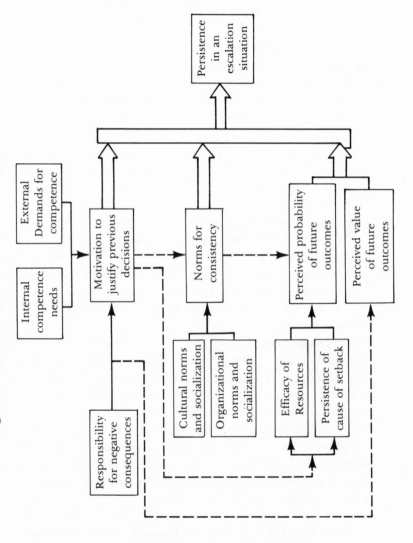

consequences may affect likelihood estimates via bias in information search and memory. The value of future returns may increase because they may be needed to cover past losses. Hence, Figure 1 shows the interplay between some of the antecedents of justification with perceived probability and value of outcomes, the accepted elements of rational behavior.

In addition to the confluence of rationality and justification, norms for consistency are shown to be of major importance in escalation decisions. Individuals may persist in a course of action simply because they believe consistency in action is an appropriate form of behavior, thereby modeling their own behavior on those they see as successful within organizations and/or society in general. Although modeling is usually viewed as a noncognitive process (compare Bandura, 1971), the effect of norms could be integrated into an SEU or expectancy model of decision making (for example, Fishbein and Ajzen, 1975) and be viewed as one element of an economically rational decision to commit resources. Likewise, norms for consistency could also be viewed as an outgrowth of individual needs for cognitive consistency (Festinger, 1957) or socialization for consistency within the general society. The possible effect of justification upon norms for consistency is depicted by a dotted line in Figure 1, as is the possible effect of norms upon the perceived probability for future outcomes.

In summary, Figure 1 shows persistence in escalation situations as a complex process dependent upon justification and normative forces as well as the standard properties of economic decision making. Research has emphasized how escalation decisions are different from simple isolated choices and why constructs other than SEU can help explain persistence in such situations. Many of the variables we have explored must still be viewed as tentative determinants of persistence because they are based as much on theoretical deduction as empirical evidence. This is especially the case for the interactive effects shown in Figure 1.

Some Leads and Cautions for Future Research on Escalation

There are numerous paths further escalation research could follow. The first path would be to set out additional parameters by which justification may promote persistence. Factors related to an internal form of justification would likely overlap with many of the variables already found to affect dissonance arousal. Likely candidates are foreseeability of negative results, the extent of participation and free will in decision making, relevance of the decision to individual self-worth, and personality variables such as self-esteem and ego defensiveness. Factors related to an external form of justification might draw on the self-presentation and impression-management literature. Relevant research questions from this perspective might center on the evaluation system of the organization and how much weight is placed upon past performance. Additional factors might relate to the administrator's role relationship with others in the organization, including norms for openness and self-disclosure as well as the pressure for dominance and competition within the organization. External justification would be heightened, for example, within highly competitive, career-oriented settings.

An alternative way to pursue escalation research would be to probe further the rational calculus of administrative decisions. Certain sequences of losses (for example, high range or variance) may provide hope for a turnaround even though the trend is distinctly negative. A second hypothesis might be that suffering losses that are not dire can allow one to put off making the more difficult decision to kill a project. A third idea would be that the experience of having worked through a negative situation and turned it around might provide a sense of confidence that is inappropriately generalized. Executives, coaches, and others who have struggled with losses, persevered, and eventually won may have difficulty in realistically appraising the likelihood of turnaround in more severe cases. A fourth hypothesis in this line of thinking would be that the costs of closing a project, both personal and organizational, might actually be larger than keeping it alive. When banks face decisions on calling an extremely large loan, the amount of the loan itself may condition the decision because a huge loss may be ruinous to the bank. Bankers in such cases often refer to the question of "who owns whom, the debtor or the creditor?" Consistent with this position, it is often the "lead bank" that tries hardest to avoid default because its own investment can be many times that of other banks in a loan consortium.

The Baseline Problem. In most of the previous work on escalation, it has been assumed that persistence in a course of action is something to decrease. This stance has been taken not only because persistence and adaptation may be negatively related, but also because a rational baseline has been assumed for persistence decisions. A third party or disinterested consultant's view of a course of action might constitute the baseline from which escalation or persistence is dysfunctional. Such baselines are often ambiguous and may differ according to individual and departmental assessments. For example, if three organizational subunits disagree about the prospects for success, it is difficult to argue for a "correct" baseline from which escalation occurs.

A concrete example of the baseline problem would be the recent Lockheed (L1011) Tristar jet program. Lockheed suffered severe financial losses and delays in the development of the Tristar jet, in part because the engine supplier, Rolls Royce, went through bankruptcy in 1971 and a higher cost contract was later negotiated with the British government. More important, Lockheed grossly underestimated the break-even point for the Tristar as well as overestimating the potential sales volume for the plane. Nonetheless, much of the corporation's prestige was staked to the plane because it was its major venture in the commercial aircraft business. Losses continued to mount over a thirteen-year period until $2.5 billion was lost on the program. Late in 1981, the company finally decided to give up on the Tristar, and the day after the announcement, Lockheed stock jumped seven and three-quarters points on the New York Stock Exchange. In examining the Lockheed example, it is evident, post hoc, that persistence was a losing proposition. It was also evident, during the midst of the program, that sales projections were overly optimistic, at least as judged by industry analysts. But establishing the exact baseline from which escalation was dysfunctional would still be problematic.

An even more difficult baseline problem confronts research within the more general framework of commitment. Although escalation research has concentrated upon instances of persistence that appear, at least post hoc, to be glaringly dysfunctional, work on commitment has been conducted from a largely positive perspective. The commitment framework has been useful in understanding the persistence of innovative programs in organizational settings (see, for example, Chapter Six in this volume) as well as the maintenance of desirable attitudes and motivations (Salancik, 1977; Steers, 1977) in organizations. Like the research on escalation, the study of commitment has been concerned with counterforces to change but has not been tied to decisions that have produced negative consequences.

From Escalation to the General Issue of Commitment

The escalation effect could be viewed as only one instance of the more general problem of behavioral commitment. The escalation situation is important because it allows cumulation of error through a series of investment-type decisions. However, many situations contain elements that bind individuals to behavior without the involvement of negative consequences or the opportunity to recoup losses through further investment. Therefore, this discussion will be enlarged to include more general forces that may hold an individual within a behavioral path, thereby reducing adaptability or willingness to change.

Nature of Commitment. As a theoretical construct, commitment has been subjected to almost as many definitions as there are researchers using the term. Roughly half of those using the concept (and especially those doing organizational research) have treated commitment as an attitudinal construct analogous to motivation, involvement, or identification. To these researchers, commitment has either been a dependent variable in its own right or an intermediate force affecting job performance, turnover, or absenteeism (for example, Porter, Steers, Mowday, and Boulian, 1974; Steers, 1977).

To a second group of researchers, primarily social psychologists, commitment has represented something different from attitude and personal conviction. To this group commitment has stood for structural conditions in which a behavior is irrevocable or difficult to change (Brehm and Cohen, 1962), the act of staking additional consequences or side bets to an original course of action (Becker, 1960), or a state of mind that makes it difficult to change attitudes and behavior (Kiesler, 1971). I follow the second definition in treating commitment as a counterforce to change. Commitment is the glue that holds individuals in a line of behavior, encompassing those psychological forces that bind individuals to an action as well as those situational forces that make change difficult.

As one of the first to outline a model of commitment, Kiesler (1971, p. 30) defined the construct as a "pledging or binding of the individual to behavioral acts." Commitment was useful to Kiesler as an organizing construct in determining which beliefs would be most resistant to change and in specifying conditions in which there would be substantial defense when opinions are attacked. However, Kiesler considered commitment motivationally inert, incapable of affecting directly the attitudes, beliefs, or behavior of individuals. Hence, in this early research commitment was always predicted to interact with other variables (such as dissonance manipulations), rather than to produce main effects on attitudes and behavior.

Salancik (1977) also used Kiesler's working definition of "binding the individual to behavioral acts," yet considered commitment to have a substantial effect upon the formation of attitudes as well as the persistence of behavior. To Salancik, getting tied or committed to an organization is what builds identification and loyalty to the firm and having undertaken a costly action is what helps develop or articulate one's beliefs supporting the behavior. Thus, in Salancik's framework, action can be viewed as having a direct motivational impact on attitudes and beliefs—which may in turn solidify or bind the behavior. I follow Salancik's lead in considering commitment an active counterforce to change and a variable that can have direct effects on attitudes and behavior.

Antecedents of Commitment. Both Kiesler and Salancik have specified a number of antecedents or contributors to commitment. They are (1) the explicitness of the act (how unambiguous and observable is the behavior), (2) the revocability of the act (whether it can be reversed or undone), (3) the degree of volition (or free choice) perceived by the person in performing the act, (4) the importance of the act for the individual (mentioned only by Kiesler), (5) the publicity or publicness of the act (mentioned only by Salancik), and (6) the number of acts performed (mentioned by Kiesler only). Unfortunately, this list of antecedents has not yet led to a formalized theory of commitment or even to a model in which the mediating process of "binding" is specified. Therefore, in Figure 2, I have recast and extended these determinants in an attempt to move closer to a causal model.

The working assumption behind Figure 2 is that commitment is built by actions in which one is *responsible for large consequences.* Examining the list of antecedents Kiesler and Salancik consider shows that most of these conditions relate to responsibility for consequences. Therefore, by specifying a unifying antecedent for commitment, it is possible to see more clearly how specific procedures relate to the construct and how these operationalizations can be logically expanded or reduced. It is also possible to tie commitment research more explicitly to previous dissonance and attribution work because responsibility for consequences is the critical variable in each of those theories. The binding process, as described by Kiesler and Salancik, is highly analogous to self-justification and attribution processes, although neither of these linkages has been spelled out by the authors.

As shown in Figure 2, responsibility for consequences has been broken into four subcategories. It is not yet clear whether these categories subsume necessary causes or whether some number of these variables is sufficient to bind behavior and belief. Therefore, I discuss each category as a separate contributor to commitment.

Responsibility for action. One of the most heavily researched variables in the area of attitude change is the construct of choice or volition. Free choice generally increases one's attitude toward an action or position; external constraints or inducements reduce it. Both dissonance and attribution theories can account for these data, and the debate between these competing processes still goes on. Responsibility is perceived through actions that are devoid of external inducements and when behavior must overcome external constraints (for example, via effort or sacrifice).

Actor-observer differences have often been found in the attribution of causality (Jones and Nisbett, 1972). Observers of an action may overestimate the influence of internal as opposed to external factors affecting an action, and such effects are thought to be due to the differential focusing of attention on personal versus environmental stimuli (Taylor and Fiske, 1978). Within organizations, actor-observer differences may also be flagrant because responsibility can easily be attributed when one has participated in private

Figure 2. The General Commitment Process.

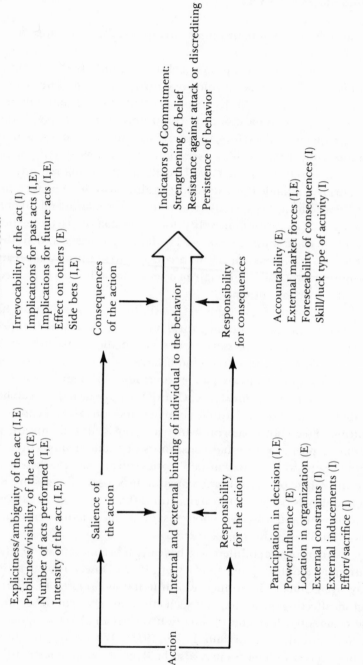

Explicitness/ambiguity of the act (I,E)
Publicness/visibility of the act (E)
Number of acts performed (I,E)
Intensity of the act (I,E)

Irrevocability of the act (I)
Implications for past acts (I,E)
Implications for future acts (I,E)
Effect on others (E)
Side bets (I,E)

Indicators of Commitment:
Strengthening of belief
Resistance against attack or discrediting
Persistence of behavior

Salience of
the action

Consequences
of the action

Action

Internal and external binding of individual to the behavior

Responsibility
for the action

Responsibility
for consequences

Participation in decision (I,E)
Power/influence (E)
Location in organization (E)
External constraints (I)
External inducements (I)
Effort/sacrifice (I)

Accountability (E)
External market forces (I,E)
Foreseeability of consequences (I)
Skill/luck type of activity (I)

Source: Based on Kiesler, 1971, and Salancik, 1977.

discussions, held a position of power, or been located in a dominant organizational department. Regardless of one's actual influence, simply standing near the origin of an action may get one labeled as the responsible party. Therefore, binding may occur when others attribute actions to the actor, even though the self-attribution of causality remains low.

Salience of the action. Explicit and public actions are more binding because they presumably are more salient to both the individual and others who are watching. In addition, actions that involve many separate acts, are long in duration, or are intense in nature might also heighten commitment because they are salient. In contrast, when decisions are diffuse (Connolly, 1977) and actions disjointed (Lindblom, 1959) or ambiguous (Weick, 1977), commitment should be minimized. Administrators who do not wish others to hold them accountable for their actions often follow such practices in "dusting the trail of their activity." Presumably, such ambiguity in action would increase the flexibility of administrative behavior.

Consequences of the action. Binding actions are thought to have implications beyond the behavior itself. They may have ramifications upon the individual's past performance or identity (for example, "if this decision does not work, it proves I have the wrong skills for this job"). They may have implications upon future acts (for example, "if we decide to develop a particular product, we must also produce and market it"). And they may have spillover effects on the life of the decision maker or others affected by his or her actions. For example, a decision to go to war, to relocate a plant, or to close a school may have many carryover effects on other aspects of one's life and entail new investments. Finally, some decisions or actions are more revocable than others. As Salancik graphically notes, marriages can be dissolved and contracts torn up, but some acts are final and irretrievable.

Previous discussions of commitment imply that it is only the individual who binds himself or herself to large and irrevocable acts. What is missing, of course, is the external binding of the person by others who are affected by the action. The binding of the individual to the act by others may be what continually "reinstates the treatment" even after one's self-attribution and justification have faded away. Therefore, the longer and more pervasive the consequences of an action, the stronger and more persistent will likely be the beliefs supporting it.

Responsibility for consequences. For some reason, responsibility for consequences has been almost completely overlooked in the commitment literature. It may have been assumed that volition necessarily implies responsibility for consequences, although this is by no means assured. One may, for example, have had little choice in an action but still be held accountable for it, and an action may be high in volition but responsibility is low because its consequences are seen as heavily influenced by external forces. Therefore, it is important in organizational contexts to distinguish when individuals will be held accountable so as to predict accurately when responsibility will be attributed by self or others. Although there is still little research on the issue, responsibility may be a key factor in the persistence of behavior, especially when there are ready opportunities to defend the action.

In summary, Figure 2, as I have described it, does two things that earlier statements on commitment do not do. First, it distinguishes clearly between action and consequences. Most of the variables discussed by Kiesler and Salancik refer only to responsibility for the act or behavior itself, rather than its consequences. For example, the notions of explicitness, publicness, and number of acts performed refer to the salience or clarity of the action to the individual, and the construct of volition refers to the free choice of the individual in performing the act. Only the notions of importance and revocability imply that the consequences of the act help in building commitment. Therefore, Figure 2 traces out many of the consequences of an action and how individuals may or may not be responsible for them. This is important for organizational contexts in which consequences are both highly monitored and attributed to individuals performing them.

Figure 2 also makes explicit whether the binding that occurs is internally or externally generated. Although past work has primarily stressed how individuals bind *themselves* to decisions and actions, it is important to address how *other parties* may bind individuals to their behavior. Especially in organizational settings, individuals may be held accountable for acts they had little choice in performing or may be held liable for consequences that were entirely unforeseen. In these situations an individual's beliefs and behavior may show correspondence only because they are bound together in the eyes of others.

Commitment and Escalation Decisions. When we reexamine escalation situations in light of the general antecedents of commitment, some interesting patterns emerge. One aspect of escalation research highlighted by the commitment model is the distribution of independent variables manipulated in these studies. Responsibility for the action, for example, has been manipulated by choice or participation in an initial course of action. Responsibility for negative consequences, however, has rarely been manipulated directly through variables such as accountability or external environmental forces (Caldwell and O'Reilly, 1982, is one exception). Likewise, the salience and consequences of the action have almost always been held constant. The magnitude or spread of negative consequences has not been manipulated, nor have various aspects of the initial decision, except for one empirical variation in which subjects wrote or did not write a statement defending their initial decisions (Bazerman, Schoorman, and Goodman, 1981). If one believes escalation situations are but one example of the more general commitment process, then many more of the variables outlined in Figure 2 should be manipulated within the escalation paradigm.

A second pattern the commitment model clarifies is how heavily escalation research has relied upon the self-justification mechanism in explaining behavioral persistence. Two reasons for this emphasis are that actions are linked in escalation settings and that there is an opportunity to recoup prior losses through additional investment in such situations. These reasons, though defensible, should not preclude the investigation of other binding forces. Having participated in a course of action, for example, can lead to self-persuasion and self-identification with a policy. Persistence in the face of failure could therefore be as much a product of firm belief as any justification motive.

Commitment and the Management of Consequences. Although escalation research has focused upon persistence in the face of negative consequences, much of administrative behavior could be characterized as the *management of consequences,* by which I mean not so much the set of actions that actually determines outcomes as the manipulation of information about those outcomes. Because few organizational activities provide unequivocal data on success or failure, much of the managerial process rests on the interpretation and communication of ambiguity (March and Olsen, 1976). Therefore, the psychological research showing that individuals try to assume credit for success and avoid blame for failure (for example, Weiner and others, 1972; Weary-Bradley, 1978) would seem especially relevant to organizational settings. Although outcomes are ambiguous in organizations, there remain strong pressures for evaluation, thus providing both the motivation and the opportunity for defensive biasing.

The observer of an action is not so subject to defensive biasing. The observer has nothing to gain by protecting the administrator whose decisions do not succeed, unless his or her own fortunes are directly tied to those of the actor. Within organizational settings the opposite pattern of bias could be expected. When a large failure occurs, a political process that ascribes blame to someone, even if that person is only marginally responsible, is often set in motion. There is some psychological research showing increased attribution of responsibility as negative consequences increase (Walster, 1966), but most evidence consists of the real-world firings of coaches following poor seasons and resignations of chief executives in times of poor performance (Grusky, 1963; Price, 1977).

Complexity is raised when negative consequences simultaneously increase external and decrease internal sources of commitment. On the one hand, the actor or decision maker may attempt to "debind" himself from an action leading to negative consequences. The observer of the action, and especially those affected by any negative consequences, may, on the other hand, seek to strengthen the attachment of the individual to the behavior. The Labour party in England, for example, has sought to identify the prime minister with the policy of tight money and cutbacks in government spending, dubbing her program "Thatcherism" ("About Face . . . ," 1981). Likewise, the Democrats in Congress have sought to highlight the identification of economic consequences with Reagan. "By adopting Reagan's tax cut bill, the House of Representatives gave him a victory and stripped him of an excuse. The economy is now his responsibility" ("Victory Puts Monkey . . . ," 1981).

Because of the complexities involved, the management of consequences is often a high art practiced by administrators. Through public speeches, meetings, and annual reports, administrators may attempt to increase their perceived responsibility for positive events and to find outside reasons for failure (such as government regulation, recession, unfair competition). When positive consequences result, the situation is not so problematic. Individuals are quick to bind themselves to successful events and others may also be willing to grant them credit. But complexity reenters when apparent successes turn into serious setbacks, causing administrators to debind themselves from an earlier commitment. In such situations negative consequences may serve to raise private doubts about a policy or decision, but the administrator may still be bound by the responsibility attributed by others. Therefore, managing both the internal and external binding process can become extremely difficult, especially because the attribution of responsibility can be closely bound to perceptions of leadership in organizations.

Leadership and Commitment. Individuals who are labeled leaders are usually prominent and visible to others. They may speak out more, have the resources to reward and punish, be experts in their fields, or occupy positions of stature and prestige (Stogdill, 1974). All these factors could be expected to predict the appointment of leaders in small group settings and to contribute to status attainment by individuals over time. What is it, however, that determines whether an individual who already holds a top position is labeled a leader rather than an ordinary administrator?

Many contributors I think are important to leadership attribution are exactly those outlined in the study of commitment. Leaders undertake actions that are both salient to others and involve large consequences. They are also the ones who bask in the responsibility for broad and sweeping actions. Hence, it is probably difficult for an individual to be labeled a leader if he or she is either only partially responsible for important actions or fully responsible for inconsequential actions.

A chief difficulty in maintaining the label of leadership comes from the necessity of performing acts that are highly binding but at the same time keeping the flexibility of good administration. Campbell (1969), for example, makes a strong case for experimentation in policy; Lindblom (1959) describes the process of intelligent administration as that of making incremental, disjointed choices. As shown by Staw and Ross (1980), however, leadership is more likely to be attributed to the individual who follows a firm, consistent course of action rather than one who tinkers with policy. Because of the inherent conflict between leadership and the need for flexibility, it is easy to see why trial balloons are so often floated, why pilot programs are disowned until proven successful, and why administrations contain trusted lieutenants who are ready to step in and accept blame when needed (that is, the "flak catcher").

When one considers the association between leadership and commitment, a related puzzle arises. Why is it that being firmly bound to a course of action can contribute to the attribution of leadership; yet at the same time leaders are also perceived to be people who move an organization or constituency from one state to another? One answer to this apparent contradiction is to note that major changes are often brought about by a *new* administration that is not bound to prior policies. A second answer is that organizational goals are often so global and diffuse that adherence to a course of action *and* movement can be perceived from the behavior of a single administrator. The savvy administrator can use movement to increase the salience and consequences of his or her actions. Yet at the same time the administrator may point out how these new actions are simply a reaffirmation of prior goals. Such orchestration is difficult but perhaps necessary when maintaining the attribution of leadership during times of change.

The difficulty of retaining flexibility in the face of commitment is highlighted by recent research on the perseverance of beliefs. As Nisbett and Ross (1980) have shown, individuals' beliefs and theories of the world can be highly resistant to change. When data that conflict with one's own view are presented, these data are frequently discredited, but supporting information is unflinchingly accepted. We tend to be hard on the methodology of opposing research and gentle on supporting studies; we tend to interpret ambiguous data in our own favor; and we pose questions that, by their very nature, provide supporting evidence (Lord, Ross, and Lepper, 1979; Snyder and Swann, 1978).

Although these perseverance effects imply a general resistance to accepting new information and beliefs, we might also expect there to be moderating effects of commitment. The greater the commitment to a particular policy or position, the more we would expect there to be perseverance of beliefs in the face of opposition. This is why it is exceedingly difficult to maintain a front of commitment while retaining the capacity for organizational learning. In absorbing the responsibility for policies, it is hard to avoid being trapped by the logic of one's own arguments and strength of one's own position. Thus, the maintenance of internal flexibility and external commitment is a tough act to follow, one that is perhaps more difficult than maintaining internal commitment at the same time as an external image of flexibility.

From Individual to Organizational Commitment. So far I have dealt only with psychological antecedents of commitment and escalation. I have assumed that the binding of belief to behavior and responsibility for negative consequences serve to hold administrators in a course of action or to restrict change. I have not considered structural impediments to change within organizations.

Standard operating procedures are difficult to change, as are administrative structures that are supported by powerful coalitions within an organization. The mechanisms by which individual commitment becomes translated into such structural sources of inflexibility are not well known. If, for example, individual administrators have supported a project to the extent that it has become embedded in the production or financial system of an organization, it will be that much more difficult to change. Likewise, when coalitions of powerful actors have supported a project or the project's administrators provide important political support for the ruling hierarchy, then change will also be hindered. Sometimes a project cannot be killed without overturning the entire organizational hierarchy. The project may be identified as the "president's baby" or become closely identified with the overall mission or goal of the firm. The latter case would seem to be especially resistant to change because its identity has transferred from any single individual to the organization as a collectivity. Ousting the chief executive may seem like a small feat compared to moving the entire mission and identity of an organization from one market to another (for example, ATT's move from public utility to a high technology firm in the communications and electronics fields). Massive turnover, restaffing, and retraining may be necessary for a major reorientation of the firm. In such cases, individual commitment to an existing policy or program may be only the tip of the structural and ideological iceberg supporting the status quo.

In Figure 3, I have sketched some of the relationships between individual and collective commitment. Individual action may be a major factor in launching collective actions such as financial outlays, procedural changes, the involvement of others, as well as the enlistment of organizational goals to support a project. These collective actions could be viewed as setting up structural barriers to subsequent change, depending upon how much a program is embedded in the financial, procedural, and ideological mission of the organization as a whole. Thus, Figure 3 outlines how individual actions can influence collective commitment to a program or course of action.

Figure 3 also shows the effect of collective actions upon individual commitment, and this is where some speculation is involved. Following my earlier discussion of individual commitment (see Figure 2), I might posit that an organizational response to a single administrator's actions might heighten the binding of policy to that person. However, collective actions might also serve to remove the individual from immediate association with the project and lessen the individual's responsibility for its consequences. The issue becomes still more complex in cases where the consequences of collective actions turn sour. Then the organization may identify the program originator as a scapegoat, just as the founder has decreased his or her own identification with the program. If forced to defend his or her original course of action, the originator may be forced out of the organization in order to make way for organizational change. Thus, as shown in Figure 3, resistance to change can be fostered by both organizational *and* individual sources of commitment. However, consequences may have a rather complex effect on change. Although positive consequences may build collective commitment to a program and impede change, negative consequences can set in

**Figure 3. Interplay of Organizational and
Individual Sources of Commitment.**

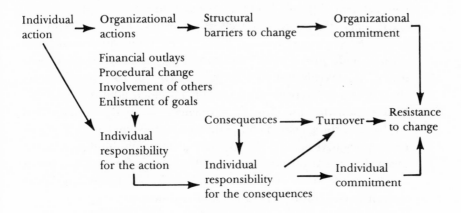

motion a scapegoating process that allows organizations to change via the turnover of selected administrators.

Some Lessons for Change. In drawing normative implications from the study of commitment, some cautions must be made. The first is that no one really knows what constitutes an optimal level of commitment to a policy or course of action. The Japanese are lauded for their long-term perspective and persistence in what can often appear to be an insurmountable task. Americans, by contrast, have often been admired for their flexibility and willingness to try almost anything as long as results are forthcoming. Both styles of action have their merits, with effectiveness no doubt determined by a fit between method and problem that we do not yet understand. A second caution for commitment research pertains to the object of commitment. Are administrators committed to a single policy, to a series of programs (for example, giving one's "all" to a program but changing if it doesn't work), or to the process of change itself? There are different implications for organizational adaptiveness depending on the answers to these questions. At present all we can say about commitment is that many cases abound where commitment appears excessive—cases where observers (and low responsibility actors) might have acted more flexibly than those most closely involved in the action.

If we accept the conclusion that there is a tendency to become overcommitted, then change and flexibility could be encouraged by following the models outlining the antecedents of escalation and commitment (Figures 1 and 2). We should, for example, be especially wary of escalation effects when behaviors are perceptually associated as parts of a single course of action because in these instances both justification and consistency influences have been found to override more objective elements of the situation. We should also be alert to any situation in which administrators are held responsible for large consequences. From the commitment model, absorbing responsibility for large consequences, be they positive or negative, sets up the internal and external binding process. From the escalation perspective, responsibility for *negative* consequences is identified as the source of justification tendencies. In my view, negative consequences are often behind the more pathological cases identified with lack of change. However, positive consequences can also produce excessive binding to behavior that may, in turn, reduce the possibility for change. The binding produced by responsibility for positive effects may set up inflexibility that can subsequently produce negative consequences for the organization as the environment shifts.

In counterbalancing commitment and escalation tendencies, individuals should seek and follow the advice of outsiders who can assess the relevant issues of a decision situation without being responsible for previous policies. Especially when organizations have experienced losses from a given investment or course of action, they should rotate or change those in charge of allocating resources. One applied instance of such a counterbalancing strategy was recently uncovered by Lewicki (1980). In a comparative case study, procedures were examined in two banks for coping with the problem of delinquent loans. The more financially aggressive bank, which had issued loans with greater risk, utilized separate departments for lending and "workout," the latter department being in charge of efforts to recover the bank's investment from problem accounts. The more conservative bank, which had fewer delinquent loans, had developed no formal procedure for separating responsibility for lending and workout, the original loan officer being charged with all phases of the loan relationship.

A second counterbalancing strategy might attempt to reduce defensiveness directly by decreasing accountability for results in the organization (for example, greater recognition of external influences on performance) or by deemphasizing the importance of past performance for the individual. For example, efforts could be placed on evaluating the future potential of individuals without such heavy reliance on past performance. By deemphasizing the all-pervasive pressure on demonstrating past success, the defense of past policies might be replaced by greater efforts on improving future performance.

A third counterbalancing strategy might involve tinkering with the perception of responsibility. Decision making, even when largely performed by a single individual, could be viewed as a shared product, thereby diffusing responsibility throughout the organization. The problem with this strategy is that what started as individually based commitment might turn into collective commitment. Although Ouchi (1981) has argued for Japanese style management in which decisions are shared widely in a firm, others (for example, Schein, 1981) have cautioned about the organizational inflexibility this may create. Having the entire organization sold on a particular long-range plan is no way to ensure change and adaptability.

A fourth strategy to reduce commitment would concentrate on neither individual nor collective responsibility. Rather than rotating projects among organizational staff or finding ways to reduce administrative defensiveness, a higher rate of turnover could simply be maintained by the organization. Bringing in new staff would be especially useful when projects have become embedded in the procedural and ideological core of the organization, making change extremely difficult. Higher turnover may be a preferable mechanism in making such difficult changes than the political upheavals and scapegoating processes that now often accompany such major alterations.

Conclusion

I have considered escalation and commitment as two counterforces to change, examined persistence of behavior in escalation situations, and broadened the analysis to consider commitment as a more general binding process. When one adds to these motivational forces the structural inflexibilities that may result from administrative commitment, some very strong counterforces to change result. In light of these forces, one must wonder not why organizations are so plodding and nonadaptive, but why they even function as well as they do.

One reason for organizational success may be that, in general, environments do not change as rapidly as critics and academics argue. For many organizations, a proven theory of how to operate within its environment may remain valid for years, while outmoded behaviors still bring results. A related idea is that organizations may survive and even prosper because adaptability is not essential to their effectiveness. Organizational purposes and procedures may be so institutionalized (Meyer and Rowan, 1977) that one need only demonstrate commitment to *something* in order to be perceived as effective. When technology is ambiguous and products are value laden, commitment to goals and procedures, whatever they are, may be sufficient for proper adjustment to the environment. At the extreme, a "school of thought" may be created (as in university life) where successful organizational leaders are those who can convince others that their own commitments are the standard to be achieved.

Commitment is very much related to adaptability and organizational success. The ways commitment is manifested in organizations may be less obvious than they appear, however. In many cases organizations and their administrators may be better at mixing commitment and flexibility than we generally give them credit for. Sometimes complexity can be maintained in private cognition and communication while simplicity is used for public communication (for example, Tetlock, 1981). Likewise, change may be able to be camouflaged as consistency and consistency presented as movement toward a new goal. Although these paradoxes will make research difficult, they comprise important questions we have barely begun to address.

A related question is whether organizational adaptability is ultimately affected more by political as opposed to psychological processes. Because there are so many forces that promote administrative inflexibility, it may be that intraorganizational politics (Pfeffer, 1981) periodically realigns the organization with its environment.

Organizations may, for example, increase their adaptability if they possess rival power centers, each with its own set of theories and views of the world. Even the presence of an "administration in exile" could help an organization adapt when conditions change so profoundly as to render prior theories useless. These possibilities deserve investigation, though they may drive our attention away from variables affecting administrative commitment and decision making.

References

"About Face: Thatcher Backs a Jobs Program." *Time*, August 10, 1981.

Aldrich, H. *Organization and Environments*. Englewood Cliffs, N.J.: Prentice-Hall, 1979.

Aronson, E. "Dissonance Theory: Progress and Problems." In R. Abelson and others (Eds.), *Theories of Cognitive Consistency*. Chicago: Rand McNally, 1968.

Aronson, E. *The Social Animal*. San Francisco: Freeman, 1976.

Bandura, A. *Psychological Modeling: Conflicting Theories*. New York: Lieber-Atherton, 1971.

Bazerman, M. H., Schoorman, F. D., and Goodman, P. S. "A Cognitive Evaluation of Escalation Processes in Managerial Decision-Making." Unpublished manuscript, Boston University, 1981.

Becker, H. S. "Notes on the Concept of Commitment." *American Journal of Sociology*, 1960, *66*, 32-40.

Brehm, J. W., and Cohen, A. E. *Explorations in Cognitive Dissonance*. New York: Wiley, 1962.

Caldwell, D. F., and O'Reilly, C. A. "Responses to Failure: The Effects of Choice and Responsibility on Impression Management." *Academy of Management Journal*, 1982, *25*(1), 121-136.

Campbell, D. T. "Reforms as Experiments." *American Psychologist*, 1969, *24*, 409-429.

Conlon, B. E., and Wolf, G. "The Moderating Effects of Strategy Visibility, and Involvement on Allocation Behavior: An Extension of Staw's Escalation Paradigm." *Organizational Behavior and Human Performance*, 1980, *26*, 172-192.

Connolly, T. "Information Processing and Decision Making in Organizations." In B. Staw and G. Salancik (Eds.), *New Directions in Organizational Behavior.* Chicago: St. Clair Press, 1977.

Crosbie, P. V. *Interaction in Small Groups.* New York: Macmillan, 1975.

Edwards, W. "The Theory of Decision Making." *Psychological Bulletin,* 1954, *51,* 380–417.

Festinger, L. *A Theory of Cognitive Dissonance.* Stanford, Calif.: Stanford University Press, 1957.

Fishbein, M., and Ajzen, I. *Belief, Attitude, Intention and Behavior: An Introduction to Theory and Research.* Reading, Mass.: Addison-Wesley, 1975.

Fox, F. V. "Persistence: Effects of Commitment and Justification Processes on Efforts to Succeed with a Course of Action." Unpublished doctoral dissertation, Department of Business Administration, University of Illinois, 1980.

Fox, F., and Staw, B. M. "The Trapped Administrator: The Effects of Job Insecurity and Policy Resistance upon Commitment to a Course of Action." *Administrative Science Quarterly,* 1979, *24,* 449–471.

Gallup, G. *The Gallup Opinion Index.* Princeton, N.J.: American Institute of Public Opinion, March 1978.

Grusky, O. "Managerial Succession and Organizational Effectiveness." *American Journal of Sociology,* 1963, *69,* 21–31.

Hannan, M. T., and Freeman, J. H. "The Population Ecology of Organizations." *American Journal of Sociology,* 1977, *82,* 929–964.

Hughes, E. J. "The Presidency versus Jimmy Carter." *Fortune,* December 4, 1978, p. 58.

Jones, E. E., and Nisbett, R. E. "The Actor and the Observer: Divergent Perceptions of the Causes of Behavior." In E. E. Jones and others (Eds.), *Attribution: Perceiving the Causes of Behavior.* Morristown, N.J.: General Learning Press, 1972.

Kiesler, C. A. *The Psychology of Commitment: Experiments Linking Behavior to Belief.* New York: Academic Press, 1971.

Lewicki, R. J. "Bad Loan Psychology: Entrapment and Commitment in Financial Lending." Working paper 80-25, Graduate School of Business Administration, Duke University, 1980.

Lindblom. C. E. "The Science of Muddling Through." *Public Administration Review,* 1959, *19,* 79–88.

Lord, C., Ross, L., and Lepper, M. "Biased Assimilation and Attitude Polarization: The Effects of Prior Theories on Subsequently Considered Evidence." *Journal of Personality and Social Psychology,* 1979, *37,* 2098–2109.

McCain, B. "Commitment under Conditions of Failure: Escalation or De-Escalation." Unpublished manuscript, University of Iowa, 1981.

March, J. G., and Olsen, J. P. *Ambiguity and Choice in Organizations.* Bergen, Norway: Universitetsforlaget, 1976.

Meyer, J. W., and Rowan, B. "Institutionalized Organizations: Formal Structure as Myth and Ceremony." *American Journal of Sociology,* 1977, *83,* 340–363.

Miller, D. T., and Ross, M. "Self-Serving Biases in the Attribution of Causality: Fact or Fiction?" *Psychological Bulletin,* 1975, *82,* 213–225.

"Money Down the Drain." *Time,* June 25, 1979, p. 26.

Nisbett, R., and Ross, L. *Human Inference: Strategies and Shortcomings of Social Judgment.* Englewood Cliffs, N.J.: Prentice-Hall, 1980.

Ouchi, W. *Theory Z: How American Business Can Meet the Japanese Challenge.* Reading, Mass.: Addison-Wesley, 1981.

Pfeffer, J. *Power in Organizations.* Marchfield, Mass.: Pitman, 1981.

Platt, J. "Social Traps." *American Psychologist,* 1973, *28,* 641–651.

Porter, L. W., Steers, R. M., Mowday, R. T., and Boulian, P. V. "Organizational Commitment, Job Satisfaction, and Turnover Among Psychiatric Technicians." *Journal of Applied Psychology,* 1974, *59,* 603–609.

Price, J. L. *The Study of Turnover.* Ames: Iowa State University Press, 1977.

Ross, L. "The Intuitive Psychologist and His Shortcomings: Distortions in the Attribution Process." In L. Berkowitz (Ed.), *Advances in Experimental Social Psychology.* Vol. 10. New York: Academic Press, 1977.

Rubin, J. Z., and Brockner, J. "Factors Affecting Entrapments in Waiting Situations: The Rosencrantz and Guildenstern Effect." *Journal of Experimental Social Psychology,* 1975, *31,* 1054–1063.

Salancik, G. "Commitment and the Control of Organizational Behavior and Belief." In B. Staw and G. Salancik (Eds.), *New Directions in Organizational Behavior.* Chicago: St. Clair Press, 1977.

Sheehan, N., and Kenworthy, E. W. *Pentagon Papers.* New York: Quadrangle Books, 1971.

Schein, E. H. "Does Japanese Management Style Have a Message for American Managers?" *Sloan Management Review,* Fall 1981, pp. 55-68.

Shubik, M. "The Dollar Auction Game: A Paradox in Noncooperative Behavior and Escalation." *Journal of Conflict Resolution,* 1971, *15,* 109-111.

Simon, H. A. *Administrative Behavior.* New York: Macmillan, 1957.

Slovic, P., Fischboff, B., and Lichtenstein, S. "Behavioral Decision Theory." *Annual Review of Psychology,* 1977, *28,* 1-39.

Snyder, M., and Swann, W. B. "Behavioral Confirmation in Social Interaction: From Social Perception to Social Reality." *Journal of Experimental Social Psychology,* 1978, *14,* 148-162.

"The State of Jimmy Carter." *Time,* February 5, 1979, p. 11.

Staw, B. M., "The Escalation of Commitment to a Course of Action." *Academy of Management Review,* 1981, *6*(4), 577-587.

Staw, B. M. "Knee-Deep in the Big Muddy: A Study of Escalating Commitment to a Chosen Course of Action." *Organizational Behavior and Human Performance,* 1976, *16,* 27-44.

Staw, B. M. "Rationality and Justification in Organizational Life." In B. Staw and L. Cummings (Eds.), *Research in Organizational Behavior.* Vol. 2. Greenwich, Conn.: JAI Press, 1980.

Staw, B. M., and Fox, F. "Escalation: Some Determinants of Commitment to a Previously Chosen Course of Action." *Human Relations,* 1977, *30,* 431-450.

Staw, B. M., and Ross, J. "Commitment to a Policy Decision: A Multitheoretical Perspective." *Administrative Science Quarterly,* 1978, *23,* 40-64.

Staw, B. M., and Ross, J. "Commitment in an Experimenting Society: An Experiment on the Attribution of Leadership from Administrative Scenarios." *Journal of Applied Psychology,* 1980, *65,* 249-260.

Staw, B. M., Sandelands, L. E., and Dutton, J. E. "Threat-Rigidity Effects in Organizational Behavior: A Multi-Level Analysis." *Administrative Science Quarterly,* 1981, *26,* 501-524.

Steers, R. M. "Antecedents and Outcomes of Organizational Commitment." *Administrative Science Quarterly*, 1977, *22*, 46–56.

Stogdill, R. M. *Handbook of Leadership*. New York: Free Press, 1974.

Taylor, S. E., and Fiske, S. T. "Salience, Attention and Attribution: Top of the Head Phenomena." In L. Berkowitz (Ed.), *Advances in Experimental Social Psychology*. Vol. 11. New York: Academic Press, 1978.

Tegar, A. I. *Too Much Invested to Quit*. Elmsford, N.Y.: Pergamon Press, 1980.

Tetlock, P. "Pre- to Postelection Shifts in Presidential Rhetoric: Impression Management or Cognitive Adjustment?" *Journal of Personality and Social Psychology*, 1981, *41*, 207–212.

Thompson, J. D. *Organizations in Action*. New York: McGraw-Hill, 1967.

Vandiver, K. "Why Should My Conscience Bother Me?" In A. Heilbroner (Ed.), *In the Name of Profit*. Garden City, N.Y.: Doubleday, 1972.

"Victory Puts Monkey on Reagan's Back." *Chicago Tribune*, July 30, 1981, p. 6.

Vroom, V. *Work and Motivation*. New York: Wiley, 1964.

Walster, E. "Assignment of Responsibility for an Accident." *Journal of Personality and Social Psychology*, 1966, *3*, 73–79.

Weary-Bradley, G. "Self-Serving Biases in the Attribution Process: A Reexamination of the Fact or Fiction Question." *Journal of Personality and Social Psychology*, 1978, *36*, 56–71.

Weick, K. "Enactment Processes in Organizations." In B. Staw and G. Salancik (Eds.), *New Directions in Organizational Behavior*. Chicago: St. Clair Press, 1977.

Weiner, B., Frieze, I., Kukla, A., Reed, L., Rest, S., and Rosenbaum, R. M. "Perceiving the Causes of Success and Failure." In E. E. Jones and others (Eds.), *Attribution: Perceiving the Causes of Behavior*. Morristown, N.J.: General Learning Press, 1972.

Wicklund, R., and Brehm, J. *Perspectives on Cognitive Dissonance*. Hillsdale, N.J.: Erlbaum, 1976.

◘ ◘ ◘ ◘ ◘ ◘ **4**

Problems of Changing White Males' Behavior and Beliefs Concerning Race Relations

◘ ◘ ◘ ◘ ◘ ◘ ◘ ◘ ◘ ◘ ◘ ◘ ◘ ◘ ◘ ◘ ◘ ◘

Clayton P. Alderfer

This chapter reports on work in progress. It describes the understanding and demonstrates the behavior I have reached after slightly more than ten years of attempting to learn about race relations in organizations of the United States. I do not feel that the learning is

I wish to express my appreciation to the people who provided comments on an earlier version of this chapter: Charleen Alderfer, Chris Argyris, David Berg, Connie Gersick, Paul Goodman, Melissa Middleton, David Morgan, Ken Smith, Leota Tucker, Robert Tucker, and Leroy Wells, Jr. This chapter is also a product of the scholars and practitioners at the workshop held at Carnegie-Mellon University to discuss the chapters in this book. I thank the members of that group for their contribution to my learning.

complete; more is to be done at both personal and collective levels. But I think my progress has been significant. What I say here represents a point of view that is not widely shared by white people. I write the chapter, nevertheless, mainly for other white people—and especially for white men. When black people read this chapter, I ask that they look at it as the effort of one white person to speak with other whites about the subject of race.

By design, the chapter is written to create two kinds of dialogue with readers. The first consists of the traditional data-theory dialectic. I present a variety of data—personal, observational, statistical—to ask the reader to consider new ways of thinking about race. I also present a series of propositions that offer a perspective on race that fits the data. My own learning about race has been much more inductive than deductive. Thus, I lead with data rather than with theory. The theory offered in three later sections of the chapter represents my current thinking about solving the problem of defining racism, formulating race relations as a special case of intergroup dynamics, and developing a theory-based perspective on changing white men.

The second dialogue, which is not totally independent of the first, is between emotions and intellect. White readers are likely to experience a range of emotions in reading this chapter. My experience with race has taught me that we whites seem to have an almost endless array of tactics to avoid facing the emotions in ourselves in relation to the subject of race. I believe it is very difficult, if not impossible, for white people to learn about race without having our emotions aroused. Whether this can happen through reading and reflecting is much more of a question for me. Writing this chapter to create a dialogue between emotion and intellect is therefore an experiment. Readers who wish to enter this experiment might keep an explicit record of their feelings as they proceed through the chapter.

In a certain sense the chapter is an attempt to re-create for the reader something like the kind of learning process I have gone through to reach my current knowledge of race. From the beginning I did not believe that mere intellectual learning would be enough. I also believed that reading and thinking would be very important because my own style relies heavily on the intellect. My self-designed strategy for learning about race was to mix experience with reflection. As a result of this process, I have had numerous painful experiences and changed very markedly the manner in which I understand human behavior in general and race relations in particular.

When Paul Goodman asked me to join his Carnegie-Mellon seminar, we discussed what I might contribute. Given a variety of options, he preferred what I considered the most novel of my professional activities. There was no question that the race work met the criterion, but I had some serious trepidation about whether I was ready to go public at this stage of the work. Furthermore, I was sure that the other participants in the seminar would be only senior white males.

As a senior white male myself, I would be presenting a paper on race relations, a problem in intergroup relations, to just one racial group. All I knew about race relations suggested that this group working without contact with a comparable black group would have difficulty understanding what I had to say about race. The historical evidence indicates that white people, especially those in power, tend not to reflect on their own contribution to racial dynamics except under the most unusual circumstances. Generally, the pattern is for whites to talk about blacks but not about themselves in order to cope with racial problems. My learning was going consistently in the direction of saying that useful knowledge about race relations for whites was much more likely to occur if we could talk about ourselves as a group *before* dealing with interracial issues. Because the conference group consisted of all senior white males, I imagined that they would find my approach unnatural.

Paul had indicated that a purpose of the seminar was to encourage exchange and learning among the participants. I liked this idea. From my perspective, this orientation itself was a very good sign about the seminar. It suggested that our joint activity could be different than most professional meetings, whose aims rarely seem to be oriented toward learning.

The seminar was designed to provide each participant with as much useful feedback about the content of his presentation as was feasible. Generally, participants came to the seminar with papers largely finished and received reactions to their nearly complete work. I came with, at most, a partially begun paper and told my colleagues that I expected to learn not only from the content of what they said to me, but also from the process of how we interacted.

In taking this orientation to the conference, I knew I was violating certain well-established norms about the behavior of presenters at such events. Not bringing a fully complete paper was one violation. People might feel I was failing to meet legitimate expectations. Asking people to reflect on their own experience and behavior was a second departure from the norm. Social scientists who are firmly committed to a positivist epistemological tradition do not easily accept the idea that examining one's own group identification can be a means to basic knowledge about social behavior. I took the stance I did because I took seriously Paul Goodman's commitment to have the conference become an opportunity for learning. But I did not expect to have an easy time during the conference, and I was not disappointed. The article incorporates data and analysis from exchanges at the meeting.

As it turns out, it is very useful for both research and consulting to do some kinds of race work in homogeneous groups (that is, groups of all black and all white members) and other kinds of activities in heterogeneous groups (that is, groups of black and white members) (Alderfer, Alderfer, Tucker, and Tucker, 1980). In content and in process, this chapter should be viewed as a homogeneous group event. It is the product of one senior white male working in and with a homogeneous group of similar people. I believe that a white person who has learned to work on racial issues from an intergroup perspective will understand this statement differently than a white person who has not. A higher proportion of black than white people will understand the statement as intended because being in a minority position tends to "teach" more about intergroup phenomena than being in a majority position. For both white and black readers, I want to indicate that learning to make this statement was necessary for me to be able to complete the chapter. Without it I was blocked by the knowledge that what I had to say was likely to be experienced very differently by most whites and most blacks. I did not know how to let readers know that. I was helped to make the statement by a conversation with Robert C. Tucker, a senior black male, with whom I have collaborated extensively for more than six years. I have made similar comments during race workshops and other organization interventions. The effect often seems to surprise people. Blacks often laugh with a sense of knowing on their faces and whites seem disturbed—almost stunned. Despite (or because of) these reactions, both groups seem freed to continue their work of learning, perhaps because I have been freed to be more myself by making the statement. I hope similar effects will occur for readers of this paper.

All that I have said in the preceding paragraphs follows from how intergroup theory deals with the problem of objectivity in social research. The tradition in much of American social research, which has been largely dominated by white men, has been to view data as independent of investigator or of what group memberships are characteristic of investigators who use particular methods. This orientation deals with the problem of objectivity by separating investigators from the phenomena they study. Intergroup theory takes a different position on this very fundamental issue. It assumes that investigators are inevitably entangled in the phenomena they study, no matter what method or combination of methods they use. Intergroup theory provides a framework for understanding the entanglements and for reasoning about how to manage and balance the relevant group forces in order to best achieve the various goals of science, practice, and policy. "Objectivity," as conventionally defined, is interpreted by intergroup theory as a sign of efforts to avoid engaging the phenomena. According to intergroup theory, the key to using one's group identities in the service of understanding is to become conscious of which group identities are likely to be evoked by whatever phenomena are being studied. Thus, in the preceding paragraphs, I note that my identity as a senior white male has shaped my approach to race relations. The perspective of intergroup theory has evolved from more than ten years of research and consultation. It has been developed more inductively than deductively from anomalous research results and from "mistakes" in consultation. It changes in response to orderly accumulation of systematic information (see Alderfer and Smith, 1982). I presented what I believe to be my relevant group identities in relation to racial dynamics as an illustration of intergroup theory in use.

From this point forward, the purpose is to establish an empirical conceptual basis for propositions about white males changing their behavior, feelings, and cognitions about race in predominantly white organizations.

The second section of the chapter begins with a discussion of the concept of racism and briefly sets its historical context. Racism is not a term with a single meaning, but that fact does not severely limit its usefulness. It is a term that also has feelings associated with it. I believe that taking a look at some of those feelings from a white perspective can be very useful for changing white males.

The third section presents the major concepts and propositions of intergroup theory along with discussion of how they are relevant to the problem of changing white males. Intergroup theory proposes to deal with a wider range of phenomena than race relations. In some specialties within social science, race relations and intergroup relations are virtually synonymous. Although I do not agree with this orientation, I do believe that race relations offer a particularly fruitful arena for gaining insight into general intergroup problems because of the severity and persistence of destructive racial dynamics in organizations of this society.

The fourth section consists of a discussion of conventional social research as a set of forces relevant to changing white males. The analysis explores how group forces within social science itself help render the field less potent than its potential in facilitating change in race relations.

A fifth section includes description and analysis of how the present subject was dealt with at the Carnegie-Mellon conference.

The sixth section presents statements toward a theory of changing white men in the context of race relations. As a stepping-off point, one may be aided by recognizing the two senses of the phrase. Changing white males can mean "White males are changing." It can also imply "Here's how to change white men." I mean the words in both senses.

The overview then draws together the various steps in the overall logic of the chapter and explains how the parts of the general argument establish a whole.

The Concept of Racism

The concept of racism plays a prominent part in most contemporary writing about race relations. It is a term used by both black and white writers (for example, Carmichael and Hamilton, 1967; Jones, 1972; Kovel, 1970; Silberman, 1964). It is also a term that many whites find extremely distasteful.

Need for the Concept. In scientific work, concepts come into use for a variety of reasons. Among them are determinations by investigators that certain data can be understood more fully, explained more completely, and predicted more accurately if specific abstract ideas are brought into the language and key statements relating the concepts to each other are used to deal with the phenomena. For example, although the concept of the unconscious existed before Freud and Jung, these two investigators used that idea in their theories because of continuing encounters with dreams and other symbolic data. These phenomena could be more easily understood, explained, and used with a concept of the unconscious than without. Although Freud and Jung became well known for making unconscious dynamics central to their theories of personality, others used the term not only because of the persuasive power of the two major theorists but also because of the large amount of data that can be accounted for by using the concept. Without the concept, one is forced either to overlook a large amount of recurring phenomena or to deal with it using less satisfactory terms.

In this context, the need for a concept of racism arises from examining the history of race relations in the United States. That study shows that the story of race relations in the United States is a series of cycles of regression and progression followed by repeated episodes of backward and forward movement (Bennett, 1962; Jones, 1972; Kerner and others, 1968; Kovel, 1970). A most poignant comment on this pattern was provided by Kenneth Clark when he testified before the Kerner Commission: "I read the report . . . of the 1919 riot in Chicago, and it is as if I were reading the report of the investigating committee of the Harlem riot of '35, the report of the investigating committee on the Harlem riot of '43, the report of the McCone Commission on the Watts riot. I must again in candor say to you members of this Commission—it is a kind of Alice in Wonderland—with the same moving picture re-shown over and over again, the same analysis, the same recommendations, and the same inaction" (Kerner and others, 1968, p. 29).

The concept of racism addresses a number of questions concerning the overall pattern of race relations in the United States.

Why does such substantial inequality between the races exist in a country manifestly committed to fairness among its people? What explains the recurrent cycles of regression and progression in changing race relations? Why does it seem to matter so little which specific individuals become involved in racial progress or regression?

Although the phases are of interest because of their overall pattern, at least as significant is the original direction of the cycle. By 1600, there were more than a half million African slaves in the Western Hemisphere of the New World. Black people were brought as slaves to the English settlement in Virginia by 1619. When the Declaration of Independence was signed in 1776, there were approximately five hundred thousand blacks held as slaves and indentured servants in the United States alone. At that time about one person in six in the United States was held in servitude. All of this was done in a country whose stated reason for being was to escape arbitrary and tyrannical rule, yet whose method of beginning was to enslave a significant proportion of its own people. This is why I say the initial phase of the race relations cycle was regressive. Outbreaks of progressive action have followed those beginnings, but the origins of the United States sanctioned black slavery, and the colonial economy depended on it. Oppression of black people by whites was a key element in the founding of the nation. The initial collective impulse of the United States was toward regressive race relations.

Since those early years there have been changes. Slavery and slave trade were abolished in the 1800s. The United States Constitution has been amended several times to reduce the legal framework of oppression against blacks. Federal legislation and judicial decision have brought further change toward more progressive relations between blacks and whites. The latest phase of this progressive action began with the *Brown* v. *Board of Education* decision in 1954 and was followed by a decade of civil rights activism during the 1960s. Blacks as well as whites indicate that barriers to blacks have been again reduced (Fernandez, 1981). But to a careful observer of the contemporary scene, it must also be apparent that we are once again living through a regressive phase at the national level.

As recently as January 24, 1982, the front page of the *New York Times* carried a story with the headline "Changes on Rights Are Starting to Have Impact." The lead paragraph of the story stated, "The President . . . is beginning his second year in office under a mounting barrage of assertions that he is undermining the civil rights and civil liberties of Americans in a broad range of means." The article contains statements by the president and interpretations by other national leaders. The president was quoted as saying, "I have been on the side of opposition to bigotry and discrimination and prejudice, and long before it even became a kind of national issue under the title civil rights. And my life has been spent on that side." The president of the Potomac Institute, a leader in civil rights since the 1950s, interpreted the actions of the current administration as, "trying to reduce the whole area of civil rights to a question of individuals" (p. 2). The assistant attorney general, in the same article, is reported to see the issue as "elevating the rights of groups over the rights of individuals," which is "at war with the American ideal of equal opportunity for each person." This Justice Department official added, "This Administration . . . is firmly committed to the view that the Constitution and laws protect the right of every person to pursue his or her goals in an environment of racial and sexual neutrality." The statements by these two senior government officials show little evidence that they perceive widespread effects of racism. The president's words give the impression that he has little awareness of racial history in the United States. He said he was opposed to bigotry before civil rights became a national issue. Surely he does not mean to suggest that he is more than three hundred years old. The assistant attorney general's statements suggest that his view is shaped by the idea, often held by white men, that attending to group-level phenomena is in fundamental conflict with the development of individual people. Furthermore, one must also wonder about the Justice Department official's sense of history. When has the United States ever been an environment of "racial and sexual neutrality"? By their words and actions, I am led to the conclusion that these two senior officials of the United States government, who happen to be white men, are helping lead the country into a period of significant regression in race relations. Within the lifetime of people who will read this chapter, we shall have lived through successive periods of progression and regression in relations between blacks and whites at the national level. The concept of racism is useful to understand not just the three-hundred-year history of race relations in the United States but also the changes we have experienced in the last twenty years.

The Present Concept of Racism. Like many ideas in the social sciences that deal with difficult and complex issues, *racism* does not have a single widely agreed upon meaning. A variety of scholars has defined the term and helped shape its meaning (Carmichael and Hamilton, 1967; Fernandez, 1981; Jones, 1972; Kovel, 1970; Silberman, 1964). In what follows I draw on their work plus my own experience to provide an extensive definition and discussion of the concept.

Racism is a series of intellectual arguments with associated actions, or one may say that racism consists of recurrent behavioral patterns with associated intellectual justifications. Virtually all concepts of racism include both beliefs (or attitudes) and behavior, but vary somewhat according to whether behavior or ideas are primary. Usually, whether one starts with the behavior and follows with the ideas or vice versa depends on whether one's group is the giver or receiver of racism.

Dominance is an essential element in racism. Mere ethnocentrism, by which one group evaluates itself more favorably than other groups, is not enough. Racism means that one racial group evaluates itself more favorably than another group and uses its superior power to resist examining that evaluation. The idea of dominance may also be found in other "isms"—sexism and ageism—but each of them is qualitatively different from racism. Although women generally are less powerful than men in the United States, the basis of male-female relations was not rooted in overt slavery. Efforts to empower women and reduce gender based discrimination do not have a history of enslavement of one group by the other to counteract. Ageism is even more complex in relation to issues of dominance. Age is not a fixed condition for the life of individuals in the same way that race and gender are; over the course of a normal lifetime, a person will be young, middleaged, and old. Moreover, which age group is more dominant in a given situation is not as easily predictable as which race and gender are usually in control.

For racism to occur, one racial group must possess significantly more power than another racial group. Members of the dominant racial group are therefore able to use their superior power to demean, subvert, or destroy the present condition or future potential of members of the subordinate racial group. The dominant racial group also uses its superior resources to maintain its dominant position at the expense of the subordinate group. Dominant racial groups have belief systems that provide ways to understand and explain their behavior. Without its racist ideology, a dominant group would probably have a much more difficult time justifying its actions. The usual content of racist ideology states that the dominant racial group is inherently superior to the other racial group based on a variety of physical, biological, social, or cultural traits. Often these hypothesized group differences are further supported by reference to scientific or social scientific research (Jones, 1979).

The somewhat different emphases on behavior versus beliefs for oppressed versus dominant racial groups arise from their intergroup relations. Oppressed group members perceive the effects of dominant group actions more quickly because the behavior has more immediate impact on them than attitudes and ideas. Dominant group members tend to have access to the ideas and attitudes more readily because the beliefs serve to shield them from a full realization of the consequences of their behavior.

In the United States, the most frequently observed form of racism is white racism. Despite periodic progressive changes over three hundred years, whites remain the dominant racial group in this country and therefore have many more opportunities to demonstrate racism than do blacks. Black racism does occur in the United States, but it is possible only in settings where blacks are the dominant racial group.

Racism also varies by level of analysis, degree of severity, and conscious awareness. In terms of level of analysis, many people view racism mainly as a personality trait. We talk about prejudiced individuals and stereotyped thinking. (Summaries of the social psychology of prejudice and ethnic relations may be found in Harding, Proshansky, Kutner and Chein, 1969.) There is a variety of studies that seek to identify such individuals and to examine the dynamics of their minds. Racism, however, is developed and maintained by more complex human systems than just individuals. We refer to organizational and institutional racism when the structures and processes that establish and perpetuate racism develop a life of their own that exists apart from whatever individuals may fill roles and responsibilities in the higher-order systems. When the *Plessy v. Ferguson* Supreme Court decision in 1896 approved of "separate but equal" facilities for blacks and whites, an entire institutional fabric for racism was created. It mattered very little which individual white people managed and controlled the schools and other organizations affected by the decision.

In terms of severity, many white people also recognize racism only when they observe it in its more heinous forms. If a Ku Klux Klan leader declares that his organization's mission is to return America to the principles established by the white founding fathers, most white people would probably view that as a racist act. But there are also many more subtle forms that people who learn to accept their whiteness can detect. Recently, a controversy about whether the Prudence Crandall School should be preserved as a historical landmark or converted into a town library arose in the town of Canterbury, Connecticut. The Prudence Crandall School is believed to be the first school in the United States for black girls. Commenting on the conflict, the first selectman of Canterbury said that the issue between the historical commission and the town was "not a race thing at all," after he noted that there were only two black families in the town's population of thirty-five hundred. How could diminishing a key landmark in the history of race relations not be racist? What relevance did the town having only two black families have, unless the action was racial? A town minister also commented, "I don't see that resentment now. It's just that Northerners who have little association with black issues and problems tend to be indifferent. I don't know that there's a great deal of sentiment one way or the other about the museum" (*New York Times*, February 7, 1982). Failing to see the racial significance of the Prudence Crandall controversy and speaking to support that denial are examples of the more subtle forms of racism that often are overlooked by members of dominant white groups.

Probably the most difficult aspect of racism for whites to accept is distinction between its conscious and unconscious forms. For a significant period, television programs had a marked tendency for janitors and criminals to be portrayed by black actors and for police and judges to be played by white people. Black-white jokes told in the locker rooms of white male establishments rarely have white people as an object of humor. Connotations of "blackness" as a color are generally negative in the English language

(Kovel, 1970). By definition, unconscious racism occurs without awareness of the institution or person demonstrating it. Identifying and changing unconscious racism is always painful. The ideology and behavior of racism violates most individuals' sense of Judeo-Christian ideals. Keeping racism unconscious preserves the ideal instead of confronting a more painful reality. Otherwise there would be little need for the covert mechanisms to keep this form of racism from awareness.

One of the more startling examples of institutional racism occurred in the form of a memorandum distributed anonymously to the desks of black managers in a major U.S. corporation. The news indicated that between November 1, 1981, and April 1, 1982, there would be *"OPEN SEASON"* on "Porch Monkeys." Readers were told that other terms for the prey were jigaboos, saucerlips, jungle bunnies, spooks, or spearchuckers. Additional statements in the document indicated that "porch monkeys" could be spotted by looking for bright colors, Cadillacs, empty wine bottles, and hookers. Readers were literally invited to hunt and kill the identified species.

When this document was brought before a group of black and white people in the corporation, reactions varied within and between the racial groups. Whites spoke first. The individual who spoke initially said he doubted whether the document was authentic. He suspected that the speaker had invented the paper for its shock value. A second white person said he was insulted to be asked to look at such an appalling piece of paper. Then a number of whites expressed their dismay and disgust that such a piece of filth should be written and circulated. Some said they were absolutely astounded to learn that such things happened. Others said that they had seen the document, had imagined that it was one of a kind, and had done nothing to intervene.

Blacks spoke second. They acknowledged not only that this document and others like it were familiar but also that learning to live with such events was "par for the course" or "part of the price of admission" in working for the corporation. There was low-keyed laughter and statements to the effect that people had to keep cool when faced with assaults of this kind; otherwise they would be unable to operate effectively in the predominantly white environment. Later, when the blacks were meeting among themselves without whites present, they questioned whether their responses had been too accepting or acquiescent. Perhaps by not showing more anger, they had not given the proper message to the whites.

Racism is one especially malevolent form of intergroup conflict. Not every form of relationship between racial groups or every form of conflict between racial groups necessarily becomes racist. Viewing racism from broad historical and cultural perspectives, writrs for the *Encyclopedia Britannica* ("Racism," 1974) noted that the relations between white Northern Europeans and black Africans represent one of the most sustained and severe forms of racism that have ever been observed. The roots of racism in the United States begin with that struggle.

Many whites have feelings about the term *racism*. I believe that the overwhelming majority of white people would prefer not to use it. Some become visibly upset on hearing the word. They experience the term as an indictment and react with a sense of guilt and defensiveness. A small proportion of whites, however, seems to have a wholly different attitude toward the racism concept. This minority of whites seems to experience a certain kind of gratification from using the term *racism* to condemn other whites. Carmichael and Hamilton (1967, p. 28), among others, comment on whites who seem to give up their whiteness and try to "be black" in the service of improving race relations. The process by which some whites accuse other whites of being racist is a special form of scapegoating. The effect is to excuse the whites who characterize others as racist from looking at their own feelings and ideas about race and from accepting their own whiteness as a collective condition. Locating racism in particular individuals discourages individual white people from examining themselves and blocks collective acknowledgment that all whites inevitably participate in maintaining the status quo of white dominance.

I do not think it is helpful for whites to deny or in other ways to escape our white racial identity. If race relations are to become less pathological, both whites and blacks must alter customary ways of acting, thinking, and feeling. Intergroup theory clearly implies that these changes must occur within each racial group as well as between them. I believe the concept of racism, including the emotional connotations associated with it, is an essential element in the intellectual equipment that whites need to participate in that change process. I do not, however, believe that racism should be used as a term for some whites to condemn others. It is necessary to explain our collective racial history and its continuing presence in contemporary events, but using the term as a means for some white individuals to demean others is to create forces against progressive change.

In summary, exploitation of blacks by whites has existed in the territory of the United States since before the country's founding. Although slavery has been abolished for more than a hundred years, patterns of economic and social discrimination against blacks in predominantly white organizations continue to exist to this day. Accompanying these behavioral patterns are intellectual arguments that both deny and justify the inequities. White leaders can be frequently observed making statements whose effect, at a minimum, discourages other white people from achieving greater consciousness of the problems.

The concept of racism serves a number of scientific functions. It helps explain why such powerful discrimination can continue to exist in a country so manifestly committed to equity among its citizens. It provides a basis for understanding the regressive and progressive cycles in our racial history. It calls attention to both individual and collective aspects of the patterns and thereby explains why certain words and actions repeat themselves even though specific individuals change roles and responsibilities.

As defined here, the concept of racism also sets directions for social and organizational change and therefore is not value neutral. Specific areas for improvement include:

- The behaviors of whites toward other whites and in relation to blacks
- The understanding of whites about race and racial dynamics
- The perceptiveness of whites with respect to the more subtle forms of racism as well as to the more blatant manifestations
- The capacity of whites to deal with both personal and collective manifestations of racism
- The willingness of whites to be alert to unconscious as well as conscious forms of racial events

Stating these directions for change from the "white side" is consistent with the orientation of this chapter being written by a white male mainly for other white people. I believe that major initiatives for change must come from whites. I also believe that whites alone cannot change the current pattern of racial dynamics. Black responses to white efforts to change will be significant in determining whether significant change can occur and, if so, in what forms.

Intergroup Theory

Intergroup theory consists of a series of concepts and propositions that offer one means to understand, explain, and predict relations between groups that are related to one another in organizations. Intergroup theory aims both to be more general in scope than race relations and to provide a basic framework for dealing with racial dynamics. From the perspective of intergroup theory, racism represents one especially undesirable quasi-stationary equilibrium condition between black and white groups.

Intergroup theory makes investigators and change agents part of the phenomena. The first section of this chapter shows how the self-reflective quality of the theory can be applied by readers and writers. The theory also provides ways of conceiving of different states than currently exist and of reasoning about how the quasi-equilibrium might be changed.

Intergroup theory consists of a definition of groups in organizations, a series of propositions about intergroup relations in organizations, and the concepts of microcosm group and of embedded intergroup relations. (This material is taken, with slight modifications, from Alderfer and Smith, 1982.)

Groups in Organizations. Within the social psychology literature there is no shortage of definitions of groups, but there is also no clear consensus among those who propose them. Because these definitions have largely depended on work done in laboratories by social psychologists studying internal properties of groups, they are limited in recognizing the external properties of groups. A definition of "groups in organizations" gives a more balanced attention to both internal and external properties.

A human group is a collection of individuals (1) who have significantly interdependent relations with each other, (2) who perceive themselves as a group by reliably distinguishing members from nonmembers, (3) whose group identity is recognized by nonmembers, (4) who, as group members acting alone or in concert, have significantly interdependent relations with other groups, and (5) whose roles in the group are therefore a function of expectations from themselves, from other group members, and from nongroup members. This conceptualization of a group makes every individual member into a group representative whenever he or she deals with members of other groups, and it treats every transaction among individuals as, in part, an intergroup event. In the context of race relations, this orientation means that neither investigators nor respondents can escape their racial identities. Racial group membership will shape both how people experience the phenomena of race relations and how they are experienced by those with whom they interact.

Intergroup Relations in Organizations. Every organization consists of a large number of groups, and every organizational member represents a number of these groups when dealing with other people in the organization. The groups in an organization can be divided into two broad classes: identity groups and organizational groups. An identity group may be thought of as one whose members share some biological characteristic (such as race), have participated in equivalent historical experiences (such as migration), are currently subjected to certain social forces (such as unemployment), and as a result have similar world views. When people enter organizations, they bring along their identity groups, which are based on variables such as ethnicity, sex, age, and family. An organizational group may be conceived of as a group whose members share approximately common organizational positions, participate in equivalent work experiences, and consequently have similar organizational views. Organizations assign members to organizational groups according to division of labor and hierarchy of authority. One critical factor in intergroup relations in organizations is that membership in identity groups is not independent from membership in organizational groups. Certain organizational groups tend to be filled by members of particular identity groups. In the United States, for example, positions in upper management tend to be held by older white males; black people tend to hold lower ranking, less powerful positions.

Both identity groups and organizational groups fit the five criteria of the definition of a human group. First, there are significant interdependencies between identity group members because of their common historical experiences and between organizational group members because of their equivalent work or organizational experiences. Second, members of either group can reliably distinguish themselves from nonmembers on the basis of common historical experience or common location in the organization. However, the precision of this identification process depends on the permeability of group boundaries, which refers to the ease with which boundaries can be crossed and members can enter and leave groups. Third, nonmembers are able to recognize members. The fourth and fifth aspects of the definition are highly linked when applied to identity and organizational groups. When they relate to individuals from other groups, group members may be more or less aware of the extent to which they are acting as, or being seen as, group representatives. Each person belongs to a number of identity groups and organizational groups. At any moment he or she may be a member of a large number of these groups simultaneously. The group that is made focal at a particular moment will depend on the representation from other groups and on what issues are critical in the current intergroup exchanges. A white person in a predominantly black organization, for example, can rarely escape representing white people in some way, no matter what her or his preference is. But if that white person is in a predominantly white organization, he or she will probably be seen as representing instead some other group, such as a particular hierarchical level. Rarely are individuals "just people" when they act in organizations. When there are no other group representatives present, individuals may experience themselves as "just people" in the context of their own group membership, but this will quickly disappear when the individual is placed in a multiple group setting. How group members relate to each other within their groups, as a function of their own and others' expectations, is highly dependent on the nature of the intergroup forces active at that time.

Research on intergroup relations has identified a number of characteristics of intergroup relations that do not depend on the particular groups or the specific setting where the relationship occurs. These include:

1. *Group boundaries.* Both physical and psychological group boundaries determine group membership. Transactions among groups are regulated by variations in the permeability of the boundaries.

2. *Power differences.* The types of resources that can be obtained and used differ among groups. The variety of dimensions on which there are power differences and the degree of discrepancy among groups influence the degree of boundary permeability among groups.

3. *Affective patterns.* The permeability of group boundaries varies with the polarization of feeling among the groups; that is, it varies with the degree to which group members associate mainly positive feelings with their own group and mainly negative feelings with other groups.

4. *Cognitive formations, including "distortions."* As a function of group boundaries, power differences, and affective patterns, groups tend to develop their own language (or elements of language, including social categories), condition their members' perceptions of objective and subjective phenomena, and transmit sets of propositions—including theories and ideologies—to explain the nature of experiences encountered by members and to influence relations with other groups.

5. *Leadership behavior.* The behavior of group leaders and representatives reflects boundary permeability, power differences, affective patterns, and cognitive formations of their group in relation to other groups. The behavior of group representatives, including formally designated leaders, is both cause and effect of the total pattern of intergroup relations in a particular situation.

The Concept of Microcosm Groups. As researchers, we can ask what methodologies are available for observing and studying intergroups in action. One technique directly derivable from intergroup theory is to create an organizationally based group in which representatives of the salient groups are present. This is called a *microcosm group*. In order for it to be a real group, the microcosm group must have an organizationally valid task. The most appropriate task for the microcosm group, which is created for research purposes, is to shape and monitor the research process on behalf of the organization as a whole. The task may include regulating the boundaries between the researcher and the organization, managing power differences between research and organizational processes, monitoring affective patterns, correcting cognitive distortions, and making the research activity beneficial for both the organization and the researchers.

The concept of microcosm group follows directly from the definition of groups in organizations and from the characteristics of intergroup relations in organizations. Using the proposition that all individuals are group representatives, the microcosm group may be designed to show the relations among the groups in or among organizations through the interpersonal relationships of its members. The boundary permeability, power differences, affective patterns, cognitive formations, and leadership behavior found in the microcosm group may then be interpreted, in part, as mirroring the analogous dynamics of the larger organization.

Because the purpose of creating a microcosm group is to have a structure that will allow observation of particular intergroup relationships within or among organizations, the membership of the microcosm group must be such that, first, the definitional requirements of a group in general are met, and, second, the critical intergroup processes within the group can be observed. For example, if an organization is experiencing interracial conflict, the microcosm group should include the major parties of the conflict in sufficient numbers and in balanced proportion so that no one subgroup of group representatives feels its perspective is significantly simplified or obscured. Or, if labor-management issues are prominent, then representatives of these groups should be included in the microcosm group in the same way. No single microcosm group, however, can adequately reflect all possible intergroup relations in an organization. Researchers and members of the organization must decide together which group relations are of primary interest and must then compose the microcosm group accordingly.

The Concept of Embedded Intergroup Relations. Embeddedness refers to interpenetration across levels of analysis; it concerns how system and subsystem dynamics are affected by suprasystem events and vice versa. Relations among identity groups and among organizational groups are shaped by how these groups and their representatives are embedded in the organization and also by how the organization is embedded in its environment. The effects of embeddedness may be observed on individual members, on the dynamics within identity groups and organizational groups, and on the intergroup transactions among diverse identity groups and organizational groups.

Effects of embeddedness derive from power differences among groups across levels of analysis. "Congruent" embeddedness means that power differences at the system level are reinforced by those at the subsystem and the suprasystem levels. "Incongruent" embeddedness means that power differences at the system level differ from those at other levels. The relations among groups are more complex under incongruent embeddedness than under congruent embeddedness. Affective patterns, cognitive formations, and leadership behavior will be less consistent and less inclined to favor one group at the expense of other groups within a level and among levels, under incongruent embeddedness than under congruent embeddedness. In particular, incongruently embedded groups will be inclined to minimize their advantages and emphasize their disadvantages in order to prevent loss of power.

Much of intergroup theory has been shaped by the concept of ethnocentrism, by which each group sees itself more favorably than it sees other groups. But we have learned that the phenomenon of the ethnocentrism does not explain the pattern of perceptions among groups when groups are hierarchically embedded with one another across levels of analysis (Alderfer and Smith, 1982). Figure 1 shows how a pattern of embeddedness might appear to black and white groups in the same organization. In this situation, *both* groups thought that they were at a disadvantage with respect to upward mobility.

Figure 1. Patterns of Embeddedness of Black and White Groups in the Same Organization.

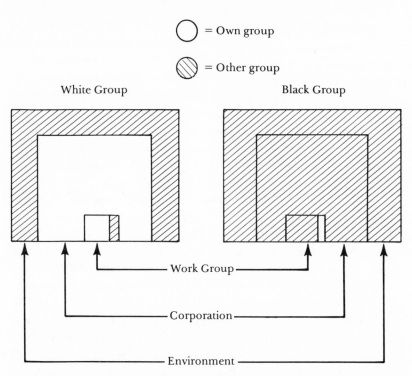

Source: Alderfer and Smith, 1982.

Applying intergroup theory to the problem of changing white males begins by asking white people in general and white men in particular to accept their whiteness as a *group*-level variable that shapes their power, affect, cognition, and behavior. Normally, that is not an easy process for white people in the United States. Northern European culture, from which the dominant U.S. norms derive, generally places *individuals* within the white group at the center of attention. There is an aversion to thinking in group-level terms. We saw that manifested previously in quotations from senior government officials. Intergroup theory interprets those statements not only as the views of the individuals who made them but also as the wishes of the group who authorized the particular officials to speak for them.

Microcosm groups provide a vehicle whereby representatives of particular groups can examine their relationships with members of other groups. The racial history of the United States has resulted in relatively few opportunities for whites to learn about race relations by participating in microcosm groups with blacks. Generally speaking, special efforts must be made if many whites, particularly those of high status, are to have the opportunities to be in mixed racial settings with blacks. Blacks regularly find themselves in mixed racial settings and have no choice except to learn about white culture if they are to survive.

The collective emphasis on individuality, coupled with minimal exposure to blacks, means that whites have far less awareness of the impact of their own group culture on other cultures than vice versa. Only when the power balance changes enough for blacks to have significant influence do whites begin to sense the effects of embeddedness. Affirmative action represents one kind of change in the pattern of embeddedness in the wider culture. Because of this change in the legal structure of our society, blacks now have more potential power than at any previous time. White complaints about "reverse discrimination," the adverse effects of quotas, and the like are signs that whites are feeling the consequences of their own embeddedness in ways that are relatively new. Blacks have had similar experiences throughout their history in the United States. The pattern of embeddedness shown in Figure 1 reflects both contemporary and historical differences between how blacks and whites view their own and the other racial group's power in a predominantly white organization.

Race Relations in Research and Consultation

Within the social science community there is debate—sometimes quiet and other times noisy—about how race relations should be studied. There is also controversy about how the results of past and present research should be interpreted and utilized. The core of this debate turns on the degree to which investigators' racial identities, both biological and psychological, affect their research and consultation. Closely linked to the core issue is a similar question: How is the nature and quality of relationship between black and white investigators related to the research results and their utilization? Different views on these matters tend to be held by black and white investigators. There are also variations in views within each racial group.

As a starting point for the examination of these questions, an empirical study by Sherwood and Natanpsky (1968) is especially interesting. These investigators sought an empirical answer to the question of "whether Negroes are or are not innately inferior to whites in intelligence can be predicted from biographical and demographic data about the investigators." Both overall effects and specific variables showed significant differences among demographic groups of researchers in terms of the conclusions they reached about the basis of black-white differences in intelligence test scores. Researchers who were older, had parents with less formal education, and had lived in urban settings as children were more likely to explain IQ differences by environmental causes. These findings suggest that investigators are likely to call upon their own experience to provide justifications for race research results, regardless of how conscious they are of doing so.

Data of a more clinical variety making a similar point can be found in Arthur Jensen's (1980) preface to *Bias in Mental Testing.* Jensen writes that he began his interest in whether intelligence tests are culturally biased with a belief that they were. Later he had an encounter with Irving Lorge, president of the Psychometric Society and editor of *Psychometrika,* the result of which was to have Jensen "feel a bit 'soft headed' for any unquestioning and sentimental resonance to the cultural bias position. Lorge let me see that one could take a more . . . incisively critical stance. . . . He became one of my favorite professors, although I must admit I never felt at ease in his presence" (Jensen, 1980, p. xii). Is it possible that Arthur Jensen's energy and role in the controversy about race and intelligence testing was substantially fueled by concerns about appearing softheaded in the eyes of one of his major professors?

I once attended a research conference composed of investigators whose work pertained to race and ethnic studies. One very distinguished investigator, a white male whose career spanned several decades and whose accomplishments included several awards for race research, described his latest series of experiments.* The studies were designed to choose among competing explanations for changing a variable he called "white negative racial attitudes." He explained how the new studies grew logically out of twenty years of previous work and how they utilized newly developed methodological techniques to resolve previously established ambiguities of results. In describing his work, he also mentioned that the experimenter was white and the assistant experimenter was black. This fact seemed very significant to me; others in the conference seemed not to notice. When I later raised a question about the design, a highly committed experimenter explained how the roles and races of the experimenter and his assistant were potential variables for other experiments and should by no means lead one to raise questions about the study just described. He suggested that having a black assistant and white experimenter was a "conservative" design (he meant that in a statistical, hypothesis-testing sense), and that reversing the races and roles would undoubtedly produce a "stronger" finding. Apparently his theory of race did not include propositions regarding how whites react to blacks in authority and therefore did not generate the hypothesis that having a black person fully in charge of the experiment might produce negative change in "white racial attitudes" due to whites' resistance to blacks having final authority. Neither this person nor the original experimenter seemed to think about the experimental setting as an organization with its own racial dynamics, which may be more complex and subtle than the experimental treatment consciously controlled and manipulated by the investigator. According to the experimental mentality, the role and race of experimenter are additional variables to be exam-

---

*I do not report the author of this study because two white male senior social scientists whom I regard highly have asked that I do not. They believe that doing so would be unfair to the man in light of his overall pattern of accomplishments. I shall provide the complete citation to any reader who contacts me directly. In making this decision, I am aware that I may be accepting the sort of pressure that is common for senior white men to exert on each other in racial matters. I report the matter in this way to demonstrate that such forces are alive as I revise this chapter and to indicate that there are conditions under which my behavior is shaped by them.

ined in future studies. This experimental logic, I would argue, is largely the product of white male positivist culture and as a result contains built-in biases that may be largely invisible to dominant white investigators who think their own racial history and identity are irrelevant to how they think and act during the conduct of race research.

The tendency for white investigators either to be unaware of the effects of their racial identity on research work or to act out their group biases through the medium of research has a long history (Boykin, Anderson, and Yates, 1979). In a book written to explore the consequences of psychology's emphasis on the individual to the exclusion of other levels of analysis, Sarason (1981) took the history of intelligence testing as a prototypical example. After an extensive review of history that documents the events leading to the construction and widespread use of intelligence tests in France and the United States, Sarason (1981, pp. 83–84) concludes:

1.   Distinguished psychologists, influenced by Binet, saw the measurement of intelligence as a significant scientific achievement.
2.   These psychologists understood well that this achievement would and should have practical social significance.
3.   Although their scientific achievement was in measuring individual intelligence, they used these tests (as did others) as a way of coming to conclusions about groups of people viewed pejoratively by more forceful segments of the social order.
4.   There is no evidence that as a group these psychologists differed in attitude from these more powerful segments; on the contrary, there is evidence that they became interrelated with them and in effect were willing agents of that part of the social order. . . .
5.   These psychologists were unable to ask and pursue the following question: In what ways and to what extent is the *substance* of my thinking and research related to who I am and where I am in the social scheme of things? . . . The last point is, of course, the crucial one for my argument because the inability of these psychologists to ask and pursue these questions insured that their theories and research would play into and reinforce the prejudiced attitudes of the dominant groups in the society, groups to which these psychologists belonged.

Nor were psychologists the only group of social scientists whose group-level identifications seem to shape how their "research results" were interpreted and promoted in the larger society. Silberman (1964) shows how Philip Hauser, a distinguished sociologist, provides sociological explanations for the lack of black upward mobility, which both supports racist beliefs in the wider society and fails to call whites' attention to alternative explanations for observed patterns of black behavior. The essential policy directive was that blacks need "acculturation." Silberman (1964, pp. 26–27) quotes Hauser as follows: "The problems which confront the Negro today . . . are essentially the same kinds of problems which confronted our migrant groups in the past. . . . Negroes have been drawn from a primitive folk culture into a metropolitan way of life . . . the older residents must teach the newcomers what is expected of them in the city. . . . A Negro in the Mississippi Delta . . . tosses his empty whisky bottle or beer can in a cotton patch, and what difference does it make? But on the asphalt pavements of a city it can make a difference, esthetically and with respect to safety. If physical violence is accepted in the south as a means of resolving conflict . . . nobody cares much; but in the urban community, such acts become felonies, with much more serious consequences."

Hauser, of course, did not speak for himself alone but for a substantial group of white male sociologists who do examine their own whiteness in the conduct of race research. They act to interpret and then to transform black people into their unexamined ideals of what good white behavior should be. We should not be surprised when blacks react with anger to a predominantly white male social science that perpetuates and promotes such ideas.

In fact, when the civil rights movement of the 1960s reached the social science enterprise, a debate between black and white social scientists was observed. In one special issue of the *Journal of Social Issues* on the white researcher in black society, Cedric X (Clark) (1973, p. 117), the editor, concludes the volume by stating: "Only when inner-oriented scientific research is seen in this general American sociocultural context, and only when the scientist has a clear understanding of the history of white American social systems vis-a-vis non-whites, will he be able to appreciate fully the genocidal fears which many educated blacks have of America's 'scientific' solutions to its racial problems. Whatever else one might conclude about the future of the white researcher in black society, one can rest assured that it will not be irrelevant. It may not be beneficial, but it will certainly be relevant. In this sense the role is not likely to change radically from its past. It will only become more *logical* to the scientists doing the observing and more *horrifying* to the people being observed."

The counterpoint to Clark is provided by the most distinguished of American sociologists writing at about the same historical period—Robert K. Merton (1972, p. 45). "A paper such as this one needs no peroration. Nevertheless here is mine. Insiders and outsiders in the domain of knowledge, unite. You have nothing to lose but your claims. You have a world of understanding to win." It turns out that Merton's paper, despite its general and abstract title, takes race relations as its concrete subject matter. A more appropriate subtitle might therefore have been "A Chapter in the History of Race Relations Research." As I read it, the paper is a carefully reasoned argument against "insider" knowledge. Merton seemed especially disturbed by the idea that black people might have access to information about black life experiences that is unavailable to whites. He seemed less manifestly concerned with the possibility that accepting the validity of insider doctrine would lead whites to scrutinize the nature of white life experiences, including the impact of white men in social science. His concluding statement suggests he is largely unaware of what "uniting" means when one group is so completely in the dominant position. Or perhaps he is aware? Then his conclusion becomes yet another version of Hauser's acculturation doctrine and provides support for Clark's hypothesis concerning (intellectual) genocide. I hope readers of this chapter will not avoid looking squarely at the implications of this ambiguity.

Merton's argument is also important for another reason: His basic precept is that taking account of the investigators' group identifications undermines American ideals and promotes Nazi-like horrors in science and practice. When observing the criticisms of some black scholars, he objects to the anticipated effects of group pride on the accumulation of knowledge about social phenomena. To the extent that one interprets taking account of one's group membership as promoting the kind of ethnocentric chauvinism that Merton

fears, I can only agree. But what Merton does in the eyes of intergroup theory is to favor explicitly the ideology of an organization
group (positivist sociology) while denying the effects of an identity
group (white men who dominate sociology). In doing so, he does
not fully escape the chauvinism he decries; he accepts the validity of
organization group claims while ignoring that identity group forces
shape his perspective. The orientation to accept and acknowledge
the parts played by organization and identity groups on one's
thoughts, feelings, and actions as a professional is not a veiled argument that one group or set of groups is superior to others. Rather,
it is a recognition that all group perspectives are limited in orderly,
systematic ways. The argument here is that we have a better chance
of discovering and correcting the limitations of our group-
determined perspectives if we recognize that they are likely to operate and attempt to determine their influence than if we cite the
canons of positivist philosophy to deny their existence. I suggest
that the implications of Merton's arguments for the kinds of issues
raised by Cedric X show the dangers of ignoring identity group
influences on both science and practice.

Events at the Carnegie Conference

At the Carnegie Conference I asked the group for a different
kind of help than most of the other presenters. My request was not
only for reactions to the written draft that all had received in advance, but also for help with a particular problem that was facing
our team in a race relations change project. The issue was derived
from the imbalance in numbers between blacks and whites in the
organization where the project was going on. Because whites out-
numbered blacks by a ratio of more than ten to one in the corporation and our intervention and education designs called for ratios
ranging from one to one to two and a half to one, before long we
would reach a point where there simply would not be enough blacks
to continue the work. The situation raised the question of whether
white-only intervention designs could be constructed. I asked this
white-only group of distinguished social scientists for their views.

In making the request, I indicated that what they said would
be used both for making revisions in the paper and as data in its own

right. Both the group and I recognized that my request was not easy. None of the people in the room was especially known for his work in the area of race, although several had conducted research or engaged in consultation that had touched racial issues, even if race had not been the primary focus of attention. I held several hypotheses about how the discussion would unfold:

1. Rarely is race not a difficult issue for white people. I expected the group to have trouble with the question I posed and with me for posing it.
2. Most of the people in the group were noted for having particular conceptual positions. I expected them to use their existing views on the problem.
3. From other encounters, I knew that intergroup theory as presented in the preceding section was not congenial to whites unless they went through certain kinds of learning experiences. Only one member in the group, as far as I knew, had had such experiences. Thus, I did not think the group as a whole would be able to use itself as a vehicle for learning about white dynamics.

I carried into the session a hypothesis, suggested several times in earlier sections of this chapter, that white social science, whether basic or applied, needs fundamental reorientation if it is to be useful in the area of race relations. I thought the process of the discussion to follow was one means to test this hypothesis. To the extent that the participants were able to engage the question on its own terms, regardless of whether they reached an answer, the hypothesis would be disconfirmed. To the extent that they were unable to deal with the question as posed, the hypothesis would receive support.

Responses provided by the group discussion, as taken from a tape recording of the meeting, were as follows:

1. The first person who spoke asked whether I had a theory to explain some of the statistical data that had been in the draft given to conference members.
2. The next person asked whether significant differences in intervention strategy would arise if gender or age were to replace

race. He said he believed a more fundamental issue was training people in how to discuss "undiscussable" issues. If people learned how to do that, they would apply the theory and skills to a variety of difficult topics, including race.

3. Someone asked for an example. I was drawn into role playing a black subordinate because no black people were present. I then pointed out to the group that I thought we knew what to do when black people were available for the intervention program. Did they mean to suggest that a way to deal with the absence of blacks was to have whites play the roles of blacks? People seemed to feel, and I agree, that there were serious limitations to this approach because of the widely shared sense that whites have limited knowledge of black experiences.

4. The next person, who was a discussant rather than a participant, professed not to understand the focus of my paper. He mentioned that there were ten thousand articles on the topic I was addressing, and the draft article cited only five. He asked if my "new slice" was how to change the racial attitudes and behavior of white managers using other whites to do it. This exchange brought other participants into the discussion. One argued that it was not possible to bring about significant change without the presence of black people. Another person asserted that he had a significant insight into "my own racism" through feedback from another white person. A third person argued that working with whites alone could affect only moderate change at best because significant change required altered behavior by whites that was perceived as such by blacks.

5. Others then joined the discussion to point out the distinction between personal and institutional racism. Another person suggested that the problem may not be a behavioral science issue at all. Perhaps it is more of a social, philosophical, and political issue, he indicated.

At this point the nature of the discussion changed markedly because of the effort one participant made to deal with the here-and-now behavior of the group.

My preconference draft article included a summary of a factor analytic study that identifies two major dimensions of racial attitudes (Alderfer, Tucker, Morgan, and Drasgow, in press). The first dimension consists of scales that measure the degree to which a person believes that "Whites and White Systems Hurt Blacks." The second dimension indicates the degree to which a person believes that "Blacks and Black Systems Hurt Whites." A major finding of the study is that, although these dimensions turn out to be relatively independent *across* black and white racial groups, *within* the racial groups the dimensions have significantly different relationships. Among blacks, the dimensions are negatively correlated, and among whites, they are positively correlated. From these results, I had suggested that one might have empirical bases for distinguishing between black progressives and black conservatives and between white progressives and white conservatives.

"Black progressives" refers to black people who believed that whites and white systems hurt blacks *but* blacks and black systems do not hurt whites. "Black conservatives" refers to black people who believed that whites and white systems do *not* hurt blacks *and* that blacks and black systems do hurt whites. "White progressives" refers to white people who believe that whites and white systems hurt blacks *and* that blacks and black systems hurt whites. "White conservatives" refers to white people who believe neither that whites and white systems hurt blacks *nor* that blacks and black systems hurt whites.

The participant who asked the group to consider its own situation spoke as follows: "I feel that I've got to come in on this one. I keep wondering what are the things that are undiscussable amongst us, now, which might be an expression of the fact that all of us as participants in this conference are white males. . . . What might they say to us about the underlying assumption that we bring to bear on this discussion, and how different might those assumptions be if half of us were black. I imagine that none of us would be sitting around the room talking and feeling as we are. It would be a radically different set of feelings and thoughts. . . . I wonder whether it would be possible for us to place ourselves into one of . . . the (categories) from your study. . . . And what would that tell us about ourselves?"

There was a five-second silence. Then a discussant stated, "I would like to mention one undiscussable thing that would be more discussable if there were more blacks in the room, and that is my feeling that this is really an extraordinary oversimplification of an extraordinary complex problem on which much has been done and researched. . . . There are differences between racism and prejudice, between behavior and belief, and between behavior in work settings and not, and between acknowledging that extra training may be needed for minority groups in certain circumstances and not, and between when certain subcultural values have to be enhanced in training and not. . . . Leadership affects the context in which these things are accepted. . . . We're kind of pretending that when we talk about this problem, there are just a couple of dimensions, and there are just not. There are a hundred, and all hundred have been investigated. The only thing you've got going for you is this notion of how you can get whites to teach whites about problems of other groups with whom they do not have much contact."

The original questioner then responded, "I think that is where you miss. It is not having whites teach whites about other groups but about their own group. We are asking, 'what can whites teach whites about white group phenomena?' That's the question."

Respondent: But the premise is across to some minority
                               group. Whether it's women or older people
                               or blacks or whatever.
Another Respondent: You raise a very important issue about my
                               own work. Assume there are 100 variables,
                               and they have been studied. . . .

The conversation proceeded for about fifteen minutes before it was time for another paper to be discussed. Other issues were raised. What can be learned from the extensive series of social psychological studies on race? Would I tell the group about what we had done when both blacks and whites were available in adequate proportions? Is it not an established fact that no change will occur unless there is organized pressure from blacks against whites? Is the answer to use black consultants with all-white groups? Should workshops be required? Just how potent are such workshops in effecting changes?

Aside from the momentary episode about three fourths of the way through the discussion, the group at no other point came close to discussion of its own behavior in the room. When one respondent suggested one means for doing that, he got no support. After a brief delay, the response he got was from a discussant whose view was that the original document gave extraordinarily inadequate attention to the existing literature. These results, at a minimum, suggest that it was not natural for this group of senior white males to reflect on their own circumstances in the present as a means to respond to a colleague asking how whites can teach and learn about race relations from other whites. We found that this group of white men did have ways to cope with the question: They asked for more information from the person who posed the question. They translated the question into another theory, which had an answer, but that answer turned out not to fit the question. They said the question could not be answered. They claimed not to understand the question. They argued that the answer already existed in literature, in studies apparently unknown to the presenter. They said the question was not relevant to behavioral science, only to philosophical, political, and social issues. Several participants did not join the dialogue at all. The variety of responses seems consistent with the initial hypotheses as to how the group might respond. Rather than providing answers as to what changes among white men might be, the conference gives additional data relevant to demonstrating what happens when senior white male social scientists are asked to help work with white people based on their own experience.

Interpreting the results of the Carnegie Conference through the lens provided by the concepts described earlier in this chapter is just one way to give meaning to the events. A person who had more positivist leanings would probably give a very different analysis. Someone of a strictly empirical orientation might suggest that *any* effort to ask people to talk about their life experiences in the here-and-now is very difficult. The fact that race was at stake was largely irrelevant. A request for a group of any demographic composition to operate in the here-and-now would face similar kinds of reluctance and resistance. Still another way to explain the phenomenon includes recognizing that many factors shape a discussion, including what happened during earlier parts of the conference, the makeup of participants in terms of their work in research and practice, and the history the individuals had with each other prior to the conference. I mention these alternative hypotheses lest readers conclude that there is only one way to interpret the happening. The Carnegie Conference was not a controlled experiment; alternative explanations were not ruled out by the design.

Propositions for Changing White Men

Because white males continue to dominate major organizations in this country, the problem of changing white males is closely tied to the nature of racism. What we say about changing white males, if it is to be helpful, should explain why the regressions in race relations continue to occur. It should also offer means to dampen, if not eliminate, the negative phases of those cycles.

The problems of changing white women in race relations are different in important ways than the problems of changing white men. White women are like white men because they are white and as a result share somewhat the benefits of being in white-dominated society and organizations. White women are also like blacks *somewhat* because their power has been limited by white men. Consequently, white women have their own special form of ambivalence toward changing race relations. As women, they identify with blacks as covictims of white male power. As whites, they resist giving up their privileged position. White women and blacks can also be provoked into competing with each other for scarce resources when change begins for either party.

The following propositions apply intergroup theory to the nature of race relations in predominantly white organizations. They focus on a specific portion of the problem of reducing racism—the question of changing white men. They draw on both statistical and experiential information about contemporary organizations.

Accepting White Racial Group Identity. The ideology of white maleness is heavily steeped in the philosophy of individualism. In its finest form, individualism is a set of values that recognizes and appreciates the full uniqueness of each person. In its most malicious and exploitative form, individualism is a philosophy that justifies those in charge playing those not in charge against one another. The destructive form rationalizes why peers can advance at the expense of colleagues who must be pushed down and back so others can move up and ahead.

For white males to accept the idea that, in addition to being individuals, we are also members of a white group is not easy—especially when the part played by that group in creating and maintaining the current state of race relations has been as powerfully malevolent as it has.

Facing the Resistance of White Groups Directly. Most progressive efforts to change race relations have attempted to dominate and overwhelm their opposition. As long as progressive forces have formal and forceful power, the change persists. But change based on coercion and surveillance is fragile. Regressions occur because reactionary forces gain in power, too. The advances made during one era may become the target of the next period's adjustments.

Theories of changing race relations should distinguish between dominating the opposition and "working through" their resistance. In psychotherapy, the concept of working through means that a client's difficulties are identified, accepted on their own terms, and then repeatedly encountered. Rather than solving a problem once and for all, the client and professional face it several times in the course of treatment. A similar meaning of the term holds for changing race relations, except that in this context the relevant exchanges are not primarily intrapersonal, as in the case of psychotherapy, but intragroup and intergroup. To contend with racism, one must be prepared to experience its subtle and diverse manifestations again and again.

In my judgment, whites in general and white men in particular need to become a significant force in the change processes. Working through by involving whites thoroughly in the process of change must, however, be distinguished from what is called *cooptation.* Cooptation implies that individuals who are opposed to a change are brought into the process indirectly; what is primarily important is that they "feel" as if they are included rather than that their points of view are an integral part of the enterprise. Working through in the race relations context means that white men feel they are part of the change process not because someone is able to establish a cosmetic method to create these impressions, but because the men have authentically engaged in the enterprise.

Such a process, of course, is risky because it allows for the real possibility that the white men may be so thoroughly involved in the change process that they can subvert it. This is the real danger. Nevertheless, I believe that only white people can take other whites thoroughly into their resistance. White people who serve in this role face formidable difficulties. Standing outside the modal white culture, they encounter misunderstanding, diversions, anger, and rejection. Reactions by whites to the "porch monkey" document and responses of the Carnegie-Mellon conference participants to my question provide concrete examples of what these phenomena look like. Whites who act to bring other whites into greater awareness of their resistance also face serious difficulties internally. I am never more aware of my whiteness and of the pressures to preserve and protect the current, conventional meaning of that whiteness than when I am working on the subject of white resistance with other whites.

Dealing with White Depression. Entering more deeply into white resistance tends to be associated with greater acceptance of white identity. Although there is plenty of statistical evidence to support a concept of white groupness, authentic acceptance of one's whiteness tends to come only from experiential group encounters with the phenomenon. As white men (and white women as well) see the meaning of their whiteness clearly, they often come into contact with a sense of despair and depression that can be quite powerful. Often the people whose resistance was most notable in the early phases of the change process show the most severe forms of depression in the later periods.

Here it is important to distinguish between a professional-clinical stance toward these phenomena and a political power orientation. A competent professional accepts rather than fights initial manifestations of resistance and provides support during periods of despair. A person with preference for political power in such moments would be more inclined to act in ways that can produce white casualties from the change process by attacking or rejecting the person who is struggling with his newly found sense of whiteness (Yalom, Lieberman, and Miles, 1969). A white person who engages in this kind of work should be prepared to aid other whites with the depression that can occur as the change process unfolds (Marris, 1974).

Dealing with Coercion and Guilt. The arena of changing race relations is fraught with problematic incentives for whites to change. The two most powerful are coercion and guilt. Both motives are problematic.

Because of the historical patterns, some degree of coercion is often necessary to begin the change process. When there are no realistic options, the lowest possible degree of coercion is clearly preferable to no change or to regression. Coercive change has severely negative side effects, however, and should be used only as a last resort and with as much awareness as is available and with as much preparation as is feasible to deal with the undesirable consequences.

Psychologically mature whites (that is, people who have consciences) cannot escape feeling guilt in connection with the state of race relations in the United States if we look clearly at the phenomena. But guilt is not a pleasant emotion, and, unless one has a tendency toward self-flagellation, it is an experience that most of us prefer to avoid. Yet a significant proportion of whites who work to change race relations do so from a strong sense of personal guilt. People motivated in this way often tend to induce guilt in other whites and, in the process, strengthen rather than weaken white tendencies to resist.

Establishing Intrinsic Incentives for White Change. The motives that seem most fruitful for whites to engage in the service of changing race relations are a sense of competence in dealing with an enormously difficult problem and a growing sense of wholeness from developing a more complete sense of one's identity as an individual and group member. Any person who seriously faces the difficulties of bringing about constructive change in race relations cannot but be impressed with the enormity of the task. To contribute even a small part toward solving this problem can be a deeply satisfying experience. Whenever people deny significant elements of themselves, a sense of disorientation and alienation results. Energy that might be available for more enjoyable pursuits is drained off into self-protection. When we can accept our whiteness more fully, we are likely to feel freer as human beings. In part this arises because it will be more difficult for others—whether white or black—to intimidate us with charges of racism or to place us in a stance where we must be coerced into changing. But probably the most important feature of accepting one's historical place as a white person is the drive it produces toward redefining and reshaping what whiteness can mean in the future. In part this can mean an enriched sense of one's own ethnicity. In part it will grow from helping form a new sense of whiteness. Needless to say, this can call forth the most creative of our impulses.

Earning the approval of blacks can also be a motive for whites to change. I have frequently observed that blacks underestimate the extent that their affection and acceptance can influence whites to change. But from my personal white perspective, this motive is highly problematic. Not all blacks want whites to change because changing whites implies changing blacks. If whites change in meaningful and concrete ways, then blacks may be faced with accepting their black identities more fully and completely and with giving up their suspicion and mistrust of at least some whites. Neither of these is an easy process. Whites who rely heavily on black approval may find their own change inhibited by blacks who themselves resist change. For whites to earn the respect and affection of blacks who accept their identities as black people can be a deeply meaningful experience.

Providing Support Systems for Progressive White Men. White men who change with respect to race relations often face isolated and alienated relationships with blacks and whites. From years of experiencing whites as dangerous, blacks learn to be wary of trusting them. Often whites are disturbed by blacks' honest expression of mistrust. Rather than seeing the disclosure as a step forward in a developing relationship, whites—particularly those whose theories focus only on individual-level explanations—interpret blacks' expression of mistrust as a sign of personal rejection. Moreover, white men who change their ideas, feelings, and behavior about race do not stop being members of the dominant majority. They cannot expect blacks to support their personal change unconditionally as long as the intergroup power imbalance persists.

White men who change face even more difficult problems from other white men, especially if they act to reduce racism. People who change are experienced as misguided, irrational, and disloyal. They are often seen as radicals whose credibility, especially on matters of race, is open to question. When white men learn to understand racial dynamics, their general understanding of human behavior undergoes a marked reorientation. It is not surprising that they would be experienced as deviant by other whites whose theories of race are more limited.

The net result of being separate from both whites and blacks will make it difficult for progressive whites to sustain their change while retaining an enriched white psychological identity. They may be pulled between attempting to identify as a black person and returning to their more conventional white position. Whites who change need the support of other progressive whites in order to shape and sustain a new white identity. They also need the continuing stimulation of blacks in order to maintain the learning process. Support systems for progressive whites should include other progressive whites who participate in forming an enriched white identity and progressive blacks who have a secure sense of their own individual and group identities. These sorts of systems can be established realistically and authentically only when whites act to reduce the imbalance of white power within predominantly white institutions and within the enterprise of social research.

To create conditions in organizations for these propositions to be operational is no easy task. In most white male–dominated organizations, it requires a fundamental change in the system's collective theory about race relations in order to accept the concept of white identity. Then it requires a special willingness to face the issues of white resistance and depression so that the problems of guilt and coercion can be addressed and the search for intrinsic incentives for change can be begun. When these changes in basic orientation toward race relations have begun, then the possibility of establishing white and black support systems for progressive white men can be realistically undertaken. Organizations do engage in such long-term processes (Alderfer, Alderfer, Tucker, and Tucker, 1980). It takes an unusual degree of commitment to change and an especially sophisticated understanding of the necessary structures and processes.

The aim of the presentation is to demonstrate what it describes. When I suggest that positivist views of social science err because they leave investigators out of the phenomena they inevitably influence, I describe a problem. When I talk about my white male senior status and its effect on writing the chapter and participating in the Carnegie Conference, I demonstrate how an investigator committed to an intergroup perspective puts the theory into practice.

This chapter has three theoretical sections. The first explains the need for a concept of racism and then presents one. The second provides the major concepts and propositions of intergroup theory and relates them to the subject of race relations in organizations. The third consists of a series of specific propositions directed to the problems of changing white men. Discussing the concept of racism identifies a social and organizational problem and provides an extensive analytical base for examining that problem. It also makes explicit the value orientation of the chapter. Intergroup theory presents a framework for understanding group and organizational behavior and makes race relations and racism a special case within the larger class of intergroup phenomena. From this, one can see some of the general characteristics of the phenomena and also realize the degree to which each intergroup issue has its unique as well as general properties. The propositions for changing white men arise from combining my empirical understanding of contemporary race relations in predominantly white organizations with the concept of racism and with intergroup theory. The propositions are designed for white men who wish to change and for all people who wish to help white men to change.

This chapter also has three empirical sections. In the first, I give data about myself as a person who has chosen to become involved in work on race relations in organizations. In the second, I present a selected review of the literature on race relations to illustrate the sorts of concerns and kinds of questions that the present perspective would raise with the prevailing views about race in contemporary white male–dominated social science. In the third, I report and analyze events at the Carnegie Conference. That event shows one outcome of mixing this point of view and way of acting with people who, for the most part, represent the perspective of contemporary senior social science researchers. It suggests that the intergroup perspective applied to changing white men is different than how most of the conference participants would go about solving the problem.

This general orientation questions how most white male social scientists in the United States deal with the problems of changing race relations. In the language of intergroup theory, one question is an organization group issue and the other is an identity group issue. The organization group question concerns the impact of positivist assumptions on the ideas and actions of social researchers and consultants. The argument is that until we investigators accept and acknowledge our entanglements in the phenomena we study, we shall continue to be blinded to regressive effects we have on the processes of advancing knowledge and of improving human conditions in organizations. This injunction therefore calls for a reorientation to the problem of objectivity when people do social research and consultation.

The identity group question concerns specifically the impact of whiteness on the conduct of research and consultation on race relations by white people and, more generally, of whatever identity and organization group memberships are evoked by the problems and settings in which we work. The argument is that our identity and organization group membership influence what we choose to address, how we structure settings to do work, and how respondents react to us in those situations. According to the theory, one corrects for the inevitable biases of intergroup transactions not by creating greater distance and separateness between investigator and phenomenon, but by developing constructive relationships between members of the relevant identity and organization groups. In that way, the different cognitive formations of the groups can be observed and documented and their influence can be monitored or changed. The vision of the lone investigator or consultant saved from her or his biases by the benefits of positivist statistical and research design methodology is therefore limited to a smaller and smaller set of social problems. Consultants who feel that their intervention designs are free of identity and organization group influences face similar questions. This chapter shows the consequences of overlooking the effects of the group identities of researchers and consultants on the subject of race relations and offers an alternative set of concepts and methods to cope with the problems of changing white men in race relations.

References

Alderfer, C. P., Alderfer, C. J., Tucker, L., and Tucker, R. "Diagnosing Race Relations in Management." *Journal of Applied Behavioral Science*, 1980, *16*, 135–166.

Alderfer, C. P., and Smith, K. K. "Studying Intergroup Relations Embedded in Organizations." *Administrative Science Quarterly*, 1982, *27*, 35–65.

Alderfer, C. P., Tucker, R. C., Morgan, D., and Drasgow, F. "Black and White Cognitions of Changing Race Relations in Management." *Journal of Occupational Behavior*, in press.

Bennett, L., Jr. *Before the Mayflower.* Baltimore: Penguin, 1962.

Boykin, A. W., Anderson, J. F., and Yates, J. F. *Research Directions of Black Psychologists.* New York: Russell Sage Foundation, 1979.

Carmichael, S., and Hamilton, C. V. *Black Power.* New York: Vintage, 1967.

(Clark), C. X. "The Role of the White Researcher in Black Society: A Futuristic Look." *Journal of Social Issues*, 1973, *29*, 109–178.

Fernandez, J. P. *Racism and Sexism in Corporate Life.* Lexington, Mass.: Heath, 1981.

Harding, J., Proshansky, H. Kutner, B., and Chein, I. "Prejudice and Ethnic Relations." In G. Lindzey and E. Aaronson (Eds.), *Handbook of Social Psychology.* Reading, Mass.: Addison-Wesley, 1969.

Jensen, A. R. *Bias in Mental Testing.* New York: Free Press, 1980.

Jones, J. "Conceptual and Strategic Issues in the Relationship of Black Psychology to American Social Science." In P. Boykin and J. F. Yates (Eds.), *New Directions for Black Psychologists.* New York: Russell Sage Foundation, 1979.

Jones, J. *Prejudice and Racism.* Reading, Mass.: Addison-Wesley, 1972.

Kerner, O., and others. *Report on the National Advisory Commission on Civil Disorders.* New York: Bantam, 1968.

Kovel, J. *White Racism: A Psychohistory.* New York: Vintage, 1970.

Marris, P. *Loss and Change.* New York: Pantheon, 1974.

Merton, R. K. "Insiders and Outsiders: A Chapter in the Sociology of Knowledge." *American Journal of Sociology,* 1972, *78,* 9–47.

"Racism." *The New Encyclopedia Britannica.* Vol. 15. Chicago: Encyclopedia Britannica, 1974.

Sarason, S. B. *Psychology Misdirected.* New York: Free Press, 1981.

Sherwood, J. J., and Natanpsky, M. "Predicting the Conclusions of Negro-White Intelligence Research from Biographical Characteristics of the Researcher." *Journal of Personality and Social Psychology,* 1968, *8,* 53–58.

Silberman, C. E. *Crisis in Black and White.* New York: Vintage, 1964.

Terry, R. W. *For Whites Only.* Grand Rapids, Mich.: Eerdmans, 1970.

Yalom, I. L., Lieberman, M., and Miles, M. B. *Encounter Groups: First Facts.* New York: Basic Books, 1969.

□ □ □ □ □ □ 5

Diffusion of Participatory Work Structures in Japan, Sweden, and the United States

□ □ □ □ □ □ □ □ □ □ □ □ □ □ □ □ □

Robert E. Cole

My focus is the evolution of participatory work structures in Japan, Sweden, and the United States. Contrary to the conventional emphasis of assessing the efficacy of such arrangements, I attend to the process of diffusion as it has occurred or not occurred. My units

This chapter was originally prepared for a conference on organizational change held at Carnegie-Mellon University, Pittsburgh, Pennsylvania, May 19-20, 1981. The data for the Japan portion were collected during my tenure as Fulbright Research Scholar, 1977-78. I am indebted to the Fulbright Commission for their support and to the Japan Institute of Labour for providing research facilities. I would also like to express my appreciation to the German Marshall Fund, which provided a research grant for my collection of the Swedish data. Research facilities in Sweden of analyses are national- and firm-level decisions and nondecisions. The latter distinction requires an analysis of the timing of available choice opportunities. The term *diffusion* refers to the spread of participatory work practices across firms and within firms. I am guided in my study of the diffusion process in the respective nations by the extent to which means are tied to ends, actions are controlled by intentions, solutions are guided by imitation of one's neighbor, prioritizing of goals takes place, feedback and evaluation control subsequent decisions, and past experience constrains present activity (see Chapter 9). In short, I contrast the utility of newly developing paradigms of organizational behavior, such as loose coupling and the garbage can model, with the heretofore prevailing rational models of decision making. In this context it will be important to examine the process by which given models of participatory management were selected over available alternatives and by what criteria and with what incentives for individuals and interest groups. It is also important to investigate whether certain characteristics of specific organizational sponsors, such as their membership, constituency, prestige, or size of budget, aid significantly in explaining the success or failure of the diffusion of given models of participation (compare Hirsch, 1972). Furthermore, in keeping with the research agenda suggested by Cohen, March, and Olsen (1976), I will seek to specify the demographic, social, economic, and political processes that affect the extent to which different groups are successful in formulating and diffusing problems and solutions. I will be alert to situations in which there is a partial decoupling of problems and choice and where solutions are actively seeking problems. Where possible, I will examine how the agenda of choice opportunities emerges among relevant interest groups and organizations.

In dealing with the political sphere, the classic literature on diffusion has pretty much ignored the politics of the process (for example, Rogers and Shoemaker, 1971). To the extent that the political process is invoked, the focus is upon the role of opinion leaders and power concentrations. The emphasis centers on the develop-

were provided by the Department of Applied Psychology at Göteborg University. Data collection for the United States portion was made possible by a grant from the Henry Luce Foundation, Inc.

ment of an appropriate infrastructure for diffusion and the receptivity of adopting units rather than how these factors are influenced by the interplay of interests in the broad political and economic arenas. My approach involves an interweaving of models of the diffusion process with the politics of diffusion.

By comparing three diverse societies, I seek first to obtain data that permit me to judge whether there are characteristic elements of successful diffusion processes. I also aim to identify those elements of the diffusion process that are unique to particular nations. Our knowledge of such unique characteristics enhances our understanding of contrasting social structures. As Reinhard Bendix (1956, p. 445) argues, if different societies over time confront and resolve a problem, then a comparative analysis of their divergent solutions will help us understand the divergent character of the respective social structures in a process of change. The rate of diffusion may be faster in one country and the form may be different than in another country, but they may all end up in the same place over time. This represents a convergence perspective based on the assumption that there are functional forms of diffusion models. I can offer no conclusive judgments on this issue because the process of diffusion is still being played out, but the evidence thus far suggests continued divergence. In making these comparisons, I will explore the possibility that different degrees of coupling and rationality were present in the linkage between national-level and organizational-level decision-making processes in the three nations.

There are many types of what the Europeans, Americans, and Japanese usually call worker participation. It can take the form of representative democracy with worker representatives serving on boards of directors and work councils (for example, the German codetermination model). It can manifest itself in worker councils having the dominant decision-making role in the firm, as in Yugoslavia (that is, workers' control and self-management). It can also take the form of direct participation of employees in the everyday decision-making process on the shop or office floor. I focus my analysis on the latter area because, first, direct participation represents an area where the Swedes and the Japanese have been most innovative. Second, scholarly research suggests it is the area that matters most to workers. Third, shop and office floor participation is the focus of what organized efforts for participatory work practices do exist in the United States. I am concerned, then, with an expansion of direct participation of employees and their increased control of the everyday decision-making process as it has developed on the shop and office floor. Yet we must keep in mind the process by which these "solutions" emerged in competition with potential alternatives, such as board representation. Moreover, we must ask why some forms of direct participation were selected over other forms and what were the implications for the diffusion process.

Most of the research on loose coupling and the garbage can model has been conducted in universities, school boards, and local government. It is assumed that the model has less applicability in private sector business firms in which objectives can be stated relatively clearly, where a technology associating alternatives with outcomes is reasonably well known, and where there is a stable division of labor by which specific individuals and groups specialize in certain decisions (Cohen, March, and Olsen, 1976, p. 24). Cohen, March, and Olsen note that the characteristics of loose coupling and the garbage can model can be observed some of the time in almost all organizations; but they appear with more frequency in organizations such as universities. Without denying these observations, it is still appropriate to ask under what conditions the garbage can model becomes applicable to private sector business firms. I will show that in such firms, for selected kinds of innovations, the garbage can model applies with considerable force. Future research might well extend the range of problems and decisions producing similar outcomes, but I will concentrate on decisions to introduce participatory work practices. These decisions represent organizational choice situations in which goals are problematic, technologies are ambiguous and only partially understood, and participation in the decision making is often fluid. I refer here not to participation in shop or office floor decision making but to participation in the decision to introduce such forms of participation in the organization. March and Olsen (1976, pp. 38–53) refer to this as "attention structures." Studying the process of participation in decisions about participation contains its own set of ironies.

Consider first the issue of goals and objectives. For management, there are many possible diverse goals that can potentially be served by participatory work practices. Among them are increasing productivity, increasing product quality, improving worker morale and reducing alienation, democratization of the work place, meeting public pressures, more effective utilization of their labor force, good public relations, reducing employee turnover and absenteeism, reducing worker grievances, weakening the unions, and developing cooperative relations with the unions. These objectives are not always additive; some are achieved only at the expense of others. Moreover, there is a variety of other organizational actions that may potentially contribute to the solution of each of these "problems." In addition, achievement of some of these objectives might have adverse consequences on the achievement of other organizational objectives. Management goals may be in fact quite different, depending on the level of management. Middle management often sees participatory work practices as a threat to their authority and prestige, and top management may see participatory practices as an opportunity to cut out some layers of dead wood in management. Other parties, such as unions and workers, will have their own objectives. In summary, the goals toward which participatory work practices are directed are problematic, with management having difficulty choosing the objectives to be served.

A similar case can be made for the ambiguity of the technology, by which I mean the technique of executing participatory work practices. The dispute over technique is considerable. Scholars have often introduced concepts of participatory work practices at a high level of abstraction so that practitioners are at a loss in how to proceed. Competing agents of diffusion will offer different solutions on how to execute the theory of participation, with the potential user again left in a confused state. If failure occurs, it can be attributed to poor technique or to the inappropriateness of the theory. The belief that every business firm as well as plant and office has a unique culture that requires a special adaptation of the technology makes it difficult to specify the appropriate technology with exactness. The difficulty of measuring the outcomes of this technology and relating them to specific inputs contributes to its ambiguity. Although some of the specific participatory work models being advocated are presented as self-contained packages, many of them tend to be diffuse. This diffuseness makes unclear just how much of an impact it will have on the organization in the long run and how much and what else will have to change in the organization as a result of adopting participatory work practices. All this further reinforces the ambiguity of the technology. Managers prefer packaged solutions whose cost and outcomes are, if not guaranteed, at least defined and limited (Cherns, 1979). One of my tasks will be to examine how the different nations handled this ambiguity in technology and whether there were variations in the degree of ambiguity of the specific technological packages chosen.

The issue of who can, should, and does participate in the decisions by the firm to innovate in the area of work redesign is also commonly unclear, at least in the initial stages. March and Olsen (1976) argue that this follows logically from a situation in which goals and technology are unclear. Although personnel departments may seem the logical place for decisions concerning the adoption of participatory structures to get made or at least recommended, in the United States this department often has an adversary relation with labor and a vested interest in conflict. Consequently, it is often ill equipped to undertake such initiatives. Other departments, such as human resource development and training and education, are possible candidates for initiatives, except that, like personnel, they are commonly low status departments without the necessary clout in the organization to ensure the acceptance of proposed work reorganization. My survey of American firms adopting quality control circles shows that sponsorship comes from a wide range of departments, from quality assurance to personnel to top management. That there is no obvious sponsor and therefore no obvious set of individuals who will participate in the decision to introduce participatory work practices adds additional ambiguity to the situation. The relative obligations and rights of staff versus line to make and/or enforce the execution of decisions relating to participatory work practices is not self-evident in many firms. Indeed, it is often a source of much conflict. On a number of occasions plant managers and line staff, unhappy with staff pressures in the participatory area, have told me, "those staff guys at corporate are like geese that fly in, drop their load, and then fly back home. And we get stuck with cleaning up the crap."

The ambiguity of goals, technology, and who is to participate in the decision to innovate all contribute to seeing the choice
process surrounding participatory work structures as one in which
loose coupling is the norm.

Three Snapshots

In the early 1970s, extensive discussions began to take place in
the United States on the need to humanize work. In connection with
job humanization, we heard about job redesign, job enlargement,
and job enrichment. Although the terms are often used loosely, the
job humanization movement focuses primarily on the redesign of
jobs. This redesign was envisioned as occurring either horizontally
(job enlargement), thereby creating more variety in the job, or verti-
cally (job enrichment), thereby expanding the range of employee
decision making. Although there are numerous similarities with the
earlier human relations movement (Berg, Freedman, and Freeman,
1978), a major characteristic of the new movement distinguishing it
from the human relations approach is its focus on changing the job
itself. Whatever the forms, the current programs and proposals designed to humanize work have one common denominator: They all
involve an attempt to reduce alienation and increase job satisfaction
by producing an increase in employee participation in work place
decisions, increasing job variety, and making more effective use of
worker potential. Ideally, these practices are supposed to serve the
twin purposes of improving organizational efficiency and productivity while enhancing the quality of work life. An improved quality
of work life is expected to involve workers in controlling those aspects of their work that directly affect their everyday lives. These
arguments find support in the social science literature, which suggests that a major factor in worker alienation lies in lack of control
over everyday decisions (Blauner, 1964; Kohn, 1976). From an organizational perspective, what is involved, above all, is a decentralization of the decision-making process.

When we examine the adoption and diffusion of participatory work structures of this sort in the United States, we are hard put
to say that many of the noble ideas I have outlined have been institutionalized in large numbers of American corporate enterprises. Self-

managing teams, for example, have won only very limited acceptance. One prominent scholar claims that there is a revolution occurring in the design of new plants that is leading to the implementation of these ideas (Lawler, 1978). On closer examination, however, the evidence is scant, the number of cases small, the labor force of such plants often atypical as a result of special recruitment procedures, and the claim seems more of an attempt to drum up support for these developments than a demonstration of their acceptance. The little that has been accomplished, especially in the 1960s and early 1970s, has commonly been carried out in nonunion plants. Generally speaking, more has been done in new plants; far less has been tried or succeeded in established plants. In addition, even in allegedly "successful" experiments, such as the General Foods plant in Topeka, Kansas, the innovation has been slow to diffuse to other plants in the company, not to speak of its offices (Walton, 1978). Finally, there is more form than substance to many of the announced programs of U.S. companies. Given the ambiguity of goals and technology, it is not surprising that it is often difficult to judge what actually has happened, why it happened or did not happen, and whether what happened is good (see March and Olsen, 1976). Organizations often develop myths about what they are doing in participatory work practices, and, because of the lack of agreement over what constitutes participation, they have a great deal of latitude to do just that. This can be used as a vehicle to encourage or discourage the diffusion process. I have attended a number of company presentations in which, when all the rhetoric is stripped away, the bulk of the participation program consists of workers being able to have lockers near their work site or the plant management having established a recreation program. In general, one sees many "programs" in the United States that have beginnings and ends, but relatively few examples where participatory practices are highly institutionalized (see Chapter 6). Moreover, ceremonial adoption of participatory work practices can be buffered from actual work activities so that little substantive change occurs (Meyer and Rowan, 1977). This allows forms to be adopted without producing significant change.

The Japanese movement began in the early 1960s and accelerated. There was an increasing emphasis on decentralization of decision making; employees were to take responsibility for a variety of everyday decisions for which management representatives had heretofore been responsible (functions like maintenance, quality control, and safety). The vehicle for these efforts was "small group-ism" *(shōshudanshugi)*, as the Japanese called it. The idea was to make the small group the responsible unit in this decentralization effort. A variety of surveys suggests that these practices are now wide-spread. Japanese experts estimate that over 50 percent of Japanese firms with more than thirty employees are practicing some form of worker participation in decision making based on small-group ac-tivities (Cole, 1979, pp. 134-135). Quality control circles represent perhaps the most innovative of these small-group activities. Further-more, a conservative estimate can be made that one out of every eight Japanese employees participates in quality control circles. The circles are relatively autonomous units composed of a small group of workers in each workshop. Ideally, they contain about ten members; they are usually led by a foreman or senior workers. The workers are taught fairly simple statistical techniques and modes of problem solving and are guided by leaders in the selection and solv-ing of problems. The circles concentrate on solving job-related qual-ity problems, broadly conceived as improving methods of produc-tion as part of companywide efforts. At the same time, they are supposed to allow for the skill acquisition of workers, the develop-ment of career potential, cooperative activity, and the like. If func-tioning properly, they should give workers a sense of control over their everyday activities on the shop floor. The circles provide a mechanism for workers to take responsibility for quality control—broadly conceived—instead of leaving it to the discretion of an elite corps of engineers. A major characteristic of the circles is that they tend not to threaten the hierarchical structure of authority as much as some other forms of direct participation. Foremen tend not to be threatened by the circles and indeed often serve as leaders of them. Evidence for these propositions is found in my preliminary analysis of survey data from 267 "early adopters" of quality circles. We asked managers the following question: "Is it the experience of your com-pany that the scope and/or content of the first-line supervisor's au-thority must be changed significantly in order to have this form of small-group activity function properly?" Only 6.5 percent of the respondents answered yes, with the remainder answering no. All this suggests that circles come packaged as relatively self-contained innovations. There is a major theoretical point embedded in these observations. Decentralization of decision making does not necessarily destroy the hierarchical structure. Authority may be delegated to lower levels with subordinates still being held accountable for their decisions. The point needs emphasizing because there has been a lot of simplistic theorizing that assumed that increased worker participation in decision making automatically broke down the structure of hierarchical control.

The Japanese approach to direct shop floor participation initially was seldom presented in terms of democratization and the value of participation per se. Rather, it was more commonly introduced as part of a corporate strategy to mobilize all resources in the firm to overcome foreign and domestic competitive threats. In this sense participation was more a responsibility, an obligation, of each employee than an opportunity to express one's talents and take charge of one's own situation and environment.

The Swedish efforts to develop participatory work structures crystallized in the late 1960s with an emphasis on autonomous or self-steering work groups *(självstyrande-grupper)* as the unit of production. These ideas on decentralization of decision making spread rapidly. There was a long and intensive public debate on these issues centering on broad issues of democratization and social justice. It is still more difficult to evaluate how well these activities are actually diffused in Sweden than in Japan. The reasons are themselves revealing; they reflect the Japanese penchant for national surveys and their organizational penchant for systems of formal registration. On the Swedish side they reflect, in part, the strategy of diffusion adopted by the technical department of the Swedish Employers' Federations (SAF). In any case, the ideal of autonomous work groups with workers making all their own decisions regarding work allocation, recruitment, planning, budgeting, purchasing, and so on is obviously very rare. It is certainly far less common than the English language public relations efforts of the SAF and the efforts of specific companies like Volvo would suggest (Gyllenhammar, 1977; Swedish Employers' Confederation, 1975). Yet modified versions of this decentralized work system are in effect in most large

Swedish firms, and, unlike the Japanese, they spread rapidly to the
public sector as well. Gunzburg and Hammerström (1979, pp. 39–
40) come to similar conclusions, reporting estimates of well over one
thousand firms with significant work reorganization efforts in the
mid 1970s. Albert Cherns (1979, pp. 360–361) ranks Sweden first
among European countries on the extent to which the quality of
working life movement has been diffused. Unlike the Japanese approach, many of the early Swedish efforts explicitly challenged the
hierarchical system. Consequently, it generated a good deal of opposition. Many employers were reluctant to experiment. Middle managers in particular opposed efforts to develop autonomous work
groups because they saw them as a threat to their own authority and
status. The Swedes adopted a top-down model of diffusion that
often made the foremen incidental to the diffusion process and thereby contributed to their alienation from new developments. The Japanese adopted a top- to middle-down model, which meant that top
management left it to middle management to formulate procedures
and to work through and with foremen and supervisors in implementing the new system. Consequently, it generated a good deal less
opposition on the part of these personnel. Even in Japan, however,
survey data suggest that management viewed middle management
support as a problematic issue.

Areas of Comparison

A standard rational model of the diffusion process generally
involves

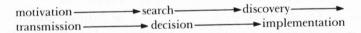

I will follow this model in rough fashion, but keep in mind the way
the ambiguity of the problems and solutions suggests different processes. This latter consideration requires that we explore the possibility that "latter" phases precede "prior" phases and in particular
the conditions under which discovery and transmission precede the
search stage. I will also focus on examining how the political dimension operates as a cross-cutting variable that impacts on all
stages.

Motivation to Innovate. The incentive for introducing new participatory work structures can be based on a variety of considerations, not all of which are equally salient at a given time and place. It would seem simple to read the record and record the problem-solving activity that led to the adoption of participatory work practices. Yet if we allow for the possibility that experience creates values, rather than the conventional emphasis on value preferences determining choices, the problem of reconstruction becomes far more difficult. The case of the diffusion of quality control circles in Japan provides a textbook example of how interpretations and explanations involving the value of participation per se were called forth long after the initial innovations (March and Olsen, 1976). This is contrary to the rational model of decision making, which sees identification of problems and evolution of the best available solution as preceding the innovation. Instead, we see a case in which the value of participation per se serves as an ex post facto rationalization. Similarly, notions of democratizing the work place, reducing worker alienation, and giving dignity to the worker must be examined carefully as possible motives. Although they are typical statesmanlike pronouncements made by high level company and government spokesmen, one must establish whether there is an incentive structure in the organization that would encourage managers to identify democratization, alienation, and dignity as problems and participatory work structures as a solution to these problems. By and large these incentives do not seem to be operative to a significant extent, except insofar as political pressures may be brought to bear. Because I am dealing with three market economies, a focus on managerial incentives seems very much to the point.

The primary motivation for innovation was similar in Japan and Sweden. Participatory work structures in Japan and Sweden were a response, in large part, to severe problems of labor shortage. But it is difficult to mobilize employees on these grounds; so broader ideologies, involving the virtues of participation as leading to self-actualization, democratization, dignity, and so on, are brought into play. Such ideologies also help the firm build legitimacy with the public and can be part of a marketing strategy for the firm's products. To pursue these issues, we need a more detailed understanding of the identification of labor shortage as a problem and how participatory work structures came to be seen as one of the solutions.

Japanese employers found themselves faced with an increasingly tight labor market in the late 1960s and early 1970s (Minami, 1973). It became more difficult for the major manufacturing firms to recruit those select employees they desired, and management came to believe that it was increasingly difficult to retain such recruits. (The evidence for the latter proposition is somewhat problematic.) Even though turnover remained low by Western standards, it occurred in the context of a severe labor shortage of male new school graduates, especially middle-school graduates. This meant replacement was both difficult and costly because of the absence of a pool of workers willing to take the most disagreeable jobs in the manufacturing sector. Between 1970 and 1973, momentum began to build to reverse Japan's long-standing policy of relying exclusively on domestic labor and to admit foreign migrant labor. The oil shock of 1973 and the deflation of Japanese economic growth, along with the decision to increase off-shore equity investments, led to a shelving of the issue.

Rising educational levels led to an increasing proportion of workers who were reluctant to accept the least demanding jobs. The educational system was producing more and more high school graduates who had been led to expect white-collar jobs commensurate with their educational achievements. Instead, an increasing number were being assigned to blue-collar jobs. Management was greatly concerned about these trends. Many predicted an increasingly militant labor force unwilling to be satisfied with menial jobs. Surveys reported that workers wanted jobs that would allow them to develop their abilities and talents, whereas in the past workers had given priority to job security. It may be that management overestimated the problem, egged on as it was by exaggerated media reports and predictions that unrest on campuses would spread to the shop floor. By the late 1960s and early 1970s, evidence that supported management fears began to surface. The labor shortage was intensified for just those firms in the manufacturing sector that had the most standardized and routinized jobs. Industries still characterized by hard physical work under trying conditions and those requiring routinized job performance had a good deal of difficulty recruiting and retaining their labor force. The auto and steel industries experienced great difficulties and had trouble meeting their expanded production schedules. A survey of 1,579 establishments in the machinery and metal manufacturing industry reports that of the new employees recruited in spring 1969, 50 percent of both the middle and high school graduate recruits had quit within a three-year period (Ministry of Labor, 1974, p. 72). These circumstances constituted a major motivational force for Japanese management to search for solutions to minimize what had become identified as a significant problem. The creation of participatory work structures that would make their firms more attractive to highly educated potential recruits and reduce the likelihood of turnover and labor unrest seemed to be a reasonable investment for the firms to make. Those firms and industries that had the greatest recruitment problems, such as auto and steel, took the lead in introducing participatory work structures. In the case of quality control circles, our survey of "early adopters" revealed that auto establishments were four times more likely to have introduced circles than would have been expected relative to their weight in the employment structure in the early 1960s. Specifically, 16.9 percent of our sample of innovators were auto establishments, although at the time they accounted for only 4.4 percent of the manufacturing labor force (unpublished survey data).

In the interwar period, Japanese firms had carried on discussion and study practices among work teams (for example, Cole, 1979). Thus, they had in their behavioral repertoire (tradition) experience with small-group participatory practices, albeit on a more authoritarian model. This experience made the selection of participatory work practices a reasonable solution to their problems. However, it was hardly the only solution. At the same time that managers were introducing participatory practices, the pace of technological innovation accelerated. Clearly, productivity improvement technology was a logical way to cope with labor shortage from management's point of view. Similarly, it was in the 1960s and 1970s that offshore investments in production facilities grew at a rapid pace as Japanese firms sought to break the bottleneck imposed by the labor shortage. So participatory work structures were only one of a number of actions designed to deal with the effects of the labor shortage. Indeed, not until the slowdown imposed by the oil shock of 1973 and the subsequent recession in 1975 did an external solution to the labor shortage appear. Thus, participatory work structures actually were at best of only modest importance in addressing the major problem for which they had been devised. There were other factors relevant to the selection of participatory work practices as a solution. Participatory work structures were part of a corporate strategy designed to mobilize all resources to deal with a heightened competitiveness in domestic and foreign markets. With much of labor as a fixed cost under the lifetime employment system, it made sense to utilize fully the abilities of that labor force. Participatory work structures were a logical follow-up to the growing interest in improving worker training and education.

The labor supply situation was even more serious in Sweden. By the mid and late 1960s, a severe labor shortage developed. Swedish workers were increasingly unwilling to take those jobs characterized by routinized tasks and poor working conditions. Educational levels rose rapidly. Most Swedish youth were graduating from the nine-year comprehensive school (age seven to sixteen), and by 1968, 80 percent of the sixteen-year-olds were continuing their education. Swedish employers sought to deal with these conditions through various approaches. First, they welcomed more women into the labor market, a policy reinforced by a variety of governmental actions, including the establishment of a national network of daycare centers and labor market training courses. The entire growth in the number of people in the labor market from 1965 to 1974, from 3.7 to 4.0 million, consisted of women, primarily married women. By the mid 1970s, they made up 40 percent of the labor force (Forsebäck, 1976, p. 97). By the mid 1970s, women made up 22.3 percent of the total number of blue-collar workers in the private sector in mining, quarrying, and manufacturing (Statistiska Centralbyrån, 1978, p. 93). A second strategy involved an increase in the employment of aliens. The number of aliens taking jobs in Sweden increased steadily from 121,747 in 1962 to 221,925 in 1973 (Statistiska Centralbyrån, 1977a, p. 257). The Nordic component of this migration has been approximately 65 percent, with the bulk of workers coming from Finland. Despite the high Scandinavian content of the migration, the Finns have presented considerable adjustment problems; for those Finns not growing up in Swedish-speaking areas, the language hurdle is considerable. Yugoslav immigrants came to constitute 10 percent of the non-Nordic inflow. In 1977, approximately half these migrants (61 percent in 1971) were concentrated in the mining, quarrying, and manufacturing industry, as opposed to only 25 percent of the Swedish labor force; migrant labor constitutes 10 percent of the total employment in this sector (Statistiska Centralbyrån, 1978, p. 195).

Moreover, within manufacturing, the migrant workers were concentrated in just those industries characterized by the most routinized jobs and poorest working conditions. In the early 1970s, only half the workers in these manufacturing sectors were Swedish and one fifth were women.

In the late 1960s, Swedish manufacturing employers became increasingly concerned that the reliance on female and foreign labor was not solving their problem. They still had difficulty finding enough workers to do the least desirable jobs and found themselves relying on the lowest quality labor. Doubts began to increase about the wisdom of relying on an increasingly larger number of foreign workers. In addition, problems of absenteeism and turnover swelled to almost unmanageable proportions. Annual employee turnover peaked in 1970 at about 50 percent in a number of large plants in metropolitan areas (Jönsson, 1979, p. 3). High unemployment and sick pay benefits made turnover and absenteeism relatively costless to employees. All these factors were responsible for management giving serious attention to strategies for restructuring work so that Swedish workers could be brought back into the factories and turnover and absenteeism cut and reduced to manageable proportions. As in Japan, major innovations in participatory work structures took place in just those industries suffering the severest recruitment, turnover, and absenteeism problems. Volvo Corporation, as the largest Swedish private firm, experienced some of the most severe problems and achieved fame as one of the more adventurous in designing participatory work structures (for a "friendly" assessment of their experience, see Jönsson, 1979).

We see here a situation in which successive choices (recruit females, recruit aliens) are associated with the labor shortage problem unsuccessfully for some time, until a new choice (participatory work practices), which is "more attractive" to decision makers, comes along (compare Cohen, March, and Olsen, 1976). However, rather than abandon previous choices, the new choice is added on in an effort to resolve the problem. As in the case of Japan, there were additional factors responsible for the identification of participatory work practices as a solution. These factors were primarily political in nature and involved other interest groups; they will be dealt with in a subsequent section. Such alleged factors as the "postindustrial ethos," to which Cherns (1979) refers, however, seem to have operated more as legitimizing ideology than causal factors in the adoption process.

     To contrast the situation in Japan and Sweden with that in the United States is revealing. A large reserve pool of unemployed labor exists in the United States. This pool is available to fill the most disagreeable jobs. Although labor turnover is remarkably high by world standards, an ever ready source of replacements is available through this pool. This has constituted a major barrier to the introduction of participatory work structures in the United States (see Wool, 1973). The differences are most obvious in a comparison of the auto industries. Per Gyllenhammar, the president of Volvo Corporation, recounts how he came to the United States in the early 1970s and found that some American auto plants had turnover figures similar to that of Swedish auto factories. That is, "at the worst, half the employees left every year." He was astounded that American managers did not perceive this as a serious problem. Rather, the American managers were accustomed to greater mobility of workers and reasoned that they could train people and put them on simple jobs so quickly that the turnover figures did not matter, even if they did require extra planning (Gyllenhammar, 1977). In short, because of this reserve pool of labor, management tolerated high turnover and absenteeism rates and had little incentive to engage in searches for new ways of organizing work. Indeed, the assumption that they had large quantities of unskilled labor being processed through the firm at regular intervals determined to a significant extent the simplifying job design specifications produced by engineers.

     For all practical purposes, participatory work practices did not represent a choice opportunity among American managers during the 1960s and 1970s. The recognized problems, the available solutions, and the direction of the attention of key policy makers combined to make participatory work a nonissue. There were isolated managers who for ideological reasons took an interest and were in a position to bring about innovation (such as at Donnelly Mirrors and Lincoln Electric). Ironically, it is only with the remarkable success of the Japanese in competing in American export and domestic markets that a more general reevaluation has begun. Suddenly everyone is looking for the key to Japanese success, and participatory work practices have been identified as part of the package. There was literally an explosion of American firms experimenting with quality circles in the early 1980s. Whether this represents another in a string of organizational development (OD) fads or an innovation with long-term implications remains to be seen.

Search, Discovery, and Transmission. The ideas adopted by the Swedish employers orginated in the Tavistock Institute in England (Emery and Trist, 1969). These ideas emphasized the development of the organization as an open sociotechnical system that focuses on the interaction of social and technical factors. The aim is to develop small work groups that maintain a high level of independence and autonomy. As a consequence, it is expected that jobs will be enriched, individual responsibility will be increased, and learning possibilities will be enhanced. English employers were slow to adopt these ideas, but they were carried to Scandinavia—specifically to Norway by Einar Thorsrud, a charismatic Norwegian scholar (see Cherns, 1979). Three of the key events that served as a transmission belt from Norway to Sweden were: a visit to Norway in 1966 by a Swedish union and management team led by the Swedish scholar Reine Hansson who was close to Thorsrud's research, the translation of Thorsrud's research into Swedish in 1969 under the auspices of a joint labor-management publication company (Thorsrud and Emery, 1969), and a grand conference (a "hallelujah conference" as the Swedes call it) held in Stockholm in 1969 with Thorsrud as guest speaker. The conference was sponsored by the technical department of the Swedish Employers' Confederation (SAF) and attended by officials of major companies as well as leading union officials. Interestingly, Thorsrud's ideas were never as fully accepted in Norway as they were in Sweden. This is commonly explained by the lack of suitable mass production industries in Norway, middle management opposition, too heavy reliance on academic consultants, and the hostility of organized labor, which saw many of Thorsrud's ideas on direct shop floor participation as a threat to the centralized decision-making power of the labor movement (compare Jenkins, 1974). Swedish scholars often say that the ideas developed in England were tried out in Norway and achieved their widest diffusion in Sweden. The sociotechnical approach is a diffuse package with far-reaching implications for the firm's organization. This diffuse quality, deriving from ambiguous operational goals and technology, undoubtedly slowed the diffusion process. It was not the packaged solution with known costs and outcomes that management preferred.

In the case of Japan, we see a similar cross-national diffusion process, but the source of the ideas was primarily in the United States. American behavioral scientists' research is well known in Japan. It is part of a broad "management boom" in the postwar period in which ideas of American management in all fields have achieved an especially exalted position among Japanese management officials. In the area of participatory work structures, the research of McGregor, Maslow, Likert, Arygris, and Herzberg, to name a few, is particularly well known in Japan (they have had their impact in Sweden as well). This is a function of an almost instantaneous translation of books and articles, a steady stream of Japanese students to the United States, and invited lecture tours of the American experts to Japan (compare Kobayashi and Burke, 1976). It would be rare to find a personnel head of a major firm who was not well versed in the various ideas of leading American scholars in this area. These ideas, combined with and adapted to indigenous values and practices, formed the basis of the Japanese effort in the area of participatory work structures.

In the history of technology transfer—and we may think of these ideas on participatory work structures as a kind of organizational software technology—the process by which the inventors of a technology are not necessarily the commercializers is common. The jet engine, for example, was invented in England but successfully commercialized in the United States (Miller and Sawers, 1970). The causes of this disjuncture became the basis for an interesting intellectual inquiry. Why has American management been so slow in adopting the ideas of American scholars? Is there a need for and what are the advantages of adopting participatory work structures? Japan and Sweden are oriented outward to an extent that is hardly duplicated in the United States. Both rely heavily on export industries to sustain their standards of living. They believe that their success, indeed, their very survival as nations, depends on their ability to search out and absorb ideas from abroad rapidly and efficiently. In both countries, if a solution to a problem is not immediately at hand, it comes as second nature to management to look for solutions outside their national borders. Mapping their foreign environment in a systematic fashion is a well-institutionalized practice in both countries.

The situation of the United States seems very different. Until recently, Americans appeared confident of their own managerial abilities and technology and not very attuned to learning from abroad. With a vast domestic market, the economy cannot be said to be export oriented to the extent of Japan or Sweden. They are accustomed to being on top, and until recently there has not been the same incentive to learn from others. The ideas put forward by American behavioral scientists seemed to fit much better with existing organizational practices in Japan and with their prevailing managerial philosophy than they did in the United States. The Japanese scholar Shin'ichi Takezawa (1976, p. 31) caught the sense of this in the following remarks: "The behavioral science model of management, however, is not perceived as an antithesis of the organizational reality as it might be in the United States. Instead, Japanese managers tend to accept the model as an idealized goal which essentially lies in the same direction as their own behavioral orientation. Often, they are puzzled to find out that American management in practice fits the scientific management model far better than that of the behavioral sciences." This difference provides an explanation for why these ideas were so eagerly received in Japan and why, once exposed to these ideas, they led to a choice opportunity. In the United States these same ideas did not lead to a choice opportunity; rather, they were seen as threatening to many managers and union leaders. The prevailing adversary relationships between managers and workers and managers and unions constitute a formidable obstacle to the adoption of new ideas about organizing work in a cooperative fashion. The notion that worker loyalty and cooperation can lead to significant improvements in productivity tends to be seen as either trivial or impossible to achieve. In short, the gap between existing practices in American industry and the new managerial philosophies is so great as to make search and adoption problematic. Participatory work practices were simply not on the agenda of solutions for most American managers in the 1960s and 1970s, nor was the issue the province of any particular managerial level or department. It is no wonder then that Japanese managers acted more quickly than American management in searching out, adopting, and diffusing ideas concerning participatory work practices.

It is of particular significance that scholarly theories and ideas provide the foundation for the movements that developed in Japan and Sweden. In the three countries, the scholars who most consistently ignored shop floor participation were the Japanese, although, in characteristic fashion, the Japanese found that they could access Western scholarly output as well as draw upon their own historical legacy. In any innovation process, some organizations take the lead and others lag behind. The early innovators in Sweden, Japan, and the United States tend to identify specific problems such as labor shortage and lagging productivity or quality and be consciously motivated to search out solutions to their problems. These early innovators saw participatory work structures as addressing selected problems. So far this is in line with the rational decision-making model. However, in all three countries, we see a process whereby participatory work structures get identified publicly as the solution to a wide range of problems. The shift to participatory work structures assumes the quality of a fad. In Sweden the 1969 "hallelujah" conference featuring Einar Thorsrud kicked off this phase; in Japan it occurred roughly in the same period; in the United States we seem to be just beginning to enter this phase, as testified by the treatment of the subject in the business journals (for example, "The New Industrial Relations," 1981). Well-known, large manufacturing firms like General Motors, Westinghouse, and General Electric are being written up widely in the business press on their participative programs. They are beginning to hold in-company seminars and workshops to diffuse these practices within the firm. The emotional character of this publicity and promotion effort tends to push careful evaluation of results to the background. At this point, companies begin adopting participatory work practices because it is the "thing to do." The public message is that your ability to compete successfully will be impaired unless you adopt this "magic" new formula. Prestige accrues to the early adopters (compare Meyer and Rowan, 1977). They are held up in the media as a model to emulate and large-scale visitations from other companies take place. The more skillful, like Volvo, the Buick Motor Division, Hewlett-Packard, and Toyota, will convert this to a public relations success, increasing their legitimacy both internally and externally.

A decoupling of motivation and search on the one hand and action-oriented solutions on the other begins to take place. Instead of problems chasing solutions, as posited in the rational model of decision making, solutions begin to chase problems. The solution is publicly dangled before companies with the promise that it will address a wide range of problems. The presumption is that the proponents have searched and found the most suitable alternative. To the extent that private consultants are operating in the market, these tendencies will be enhanced. To be sure, over the long haul the innovation may be dropped if it is not found to address specific problems faced by the company, although not necessarily so.

Decision and Implementation. In both Sweden and Japan, a similar infrastructure developed to diffuse ideas and practices concerning participatory work structures in the private sector. We may think of this infrastructure as composed of facilitating organizations. In some cases, new freestanding organizations develop for the purpose of diffusing ideas on participatory work structures; in other cases, new sections and departments are added; and in still other cases, existing sections and departments are given new functions. In Japan, the Japan Federation of Employers' Association (Nikkeiren) played a major role in legitimating the new ideas.* In addition to

---

*Nikkeiren, although analogous in function to the National Association of Manufacturers in the United States or the Swedish Employers' Confederation, is a good deal more specialized in labor and personnel matters and more prestigious and powerful in this area than its U.S. counterpart. Keidanren (Federation of Economic Organizations) stands as the most powerful multipurpose employer organization. The SAF is comparable to Keidanren in scope and power but would also include Nikkeiren's functions under its mandate. With regard to policing labor contracts, the

Nikkeiren's role, specialized organizations such as the Japan Union of Scientists and Engineers (JUSE) developed departments designed exclusively to propagate specific small-group activities. JUSE is a national nonprofit organization dedicated to providing services to participating Japanese companies in the areas of quality and reliability. It is composed of university professors in engineering and science and engineers from leading firms. JUSE is closely tied to business circles. These linkages provided legitimation for JUSE initiatives; JUSE assumed the major leadership role in developing and diffusing the concept and practice of quality control circles. Its low-priced magazine, *Quality Control for Foremen,* was a major factor in promoting quality control circles. Training programs were organized using not only textbooks but also radio and television. QC circle conventions, to which companies send circle members to present their successes, were begun in 1963. By 1978, a QC circle convention was being held once every three days in Japan. In the early days of the movement, the conventions were an important device for diffusing the movement through the procedure of inviting representatives of companies which had not yet adopted the QC circles. Nowadays the conventions serve more to reinvigorate existing circles by showing new methods and applications. Local level branches of JUSE were established and helped insure that local users and potential users could learn from one another. JUSE began a national registration system in 1964 with 1,000 circles affiliating in that year. The number registered with JUSE rose to 110,000 in 1980. With an average of almost ten members a circle, the membership totaled one million. These figures overestimate actual membership because they do not reflect deregistrations (including those circles in companies which go out of business); there is little incentive for companies to report the deregistration of a circle. However, in addition to registered circles, unregistered QC circles—more heavily concentrated in small and medium size firms—are estimated conservatively to total an additional five times the number of registered circles, with a membership of some four million. Nonetheless, it is

---

SAF has the most power in a formal sense; it has fined member companies for wage agreements that go beyond its guidelines.

difficult to know exactly how many workers participate in circles and with what degree of consistency.

In the case of Sweden, we see some similar developments, although their diffusion efforts are not as imaginative as those of the Japanese. As in Japan, the employers' federation made a high level decision in the mid 1960s to support participative activity. The high level conference run by the technical department of SAF for its member companies in 1968 to introduce Thorsrud and his ideas symbolized this commitment. Unlike the Japanese, the Swedish Employers' Confederation decided to keep more of the initiation of small-group activities in its own ranks. The technical department of SAF engaged in a large scale training and publications program. It conducted detailed case studies of carefully selected companies and disseminated their reports widely. In 1975, the technical department published a report based on the experience of more than 500 participative work structure experiments carried out in several hundred companies (Swedish Employers' Confederation, 1975). They have also published their detailed vision of the factory of the future.

In the critical early years of the movement, to spread direct participation in shop floor decision making, two other instrumentalities were important. The first was the Development Council for Cooperation Questions (Utvecklingsrådet för Samarbetsfrågor). The council was established in 1966 by SAF and the two major union federations, the Central Organization of Salaried Employees (TCO) and the blue-collar Swedish Trade Union Confederation (LO). The council was begun as an attempt to explore new possibilities for the existing workers' councils.

The Development Council built a special group for research called URAF, composed of psychologists, sociologists, engineers, etc. URAF's task was to make clear what stimulated democratization of the workplace and what hindered it. Its specific purpose was to initiate and supervise projects and carry on research. These efforts were anchored, as in Norway, in development groups at the company level in which the various interest groups—management and labor—were represented. These development groups had at their disposal the research results of social scientists and technicians associated with URAF. Based on these resources they made decisions on the implementation of participatory work structures. URAF sponsored some ten key pilot projects in the period 1969–70. These pilot projects have been widely reported and in a strongly positive manner by management groups and in a cautiously favorable fashion by labor groups (for example, Landsorganisation, 1976). Yet, by the early 1970s the level of cooperative activity within URAF fell off markedly. Both parties accused the other of sabotaging the joint effort and blamed the other for the failure to operate more effectively. It is clear that the employers' confederation felt shackled by the cooperative activity and preferred to proceed on its own with a freer hand. Thus, the employers' confederation increasingly shifted its main initiatives to its technical department and away from cooperative activity with the unions. Nor was the union totally innocent in regard to the gradual crippling of URAF. Militants within LO received increasingly stronger support for their views on industrial democracy in the early 1970s; LO turned more and more to legislation for the implementation of their goals. Consequently, they saw cooperative activities with the employers as less and less relevant to the meeting of their goals. URAF formally went out of existence in 1978.

A second instrument for diffusing ideas and practices concerning participatory work structures was the Personnel Administration Council (Personaladministrativarådet), set up by SAF. In the early 1960s, it was primarily concerned with personnel questions such as how to improve recruitment and selection procedures. It is primarily a consultant organization that, through its professional staff and associated consultants (primarily academics), provides services to individual firms. With the shift in public and employer interest in the late 1960s toward participatory work structures, the council moved heavily into this area. It guided several important projects and played a key liaison role between academic research and managerial concerns (see Björk and others, 1973). The Council was formally made independent of SAF and solicited LO and TCO representatives on its board of directors. However, many managers and SAF officials found the Council's recommendations too abstract and divorced from managerial concerns and orientations (for example, sensitivity training). This again had the effect of shifting the major thrust of employer initiatives back to SAF's technical development. In summary, although two major organizational instruments developed more or less outside of SAF, the nature of the developments has been such that they have increasingly played a diminished role in the diffusion of participatory work structures after having been important in the early 1970s.

One of the most significant similarities to emerge in this comparison is the important role played by the technical staff (that is, trained in the engineering disciplines) in the diffusing organizations. Although nontechnical personnel may play a significant role in legitimating the new practices, in both countries the technical staff play the decisive role in converting academic theories into what is seen as usable, practical knowledge. They digest and purge academic theories from their more radical connotations and make them compatible with existing managerial orientations. It may be thought of as a sanitizing function. In Sweden, SAF's technical department assumed a larger and larger role in the diffusion process. The department is composed of a select group of engineers who taught themselves as much behavioral science as they felt they needed to make their contribution. In Japan, JUSE is composed almost exclusively of technical people. Moreover, the quality control (QC) circles are commonly initiated and operated in companies under various technical departments, such as quality assurance and the production control department, rather than personnel departments. Of 267 early adopters surveyed, 60 percent report that at the time of their initiation, circles were under the jurisdiction of technical personnel, 5.6 percent under nontechnical personnel, and top management had direct responsibility for 30 percent. The key role assigned to technical personnel means that you had technical personnel in JUSE talking to technical personnel at the adopting companies. This is a strong setup for ensuring maximum communication between the respective parties. In both countries, company officials are likely to be receptive to the suggestions and recommendations of technically trained individuals—both within and outside the firm—who are seen as basically sharing the same values. Academics and management consultants are more likely to be seen as outsiders with views that are incompatible with organizational needs.

We may consider now the institutional infrastructure for the diffusion of participatory work structures in the United States and compare it with developments in Sweden and Japan. Since progress in moving toward shop floor participation of workers has been slow in the United States, it is not surprising that the development of a comparable infrastructure has also been retarded. (This section draws on Dickson (1975) and Davis (1977) as well as on interviews with selected participants and examination of Ford Foundation records.)

The National Commission on Productivity grew in almost accidental fashion out of the National Commission on Prices and Productivity. To improve the quality of the workplace and raise productivity, they planned ten to twenty demonstration projects at work sites in manufacturing, service, and government. The commission envisioned "seeding" these projects and one of the major building blocks was expected to be participative work structures.

Erratic government funding and executive action by President Carter eventually led to the disbanding of the commission in 1978. Despite some innovative projects and an active publications program, it cannot be said that the commission came very close to achieving its ambitious goal of widescale diffusion (see Goodman, 1979). It never functioned as a permanent resource for organizations contemplating innovation or as an effective diffusion agent.

The American Center for Quality of Working Life was set up by Edward Mills, formerly of the National Commission on Productivity and, prior to that, an advertising executive. Public and private grants provided the initial funding, but again financial support has been erratic. The center concentrated on developing labor management committees at selected factories and worksites to tackle workshop problems. A major condition of center activity was that the parties agree to have developments monitored by an external evaluation group from the Institute of Social Research at the University of Michigan. The evaluation process was carried out independently and involved detailed measurements. The center initiated or sponsored eight such arrangements (Davis, 1977). Mills was later to lose enthusiasm for evaluation activities.

A similar path was taken by the Ford Foundation (Ford Foundation, 1975). They began their support for participative activities in 1970 and by 1978 had spent over one million dollars. They have now discontinued major support for such participative activities. Grants were made to the Quality of Work Program at the University of Michigan, the American Center for Quality of Working Life at the Institute for Industrial Relations at the University of California (Los Angeles), and to the Work in America Institute. Although these organizations have shown promise, none has been able to assume leadership, alone or in cooperation with others, in the movement to diffuse participatory work structures. Lack of sustained financial support is a continuing problem. A recent entry in this arena is the American Productivity Center established in 1977. Privately funded through grants from 120 major corporations (which totaled ten million dollars in Fall 1978), it includes high level business executives and some union leaders on its board of directors. It is the first major entry of corporate America into this field, but with its primary focus on improving productivity it gives only limited attention to work reform.

In addition, some twenty state level organizations established quality of work projects with labor-management participation. The initiatives have often come from universities. These statewide quality of work committees hold great promise for tying demonstration projects into a local network of labor and management. Yet, such state committees as well are still struggling to survive and appear far from achieving a self-sustaining momentum. Local networks through which users and potential users can learn from one another have yet to be put into place.

What conclusions can we draw from this treatment of infrastructure in the three nations? The organizations set up to diffuse participatory work practices in Japan and Sweden had the high level support of prestigious business firms and organizations, and, in the case of Sweden, at least initially, labor organizations. This high level support of a particular form of direct participation tended to drive out other possible interpretations of the problems and alternative solutions. However, in Sweden the Swedish Trade Union Confederation (LO) changed its position and began advocating legislative solutions calling for worker participation on boards of directors. This led to a new broadened agenda.

The high level of support, available to these organizations designed to diffuse participatory practices in Japan and Sweden, ensured that their proposals would receive a serious hearing. The involvement of technical personnel meant that there was a cadre of influential decision makers who would participate in the diffusion effort and had counterparts in industry. All this stands in marked contrast to the United States. Instead of key organizations with high legitimacy and prestige emerging as the advocates of participatory work practices, we find an array of often squabbling kingdoms, with few having a kind word for any of their "competitors." Funding was erratic and made difficult the implementation of long-term strategies, regardless of the high sounding pronouncements. The array of backgrounds of those heading these organizations suggest that the movement was unable to command the attention of any single key policy-making counterpart group in industry. Notable is the absence of technically trained personnel (engineering staff) in the U.S. effort at either the infrastructure or the firm level. Finally, no effective local networks were set up to highlight given problems and to associate with these problems participatory practices as the appropriate solution.

Structure of Diffusion and Diffusion Strategies. One characteristic of the American effort to build an institutional infrastructure is the relative stress on measurement of results, often with the active involvement of scholars. A great deal of the limited efforts in the 1970s were invested in developing systematic scientific evaluations of ongoing innovations in participatory work practices. The joint effort between the Quality of Work Program at the University of Michigan and the American Center for the Quality of Working Life represented the key initiative—it has now come to an end. In the context of the limited efforts being made at the time, scarce resources were diverted from direct efforts to introduce participatory work practices. A comparison with the Swedish and Japanese approaches reveals a different approach. The Swedes and Japanese plunged ahead with less interest in formal evaluation and measurement systems. They were concerned with getting things done, in getting on with their initiatives, in experimenting with a wide range of techniques and writing fairly sketchy reports to spread the lessons. This is especially the case with the Japanese; when managers are pressed as to evidence for the success of the QC circle programs, they are often at a loss to provide it. Their responses tend to rest on intuitive evaluations. They will often mention successful case studies and the number of implemented QC circle suggestions to illustrate the effectiveness of the program, but they seldom have engaged in costing out the full program and weighing it against benefits derived. The same is true for the Swedish employers, although to a lesser extent. The technical department of the employers' federation has written up a larger number of case studies depicting successful operations, but they are remarkably devoid of hard evidence on program success. Indeed, SAF's technical department has made it clear that they are not engaged in scholarly research but in purposeful selection of case studies ("demonstration projects") to advance the diffusion of participatory work structures. They have been severely criticized by some Swedish scholars in this connection. SAF officials reply that they are not in the business of testing hypotheses and theories and that is why the projects described in their reports succeeded (Myrdal, 1977).

The implicit assumption of American evaluation efforts seems to be that management will adopt participatory work initiatives only if they are scientifically proven to be effective. Witness the statement by Louis Davis (1977, p. 63) that American society prides itself on pragmatism and demands demonstration projects or experiments to prove the effectiveness of quality of working life concepts. Although the emphasis on demonstration projects has its counterpart in Japan and Sweden, the emphasis on experimental design with complex measurement is distinctively American. Marty Rein (1976) notes the prevalence of the view that if we are to produce better information about which government interventions work and which do not, it is necessary to design social programs deliberately as experiments. The experimental approach based on random selection will allow us to gain reliable and valid information about the effectiveness of innovative social programs. The Swedish and Japanese efforts lead us to question these assumptions. Herbert Simon (Williams, 1978) points to the interesting case of the adoption of computers by major American firms. He found that major firms often made the decision to buy or rent one not on the basis of a rational assessment of costs and benefits. Often the executives with decision-making authority knew remarkably little about the possible benefits. Rather, it became the thing to do. One had to have one because one's competitors had one. It was hard to show up at a business lunch without one. The inference that Simon drew from these observations was that when innovations came along, the forces that result in their acceptance are not necessarily economic ones. He concluded that economic decisions based on rational evaluation of carefully sorted and weighted criteria were no match for the emotion and excitement triggered by a technical or business innovation.

Similar situations have recently been reported in the adoption of Computer Aided Design and Computer Aided Manufacturing (CAD-CAM). George Strauss (1976) documents the faddish quality of successive management adoptions of organizational development programs and the noneconomic motivations for adoption, especially with the kind of software organizational technology under consideration. If we take the issue to be the speed at which best practice is diffused, the identification of best practice is difficult and subject to differing interpretations. Moreover, expected profitability, a major determinant of rate of adoption of technological innovations, is extremely difficult to estimate for this kind of software technology (compare Mansfield, 1968). This further increases the ambiguity. Under these conditions, whether a given practice, such as participative management, is the best practice or has high expected profitability becomes less important than the evolution of a consensus that identifies it as the best practice and profitable. Facilitative organizations such as the Japan Employers' Federation, JUSE, and SAF have played a central role in determining what constitutes best practice at any given time and rapidly diffused this information to the most important of the potential users. Given these characteristics, the "emotion and excitement" triggered by the innovation will be far more powerful factors than rational evaluation processes. The "hallelujah" conference at which SAF introduced Thorsrud was a far more powerful stimulus than a hundred carefully executed studies with their arcane language and concepts.

Many American advocates of participative work practices have accepted a model of managerial adoption and diffusion based on the experimental approach. This rests on the assumption of the prior need for calculation of the net benefits to be derived based on scientific verification. We reject the intuitive evaluations with which the Japanese seem so much more comfortable. March (March and Olsen, 1976) argues that the American cultural heritage gives primacy to the ethic of rationality at the expense of intuition, impulse, faith, and tradition. Measurement establishes an organization as appropriate, rational, and modern. Its use displays responsibility and avoids claims of negligence (compare Meyer and Rowan, 1977).

Some American observers have seen measurement as problematic. Irving Bluestone, former vice-president of the UAW, expressed the matter to me in the following fashion: "I don't see the need for all this complex measurement and evaluation. If the local union leader and the plant manager like the new work arrangements, then it works."

For all the claim that those doing evaluation studies make to provide scientific verification, it is doubtful whether a "true" evaluation of results is possible. The ambiguity of goals and technology of participative work practices means that all participants in an evaluation effort will interpret the multitude of "facts" they have available to them in a variety of ways, depending on their social position and values. The aggregation of these facts into consistent explanations for what happened and did not happen, why it happened or did not happen, and whether it was good or bad will further increase the probability of discrepancies in accounts. Put differently, the objective reality allows for a variety of interpretations, and these interpretations may be just as important or more important than the objective reality (March and Olsen, 1976).

Many evaluation studies take a long time to complete. This often delays the point of decision making to a time when initial enthusiasm has evaporated. In summary, evaluation studies may inhibit the adoption and diffusion process by diverting scarce resources from alternative uses, creating "noise," making it difficult to communicate to a wider public, and unnecessarily complicating the decision-making process by which management makes adoption decisions.

We have here a case of both push and pull. On the one hand we have an academic community with strong measurement capabilities, entrepreneurially inclined, and capable of arguing for the importance of evaluation in assessing the utility of participative work structures. During the 1970s, many of these academic proponents of participative work practices saw evaluation studies as the only available strategy open to them to convince a skeptical management. In contrast, Japanese scholars, throughout the 1960s and 1970s, pretty much ignored shop floor participative work practices. Those with Marxist sympathies saw it as part of a continuing management effort to break down worker collective loyalties and rebuild work structures based on commitment to managerial goals.

American scholars were responding to a suspicious management that demands measurable bottom-line results from such innovations. Wayne Rieker, formerly manufacturing manager of Lockheed Air Missile and originator of their quality control circle program and later a successful consultant on circles, adds an additional perspective: "It seems to be considered a weakness in the United States if we cannot apply some scientific measurement to the investment in an activity where *workers* [author's italics] are involved, such as QC circles. Yet, it appears quite acceptable to invest in *professional* or *management personnel* [author's italics] by providing training or sending them to 'charm school' at Stanford, Harvard, Yale . . . without being required to provide scientific proof of the return on the investment" (Rieker and Sullivan, 1981, p. 29). We can see how a suspicious management enforces the measurement role in the following example from a major aerospace corporation. A division manager called the staff that implemented a participatory work program and gave them one day's notice to make a presentation to a high level management team on the benefits being provided by such activities. As the staff person in charge told me, "This is using measurement as a terrorist tactic. If they had given us a month to prove our case, at least it would have been a reasonable request." These sentiments, interests, and capabilities on the part of a suspicious management strongly reinforce the measurement role.

With respect to the setting up of an infrastructure to accomplish the objective of collecting, standardizing, and feeding back information to the field, the Swedish and the Japanese managers adopted highly "rational" vehicles tailored to this end. The means were closely tied to the desired goals. SAF, Nikkeiren, and JUSE acted to ensure that firm-level solutions would be as "guided by imitation of one's neighbor" as mediated by them. The Americans have yet to develop such vehicles. However, with regard to the measurement and evaluation of results, the Swedish and the Japanese managers rejected the rational decision-making model. This is not to say they rejected feedback and evaluation as a basis for controlling subsequent decisions. Rather, they have been willing to take much "softer" measures of feedback as a sufficient basis for decision making and not push for quantifiable, short-term, bottom-line paybacks. If we ask the hard question of why the American managers seem inclined to push for more rigorous measurement of results, I suggest that when the nature of the intervention is such as to threaten strongly held values, there is a tendency to require measurement and evidence to justify the intervention (compare Rein, 1976). American managers often make decisions on technological changes without such requirements. Yet efforts to begin creating participatory work structures, often costing very modest sums of money, are subject to strong evidential requirements. Measurement, in turn, has a strong tendency to turn into a punitive control system that discourages risk and innovation. The Swedes and the Japanese seem less threatened by these innovations and therefore were less inclined to require strict measurement and short-term paybacks.

A second area of comparison lies in the union role. In the case of Japan, the unions have not been significantly involved in the diffusion of participatory work structures involving increased employee participation on the shop or office floor. At best, they have monitored the programs to ensure that workers were not exploited or coerced with respect to meeting times and payment. They have made no explicit attempt to see to it that workers receive a share of the increased productivity associated with these efforts. Because these innovations were seen as within managerial prerogatives and consistent with union goals to create a bigger pie, the absence of a larger and more active union role was not a serious impediment. Moreover, the unions had a different agenda for participation; it involved cooperating with management to create a labor-management consultation system at the plant and firm level. These councils grew rapidly from the mid 1960s to the mid 1970s and are now well institutionalized.

The situation has been different in Sweden. Faced with a powerful labor movement, Swedish management moved early to involve the unions in the shop floor participation movement. The special group for research, URAF, was just one mechanism for this. Union officials were as a matter of course invited to various management-run conferences on the subject and cooperated with management at the plant and office level. The unions began to go their own way with an emphasis on legislation and other modes of worker participation, but in the critical early years of the movement, the unions were publicly committed to the goal of instituting self-steering work groups. In the United States, the organizations designed to facilitate the diffusion of participatory work structures have failed to develop union support. In 1973, the United Auto Workers (UAW), on its own, negotiated a clause in its contract with the major automobile manufacturers calling for joint labor-management quality of working life committees. The task of these committees is to stimulate experimentation with work forms designed to enhance the quality of working life and to disseminate these experiences so that they can be applied more widely. Even here the primary success has been with General Motors, with Ford, Chrysler, and American Motors lagging far behind. Within the UAW national leadership, not to speak of the locals, there is by no means uniformly strong support for these cooperative efforts. Outside the UAW, union leaders have on the whole been much more suspicious of managerial motives, seeing participatory work structures as just another management technique designed to get more production out of workers without sharing the rewards with them. Because so many of management's initiatives have been in nonunion firms, the union leaders see the participatory work structures as a device to avoid unionization. Indeed, this is often the case. The unions also fear that participatory work structures will be used to reduce manpower requirements. At the same time the unions often have the power to sabotage such initiatives.

A third characteristic that distinguishes the U.S. initiative from those of Japan and Sweden is the heavy reliance on outside consultants. Japanese management has tended to eschew outside consultants. Those used in connection with the development of QC circles have commonly been company managers associated with JUSE who are loaned on contract to business firms. My recent (unpublished) survey of early adopters of QC circles reveals that at the time of adoption 60.5 percent did not use outside consultants and half of those that did relied on staffing from JUSE, with only 19 percent relying on private consultants. JUSE's services include training materials, QC circle conventions, and seminars for all levels of personnel. These materials have been utilized by company personnel to institute and execute the QC circle programs. JUSE's national reputation enhanced the credibility of its training programs. The assumption is that company personnel are capable of learning what is necessary to run these programs.

In Sweden there also has been a tendency to minimize reliance on outside consultants to initiate participatory work structures. Kondo (1976) arrives at the same conclusion in his comparison of Swedish job reform and Japanese quality control circles. The Personnel Administration Council has been the major avenue for consultant participation. That many consultant activities have been channeled through the council constitutes a form of quality control in that the council operated as a standard-setting body. A 1972 unpublished survey of SAF members conducted by the Development Council reveals that of the 628 firms judged to be conducting interesting efforts toward work restructuring and worker participation in management, 45 percent reported using external assistance. Of the 280 firms so reporting, 70 reported working through the Personnel Administrative Council.

Although Swedish managers have used consultants, they have been extremely conscious of the Norwegian experience, where it was felt that outside consultants too closely supervised the experiments. Because of this, the participatory work structures were never fully integrated into company operations. Because this was seen as an "exotic" area by many Norwegian managers, it was easier to leave it to the outside specialist; as a consequence many managers never explored and assimilated the new ideas. Finally, all this outside specialist control of the work tended to prevent knowledge of the experiments from being conveyed to the general public, presumably because of proprietary interests as well as the specialist's arcane language. David Jenkins (1974), a well-known student of the direct worker participation movement in Western Europe, concludes that this latter problem reduced the diffusion of ideas on participatory work structures. These various observations were well publicized in Sweden, and as a consequence a rule of thumb emerged to keep the initiative with company officials and employees and hold consultants in close rein.

The heavy reliance on consultants in the United States is striking. Both management and academic consultants play large roles. There is an almost overwhelming assumption that the initiation of participatory work structures requires the use of third-party consultants, who are necessary to build trust between management and workers and to facilitate cooperative activities. It permeates the literature (see the *Journal of Applied Behavioral Science*). In 1973, there were an estimated five hundred to one thousand external OD consultants in the United States (Strauss, 1976, p. 617). To be sure, not all OD consultants are concerned with the initiation of participatory work structures. In 1976, there were estimated to be no more than a dozen external OD consultants in Japan (Kobayashi and Burke, 1976, p. 119). The recent spread of quality circles in the United States provides an example. There has been an exponential increase not only in firms installing circles but in the number of private consultants installing and giving advice on circles between 1979 and 1982. In 1979, there were three consultant firms; the number exploded to over thirty by January 1982. The two leading consultant firms reported at this time that they were working with fifty organizations at any one time, with each business having tripled in 1981 over the preceding year. They each reported $1.5 million in annual revenue for 1981 and each had at least nine full-time consultants on its payroll ("Two California Firms . . . ," 1981).

Professional associations, as has been seen in the role of JUSE, have the capacity for standard setting and education of potential users. In the United States, consultants play a disproportionately large role in such organizations and operate to achieve association policies that at a minimum do not inhibit their proprietary interests and at a maximum enhance their earning potential. Two reasons consultants are able to achieve such key roles in professional associations are that they have greater control over their time allocation than company employees and they can see a financial advantage to being active. That is to say, they have a strong incentive to be active. Consultants have been successful in getting professional associations to limit their role so as not to compete with private consultant services. In the case of quality circles, the International Association of Quality Circles (IAQC), founded in 1977 by two consultants, and the American Society for Quality Control have been active in providing services relating to quality circles. Yet both organizations have an informal rule that no in-plant consultant services be offered to business firms. They thus implicitly reserve the in-plant market for private consultants. In the case of IAQC, some of the consultants fought to keep the organization from creating its own training materials. Their self-interest in this outcome is evident. These organizations struggle on a routine basis with the problem of how to limit consultant power in their organizations, and it is often a matter arousing considerable concern among members.

Without a power base in the firm, outside consultants are often handicapped in what they can do (Alderfer and Berg, 1977). The probability of diffusion within the firm is also thereby reduced. There also does not appear to be sufficient recognition of the problems created by dependence on consultants. Internal initiative is often sapped and the diffusion effort crippled. A related problem is that a strong market for consultants has arisen, so that many of the key personnel of successful participatory work efforts have left their original employer to enter the consulting business. This often creates problems and loss of momentum in the original program, as Walton (1975) has documented in a number of cases. A not unusual case may be seen at Lockheed Air Missile Division, which pioneered in the development of quality circles in the United States. The three key staff members responsible for its successful implementation left the firm and established their own consulting firms. The loss of this support and expertise crippled the circle activities at Lockheed.

A distinguishing characteristic of the U.S. approach relative to Japan and Sweden as it affects the diffusion of participatory work structures is the proprietary character of information. In Japan, the centralized character of the QC circle movement is seen in the national registration system operated by JUSE. JUSE is dedicated to providing a sharing of resources and experiences, charging just enough in fees to cover its costs. Sharing is done in a variety of ways. Some of the primary methods are a monthly magazine devoted to reporting short sketches of successful case studies in different companies, QC circle conventions designed to bring workers and foremen from different companies to exchange their experiences, intercompany visits by groups of workers organized by JUSE, a variety of seminars for employers at all levels that bring together employees from different companies, and a variety of training materials reporting on the experiences of various companies. One of the striking characteristics of JUSE is the voluntary leadership provided by various managers in leading companies for its various functions, such as QC circle conventions. Companies show no hesitancy in having their managers offer their services and share their experiences with workers and staff from other companies. Professor Ishikawa Kaoru, the leader of the QC circle movement, recounted the difficulty they had in the beginning in arranging for company visits and having companies send representatives to QC circle conventions. He explained, however, that the problem was not secrecy, but rather the lack of precedent for such activity. It was not clear that companies would be willing to provide the budgets for these innovations. Managers do not appear fearful that company secrets might be revealed in presentations to QC circle conventions. Presentations are screened routinely by the company and only occasionally do they withhold a presentation for this reason. Most presentations involve alterations in micro kinds of process, often unique to a particular workshop; therefore no competitive edge is lost in having these presentations made public. In summary, JUSE's leadership role in organizing the sharing of company resources and experiences with QC circles ensured the rapid diffusion of this software technology. It became relatively simple for any company to find out how to do QC circles. Ultimately, this public character must be understood in the context of an overall management consensus arrived at by opinion leaders in Japanese management. They agreed that small-group activity of this kind was the direction that Japanese management should be moving for the good of the nation and the health of the private corporation. They endorsed JUSE, in effect, as the major repository of wisdom on the subject. In this atmosphere proprietary information and private consultants could be expected to play a minor role.

A similar tendency appears in Sweden, although the effort is not as tightly organized by SAF's technical department as it was by JUSE. In Sweden there were many more sources of competing solutions. There emerged a national consensus that organizations providing employment should move toward industrial democracy. There was an enormous public debate of high quality. Under these conditions, there was pressure on companies to innovate and to make public their achievements. Because the unions and sometimes the government were involved in many efforts, it was difficult for managers to unilaterally treat information as proprietary and to be secretive about their innovations. Indeed, the unions have been pushing for guaranteed access to research sites. SAF's technical department, by its determination to spread the innovation, sought to publicize each successful effort as a means of securing further diffusion. Underlying the nonproprietary character of information flows is first, as in Japan, a national management consensus that these innovations were important for the future of Swedish industry. Second, and contrary to Japan, a national consensus developed in Sweden that this was an important direction to move in order to enhance societal justice.

In the United States, neither a national nor a management consensus has yet developed that the adoption of participatory work structures is in the interests of the nation or American management. Many companies treat information gained in their experiments as proprietary or "semiproprietary." Notable is Procter & Gamble in this regard, but a host of other companies, such as IBM, Cummins Engine, and Polaroid, are reluctant to talk about their experiences or allow reports to be made about them.

In one sense these restrictions may be seen as a sign of their success, for if these innovations are seen as proprietary, that means they are successful. That is, they have valued structural arrangements that allow their company to have a competitive edge insofar as the innovations lead to higher productivity, reduced turnover and absenteeism, and greater company loyalty. However, this kind of attitude has a significant negative impact on the diffusion process by restricting information flows. Just how proprietary information on these innovations has become is made clear by the fact that a number of the firms that pioneered in these processes have set up special consulting departments. Such unlikely companies as the Travelers, American Airlines, and Ralston Purina have become job-restructuring consultants. The proprietary treatment of information has been both the cause and effect of the growth of consultants in the field. One can argue that the presence of large numbers of consultants stimulates the diffusion process as they fly about "fertilizing individual flowers." But one may ask how efficient is this mode of information transfer? It introduces a significant cost to obtaining such information, which inhibits the diffusion process as compared to acquiring the information by less costly methods. A recurrent theme among managers concerns how to separate the charlatans from the competent consultants (for example, Patchin, 1981). The screening process can be extremely costly because there is a large amount of bad as well as good information in the system. Because information is proprietary and one consultant's system does not easily build on another's, one must test each new approach to see if it works, a costly matter in terms of time and money. In one sense the use of consultants to diffuse information is extremely efficient; it ensures rapid diffusion. After all, each consultant is a marketer. However, each consultant is devoted to creating a differentiated product; the more successful consultants will become knowledgeable in a narrow area and sell that expertise over a broad client base. They will develop a "package" with strong knowledge content so that clients will interact with a self-contained package and then market it over a wide area. With continual development of new packages, they are able to build repeat business. The Kepner-Tregoe problem-solving package and the Blake-Mouton managerial grid are two prominent examples. Many consultants, however, have difficulty proceeding in this fashion and stress instead client interaction with the consultant. Some reasons for this decision are:

1. Consultants often have strong ego investment and a sense of mission in services they provide, especially in small consultant firms, which are the norm in the area of participative management. Those with such a sense of mission think the client will misuse the package without proper instructions and often disparage those consultants who sell their materials outright without requiring any client interaction.

2. Consulting firms may have the shortsighted goal of building client dependency at the expense of broadening the market. This clearly limits diffusion.

    Given the difficulty of establishing copyright protection in this area, there is a constant need to generate new refinements and programs. Managers feel a need to be seen doing something new and fresh all the time. There is, consequently, an enormous amount of information available from consultants for managers who want to be seen as innovative. Yet managers have little basis for separating the bad from the good information. This sharply increases the ambiguity and uncertainty associated with adopting a particular participatory technology. There is no public body, as in Sweden and Japan, that makes available standardized information and a "public testing" of strategies and programs and feeds back that information to individual firms. That is, there is no "public" test of the quality of information. The absence of such public bodies makes it extremely difficult to develop a consensus on the best procedures. Without a centralized information clearinghouse, you have a breakdown in standard forms at the firm level. The template being offered must be flexible enough to allow adaptation to local conditions. People at the firm level must have sufficient input over implementation mode that they develop a sense of "ownership."

Company reports of their experiences are of little help. At best, published reports are sterile and gloss over the difficulties. At worst, these company reports distort their experiences and serve primarily as vehicles for company public relations.

In short, there may be rapid diffusion but not necessarily rapid diffusion of the best practice. This can lead to high rates of failure and jeopardize future initiatives. Understandably, consultants do not like to talk about failure; yet there is much we can learn from failure (Mirvis and Berg, 1977). Despite the proliferation of consultants, the rate of diffusion has been remarkably low in the United States. One might suggest a lag hypothesis based on the notion that as consultants become more experienced and receive better training, this will eventually lead to greater success in producing diffusion. I postulate, to the contrary, that the basic reason for their lack of success lies first in the lack of a management consensus that participatory work practices are a desired solution to specific problems managers face and second it is due to the inherent contradictions in the consultant role.

What does this tell us about the rational model of decision making? Consultants are advocates of solutions. By definition, they represent solutions in search of a problem; their market interests push them strongly in that direction. Consultants are advertising participatory work practices as a solution to a broad range of problems that they see management as facing. This includes just about all the objectives of participatory management discussed in the first section. In the case of quality circles, they are being marketed by many consultants as a panacea to all problems management has or could have with its employees. Consultants link organizations to information in rather a precarious fashion because their interests cannot be totally identical to the organization's. Although their formal role may be to reduce uncertainty and risk for the business firm, the actual consequences of companies following their advice may be quite different. Thus, the interposition of consultants into the decision-making process suggests the ingredients of the garbage can model, with individual decision makers, problems, and solutions all thrown into the mix.

One reason quality control circles spread so rapidly in Japan and seem to have attracted so much attention recently in the United States, compared to other direct participatory approaches, is the seemingly self-contained nature of circles. Independent of the role of consultants, this self-contained character would seem to facilitate diffusion. I would argue that the circles are less self-contained in practice than they initially appear. Nonetheless, if the contents can be marketed as self-contained, then potential users will see it as less disruptive to the existing organization. This suggests a mechanistic model of organizations in which "part replacements" are available for specific defects. This contrasts with an organic model, in which a change of one part requires adjustments of all others as the changes reverberate throughout the system. Advocates of participatory work practices in the United States often present participative work innovations in terms of an organic model. They may be correct, but insofar as it is presented in this fashion, management will see it as threatening and diffusion may be hampered. Japanese management treated circles and related innovations as a relatively self-contained package and in the context of a mechanistic model. Sweden is an interesting mixed case in which the unions saw the autonomous work groups in terms of an organic model with an eye to changing the whole structure of power and authority in the business firm. They did not see it as a self-contained package. Managers saw shop and office floor participation in terms of a mechanistic model; they preferred to limit the impact of changes to the shop and office floor. This set the stage for a major political confrontation in Sweden.

Political Dimension. Thus far my observations point to similarities in the Swedish and Japanese approaches relative to the American effort to introduce participatory work structures. Yet there are some fundamental differences that distinguish the Swedish from the Japanese approach. These distinguishing characteristics arise from the different parameters established by the political dimensions of the efforts; these parameters determine the scope of the effort, the shape and volume of information transmission, and the very form of the movement. They determine the timing of choice opportunities and who participates in the choices that are made.

The political dimension assumes the "fullest" possibilities in the Swedish effort. In Sweden a national consensus that fully endorsed employee shop floor participation in decision making emerged in the late 1960s. To understand the nature of this consensus and its implications requires an analysis of the respective motivations and activities of the major institutional actors: management, unions, and government. I have already considered managerial motivations; so I turn now to union motivations. The potential significance of the union role is clear when we consider the ratio of organized workers to the labor force in Sweden. In 1970, about 95 percent of the entire Swedish labor force was organized in unions, with roughly the same rate of organization for white-collar as for blue-collar workers. This is well above the overall organization rate of other Western European, the North American, and the Japanese economies.

The highly centralized Swedish union movement historically has been uninterested in direct workshop participation by workers. This lack of interest stemmed in part from the continual struggle of the Social Democrats with the Communists in the local and national unions over many decades. Because the Communists were strong in many local and national unions, centralization was a means of minimizing their impact. In the same vein, participation in work place decisions seemed to favor Communist interests, and therefore the Social Democrats showed little enthusiasm for it. Employee participation in decision making at the work place, insofar as it was handled structurally, was channeled mainly through the works councils. Notwithstanding an expanded role for the works councils during the postwar period, surveys showed that the rank and file workers felt little benefit from the works councils. URAF was originally established in 1968 as a way of combining shop floor participation with the works·councils.

Clearly, the strongest galvanizing force that gave new impetus to union support of direct worker participation in the work place developed in December 1969 with the two-month wildcat strike at the LKAB iron mine. The well-paid miners were concerned about poor working conditions and their loss of wage advantage compared to other occupational groups (Hammerström, 1975). It would be hard to convey in a few sentences the impact of this strike on the Swedish public, government, management, and unions. It attracted enormous media coverage, with surveys showing some 70 percent of the public in sympathy with the strikers. But this was hardly simply a strike against management, for the LKAB mines were state owned. Moreover, the local union officials were portrayed as both powerless and totally unresponsive to the rank and file demands. Thus, the strike and the public support it gave rise to was as much an attack on insensitive government and union bureaucracies as it was against traditional management. The strike was followed by a wave of wildcat strikes throughout the country in 1970 and 1971.

The strikes set in motion a national debate on the meaning of work, the proper trade union role, what employees had a right to expect from work, and a consideration of the possibilities for restructuring work and authority relationships. Media coverage was intense. Journalists like Göran Palm (1972, 1974, 1977) ventured into the factories and wrote about their experiences. An endless number of TV and radio documentaries and dramas took up the theme of the meaning of work and its impact on individual employees. Newspapers ran series after series on the subject and it was often the subject of editorials. Left-wing Social Democrats and unionists seized upon the discontent manifest in the strikes to advocate a larger role for workers (Karlsson, 1969). This was the period in which radical protest was at its heights. The anti-Vietnam movement was in full swing; the student revolt was flourishing. Under these circumstances a call for a radical restructuring of work relationships seemed appropriate to many Swedes. It was within this context that choice opportunities developed. Direct work place participation by workers seemed to be a means to meet the needs of a disaffected rank and file and to redress authority relationships in favor of the workers. These were powerful factors leading to early union cooperation with management to introduce direct worker participation in work place decisions. This cooperative activity extended to white-collar employees as well as blue-collar workers.

As the momentum for change developed, however, the political events required outcomes that were beyond the capacity of the early experiments at shop floor participation. LO was dissatisfied that shop floor democracy had not served as a stepping-stone to their goal of democratizing the entire firm. In their 1971 convention, LO endorsed a historic reversal in its policies when they fully committed LO to the worker participation movement, demanding that power for workers at all company levels be guaranteed through legislation. The new policy symbolized an end to the policy of cooperation between SAF and LO in this area and a turn to legislation. It rewrote the agenda of solutions and changed the locus of decision making. The LO policy, which the Central Organization of Salaried Employees (TCO) also endorsed, eventually led to the passage of the democracy at work law (Medbestämmandelagen), which came into effect in 1976. The new law provides Swedish workers and their unions with legal authority to bargain collectively over a wide range of management decisions that had heretofore been managerial prerogatives. The period around 1971 constituted a watershed. One of the hallmarks of Swedish trade unionism has been that labor and management have been able to agree on particular areas in which their respective interests could be advanced through cooperative action. They have been able to identify several such areas and remove them from the traditional bargaining relationship. Worker participation in decision making has run the opposite course. It was traditionally a low-priority area for the unions, which adopted a cooperative approach, reflected in their setting up the works councils and subsequently their cooperation in URAF with experimental programs designed to increase worker participation in shop floor decision making.

In the early 1970s, this cooperative approach began to give way, culminating in the historic 1971 LO convention. Legislation came to be seen as the key to making worker participation function by expanding the arena for union negotiations. Although the unions still officially support direct shop floor participation, they emphasize more the intervening role the unions should play. One senses a greater ambivalence by national union leaders in the 1980s toward direct worker participation in work place decision making. Many union leaders see the decentralization inherent in the movement as a threat to the centralized union bargaining structures that have been built up over the years. Consequently, they see it as an employer strategy to divide and conquer. Although LO and TCO national officers still endorse worker participation at the work place, the unions on the local level tend to be fairly passive. Consequently, much of the initiative is left to management. In one fundamental sense, direct work place participation in decision making has been a casualty of the LO and TCO policy shifts, for these shifts meant that direct work place participation in decision making became only one of several modes of worker participation LO endorsed. This broadened agenda of solutions brought it into competition with the movement for board membership for workers and a variety of other representative forms of participation, such as expanded works councils. Employee representatives on the boards of directors in limited liability companies and economic associations having more than one hundred employees became a law in 1972 (one of the demands of the 1971 LO congress). In principle, participation in various forms and levels of the company is complementary. In practice, there has often been strong union infighting over the priorities they should assign to the different forms of participation. The worker participation movement in Sweden has been multilevel and taken a variety of forms. This can be directly attributed to union involvement.

During the national debate that ensued in the early 1970s, each of the political parties came to take political positions on worker participation. The Social Democratic party, the ruling party in Sweden for over forty years until 1976, accepted and pushed the union's legislative proposals in the area of worker participation. Without a Social Democratic majority the unions could not have achieved their aims. Indeed, the significance of having a ruling party sympathetic to union interests is apparent in the events since the Social Democrats lost power. Previously, the unions could bargain hard with the threat that if the employers were not willing to compromise, the unions would turn to legislative solutions. After 1976, the unions had to compromise. After 1971, the Social Democratic party and the unions abandoned their historic position. They were no longer prepared to rely on the negotiation process among the private parties in the labor market operating through their centralized organizations to solve whatever issues came up. Instead, the Social Democrats, with strong union encouragement, embarked on a remarkably ambitious legislative program that has transformed and will continue to transform labor-management relationships in Sweden. This legislation included board of director membership for workers (1972), a stringent employment security act (1974), an act requiring public notification of planned dismissals and requiring consultation with public officials in specified circumstances (1974), legislation regulating the status of shop stewards at the work place (1974), legislation reorganizing dispute settlement rules (1974), a new work environment act that is revolutionary in many respects (1978), and above all the democracy at work law (1977).

One of the distinguishing characteristics of the work place participation movement in Sweden is its extension into the public sector, particularly in the approximately forty state-owned joint stock companies. Those politically committed to worker participation felt it was absolutely necessary to move the participation movement into the public sector and show that it could work there. The LKAB strike was an enormous embarrassment for the ruling Social Democratic party. The chosen instrument for removing this embarrassment was the Delegation for Company Democracy (Företagsdemokratidelegationen), appointed originally in November 1968 (before the LKAB strike) under the Department of Industry. Its staff was composed of young Social Democratic radicals and academics who were committed to using the public sector to set the norms of participation in the entire private sector.

The delegation developed five projects in which they sought to apply the sociotechnical principles to ensure direct worker participation in shop floor decision making. One of the experiments, at

Arvika, a tobacco factory operated by the Tobacco Monopoly, is generally considered to have been a success and has been widely publicized as such by the unions (Landsorganisation, 1976). Three of the projects were considered failures by members of the delegation themselves.* From the beginning the delegation's activities were extremely controversial. Conceived in a political atmosphere and with a staff motivated as much by politics as organizational reform, they required quick and public results. This was incompatible with the long, slow, and painful process involved in introducing and institutionalizing fundamental organizational change. Indeed, one of the maxims of top strategists of work place participation movements in Sweden and Japan stresses the long time periods needed to introduce and institutionalize change; attempts to force a speedup of the process are seen as likely to have negative consequences. Such seems to have been the case with the delegation's activities; they politicized all their activities. They had access to high level politicians and tried to use this political support for maximum leverage and immediate action. They spent much energy in making public accusations against directors of state enterprises for obstructing their plans. In order to set norms for the entire labor market, they sought to diffuse information on successful examples. Consequently, far more than the private sector, they adopted a policy of maximum public exposure; often the exposure was premature even when the results were promising.

The delegation tried to stay five years ahead of the experiments in the private sector, innovating with both direct and indirect forms of participation at various levels of the firm. Growing opposition made it increasingly difficult to fill this leadership role. In its 1971 convention, when LO inaugurated its legislative strategy, union interest in the bottom-up model of direct participation diminished. At the same time, opposition from the managers of state enterprises hardened; they resented the public attention and the implication that they were doing things wrong. It became difficult to recruit new managers who would accept existing or planned participatory schemes. It was rumored that SAF officials encouraged such

*Personal interview with Olle Hammerström, a former staff member of the delegation, August 17, 1978, Uppsala, Sweden.

opposition to avoid having the public sector set the norms for the private sector. Opposition political parties criticized the poor financial performance of state enterprises and the state enterprises came under constant scrutiny. Experiments were difficult to conduct under these conditions. Between 1972 and 1974, state enterprises effectively boycotted the delegation and union and political support dried up. It was no surprise that the delegation terminated its activities in 1975.

Although the Swedes have had some success in spreading the movement for work place participation to the public sector, many of the delegation's efforts can be seen as counterproductive to the diffusion of this innovation. They relied on external political support to carry through their program, and when the political support evaporated, so did any chance of success. Yet expectations for participation of public employees in work place decision making achieved and sustained a high level in Sweden. Precisely because there developed a national consensus based on a public debate of enormous proportions, it has been possible to sustain some of the momentum. Political considerations led to the delegation concentrating on maximum public exposure to facilitate the diffusion effort; this proved to be self-defeating. To be sure, such exposure is in a sense the epitome of nonproprietary information flows, which I previously espoused. The difference is that a policy of maximum, and often premature, public exposure was used to batter down obstacles to implementation and adoption and generate political support, rather than facilitating information flows per se. Such obstacles might better be overcome with quiet, behind-the-scenes negotiation.

Several characteristics emerged in Sweden as a result of the parameters set by the political dimension. Above all, the work participation movement in Sweden developed as a result of a national consensus; government, unions, and managers, all for somewhat different reasons, committed themselves to the worker participation movement. They all became actors in the political bargaining process culminating in key choice opportunities along the way. Second, it was a movement that operated at many levels in many forms, so that direct workshop participation was only one of many solutions. Yet it was a solution that had the support of all major actors in the late 1960s. This support was later diluted as the unions explored other directions and the Social Democrats lost their position as ruling party. Third, because a national consensus emerged, the movement was not limited to blue-collar workers in the private sector. White-collar employees and public sector employees were also included in the initiatives.

The political aspects of the participatory work structures movements in Japan and the United States are markedly different from that of Sweden. In Japan no national consensus on the desirability of introducing participatory work structures has been reached. Not surprisingly, then, there has been no national debate on the subject. A debate did surface among management experts on the proper strategy to pursue, but this was by definition a debate of narrow scope. A stable number of individuals and organizations allocated their attention to major choices. A management consensus developed on the need to adopt participatory work structures for primarily blue-collar workers in the manufacturing sector. In the case of QC circles, only in the last few years have some breakthroughs to white-collar workers been made. No initiatives have been undertaken in the public sector, in part because of the militancy of public sector unions, which see such efforts as a management effort to raise productivity at the workers' expense. The Japanese government has been almost totally noninvolved in the worker participation issue. The political parties, including the Socialist and Communist parties, have not taken any position on the shop floor participation issue. Board membership for worker representatives has been advocated by the Domei labor federation, the dominant labor organization in the private sector. Without the support of a ruling political party, however, this position stands no chance of being adopted. Indeed, Domei abandoned the proposal in 1978 and now advocates the expansion of the scope and power of labor-management consultation councils. In opting for this indirect form of worker representation, the unions ignored direct shop floor participation, and it never led to a choice opportunity even within the movement.

In Japan, participatory work structures have diffused heavily in the private sector among the blue-collar workers but have had almost no impact in the public sector and minimal impact on white-collar employees. This reflects the nonpolitical character of the innovation in Japan in the sense that unions, the government, and political parties have not participated in the key choices. The institution of participatory work structures has been almost entirely the outcome of the exercise of managerial prerogatives. Consequently, they could carefully control its direction, scope, and content in a way not possible in Sweden.

The situation in the United States is similar to that of Japan, although there has been some initial government involvement through the National Commission on Productivity and Quality of Working Life and the support provided by HEW for research on the book *Work in America*. A consistent high priority policy of government support, however, never emerged; broad union support also was not forthcoming. Furthermore, a management consensus on the desirability of instituting participatory work structures has yet to develop. Again not surprisingly under these conditions, no national debate emerged to broaden the claims being made by isolated intellectuals and foundation officials. Neither the Democratic nor Republican parties or the unions have a platform dealing with the quality of work. The lack of such an agenda precludes the development of choice opportunities involving more comprehensive forms of worker participation. In one major corporation the director of the participatory work program informed me in the late 1970s that their motivation was in part to ensure that the quality of work did not become a political issue leading to legislative solutions. That is, by engaging in voluntary programs, he thought his company would help avoid such an outcome. What we have thus far in the United States is a number of scattered company efforts to introduce worker participation in decision making at the work place. Until recently, these efforts have concentrated mostly among blue-collar workers in nonunion manufacturing plants. Knowledge is often treated as proprietary and information flows between firms are erratic.

Conclusion

First, the more of the major institutional actors (management, labor, and government) committed to innovate in the area of participatory work structures, the more difficult it is to control processes to the satisfaction of each of the parties. There exist multiple realities, based on differential interests (compare Chapter Nine in this volume). As the movement developed in Sweden, both management and labor became increasingly dissatisfied that the means used were not tied to *their* ends, actions were not controlled by *their* intentions, solutions were not guided by imitation of the *right* examples, priorities were *misplaced, proper* feedback did not control subsequent actions, and *proper* lessons were not being drawn from past experience. This dissatisfaction led management to fall back to its own initiatives under the guidance of the technical department of SAF so that a "tightness" in the decision making could replace the "looseness" that prevailed. Similarly, the unions turned to their own legislative initiatives as well, as a means to tighten the system of actions so that their interests might better be served.

In Japan, consensus on the need for participatory work structures developed among managers of major firms without the active involvement of unions and government. This made it considerably easier for management to maximize its perceived interests, using organizations such as Nikkeiren and JUSE as its policy instruments. Thus, they were able to develop a tight system in which means and ends were in harmony and intuitive judgments about the correctness of their direction could replace hard measurement of results.

In the United States, with no consensus among any of the major institutional actors, we have a loosely coupled system of firms operating in an environment of great uncertainty. There is no legitimate infrastructure to guide action. The uncertainty and risk involved in innovating encourages tight measurement of results, which in turn tends to increase the risks for personnel involved. Consultants address this environment with a variety of solutions, with managers at a loss to judge the effectiveness of one rather than another product. Solutions, problems, firms, employees, and consultants all float in the system so that there is a quasi-random character to the choice processes, as postulated by the garbage can model. In one sense, because one product (called a "program") succeeds another with regularity, it is assumed that the decisions will be of small consequence.

There are a number of striking similarities in Swedish and Japanese practices with respect to motivation, search, implementation, and evaluation procedures. In both nations there is a relatively tightly organized process of diffusion taking place, especially in Japan, where the self-contained package of participatory practices lent itself to more certainty with respect to inputs and outputs. Here tightness would appear to have been an asset. This is in strong contrast to the U.S. situation, where a certain looseness between means and ends has prevailed, and it would seem to have delayed the diffusion process. Put differently, the Swedish and Japanese cases display fewer of the characteristics of the garbage can model and more of the characteristics of the rational model. Yet, at the same time, in the area of evaluation and measurement, both the Japanese and Swedish managers displayed a relaxed approach, which seemed to facilitate their efforts. In the United States a more demanding approach to measurement and evaluation prevails. I traced this difference to a lack of consensus on the part of the major institutional actors and a mistrust of the utility and feasibility of participatory work structures. In this case, looseness appeared as an asset and tightness, a liability.

Under what conditions does tightness of organization seem to be an asset or a liability in the case of organizational change? Once the Swedes and the Japanese agreed upon basic goals and objectives, it appears that tightness proved an asset in the diffusion process. The building blocks were put into place to achieve the necessary results. There was trial and error learning, but by and large there evolved a set of means appropriate to the intended outcomes. Yet precisely because of the emergent consensus and the rational character of the strategy that developed, they could tolerate considerable looseness in the feedback process. Selective measurement and intuitive evaluations provided the necessary feedback to keep the diffusion process on course. This was in contrast to the United States, where there was a tendency to use measurement to question the very goal of participatory work practices.

It has been noted in previous research that decentralized structures (implying loosely coupled systems) are an asset in the initiation stages of the innovation process, but centralization (implying the possibility of tightly coupled systems) is an asset in the implementation stages (for example, Zaltman, Duncan, and Holbek, 1973). My analysis suggests that even in the implementation stage, looseness can be an asset. For the diffusion process to go forward, the basic questioning of the innovation itself must cease. This implies a certain looseness in the system as relates to evaluation and feedback. But this will not be achieved if there is no basic consensus at least among managers on the advisability of such practices. Herein lies the dilemma: There can be no looseness without consensus and it is difficult to develop consensus without tightness.

The process of diffusion of participatory work structures does not involve a "rational process" whereby large numbers of individual firms spontaneously adjust to new environmental conditions. Rather, organized efforts were involved in spreading information across firms, persuading managers there was a problem to be remedied, and helping them put new practices in place (Cole and Walder, 1981). The process is better described as a social movement in a national polity than one of organizational adjustment. Yet this organized effort is filled with ambiguities with respect to the objectives, technology, and determination of who is to participate in the decisions to innovate. These ambiguities seem particularly strong in the United States, where no high level consensus developed among any of the major institutional actors to create choice opportunities that would lead to the adoption of participatory work practices.

References

Alderfer, C., and Berg, D. "Organization Development: The Profession and The Practitioner." In P. Mirvis and D. Berg (Eds.), *Failures in Organization Development and Change.* New York: Wiley, 1977.

Bendix, R. *Work and Authority in Industry.* New York: Wiley, 1956.

Berg, I., Freedman, M., and Freeman, M. *Managers and Work Reform.* New York: Free Press, 1978.

Berglind, H., and Rundblad, B. "The Swedish Labor Market in Transition." Unpublished manuscript, Department of Sociology, University of Gothenberg, 1975.

Björk, L., Hansson, R., and Hellbert, P. *Ökat inflytande i jobbet [Increased Influence on the Job].* Stockholm: Personaladministrativa Rådet, 1973.

Blauner, R. *Alienation and Freedom.* Chicago: University of Chicago Press, 1964.

Cherns, A. *Using the Social Sciences.* London: Routledge & Kegan Paul, 1979.

Cohen, M., March, J., and Olsen, J. "People, Problems, Solutions, and the Ambiguity of Relevance." In J. March and J. Olsen (Eds.), *Ambiguity and Choice in Organizations.* Bergen, Norway: Universitetsforlaget, 1976.

Cole, R. E. *Work, Mobility, and Participation: A Comparative Study of American and Japanese Industry.* Berkeley: University of California Press, 1979.

Cole, R.E., and Walder, A. "Politics of Participative Work Structures in China, Japan, Sweden, and the United States." Working paper. University of Michigan, 1981.

Davis, L. "Enhancing the Quality of Working Life: Developments in the United States." *International Labour Review,* 1977, *116,* 53–65.

Dickson, P. *The Future of the Workplace.* New York: Weybright and Talley, 1975.

Emery, F., and Trist, E. "Socio-Technical Systems." In F. Emery (Ed.), *Systems Thinking.* London: Penguin, 1969.

Ford Foundation, "The Quality of Working Life." *Ford Foundation Letter,* September 1975, pp. 2–3.

Forsebäck, L. *Industrial Relations and Employment in Sweden.* Stockholm: Swedish Institute, 1976.

Gardell, B. *Produktionsteknik och arbetsglädje [Production Technology, Alienation and Mental Health].* Stockholm: Personnel Administrative Council, 1971.

Gardell, B. *Arbetsinnehåll och livskvalitet [Work Content and the Quality of Life].* Stockholm: Bokförlaget Prisma, 1976.

Goodman, P. *Assessing Organizational Change.* New York: Wiley, 1979.

Gunzburg, D., and Hammerström, O. "Swedish Industrial Democracy, 1977: Progress and New Government Initiatives." In International Council for the Quality of Working Life (Ed.), *Working on the Quality of Working Life.* Boston: Martinns Nijhoff, 1979.

Gyllenhammar, P. *People at Work.* Reading, Mass.: Addison-Wesley, 1977.

Hammerström, O. "Joint Worker-Management Consultation, the Case of LKAB, Sweden." In L. Davis and A. Cherns (Eds.), *The Quality of Working Life.* New York: Free Press, 1975.

Health, Education, and Welfare Special Task Force. *Work in America.* Cambridge, Mass.: M.I.T. Press, 1972.

Hirota, K., and Ueda, T. *Shōshudan katsudō no riron to jissai [The Theory and Actual Practice of "Small-Groupism"].* Tokyo: Japan Personnel Association, 1975.

Hirsch, P. "Processing Fads and Fashions: An Organization-Set Analysis of Cultural Industry Systems." *American Journal of Sociology,* 1972, 77, 639–659.

Industrial Union Department, AFL-CIO. *Viewpoint,* 1978, 8 (Third Quarter).

Jenkins, D. *Industrial Democracy in Europe.* Geneva: Business International, 1974.

Jönsson, B. "Various Corporate Approaches to the Quality of Working Life—The Volvo Experience." Paper presented at the Third National Conference on Business Ethics, Bentley College, Waltham, Massachusetts, 1979.

Karlsson, L. E. *Demokrati på arbetsplatsen [Democracy at the Workplace].* Stockholm: Prisma, 1969.

Kobayashi, K., and Burke, W. "Organizational Development in Japan." *Columbia Journal of Business,* Summer 1976, pp. 113–123.

Kobayashi, S. *Soni wa hito o ikasu [Sony Revives Its Employees].* Tokyo: Japan Management Publishing Company, 1965.

Kohn, M. "Occupational Structure and Alienation." *American Journal of Sociology,* 1976, 82, 111–130.

Kondo, Y. "Common Lines [sic] and Differences in the Swedish Job Reform and Japanese QC Circle Activities." *European Organization of Quality Control,* May 1976, pp. 9–16.

Kornhauser, A. *Mental Health of the Industrial Worker.* New York: Wiley, 1965.

Korpi, W. *Varför strejkar arbetarna? [Why Do Workers Strike?].* Stockholm: Tidens Förlag, 1970.

Landsorganisation. *Arbetsorganisation [Work Organization].* Stockholm: Tiden, 1976.

Lawler, E. "The New Plant Revolution." *Organizational Dynamics*, Winter 1978, pp. 3–12.

Lindestad, H., and Norstedt, J. P. *Produktionsgrupper och premielön* [Production Groups and Premium Wages]. Stockholm: Swedish Employers' Federation, 1972.

Mansfield, E. *The Economics of Technological Change.* New York: Norton, 1968.

March, J., and Olsen, J. (Eds.). *Ambiguity and Choice in Organizations.* Bergen, Norway: Universitetsforlaget, 1976.

March, J., and Simon, H. (Eds.). *Organizations.* New York: Wiley, 1958.

Meyer, J., and Rowan, B. "Institutionalized Organizations: Formal Structure as Myth and Ceremony." *American Journal of Sociology,* 1977, *3*, 340–363.

Miller, R., and Sawers, D. *The Technical Development of Modern Aviation.* New York: Praeger, 1970.

Minami, R. *The Turning Point in Economic Development: Japan's Experience.* Tokyo: Kinokuniya Bookstore, 1973.

Ministry of Labor. *Koyō kanri shindan shihyō [Indicators of the Conditions of Employment Administration].* Tokyo: Employment Security Office, 1974.

Mirvis, P., and Berg, D. (Eds.). *Failures in Organization Development and Change.* New York: Wiley, 1977.

Myrdal, H. G. "SAF's rapporter ingen forskning" ["SAF's Reports Are Not Research"]. *Dagens Nyheter,* November 22, 1977.

Nakayama, S. (Ed.). *Zen'in sanka keiei no kangaekata to jissai [All-Employee Participation in Management: Viewpoints and Practices].* Tokyo: Japan Federation of Employers Association, 1972.

"The New Industrial Relations." *Business Week,* May 11, 1981, pp. 84–98.

Odaka, K. "Shōshudan jishukanri taisei o mezashite" ["Toward a System of Autonomous Work Groups: A Guideline for Workers' Participation at the Shop Level"]. *Nihon Rōdōkyōkai Zasshi,* 1977a, *19*, 2–15.

Odaka, K. "Shōshudan jishukanri taisei o mezashite" ["Toward a System of Autonomous Work Groups: A Guideline for Workers' Participation at the Shop Level"]. *Nihon Rōdōkyōkai Zasshi,* 1977b, *19*, 21–34.

Odaka, K. "Shōshudan jishukanri taisei o mezashite" ["Toward a System of Autonomous Work Groups: A Guideline for Workers' Participation at the Shop Level"]. *Nihon Rōdōkyōkai Zasshi*, 1977c, *19*, 2-16.

Ozawa, T. "Technical Adaptations in Japan's Synthetic-Fiber Industry." Paper presented to the Conference on Japanese Technology Transfer, sponsored by the Social Science Research Council, Kona, Hawaii, 1978.

Palm, G. *Ett år på LM [A Year at L.M. Ericsson]*. Stockholm: Författare Förlaget, 1972.

Palm, G. *Bokslut från LM [Final Account from L. M. Ericsson]*. Stockholm: Författare Förlaget, 1974.

Palm, G. *The Flight From Work*. London: Cambridge University Press, 1977. (This volume is an English language abridgement of the two Swedish volumes.)

Patchin, R. "Consultants: Good and Bad." *Quality Circles Journal*, 1981, *4*, 11-12.

Rein, M. *Social Science and Public Policy*. Harmondsworth, England: Penguin, 1976.

Rein, M., and Marris, P. *Dilemmas of Social Reform*. (2nd ed.) Hawthorne, N.Y.: Aldine, 1973.

Rieker, W., and Sullivan, S. "Can the Effectiveness of QC Circles Be Measured?" *Quality Circles Journal*, 1981, *4*, 29-31.

Rogers, E., and Shoemaker, F. *Communication of Innovations*. (2nd ed.) New York: Free Press, 1971.

Statistiska Centralbyrån. *Statistisk årsbok 1977 [Statistical Abstract of Sweden 1977]*. Örebro: National Central Bureau of Statistics, 1977a.

Statistiska Centralbyrån. *Statistiska meddelanden [Statistical Communication]*. Series AM-Arbetsmarknad ISSN 0082-0237. June 9. Örebro: National Central Bureau of Statistics, 1977b.

Statistiska Centralbyrån. *Arbetsmarknads-statistisk årsbok 1977 [Yearbook of Labour Statistics 1977]*. Örebro: National Central Bureau of Statistics, 1978.

Strauss, G. "Organizational Development." In R. Dubin (Ed.), *Handbook of Work, Organization, and Society*. Chicago: Rand McNally, 1976.

Swedish Employers' Confederation. *Nya arbetsformer [Job Reform in Sweden]*. Stockholm: Swedish Employers' Confederation, 1975. (English edition available.)

Takezawa, S. "The Quality of Working Life: Trends in Japan." *Labor and Society*, 1976, *1*, 29–48.

Thorsrud, E., and Emery, F. *Medinflytande och engagemang in arbetet [Participation and Engagement in Work]*. (Original title *Mot en ny bedriftsorganisasjon.*) Stockholm: Utvecklingsrådet för samarbetsfrågor, 1969.

"Two California Firms Find That Attention to Quality Pays Off." *New York Times*, December 8, 1981, p. D4.

Walton, R. "The Diffusion of New Work Structures: Explaining Why Success Didn't Take." *Organizational Dynamics*, 1975, Winter, pp. 3–22.

Walton, R. "Teaching an Old Dog Food New Tricks." *Wharton Magazine*, Winter, 1978, pp. 38–47.

Williams, J. "A Life Spent on One Problem." *New York Times*, November 26, 1978, p. F5.

Wool, H. "What's Wrong with Work in America." *Monthly Labor Review*, 1973, *96*, 38–44.

Zaltman, G., Duncan, R., and Holbek, J. *Innovations and Organizations*. New York: Wiley, 1973.

□ □ □ □ □ □ □ 6

Creating Long-Term Organizational Change

□ □ □ □ □ □ □ □ □ □ □ □ □ □ □ □ □ □

Paul S. Goodman
James W. Dean, Jr.

This chapter is about the institutionalization of organizational change. It is concerned with the persistence of organizational change. Lewin (1951) describes change in terms of three processes —unfreezing, moving, and refreezing. Institutionalization is concerned with the process of refreezing. After a new policy or program is introduced into an organization, we plan to focus on factors that affect its persistence. A whole series of questions underlies this problem statement: What does institutionalization or persistence mean? How do we describe different degrees of institutionalization? What critical processes affect institutionalization? What are the critical predictors? These questions serve to organize this discussion.

In this, as in any study, it is important to limit the scope of inquiry. First, we will examine only the persistence of behavior within organizations. Persistence of individual behavior or social

This chapter and the Organizational Change Conference held at the Graduate School of Industrial Administration, Carnegie-Mellon University, Pittsburgh, Pennsylvania, on May 19–20, 1981, are supported in part by ONR Grant N00014-79-C-0167.

institutions (Meyer and Rowan, 1977) is excluded. Second, we will limit our inquiry to instances of planned organizational change. That is, we are interested only in the case in which some planned change is introduced by any of the organization's constituencies; changes emanating from random variation or maturation are excluded. Third, we will examine only cases in which the change was intended to be long term. There are many organizational situations where change is intended to be temporary or short run; these situations also are excluded.

Significance

If one is interested in creating long-term organizational change, an understanding of the processes that bring about this long-term change is critical. Unfortunately, a review of the literature indicates there are few, if any, well-developed models to explain or predict degrees of institutionalization (Goodman, Bazerman, and Conlon, 1979). This is not to say that there are not intellectual pieces that deal with the persistence of change. Berger and Luckman's (1966) concept of reciprocal typification, Granovetter's (1978) threshold concept, Kiesler's (1971) discussion of commitment, and Walton's (1980) human resource gap are just some of the ideas that bear on the persistence of change. Some of these references deal with definitions of institutionalization, some with processes that affect institutionalization, and some with predictors. Our focus is to develop a unified explanatory model that deals with degrees of institutionalization, processes, and predictors.

There has been a recent spurt of interest in the empirical literature in organizational failures (for example, Mirvis and Berg, 1977). Analyses of change programs' failures represent one way to look at reasons for persistence. Unfortunately, most of these research reports are ex post in their explanations, and those reports focusing solely on failures pick up only pieces of the puzzle. One needs to look at successes as well as failures in similar organizations in order to identify critical predictors. Our focus is to expand the success-failure dichotomy to examine degrees of institutionalization of planned organizational change. It is unlikely that the "success-failure" labels describe the persistence of change.

There are practical reasons for examining the concept of institutionalization. Over the last ten years there has been a proliferation of projects designed to improve overall organizational effectiveness. Many viewed these change efforts in a policy context, as they had potential for improving productivity and quality of working life at the national level. Many of these projects were bold and innovative. Unfortunately, the most optimistic "bottom line" is that these projects, although initially successful, often did not persist over time (Goodman, Bazerman, and Conlon, 1979; Mirvis and Berg, 1977; Walton, 1975, 1980). If organizational innovations and change are to represent one strategy for improving productivity and quality of working life, then we need to understand the forces that lead to long-run organizational change. Our orientation is not specifically toward large-scale productivity or "QWL" change projects, but toward any type of organizational change. The persistence of organizational change is a pervasive organizational problem. It is important in dealing with the introduction of new technology, new information systems (Keen, 1981), or new financial systems.

Chapter Organization and Orientation

The chapter is divided into two sections—a theory section and an empirical section. In the first section we will outline a definition and a framework for studying institutionalization and then detail the critical processes. In the second section we will present data from nine organizations that were included in a study of planned change. The information from these case studies can be used to illustrate degrees of institutionalization. Other studies on institutionalization will also be incorporated into this analysis.

The products of this chapter flow from an earlier work on institutionalization (Goodman, Bazerman, and Conlon, 1979). In that endeavor we constructed a framework for institutionalization and then presented a literature review organized around that framework. The next step was to use that framework for organizing data collected in the nine organizations. Both collection and analysis of these data provided new insights into the processes of institutionalization, which in turn led to revisions in our theoretical orientation. This chapter, then represents an evolution from our first effort and is more a product of both inductive and deductive processes.

Conceptual Framework

Institutionalization Defined. Institutionalization is examined in terms of specific behaviors or acts. We are assuming here that the persistence of change programs can be studied by analyzing the persistence of the specific behaviors associated with each program. For example, job switching is a set of behaviors often associated with autonomous work groups. To say that the behaviors associated with a program are no longer practiced is to say that the program no longer persists. An institutionalized act is defined as a behavior that is performed by two or more individuals, persists over time, and exists as a social fact (Goodman, Bazerman, and Conlon, 1979). Behavior as a social fact means that it exists external to any individual as part of social reality, that is, it is not dependent on any particular individual. An institutionalized act is a structural phenomenon. Persistence in the context of planned organizational change refers to the probability of evoking an institutionalized act given a particular stimulus and the functional form of that response rate over time. Persistence is not an all-or-nothing phenomenon; there are clearly degrees of persistence that can be identified in terms of response rates over time (Goodman, Bazerman, and Conlon, 1979).

The defining characteristics of an institutionalized act are *performance by multiple actors, persistence,* and *its existence as a social fact.*

Degrees of Institutionalization. An act is not all or nothing; it may vary in terms of its persistence, the number of people in the social system performing the act, and the degree to which it exists as a social fact. The problem in some of the current literature on change is the use of the words *success* or *failure.* This language clouds the crucial issue of representing and explaining degrees or levels of institutionalization. Most of the organizational cases we have reviewed cannot be described by simple labels of success or failure. Rather, we find various degrees of institutionalization. Indeed, an issue in collecting data about institutionalization is knowing how to operationalize this variation. That is, the problem in the field is not whether a change program persists, but how to represent the degree of its persistence. Although this problem confronted us in deciding how to measure institutionalization, its resolution is more conceptual than empirical.

The basic questions are, then: What do we mean by degrees of institutionalization? How do we represent these variations? Our conceptualization is based on the following five facets of institutionalization. The presence or absence of these facets explains the degree of institutionalization.

The first is knowledge of the behavior. Institutionalization is defined in terms of acts or behaviors. This facet focuses on the extent to which an individual has knowledge of a particular behavior. In other words, does the individual know enough about the behavior to be able to perform it and to know what to expect to happen if he or she does? For example, in several of the organizations in which we collected data, the change programs were directed toward the development of autonomous work groups. Within the label of autonomous work groups there is a wide range of new behaviors, such as job switching, and group decision making on bringing in new members, disciplining members, and planning work. Knowledge refers to the cognitive representations people have of these behaviors. Because institutionalization is a social construction of reality, we are interested in the extent to which there are common cognitive representations of each behavior among participants in the relevant social system.

The second facet is performance. In any change program there are new behaviors to be performed, given some common stimulus. One measure of the degree of institutionalization is the extent to which each behavior is performed across the participants in the social system. If job switching or intergroup communication were part of the intended change, we could look for the number of people performing the behavior as a measure of institutionalization. Behavior frequency might be another indicator, but there are certain cautions to keep in mind. In some change situations certain behavior may be low-frequency events. Failure to observe these behaviors at any point does not indicate they are not institutionalized. For example, in an autonomous work group, production decisions may be made daily, but hiring decisions may be made very infrequently. Also, some behaviors may be displayed early in a change program, but their frequency may decline over time. This does not necessarily mean that they are less institutionalized. For example, one dimension of most autonomous work groups is that everyone learns all the other jobs via job switching, a change from the traditional one person–one job format. As a group moves from the traditional structure toward autonomy, there is bound to be a high frequency of switching if the program of change is accepted. Over time, as each person learns all the jobs, people remain on one job but now have the potential to work on other jobs, as in new work configurations. At this point the frequency of the job switching behavior has decreased. This, however, does not mean that the behavior is less institutionalized. The potential for job switching is still in place (that is, known and accepted by social system members), although the actual number of job switches has declined.

A similar problem concerns the evolution of behavior. A particular behavior may be set in place during the early phases of the change program, but it may evolve over time. In one account of an organizational intervention, Goodman (1979) reports that intershift communication was introduced to improve organizational effectiveness. The organizational participants adopted this behavior, and an observer would see each crew member from one shift talking to his counterpart from the next. During the second year of change, crew members talked to their counterparts only if there were production problems. Later, a crew appointed a representative to talk with the representative from the other crews during the shift changes. In this case not only the frequency of the behaviors declined, but the form of the behavior itself changed. Nonetheless, we cannot infer that the behavior is less institutionalized. The function of intershift communication is still being performed.

This discussion of the frequency and evolution of the behavior is important to illustrate the complexity of using behavior as a criterion of institutionalization. Simple frequency counts may not be a useful measure. Delimiting the range of acceptable responses to a stimulus (for example, shift time) is difficult. Unfortunately, there are no general rules for resolving these two issues. Basically, one has to be aware of the complexities of measuring behavior and perform the analysis on a case-by-case basis. In regard to frequency, one should be able to hypothesize about differential behavior rates over different phases of change.

The third facet is preferences for the behavior, which refers to whether the participants like (or dislike) performing the behavior. We introduce this facet because we want to distinguish between private acceptance of a behavior and public performance of that behavior (compare Kiesler and Kiesler, 1969). Performance of a behavior may result from individual or group sanctions. In neither case would the performer privately accept the behavior or be positively disposed to it. We assume some level of private acceptance as reflected in positive dispositions as a necessary condition for institutionalization. The sign and intensity of these dispositions across the participants in a social system represent a way to operationalize this criterion.

The fourth facet is normative consensus. This criterion refers to the extent to which (1) organization participants are aware of others performing the requisite behaviors and (2) there is consensus about the appropriateness of the behavior. The wider the awareness that others are performing the behavior and the wider the consensus that the behavior is appropriate, the greater the degree of institutionalization.

This facet is a representation of social structure. It reflects the extent to which a new behavior has become part of the normative fabric of the organization. The first three criteria are aggregated individual phenomena.

The fifth facet is values. It refers to the social consensus on values relevant to the specific behaviors. Values are conceptions of the desirable, statements about how one ought or ought not to behave. Values are abstractions from more specific normative beliefs. Many of the change activities over the last decade have been based on values of providing people more control over their environment, more freedom and responsibility. The programs themselves have created specific opportunities or behaviors to express these values. The degree to which individuals generalize about these specific acts to endorse these or other values is an important facet of institutionalization. The critical factors for this criterion are the existence of individual values and the awareness that others hold these same values.

The reason for postulating these five facets is to enable us to deal with the question of how to represent different levels of institutionalization. We do not view behaviors as either institutionalized or not, but in terms of degrees of institutionalization. Our use of the five facets is one way to represent the degree or level of institutionalization.

Because the concept of degrees of institutionalization is critical for subsequent analysis, some other distinctions about facets are needed. First, all five facets are analytically independent. Cognitions, behaviors, preferences, norms, and values are independent constructs. Second, there may be an order among the facets that reflects a unidimensional structure. Our argument is as follows: People probably have some cognitive representations of a behavior before it is performed. Performance of a behavior generates experiences, as well as rewards and punishments, that affect people's disposition toward that behavior. As many people perform the behavior, they become aware of others' performance, which leads to consensus about the appropriateness of the behavior. If there is normative consensus about a class of behaviors that reflects a particular value, over time we expect some consensus on that value among organizational participants. Or, stating the obverse, if a new value consensus emerges over time, we would expect that value to be derived from a set of normative behaviors. The normative consensus in turn depends on the private acceptance of that behavior, which in turn reflects experiences from the performance of that behavior. The facets are therefore ordered: knowledge, performance, preferences, norms, and values. We would not expect an act to meet one of the latter criteria without meeting all of those that precede it. This thesis about the structure of the criteria is based on a developmental view of institutionalization that is elaborated in the Appendix to this chapter. Basically, we view the organization in some equilibrium state. Initially, change is introduced primarily through cognitive means (for example, communication). Initial impacts are on individuals' cognitions, behavior, and preferences. Over time, collective awareness and reinforcements lead to normative and value consensus.

A third issue concerns whether we could be more parsimonious with our facets of institutionalization. Given that our definition requires that the behavior be a social fact and that facets four and five are social facts, why could we not use only these two? It is true that the first three facets are more necessary conditions for institutionalization. It could be that all members of a social system have cognitions about a behavior, perform that behavior, and prefer that behavior, and still we would not label that behavior institutionalized.

The argument for using all five criteria is better to understand the process by which behaviors become fully institutionalized, as well as deinstitutionalized. The process is critical. We want to trace through the process by which behaviors become institutionalized or deinstitutionalized. The first three facets can provide better understanding about why a behavior becomes institutionalized. Similarly, changes in cognition, behavior, and preference can contribute to deinstitutionalization. Conceptually or empirically identifying degrees of institutionalization is a complex task. Including facets one through three (which are necessary conditions for institutionalization, not definitions) with facets four and five provides a sharper set of analytical tools to identify degrees of institutionalization. Institutionalization occurs only when facets four (norms) and/or five (values) are in place—meaning that these two facets are part of our definition. All five facets are used to examine the developmental process of institutionalization.

A fourth issue concerns the specification of the set of behaviors used to determine degrees of institutionalization. How do we identify the relevant behaviors to examine the degree of institutionalization? Most change activities have multiple behaviors, some intended, others unintended. The problem is further complicated by the dynamic aspect of change where behaviors continually evolve. If we do not specify the right set of behaviors, we cannot assess the degree of institutionalization. If we assess the degree of institutionalization in terms of five behaviors when the actual set is ten, we would misspecify the level of institutionalization.

There is no easy prescription for this problem. In our earlier work (Goodman, Bazerman, and Conlon, 1979) we addressed this by understanding the model of the change agent and the constituencies supporting the change, as well as the target population. Such an analysis of characteristics of the change activity should shed light on the modal behaviors.

The last issue concerns identification of the relevant social system for measuring degrees of institutionalization. One way to measure institutionalization is the *extent* to which (1) people are aware of others performing behavior and (2) there is consensus about the appropriateness of the behavior. The measure of "extent" requires delineation of the appropriate social system. If the system is misspecified, the assessment of institutionalization will be incorrect. The basic problem is in identifying whether the change should be defined at the subsystem or system level. If the degrees of institutionalization are measured at the subsystem level but the system level is more appropriate for analysis, the assessment of institutionalization will be incorrect. Again, knowledge of the model of the change, the constituencies' views of the change, and observing the process should permit the appropriate identification.

General Framework. Now that we can represent the degree or level of institutionalization, our attention turns to the explanation of this phenomenon. We start with the degree of institutionalization represented by the five facets. Our picture is intentionally simple. For examples, we focus on two behaviors—A and B. A is fully institutionalized in that everyone understands the behavior, performs it, prefers it, and acknowledges that it is held by others, deemed appropriate, and represented by broader value. Although behavior B is understood by all, it is performed by a minority, is not well liked, and exhibits no broad normative consensus. Hence B is less well institutionalized. The question is why we find differences in the degree of institutionalization.

The main independent variables are a set of processes. These have a direct effect on the five institutionalization facets. The processes include

1. *Socialization.* A broad category, socialization includes transmission of information to organizational members about the requisite behaviors and learning mechanisms within individuals that affect the interpretation of information.

2. *Commitment.* Commitment refers to the binding of the individual to behavioral acts. It is a function of the degree of explicitness or deniability of an act, the revocability of the act, whether the act was adopted by personal choice or external constraints, and the extent to which the act is known by others (Kiesler, 1971; Salancik, 1977).

3. *Reward allocation.* Reward allocation refers to the types of rewards related to the behaviors as well as the schedule of their distribution. The allocator could be a proponent or an opponent of the change, and rewards can be allocated to individuals or groups.

4. *Diffusion.* Diffusion refers to the extension and adoption of a new work behavior into a new social system (compare Rogers and Shoemaker, 1971). That is, it concerns the spread of forms of work organization from one setting to another.

5. *Sensing and recalibration.* Sensing and recalibration refers to the processes by which the organization can measure the degree of institutionalization, feed back information, and take corrective action. One of the major themes from our research on institutionalization is that most of the organizations we visited had no mechanism to sense the degree to which their change programs were in place. Therefore, they had no ability to take corrective actions.

Two other classes of variables are incorporated in our framework. The first refers to the *structural aspects of change.* The goals of the change and critical roles (for example, autonomous work groups, survey feedback, team building, and so forth) represent features of the structural aspects of change.

The second category refers to the *characteristics of the organization.* These represent the social context in which the change is introduced and evolves. Existing values, norms, character of labor-management relationships, and skills of the work force all represent factors in this category. (See Figure 1.)

Our framework reflects two assumptions. First, the processes have a direct effect on the facets of institutionalization. Second, the structure of the change and the characteristics of the organization have indirect effects on the criteria through the processes. That is,

Figure 1. A Simple Model of Variables Related to Institutionalization.

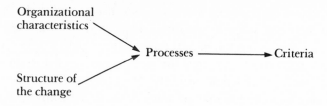

the two structural categories serve as moderators of the change process.

We intentionally have drawn a simple framework in Figure 1; there are no complicated feedback loops to represent the dynamic features of change. Rather, we wanted to create a general map to understanding institutionalization. In the following section further detail will be provided to produce a more "fine grained" understanding of the concept.

Theoretical Processes of Institutionalization

Our focus is on the persistence of change; so we will not consider here the introduction and initial adoption phases of a change program. Our analysis begins with the following general assumptions about the state of the program: Some individuals have adopted the behaviors. These individuals have progressed through the first three degrees of institutionalization. They have some knowledge about the behaviors; they have performed them; and they have some feelings or preferences concerning the behaviors. Others have not adopted the behaviors. They are at the very first stage of institutionalization, that is, they probably have some knowledge of the behaviors. A third group of individuals has entered the organization or department after the change program was introduced. They may have some knowledge of the behaviors, but they have not performed them. Our explanation of the processes of institutionalization will detail the effects of the five processes on these three groups of individuals. To the extent that the processes move them from lower to higher degrees of institutionalization, the change program will be institutionalized.

Socialization. Socialization refers to the transmission of information about beliefs, preferences, norms, and values with respect to the new organizational form. In most discussions of change, socialization plays a major role during the initial introduction phase. However, our interest is in maintaining change over time. In this context, there are two targets for socialization: existing organizational members and new entrants. New forms of work behavior often involve concepts that are both abstract and complex (for example, autonomy). As these concepts often evolve throughout the change program, a continual process of focusing attention on them and their enduring meaning seems a necessary condition for developing higher levels of institutionalization. Failure to resocialize may lead to a decline in beliefs, behaviors, and preferences and hinder the development of norms and values.

A more critical target is the new organizational members. Organizational life is characterized by a continual procession of people through positions. Failure to socialize these individuals formally into the new work behaviors is a major cause of deinstitutionalization. If there is an increasing number of nonparticipants (that is, unsocialized new members), the percentage of those performing the behavior will decline, and the costs of not participating might decline. Granovetter (1978) has argued that as the number of individuals participating in a social act declines, the potential penalty for not participating will also decline, which in turn reduces the number who are participating. Also, there may be more similar others who are not performing the behaviors. This might stimulate social comparison, which would also induce decline. That is, as more similar others decline to participate, the social legitimation for participation also declines. An important determinant of institutionalization is the transmission of knowledge, beliefs, norms, and values across generations. This transmission is critical not only because of the passing of information. The *act of transmission itself* reaffirms validity of that knowledge, those beliefs, and those values. This reaffirmation should both maintain and enhance the level of institutionalization. If old members socialize the new members, the new members will also see that the old members consider the behavior appropriate, thus facilitating norm development.

Commitment. The process of commitment is important to all three of the groups involved in the change. For older members who have adopted the behavior, multiple opportunities for recommitment should be made available, thus enabling this commitment to be strengthened and leading to the development of norms and values. It is also necessary to be careful that those older members who have not adapted do not become committed to *not* performing the behavior. This might happen if they were somehow forced to make explicit public statements that they do not intend to adopt the behavior. This should be avoided because it would make it less likely that these individuals would ever adopt. Finally, commitment opportunities, in which they may select the behavior freely (not as an organizational requirement), explicitly, and in public, should be provided to new members (Salancik, 1977). This generates high commitment, which will lead to stability of change and resistance to change in that behavior.

Another dimension of commitment is the degree to which it exists throughout the total organizational system. Using the hierarchy as one way to represent an organization, we would examine the extent to which participants of all levels were committed to the new form of work behavior. Our basic hypothesis is the greater the total system's commitment, the higher the degree of institutionalization.

Reward Allocation. Reward allocation is another critical process of institutionalization. Three issues seem important. First, the nature of the reward schedule over time should have an effect on the level of institutionalization. The distribution of similar rewards over time may be correlated with declining values. Using a simple adaptation paradigm, we might expect that the attractiveness of rewards, such as variety or pay, may gradually decline over time. This raises another issue concerning the mix of rewards. It may be that the mix of rewards (for example, extrinsic and intrinsic) would impact on the level of institutionalization. If different types of rewards exhibit different functional forms between amount allocated and degree of attractiveness (Alderfer, 1972), then the type of reward should affect the attractiveness of performing a new form of behavior and, hence, the level of institutionalization. Implicit in this discussion of issues one and two is that the effects of reward systems are not constant over time. In particular there may be a need to revise these systems to maintain the level of institutionalization.

The need to revise the reward system depends to some extent on the degree of crystallization of the critical norms and values that support the new forms of work organization. As the norms and values become more pervasive, the role of the explicit reward system may become less pronounced and less in need of revision.

A third issue concerns the degree of equity of the reward system. The acquisition of beliefs and preferences may be hampered by a system with identifiable inequities. Similarly, the development of norms and values is probably facilitated in a system with minimum levels of conflict (inequities) among the members. These issues principally apply to those who have already adopted the behavior.

Diffusion. Diffusion refers to the process by which innovations in one system are transferred to a new system. If change is introduced into a subsystem and the behavior becomes institutionalized, there is some question about the stability of this change within the large system. If the change is incongruent with some of the values, and with the normative preferences of the larger system, forces of counterimplementation may be evoked (Keen, 1981). There is evidence from change studies (for example, Walton, 1980) that these forces can undermine the levels of institutionalization in the target system. Diffusion represents a maintenance and growth strategy and serves two functions. First, by spreading the institutionalized behaviors into other subsystems, the area for counterimplementation strategies is decreased. Second, diffusion requires the affirmation (transmission) of the institutionalized behavior, which should reinforce all five facets.

An alternative to diffusion is to draw a barrier around the initial target system for change (Levine, 1980). This strategy may be viable in loosely coupled systems.

Sensing and Recalibration. We expect variation in the performance of institutionalized acts as well as in the knowledge preferences, norms, or values. Sources of the variation may be random, caused by permanent changes in the organization or environment, or evolutionary. One of the factors we have observed in our empirical cases is that rarely is there any sensing mechanism to measure this variation. Absence of any mechanisms prevents possibilities for recalibration. If forces initiate a process of deinstitutionalization and if no sensing mechanism exists, nothing will abate the decline. The role of sensing and recalibration is to activate the other process (for example, socialization), rather than directly affecting the five facets of institutionalization.

Processes and Antecedents

Before we move to some empirical data, some comments about the relationship between the two classes of antecedent variables and the processes are necessary. (See Figure 1.) The structure of change refers to the modal goals, strategies, tactics, and programs of change. These may vary over the different phases of the change. The basic hypothesis is that the structure of the change affects the processes, which in turn affect degrees of institutionalization. For example, change projects that develop very dependent relationships with external consultants probably will find it more difficult to maintain levels of institutionalization after the consultants leave because the projects will not have developed internal capabilities of resocialization, creation of new commitment opportunities, diffusion, and so forth. Sponsorship probably has a direct effect on the reward allocation process. The departure of a sponsor can change the level and type of reward, which may induce deinstitutionalization. We will trace similar relationships between the variables in this category and the processes in the next section.

The other class of antecedent variables—organizational characteristics—moderates the effect of the processes or the structure of change on the processes. For example, a high degree of environmental instability should affect the size and distribution of the work force. High work force stability should affect the ability to socialize new members into the new forms of work behaviors. Introduction of new behaviors that are at variance with employee skills or values increases the costs of performing these behaviors. We trace these and other effects in the following section, which presents data from our study and from previous work about degrees of institutionalization.

Data

Our theoretical discussion is a product of prior work (Goodman, Bazerman, and Conlon, 1979) and some empirical work we did for this chapter. Our strategy for the empirical work was to become immersed in some organizations that were at different levels of institutionalization in regard to a change effort. We hoped that the interaction between the prior theoretical work and data would generate new ways of thinking about institutionalization. Although in other cases we have argued for formal model testing (Goodman, Atkin, and Schoorman, 1982), in this case we are using data to generate ideas. We have also included in this section results of other research that is related to our model. We have provided a brief summary of the information we collected and its relationship to the previous theoretical discussions, as well as to the results of other studies.

Data were collected from nine organizations that had been involved in some major change effort generally focused on improving quality of working life and productivity. Because our sampling strategy determined the kinds of data we collected and subsequently our views on institutionalization, it is necessary to be explicit about the plan. First, we selected organizations involved in some substantial organizational change (*substantial* means that the change led to a modification in multiple organizational dimensions, such as authority, decision making, or communication). Second, we looked at organizations that were four to five years into their change effort. In all cases, many of the change activities were in place and some data on consequences (generally positive) were available. Therefore, we are not looking at organizations in which the change activities were initially blocked and never really got started. Third, we selected organizations in which there was documentation over the life of the change effort. Because we were taking only a brief snapshot, it was important to be able to understand the total historical context of the program. Fourth, we selected a sample that was heterogeneous in terms of type of organization, target population, and type of change. The nine firms are drawn from both the private and public sectors. Some are unionized; others are not. The target population ranges from primarily production workers to primarily managerial, with varied mixes among blue-collar, white-collar, professional, and managerial workers.

Data were collected by interviews. The framework for the interview schedule was designed from our first essay on institutionalization (Goodman, Bazerman, and Conlon, 1979) and focused primarily on measures of the degree of institutionalization and predictors of degrees of institutionalization. Because the change activities were different across organizations, the schedule had to be changed to fit the setting. However, in all cases, we looked for criteria of institutionalization. Therefore, if we learned that a labor-management problem-solving team was part of the change, we developed questions concerning people's knowledge of the team's existence, its functioning, and its consequences. There are some common predictors of institutionalization, such as learning mechanisms used to socialize new members, reward allocation mechanisms, and sponsorship. Questions for these concepts were tailored to the specific site. For each organization, twenty-five to thirty hours of interviews were conducted, with time per interview ranging from thirty minutes to one hour and a half.

Before we examine some of the data on institutionalization, we will briefly review some characteristics of the change programs utilized in these different organizations.

Autonomous work groups were introduced into some of our organizations. Basically, these are self-governing groups organized by process, place, or product. There is a substantial shift in authority and decision making as the group takes over decision making on hiring, discipline, allocation of production tasks, and so forth. Most autonomous groups encourage job switching and pay is by knowledge rather than activities (Goodman, 1979).

Problem-solving hierarchies were another common form of change. In this type of program, a hierarchy of linked problem-solving groups is superimposed on the existing organizational structure. The groups are generally arranged following the current organizational structure, with lower level groups dealing with problems specific to their areas and higher level groups dealing with problems that cut across multiple organizational units. In our sample, these groups met regularly. Products from these groups include

work simplification, flextime projects and new performance apprais-
al systems.

One organization introduced a matrix organization with
quality control circles. At the factory level, all work was organized
by business teams that generally reflected products or processes. The
team was located in one area, and its membership was composed of
staff and line personnel at the exempt level. The matrix was created
to be sure staff people (engineering) reported to the business team
leader as well as to the staff manager (for example, the head of
engineering). QC circles were linked to the teams and introduced at
the production worker level.

Another organization introduced an elaborate hierarchical
system of teams for strategic planning. This system was called the
parallel organization. The target population in this program was
managers and staff personnel. The parallel organization was a separate organization from the traditional line and staff group. It was
a permanent organization. All members belonged to both the traditional line and staff organization and to the parallel organization,
and each participant had two bosses. Within the parallel organization, there is a mechanism for generating new strategic problems
and a mechanism for auditing the implementation of the plans
adopted to deal with these problems.

One of our organizations introduced a variation of a Scanlon
Plan—a labor-management productivity plan with plantwide
bonuses.

Degrees of Institutionalization. Table 1 summarizes some of
our interview data in terms of degrees of institutionalization. Five
different organizational forms were introduced into our sample of
nine organizations. Autonomous work groups and problem-solving
hierarchies were the most common forms, but their specific form
varied by organization. Within a given form, such as problem-
solving hierarchies, we find organizations producing very different
products or services.

The table is also arranged according to the facets of institutionalization. *Knowledge* refers to the degree to which organizational participants understand the proposed organizational form
(for example, autonomous work groups) and its requisite behaviors
(job switching). *Behavior* refers to the extent to which a behavior is

Table 1. Degrees of Institutionalization.

Organizational Form	Knowledge	Behavior	Personal Dispositions	Normative Consensus	Value Consensus
1. Autonomous Work Group	very low	none	none	none	none
2. Problem-Solving Hierarchy	very low	very low	very low	none	none
3. Problem-Solving Hierarchy	medium	low	mixed	very low	none
4. Problem-Solving Hierarchy	medium-high	low-medium	mixed	low	none
5. Matrix-Production Business Team	medium-high	low	low	very low	none
6. Problem-Solving Hierarchy	high	medium-high	medium	medium	low
7. Autonomous Work Group	high	moderate	medium	low-medium	none
8. Parallel	high	high	medium-high	medium	none
9. Bonus Productivity	high	high	medium-high	medium-high	low

performed. *Personal disposition* refers to the extent to which people like and privately accept the new behavior. *Normative consensus* refers to the degree to which multiple others view the behavior as appropriate. *Value consensus* indicates the degree of consensus concerning an abstracted concept (for example, autonomy, cooperation) derived from specific behavior included in the other criteria.

We operationalized the criteria by estimating the percentage of people (that is, those we interviewed) in each of the five categories. Because the data do not provide opportunities for refined measurement, we used gross categories—low (0-33 percent), medium (34-66 percent), high (67-100 percent). Also, our judgments are aggregated across behaviors for any site. That is, there is a large number of behaviors included in the form designated as autonomous work groups. A low rating means that less than one third of the people are performing any of the behaviors. A high classification means that most of the people are performing all the behaviors. The only other code used is mixed, and it appears in the personal disposition category. *Mixed* means that, although the new behavior has acquired a certain amount of support, there is also a clearly recognizable opposition to it.

Table 1 is ordered in terms of degrees of institutionalization, with a program of autonomous work groups exhibiting no signs of institutionalization five years after its inception and a bonus productivity plan exhibiting the highest level of institutionalization. Most of the nine organizational forms were introduced at the same time, and all experienced a period of success.

The first significant observation from this array of data is that five of the nine sites exhibit low levels of institutionalization, as measured by the behavior criterion. Only two of the nine exhibit moderate to high levels of institutionalization. These are congruent with other reports (Hinrichs, 1978; Walton, 1980) that it is difficult to maintain organizational change over time.

A second observation is that there is some order among the institutionalization criteria. If knowledge is not present (that is, medium or above), the other categories are labeled low or none. If behavior is not present, the remaining categories are similarly labeled. If behavior is present, the knowledge category is present. If the personal disposition category is not present, the remaining categories are not present. If personal dispositions are present, so are the preceding categories. Basically, there appears to be some unidimensionality among the criteria, resembling a Guttman scale.

Degrees of Institutionalization and Critical Processes. Table 2 presents the organizational forms arranged by degrees of institutionalization and by the critical processes. The basic theme in our theoretical discussion is that the critical processes have a direct effect on the degrees of institutionalization. The table is not presented for hypothesis testing. Rather, we are looking for trends and gross associations.

Socialization. Socialization refers to the transmission of information to organizational members about the new forms of work behavior. Of critical interest for us is transmission after the new

Table 2. Degrees of Institutionalization by Critical Processes: Socialization.

Organizational Form	Socialization— Initial	Socialization— Retraining Old Members	Socialization— Training New Members
1. Autonomous Work Group	high	limited	low
2. Problem-Solving Hierarchy	high	none	none
3. Problem-Solving Hierarchy	high	none	none
4. Problem-Solving Hierarchy	high	none	none
5. Matrix-Production Business Team	high	none	low
6. Problem-Solving Hierarchy	high	none	none
7. Autonomous Work Group	high	none	medium—indirect
8. Parallel	high	none	medium—indirect
9. Bonus Productivity Teams	high	none	medium—indirect

behaviors are in place. The extent to which organizational members must explain to new participants the rationale for the work behaviors should reinforce the existence (or institutionalization) of these behaviors.

As Table 2 indicates, there were no differences among the organizations in their initial socialization programs. All were relatively extensive, as one would expect. The next question was whether formal training programs were planned over time. The idea behind this measure is that some of the knowledge presented early in the program might decay and some form of retraining might be necessary. All these programs had some form of committee structure meeting over time, which obviously would provide some socialization experiences, but only for a few members. Here we are referring to intentional periodic retraining for *all* organizational participants. In the first autonomous work group, there were plans to provide retraining over time. As we moved into year two of that program, there was a noticeable decline in the number of meetings. The other programs did not have a schedule of retraining activities for existing organizational participants.

Golembiewski and Carrigan (1970) report that retraining can facilitate persistence. In a program designed to change the practices of high-level managers in the sales division of a manufacturing firm, they found that a retraining exercise several months after the program was instituted strengthened the persistence of the program. In a similar vein, Ivancevich (1974) compared Management by Objectives programs in two large manufacturing firms. One firm had a retraining exercise; the other had none. After three years, the program in the former plant exhibited greater persistence. There were, however, some differences in the two plants, which makes it difficult to conclude unequivocally that the retraining caused the difference in persistence.

The next question concerns the socialization of new participants who came into the organization after the program was on line. We did not see that any of the programs offered training to these new members that was comparable to the training when the programs were initiated. The features of the organizational forms might have been mentioned in an orientation meeting, but the intensity of this training was much lower than in the introduction of the program.

Given that all the organizational forms are very complicated in terms of operations, beliefs, and values, it is surprising that these organizations did not pay more attention to socialization of new members—a critical feature of institutionalization. A number of laboratory studies have focused on the transmission of organizational culture to successive generations through the passive socialization of new members. Jacobs and Campbell (1961) showed that extreme judgments of the magnitude of the autokinetic effect (introduced by confederates) could be reiterated through several "generations" of subjects. This was accomplished by placing new subjects, one by one, into groups in which the extreme norm existed. Over time, then, the "socialized" became the "socializers." However, the estimates converged on the natural autokinetic norm over successive generations, and all the experimental groups' estimates equaled those of the control group by the tenth generation. This is similar to the decline over time often observed in programs of organizational change. Jacobs and Campbell infer from this that subjects' announced judgments are averages of tradition and their own judgments. Therefore, a norm that has no basis in reality (that is, no "function") is unlikely to become institutionalized. However, one should also observe that there was no formal socialization procedure for the new participants; this may also be important in understanding the decline.

Weick and Gilfillan (1971) employ a similar but slightly different experimental paradigm, dealing with strategies groups use in a game. Two strategies of equal potential effectiveness were used: one easy and one hard. Groups initially assigned the hard strategy eventually abandoned it in favor of the easy one; groups initially assigned the easy strategy were able to maintain it over successive generations. Weick and Gilfillan call the hard strategy "unwarrantedly arbitrary" and argue that such strategies in general will not become institutionalized. The argument is similar to that of Jacobs and Campbell (1961): that tradition alone will not be sufficient to perpetuate a norm if there are better, that is, more functional, norms available. These findings were echoed in a somewhat more complex experiment by MacNeil and Sherif (1976). We may therefore revise our statement about the necessity for socialization of new members. Socialization mechanisms may not be necessary if the desired behaviors are easy, comfortable, and obviously functional from the new participant's perspective. But programs of organizational change often contain elements that go against the grain of existing work cultures. It is in this situation that socialization programs are badly needed but are rarely found. The decline of work innovations and the reversion to more commonly accepted forms of organization as new members are introduced should therefore not be surprising.

Another way to conceptualize training of new members is to determine the extent to which they would be forced to learn about the new organizational form. In the organizations with the highest level of institutionalization (refer to organizational forms 7–9 in the tables), it would be very difficult for a new participant not to learn about the program. In the bonus productivity teams, a monthly bonus meeting is held with all participants. The new participants are forced to be aware of that organizational form. In the parallel organization, most new participants (given a particular job level) have to participate in one of the parallel problem-solving groups. Because these groups are independent and permanent and are supervised by a different person from the one on their line job, it is hard not to learn about the parallel organization. Also, this organization has extensive manuals explaining the functioning of this form, as well as audiovisual presentations that facilitate the training of new members. In the autonomous work group program (organizational form 7), the pay system is designed to force people to learn about the functioning of autonomous work groups. In the other organizations, it is easier to enter the organization without learning about the organizational form. In problem-solving groups, for example, it is unlikely that a new member would participate in one of the groups. Unless the participant conversed with an active participant, learning would not occur.

Commitment. Commitment refers to the binding of individuals to behavioral acts. Higher levels of commitment should enhance the degrees of institutionalization (see Table 3). We divided commitment into three categories. To what extent did the adoption of the new behavior reflect personal choice or an organizational requirement? The more it reflected personal choice, the greater the commitment. The data, not surprisingly, show a greater frequency of personal choices. What is different is that one of the most institu-

Table 3. Degrees of Institutionalization by Critical Processes: Commitment.

Organizational Form	Source	Commitment Opportunities	Target
1. Autonomous Work Group	personal choice, organizational requirement	initially limited, later total	lower
2. Problem-Solving Hierarchy	personal choice	lmited	lower
3. Problem-Solving Hierarchy	personal choice	limited	lower
4. Problem-Solving Hierarchy	personal choice	limited	lower
5. Matrix-Production Business Team	personal choice, organizational requirement	total	total
6. Problem-Solving Hierarchy	personal choice	limited	total
7. Autonomous Work Group	personal choice	total	lower
8. Parallel	organizational requirement	total	total
9. Bonus Productivity Teams	personal choice	total	total

tionalized programs are initiated by organizational requirements. The first autonomous work group program demonstrates a more expected trend. The program seemed to grow and develop when personal choices were carried out freely. Later in the program, when organization requirements caused participation, the program began to decline.

We also explored opportunities for commitment, that is, the extent to which an individual had the opportunities to make commitments to the program. Some of the programs created the opportunities for *all* members to participate; others did not. Higher degrees of institutionalization seem to result from total rather than limited opportunities.

If we hold constant the opportunities for commitment, another issue concerns the target of commitment. Organizations varied in terms of whether they tried to get total organizational commitment versus the commitment of a specific group or organizational level. The data seem to indicate that lower levels of institutionalization result from targeting specific groups. Basically, we found that in the first four organizations, most of the focus was on bringing the lower-level participants around to the new organizational culture. Unfortunately, middle and lower-middle managers were either ignored or threatened by the change. Later they introduced counter-implementation strategies (compare Keen, 1981), which worked against institutionalization of the change. Resistance by lower management has been a chronic problem with many QWL programs (Goodman and Lawler, 1977).

Several other studies have noted the impact of commitment on institutionalization. For example, Ivancevich (1972) attributes the failure of one Management by Objectives program to a lack of commitment by top management. Walton (1980) notes the high level of commitment in several successful programs of work innovation. Research on commitment is not limited to organizational studies. Kiesler (1971) and his associates have performed several experiments on commitment that bear directly on institutionalization. In one set of experiments, it was demonstrated that attacking someone's beliefs will have differential effects, depending on the strength of the commitment. If someone is weakly committed to a belief, attacking the belief will make the commitment weaker. However, individuals who are strongly committed will become even stronger when attacked. New individuals in the work group may represent an attack on the group's beliefs because they have not yet been socialized. If group members are only weakly committed to the change program, this mild attack may further weaken their commitment. However, groups that are fairly strongly committed will become even stronger when new members are added. This has obvious policy implications for the timing of the entry of new members, as well as for the choice of socialization agents.

Reward System. The type of reward system can affect the degree of institutionalization. Our first subcategory concerns whether the rewards are primarily intrinsic or extrinsic. Although there may be some controversy about classifying rewards this way, we were basically interested in whether rewards that were internally mediated, externally mediated, or some combination of these were related to the degrees of institutionalization. Table 4 seems to indicate that organizational forms that mixed both internally and externally mediated rewards exhibited higher levels of institutionalization. This finding is not so obvious if you examine the context in which most of these plans were introduced. The major themes were to provide workers more autonomy, responsibility, control over their environment, challenge, and feelings of accomplishment—all internally mediated rewards. The assumption was that these rewards would be sufficient to drive any new organizational form. The information in Table 4 questions that assumption. Goodman (1979) and Walton (1978) also question the assumption that internally mediated rewards are sufficient to facilitate institutionalization. In both of the programs studied by these authors, the lack of extrinsic rewards seriously hampered the process. The rationale for both sets of rewards may be as follows: I will increase my effort and performance quality with new opportunities for accomplishment and challenge. Over time, the organization should benefit from my new contributions. Given a general contributions inducements framework, I might expect some additional inducements to compensate for my contributions.

A second issue concerns the contingency between behavior and rewards. That is, if a person adopts one of the requisite behaviors (attending group meetings, solving problems, assuming leader-

Table 4. Degrees of Institutionalization by Critical Processes: Reward Allocation.

Organizational Form	Types	Reward Allocation Contingency Behavior—Reward	Problems of Inequity
1. Autonomous Work Group	primarily intrinsic	medium	yes
2. Problem-Solving Hierarchy	primarily intrinsic	medium	no
3. Problem-Solving Hierarchy	primarily intrinsic	medium	yes
4. Problem-Solving Hierarchy	primarily intrinsic	medium	no
5. Matrix-Production Business Team	primarily intrinsic	medium	no
6. Problem-Solving Hierarchy	primarily intrinsic	medium	no
7. Autonomous Work Group	intrinsic/extrinsic	high	no
8. Parallel	intrinsic/extrinsic	high	no
9. Bonus Productivity Teams	intrinsic/extrinsic	high	no

ship roles), to what extent is that behavior linked with a reward? Although our interview data are not as robust in this area, some observations can be made. First, all nine programs have a common set of internally mediated rewards—autonomy, responsibility, challenge, variety, accomplishment. Second, some of these rewards are more related to participating in a program than to producing (see March and Simon, 1958). That is, the amounts of autonomy do not covary with the amounts of problem-solving behavior, job switching, and so forth. Some internally mediated rewards (for example, accomplishment) do covary with successful problem solving or job switching. The point is that there is not as high an across-the-board contingency between behaviors and the internally mediated rewards found in most of these organizational forms as one might expect. Hence the rating of medium for this column.

The extrinsic rewards, particularly pay, are more closely linked to the requisite behaviors. In the bonus productivity teams plan (organizational form 9), production behaviors such as effort, coordination, and suggestion making are linked to monthly bonuses that serve monetary and recognition functions. In the autonomous work group (organizational form 7), both group and production behaviors are clearly linked to a pay system. Therefore, it seems that there are closer contingencies in the last three organizations. This occurs not because extrinsic rewards are more prevalent, but because there was a conscious attempt to link them to program behaviors. The importance of this link between performance and outcomes has been a dominant theme in the literature on motivation (Vroom, 1964) and effectiveness of pay systems (Lawler, 1971). In general, the stronger and more consistent this link, the more adherence there will be to the behaviors in question.

A final concern under reward allocation processes is the potential for problems of inequity. In a change program with the scope of those we are studying, new behaviors are undertaken, new skills are acquired, and new rewards are provided. It is therefore extremely difficult for an organization to maintain the delicate balance that marks an equitable reward system. Inequity may be perceived among subsystems if one group has started to accumulate new rewards unavailable to other groups. It may also occur within a given subsystem as new and inequitable patterns of reward allocation become obvious to those working closely together. In the present study, we noted the occurrence of problems of inequity (Table 4). These problems were found in only two of the sites, neither of which exhibited very high levels of institutionalization.

Results of other studies have shown that new programs often become complicated by questions of equity. For example, Locke, Sirota, and Wolfson (1976) report that a job-enrichment program in a government agency did not become institutionalized, mainly because the workers were not compensated financially for the new skills they had learned. They had never been promised more money, but the fact that they were accomplishing more for the same pay was perceived as inequitable. Goodman (1979) reports similar problems in a program to develop autonomous work groups in a coal mine. Part of the program involved job switching, whereby everyone would eventually learn all the jobs in the crew. The problem was that the entire crew was to be paid at the same (higher) rate, which originally was paid only to certain crew members. Because it had taken years for some of the men to attain this rate, they felt it inequitable that the other crew members should come upon it so easily. This led to resistance to the program.

The third issue we considered is whether any of the programs had developed mechanisms to deal with the "novelty" problem. In the theoretical discussion, we examined the diminishing value of rewards over time. When a program starts, the new rewards have a high novelty and attractiveness. But as one adapts to the level of these rewards, they may be perceived as less valuable (Lawler, 1971). We wondered whether any of our programs had mechanisms to revise the type and schedule of reward. None of our sites used such a mechanism. Walton (1980) shows how adaptation to reward levels can lead to increasing perceptions of inequity; so in the absence of this type of mechanism, perceptions of inequity are increasingly likely over time.

Diffusion. Diffusion refers to the spread of an innovation from one system to another. The significance of diffusion is that it helps lock in behavior. As other systems perform the new behavior, it legitimates the performance of that behavior (that is, enhances normative consensus) in the focal system. If the new behavior is performed in isolation with respect to other adjacent systems, counterimplementation strategies may be evoked in these other systems against the new behavior.

In our analysis, we distinguished between diffusion within the target system and diffusion external to that system. *Within* target diffusion means that the change was introduced into one section of the target system and would be spread throughout the target system. Diffusion external to the target system refers to spreading the organizational form to other independent organizational units that have some formal connection to the focal unit. For example, the organization with the bonus productivity plan is one of nine plants in a common division. Diffusion in this context refers to whether those eight organizational units adopt the bonus productivity plan or some variant.

Table 5 shows our rating of the extent of diffusion. The label NR (not relevant) means that no diffusion would be expected. If an organizational form were introduced into the whole target system, there would be no room for diffusion. If an organization were not linked to other external units, there would be no room for external diffusion.

For *within* target diffusion, the data are difficult to interpret because of the frequency of the NR. Remember, however, that the NR in this context means that, in those organizations, there has been a total system intervention. In cases one through four, there has been an initial partial system intervention with only low to medium levels of success in further diffusing the new forms of work organization. Also, in these organizations there were either negative attitudes displayed toward the new behaviors by members of the "out" group or counterimplementation strategies directed against the "in" groups performing the new behaviors. It would seem that in partial interventions, failure to diffuse may lead to a decrease in institutionalization. Goodman (1979) has demonstrated this. In this study, when the intervention failed to diffuse beyond the original target group, it was perceived as inappropriate and failed to become institutionalized.

In the column on diffusion to external systems, there are no clear trends. The most- and least-institutionalized organizations conform to our expectation that greater diffusion would facilitate

Table 5. Degrees of Institutionalization and Diffusion.

Organizational Form	Within Target System	External Target System	Sensing Follow-Up
1. Autonomous Work Group	low	none	none
2. Problem-Solving Hierarchy	low	NR	none
3. Problem-Solving Hierarchy	medium	low-medium	none
4. Problem-Solving Hierarchy	medium	NR	none
5. Matrix-Production Business Team	NR	none	none
6. Problem-Solving Hierarchy	NR	low-medium	none
7. Autonomous Work Group	NR	none	low-medium
8. Parallel	NR	low	high
9. Bonus Productivity Teams	NR	high	high

institutionalization, but the data on other organizational forms are too varied.

Sensing and Recalibration. Sensing and recalibration refer to the processes of determining whether the new forms of work behavior are performed and generating corrective actions to ensure that the behaviors are in place. A striking but not unusual finding gathered during our data collection was that there often was a wide discrepancy between the behaviors intended by the specific organizational form and the actual behaviors. Most of the organizational forms identified in Table 5 did not have sensing or feedback mechanisms to examine the performance of the new forms of work behavior. Only in organizations nine and ten do we find both auditing mechanisms and specific mechanisms to recalibrate the change. Walton (1980) claims, on the basis of four case studies of innovation, that the absence of such mechanisms is a major impediment to the process of institutionalization.

Structure of Change. In our theoretical discussion, we identified two antecedent variables that affect the degree of institutionalization through their impact on the process variables: the structure of change and organizational characteristics. The structure of change refers to some of the unique characteristics of the change activities. Table 6 presents the organizational forms by structural characteristics of the change program.

The goals for each program were analyzed in terms of whether they had a broad or a specific focus. We speculated that a broad, multiple set of goals would complicate the process of socialization and reward allocation. A problem in any analysis of goals is whose perspective is most valid because different perspectives or constituencies provide different goal statements. We took the point of view of the dominant coalition in determining the set of goals for analysis. Another problem in measuring goals is whether to accept stated goals or operational goals. We accepted the publicly stated goals that generally appeared in some written document. The data in Table 6 seem to indicate that change programs with more specific goals exhibit higher levels of institutionalization. Specificity means that there is greater attention to fewer goals and/or the goals that are more easily operationalized. In the case of the bonus productivity teams, the principal focus is on increasing productivity. The bonus

Table 6. Degrees of Institutionalization and Diffusion.

Organizational Form	Goals	Change Program	Initial Target	Consultant	Sponsor	Internal Support System
1. Autonomous Work Group	diffuse	medium programmed	subsystem	external	present	none
2. Problem-Solving Hierarchy	diffuse	medium	subsystem	external	absent	none
3. Problem-Solving Hierarchy	diffuse	medium	subsystem	external	absent	none
4. Problem-Solving Hierarchy	diffuse	medium	subsystem	external	absent	yes
5. Matrix-Production Business Team	specific	low-medium	total	external-T	absent	yes
6. Problem-Solving Hierarchy	diffuse	medium-high	total	external-T	present	none
7. Autonomous Work Group	specific	high	total	internal	present	yes
8. Parallel	specific	high	total	internal-external-T	present	yes
9. Bonus Productivity Teams	specific	high	total	external-T	present	none

formula provides a monthly account of whether that goal was achieved. The diffuse label was attached to programs with (1) multiple primary goals (one program had five goals, which included measuring productivity, safety, job skills) and (2) less operational goals, such as personal growth, individualization.

We looked at other characteristics of goals, such as whether they were written, and found no relationships with institutionalization. Another characteristic was whether goals were common or complementary (Goodman, 1979). Common goals are congruent with the interests of all participants (for example, safety). Complementary goals are trade-off goals; one party gets one goal (for example, increased productivity) and the other gets a different goal (increased income). We found no relationship between institutionalization and the common/complementary distinction.

The next factor reflects the extent to which the mechanisms of the change are programmed. By *mechanism* we refer to structural features of the organizational form. The parallel organization is composed of a hierarchy of groups. An autonomous work group is defined by the set of self-governing decisions made by that group. In highly programmed organizational forms (for example, the parallel), the design, composition, meeting time, intergroup relationships, and procedures for initiating a meeting would appear in detail and in written documents. The information in Table 6 indicates that programs that are more highly programmed are also more institutionalized.

The third factor concerns whether the target of change was the total system or a subsystem. The problem with subsystem change is that it is more susceptible to counterimplementation activities and hence lower levels of institutionalization. Table 6 indicates that organizational forms with total system interventions appear to persist longer than those with subsystem intervention. In organizations one through four, there were counterimplementation strategies initiated against the proposed new forms of work organization.

We also looked at the role of the consultant in terms of whether change was initiated by external or internal consultants. We were also interested in whether the external consultant created a long- or short-term relationship with the organization. In the latter case, the role was to provide expertise on organizational forms, to train organization participants to manage the change, and to legitimate the process via expertise. Most of the organizations used external consultants. Two of the three most institutionalized forms used an internal consultant. Those organizations using a short-term external consultant exhibited higher levels of institutionalization. In organizations using external consultants over a long time period, we found little development of an internal capability for managing change; so when the consultant left the organization, there were major problems in managing change.

Another factor that appears to affect the degree of institutionalization is the presence of a sponsor. The sponsor's function is to initiate, legitimate, and allocate resources to the change. If the sponsor leaves the organization, these functions will no longer be performed, and processes such as commitment and reward allocation will be altered. It appears (Table 6) that the initial sponsor is still present in organizations six through nine, but the initial sponsor has left in organizations with lower levels of institutionalization.

The withdrawal of sponsorship can follow from common organizational practices rather than be inherent to the change project. For example, Crockett (1977) reports a major organizational intervention in the State Department in which substantial changes were observed to persist for years. However, when the project initiator, a political appointee, left office, the organization reverted to its traditional form. The new administrator was not sympathetic to the values and structure of the change program. As program support and legitimacy decreased, the degree of institutionalization declined. Similar effects were reported by Walton (1978) when the sponsors of the famous Topeka Experiment left the organization, and by Levine (1980) when an innovative college president left after instituting a new structure for the school. In some cases, the sponsor left temporarily (Frank and Hackman, 1975); in other cases (Miller, 1975; Walton, 1975), the sponsors focused attention on other organizational matters. A study by Scheflen, Lawler, and Hackman (1971) showed that sometimes middle management will withdraw support from a program because they were not involved in planning for it. This finding is potentially of great importance because many organizational innovations are planned at very high levels of the organization and implemented at the lowest levels. In all cases, however, the persistence of the new structures declined.

The last factor was whether the organization had introduced an internal support system to facilitate the change process. The support system was generally identified by the role of a facilitator who worked directly with the organizational participants included in the change and who could move across different organizational levels to gain commitment, resolve conflicts, and legitimate the change activities. The findings on this factor seem inconclusive.

Organizational Characteristics. There is a set of organizational characteristics that can moderate the impact of the change processes. That is, there can be an interaction between the effects of the structure of change and the effects of the organizational characteristics on the change processes. The organizational characteristics are given and they exist prior to the change activity.

The first factor concerns the congruency between the structure of change and the existing management philosophy and structure. Organization one had a very authoritarian philosophy and clear hierarchical structure. The proposed change moved the organization toward a more democratic mode and authority was pushed down to lower organizational levels. We label this condition as a low congruency. Change was introduced in this organization and did persist with some degree of success over a three-year period, but the management philosophy and organizational structure did not change. We hypothesize that over time this discrepancy increased the forces of deinstitutionalization. In Table 7 we see that greater levels of congruency may be related to greater levels of institutionalization.

Walton's (1980) data show that in some change efforts there is a gap between the requirement inherent in the structural features of the change and the employees' skills and values. The lower the congruency (or greater the gap), the lower the levels of institutionalization. Unfortunately, we cannot discern any trends in our data because of the lack of variability in the congruency variable.

We did gather some information from one of our companies that had introduced an autonomous work group into a new organization. The employees were just in the process of learning their basic job skills. The rewards for doing both self-governing activities and job activities far exceeded the employees' capabilities, and the change failed. The gap in this instance worked against the long-run viability of the program. Levine (1980) describes a set of innovations attempted at a state university. Some of the innovations were more

Table 7. Organizational Characteristics.

Organizational Forms	Congruency		Stability		Union
	Management Philosophy Structure	Employment Values Skills	Environment	Technology	
1. Autonomous Work Group	low	high	stable	stable	yes
2. Problem-Solving Hierarchy	low-medium	medium-high	stable	stable	yes
3. Problem-Solving Hierarchy	low-medium	high	unstable	stable	yes
4. Problem-Solving Hierarchy	low-medium	medium-high	stable	stable	yes
5. Matrix-Production Business Team	high	high	unstable	stable	yes
6. Problem-Solving Hierarchy	high	high	stable	stable	yes
7. Autonomous Work Group	high	medium	stable	stable	no
8. Parallel	high	stable	stable	no	no
9. Bonus Productivity Teams	high	high	stable	moderately stable	no

congruent with organizational norms and values than others. Over time, those innovations that were congruent were more likely to persist than those that were incongruent. Similar conclusions were drawn by Warwick (1975) and Crockett (1977) concerning a major organizational change undertaken in the State Department. The new structure favored the taking of initiative by lower-level officials, which was incongruent with both the reward system and received wisdom about how to be successful at the State Department. Not surprisingly, the change did not last. Finally, Miller (1975) showed that a change program must be congruent with cultural norms and values, as well as with those peculiar to the organization. An organizational innovation in several Indian weaving mills was hampered because it did not provide for the workers' need for recognition by superiors, which is strong in the Indian culture.

Another issue that appears to affect the level of institutionalization concerns the stability or variability in the environment. In an earlier literature review (Goodman, Bazerman, and Conlon, 1979), evidence was cited that high variability without some boundary buffer mechanism works against institutionalization. In our data there were only two instances of instability in the environment. In these cases there was a major decrease in demand for the organization's products, which led to curtailments in the work force. These changes in the work force in turn changed the composition of many of the groups that were an integral part of the change mechanism. Because these economic changes were not buffered, they decreased the effective function of the groups, which lowered levels of institutionalization.

We thought that variations or instability in technology would have a similar effect. However, there were few changes in technology. In case nine, there were some technological changes, but these were easily incorporated into the organization without affecting the change activities of lower levels of institutionalization.

The next factor concerns whether the organization was unionized. We have argued elsewhere (Goodman, 1979, 1980) that there may be some inherent conflict between an organizational form that is based on labor-management cooperation and a labor-management system based on an adversary relationship. This inherent conflict may work against the long-run viability of the new organizational form. The data do indicate this type of relationship; firms whose programs were most institutionalized were nonunion. However, it would be a mistake to infer from the data that union versus nonunion is a principal cause of institutionalization. There are too many other independent variables, which we have presented to the reader, that affect institutionalization. One cannot assert that the institutionalization of change will not occur in a union-management system. All we have argued for, theoretically, is that it will be more difficult.

There are other organizational characteristics, such as size, age, and location, that might be included in this table. They were excluded because we did not identify theoretically, or through a literature review, how the variables would moderate the processes in Table 7.

Conclusion

We have presented a definition, a conceptual procedure to analyze degrees of institutionalization, and a framework to explain or predict the level of degrees of institutionalization. Now that an analysis is completed, it may be useful to identify ways in which this analysis differs from other discussions of institutionalization (compare Berger and Luckman, 1966; Zucker, 1977; and Walton, 1980).

Conceptualization of Degrees of Institutionalization. Institutionalization is not an all-or-nothing phenomenon. More likely, we find degrees of institutionalization in any social context. We have proposed five criteria to represent the degree of institutionalization: cognitive consensus, common behavior, common preferences or private acceptance, normative consensus, and value consensus. The criteria are not simply a list of five isolated factors. Rather, we have argued that they are interrelated and developmentally may appear as a unidimensional structure. That is, cognitive consensus should precede the appearance of common behaviors, which should precede a common set of preferences toward those behaviors, and so forth. Similarly, if value consensus appears, the other four criteria should be operating with regard to a particular act.

Operational Procedure for Measuring Degrees of Institutionalization. Following a conceptual identification of criteria for institutionalization, we have suggested that it is possible to represent this concept empirically in an organizational context. The major problem we faced in going into the field was to measure the degree of institutionalization in the different settings. Although this chapter does not represent a psychometric guide to resolving this operational issue, it did appear possible to measure the level of institutionalization in the nine organizations. After defining the appropriate social system, the task is to develop questions to measure beliefs, behavior, and preferences with respect to a given act and then to ascertain the level of normative and value consensus. Questionnaires and interviews represent two methods; observation analysis could be used for measures of behavior, normative consensus, and value consensus. The point is not to suggest that the task of operationalizing degrees of institutionalization is easy. Indeed, there are tough measurement problems, to which we have offered some solutions (pp. 229–235).

A Precise Framework. In reviewing the literature on institutionalization, it is easy to find factors that affect institutionalization. Some studies suggest the degree of sponsorship, the type of reward system, whether the organization is unionized, and so forth. One can generate a long list of factors. Our position has been that there are five critical processes: socialization, commitment, reward allocation, diffusion, and sensing and recalibration. These processes are the *main* predictors of the degree of institutionalization. We have acknowledged other factors, such as characteristics of the change and characteristics of the organization, but these variables are important only as they moderate the processes.

Some Hypotheses. This was a hypothesis-generating rather than hypothesis-testing chapter. Each of the tables represents possible hypotheses. Some of the tables identify some fairly clear relationships. For example, high levels of institutionalization are associated with training new members, opportunities for commitment, types of rewards, and behavior-reward contingency. In other tables, the relationships are mixed. In either set, these represent possible hypotheses for testing. If we count across tables, some eighteen hypotheses are posed.

Development of Social Facts. An important part of an analysis concerns how acts become social facts, that is, how behaviors become part of social structure. We have adopted a developmental perspective that begins with the individual and moves to a structural level of analysis. The novel aspect of our approach is integrating several diverse learning mechanisms, such as social comparison, social thresholds, attributions, and lateral and vertical generalization (see the Appendix to this chapter).

The problem of maintaining change is itself persistent problem. Our data painted a pessimistic picture. Change had been successfully introduced; some benefits had appeared; but over time the majority of the programs had become deinstitutionalized. These findings may represent a unique sample, but others (for example, Mirvis and Berg, 1977; Walton, 1980) have reported similar findings in different settings with different types of change. Our hunch is that difficulty in maintaining change will remain a fairly persistent phenomenon. We hope that the ideas in this chapter will provide some guidance to those conducting research on change as well as to those planning and implementing it.

Appendix

This appendix details the processes by which behaviors become institutionalized by examining different phases of change at different levels of analysis.

There are many ways to characterize phases of change. We assume there will be some type of introduction, followed by a temporary adoption of the proposed behavior. Over time the behavior will become established and routinized. The next phase may be one of maintenance or revitalization, or one of decline. We propose these phases merely as a way to organize this discussion; they are not independent entities with one ending and the other beginning or some closed cycle. The phases can occur at different points. Decline might follow adoption or occur during the revitalization phase.

Level of analysis is another issue that will organize this analysis. We believe that the development of institutionalized behavior must be understood at the individual and collective levels. According to our definition, an institutionalized act is a collective phenomenon. However, to understand the development and decline of this act, it is necessary to understand why individuals adopt new work behaviors because these individual adoptions represent the "raw material" for the institutionalization process.

Individual Level of Analysis. The individual analysis begins as a new behavior is introduced. The focus is on a single individual operating in an isolated context. We will trace the individual through the different phases of change. In each phase we will try to link the relevant theoretical processes to the five facets of institutionalization.

The critical behaviors acquired during the introduction are the beliefs about the new behavior. The critical process is socialization, which provides information for these beliefs. From other literature (compare Goodman, 1979; Oskamp, 1977) we know that (1) the credibility and trustworthiness of the communicator, (2) the content of the communication (for example, one-sided, two-sided), and (3) the relationship between the content and the receiver's prior experiences or current attitudes and beliefs all bear on whether the information will be received, modified, or rejected. These new beliefs are important because they may determine whether the new behavior will be adopted (Goodman and Moore, 1970).

The *adoption* decision concerns whether the individual will perform the new behavior. This decision is based on three things.

1. Beliefs concerning the perceived ability to perform the new behavior. In a study of a Scanlon Plan installation, Goodman and Moore (1976) reported that people who felt capable of performing a new behavior did so and others who did not feel capable did not.
2. The perceived relationship between new behavior and the resultant outcomes. If an individual does not see rewards flowing from the new behavior, it is unlikely it will be adopted.
3. The attractiveness of the rewards. A variety of rewards may be promised. Extrinsic rewards, those mediated through some external source, are probably the dominant reward in the adoption decision. Intrinsic rewards may be used, but their effect is probably weaker because it is harder to assign valences to expected internally mediated rewards (for example, feelings of accomplishment) than to expected amounts of money.

Forms of identification (Kelman, 1958) can also be used in the adoption decision because people may adopt a behavior to maintain a satisfactory relationship with the person requesting the behavior.

There are many complexities in this decision process, but because it is not central to our theoretical framework, it will not be elaborated. The basic idea is that the adoption decision (a behavior) follows from beliefs developed from the socialization processes.

The adoption decision is based on expectation of rewards; the *continuation* decision is based on the prior commitment process and the receipt of rewards.

If there is congruence between expected and actual outcomes, the adopted behavior should continue. The expectation level is dynamic and adjusts over time. For example, if actual outcomes become less than the expected rewards, but this discrepancy occurs slowly, predictably, and equitably, the expectation level should adjust, and the behavior should persist. Adjustment upwards should follow a similar pattern.

Another critical process in this phase is commitment. The social context in which the adoption decision is made is as important as the decision itself. The level of commitment is highest when the adopted behavior is (1) selected freely (not because it is an organizational requirement), (2) explicit (that is, not easily deniable), and (3) publicly known (Salancik, 1977). High commitment leads to the stability of the behavior and resistance to change in that behavior. In this phase, then, reward allocation and commitment are the critical processes. Performance of the behavior and preference of that behavior are the relevant facets. As the individual continues to perform the behavior over time, affective orientations will probably be developed toward that behavior. Similarly, the greater the freedom in selecting the behavior, the more likely that private beliefs will be congruent with that behavior.

The decision to continue, as compared with the decision to adopt, occurs at a less conscious level. The decision to adopt, given limits on rationality, requires some explicit examination of the benefits and costs of the new behavior. The continuation of the behavior occurs by default. If high commitment is induced in the adoption decision, the behavior should continue. If actual outcomes are in line with expected outcomes, no explicit reevaluation of the adoption decision occurs. Indeed, over time the behavior becomes routinized, that is, performed with a low level of attention. The advantages of routinization are that it reduces the costs of decision making and provides opportunities for considering other decisions.

Over time there may be a *decline* in the perceived value of the rewards that sustain the new behaviors. This diminishing utility may vary the type of rewards (Alderfer, 1972; Hall, 1976). To *maintain* (or revitalize) the cognitive behavior and/or preferences, new processes must be introduced. First, resocialization of organizational participants may strengthen earlier beliefs or preferences and focus attention on new outcomes. Second, recommitment processes may be introduced to strengthen cognitions, behaviors, or preferences. For example, in some programs workers vote annually to reaffirm their commitment (Moore and Ross, 1978). The third alternative may be to revise the reward system to provide different types or schedules of rewards. There is a tendency to think of reward systems as fixed rather than as a mechanism in need of constant revision. New rewards may strengthen behaviors and preferences.

This brief discussion at the individual level of analysis is intended to highlight (1) the role of the individual in the institutionalization of change and (2) the link between some of the critical processes and facets of institutionalization. The discussion, however, is somewhat artificial in that it treats the individual in isolation. (It is probably more accurate in depicting so-called "early adopters," who adopt the behavior before strong norms and values concerning it have developed.)

Collective Levels of Analysis. At the collective level we want to explain the development of degrees of institutionalization. Our definition requires that institutionalization be examined in a collective context where multiple individuals are objects of change. How does an act become institutionalized? What enhances the level of institutionalization? What contributes to deinstitutionalization? The facets of collective knowledge, behavior, preferences, normative consensus, and value consensus are the objects to be explained. The processes are the explanatory variables.

Introduction and Adoption Phases. The introduction and adoption phases and the corresponding processes are almost identical to those discussed at the individual level of analysis. One difference is that the socialization and commitment processes are directed to collections of individuals rather than to one person. Also, the social context of most planned organizational change ensures that individuals will be aware that they are objects of the same socialization and commitment processes. The products from these first two phases should be common knowledge of the requisite behaviors and common adoption, at least on a trial basis, of the proposed new form of work behavior. Of course, we would expect individual variation in both the acceptance of the knowledge and performance. We acknowledge the importance of the literature about resistance to change and the effect of such resistance on any adoption decision. But our interest is in explaining degrees of institutionalization, and this requires that the behavior be adopted and initially persist over time.

Continuation. The critical development of an institutionalized act occurs in the continuation phase. Our setting for this analysis is some people with common knowledge about a new form of work behavior and a smaller percentage of people who have adopted the behavior. The question is How does the new form of work behavior become institutionalized? The explanation is based on a set of socialization or learning mechanisms that affect common beliefs, behaviors, and preferences as well as *normative and value consensus*. (Contrast this with the individual level of analysis. At the individual level of analysis, reward allocation and commitment were the major processes; beliefs, behavior, and preferences were the major facets.)

The first mechanism is *social comparison*. Much of the current social comparison literature (Goodman, 1977) focuses on how people make evaluations of outcomes (for example, pay). That is, information about others' input/outcome ratio permits the evaluation of the focal person's ratio. The more general use of social comparison processes has been to validate the social reality of beliefs. That is, people validate their own beliefs by comparing their beliefs with relevant beliefs of others.

The availability of information on others' behavior is an important way to confirm one's beliefs about the costs and benefits of a new form of work behavior. Goodman and Moore (1976) have reported that, in an installation of a Scanlon Plan, the availability of information about others may change people's belief about their ability to make suggestions, their belief about behavior-reward contingencies, and hence their behavior. In another context, for those people who have adopted the behavior, the availability of information can confirm existing beliefs and ensure the continuation of the behavior.

The effect of social comparison processes on confirming or changing beliefs, behavior, or preferences occurs at the individual level. Because we are describing the effect of social context on individual behavior, the process of institutionalization has not begun.

The second mechanism is *social threshold*. Granovetter (1978, p. 1422) postulates that a threshold is "that point where the perceived benefits to an individual of [joining some collective behavior] exceed the perceived costs." The threshold is conceptualized in terms of the percentage of people in a group performing the behavior. As the percentage changes, so do the benefits and costs, until the threshold is eventually passed. Granovetter uses this concept as a general explanation for why people engage in collective behavior.

Our use of the threshold idea is limited to cases in which it explains the amount of costs associated with not performing a new form of work behavior. Consider the following example: A new form of work behavior, "X," is introduced into an organization. Ten percent of the work group adopts the behavior. Some of the nonperformers observe the performers, modify their beliefs, and adopt behavior "X." If this process continues, the percentage of performers should increase. The threshold concept can come into play when the majority of people are engaging in the behavior and the nonperformers are becoming more visible. Increased visibility of nonperformance increases the probability of receiving some form of punishment. As the amount of participation in the new behavior increases, so will the costs of nonperformance. The relationship is not linear; only at rather high levels of participation (or visibility of nonperformance) will the costs appear. The threshold idea does not explain levels of institutionalization. Rather, it explains at the collective level how social forces bear on individual beliefs, behavior, and perhaps, indirectly, preferences. Both the social comparison and threshold processes are necessary for the development of institutionalized behavior.

The third mechanism is *attribution about appropriateness*. As individuals become aware of others performing the new work behavior, it is reasonable to expect some attributional processes will be generated to explain why multiple others' behavior is evoked. Our focus is not on a single other's performance, because we discussed that under the social comparison processes and made inferences about the individual's cost and benefits assessments. In this context, we are interested in the attributions about collective behavior. Why do multiple others perform the new behavior? An attribution about appropriateness is derived from the following observations: I am performing the behavior. I am aware that others are performing that behavior. Others are aware that other people are performing the behavior. The behavior appears predictable and persistent. I like performing the behavior. Others probably perform the behavior because they also like it *and* because it is appropriate.

One attribution about this collective behavior is that it persists because the participant feels it is appropriate. Social psychological research (Jones and others, 1972) has shown that individuals generally attribute the causes of others' behavior to internal or dispositional characteristics of those others but often attribute their own behavior to forces in the environment. It is therefore not unreasonable to believe that, when individuals see others performing behaviors consistent with the change program, they will assume that others like the behaviors and/or find them appropriate. Their own behavior, however, may well be attributed to group norms. The target of this attribution process then is the development of normative consensus.

The fourth mechanism is *lateral generalization*. Organizations are collections of norms, which represent rules or statements about appropriate behavior. Assume that a new work behavior that appears similar (and congruent) with an existing norm is introduced. Following the work of Breer and Locke (1965), we expect the "appropriate" label attached to the normative behavior to generalize to the new work behavior, assuming that there is common knowledge of the new work behavior, that people have adopted it, that they privately accept the behavior, and that they are aware of others' performance of that behavior. Consider the following example: There is a work group that embraces the norm of intragroup cooperation. Assume that this group has little interaction with other groups. As planned organizational change is introduced to bring about intergroup cooperation, the lateral generalization process from intra- to intergroup cooperation should facilitate the institutionalization of the latter form of cooperation. Lateral generalization, then, contributes to the degrees of institutionalization by creating some level of normative consensus.

The fifth mechanism is *vertical generalization*. The Breer and Locke (1965) theory of attitude and values argues that behavior precedes attitudes and values. The individual is faced with a task. Through trial and error, the instrumental task behavior (say cooperation) is identified and thus a cognition about this behavior (or knowledge, in our terms) is formed. As similar tasks are presented, the individual may generalize laterally and try the cooperative behavior in the new task. If the behavior "works" over a variety of tasks, Breer and Locke argue that a vertical generalization process will be evoked that would move from "cooperation works" (cognition) to "I prefer or like cooperative behavior" (personal preference) to "cooperation is good; people ought to cooperate" (a value). In the context of institutionalization, if there are select acts that exhibit some level of normative consensus and these acts represent a generalized value, then we would hypothesize, through a process of vertical generalization, that this value would be created. To the extent to which others experience this process and communicate with each other about it, some degree of value consensus will be developed.

The sixth mechanism is *communication and persuasion*. The effects of the five mechanisms will be augmented as system members communicate with each other about beliefs, behaviors, preferences, norms, and values. Until now we have treated the first five mechanisms in a passive context. However, the power of group communication, particularly in the context of a cohesive group, has been well documented (Kiesler and Kiesler, 1969) as a means of developing beliefs, behaviors, preferences, norms, and values.

Maintenance or Decline. Given some degree of institutionalization, the next question concerns what affects its maintenance (or growth) or decline. The independent variables that bear on this question are the processes of socialization, commitment, rewards, diffusion, and sensing and correcting. We discussed the impact of these processes on adopters and nonadopters in the chapter.

References

Alderfer, C. P. *Human Needs in Organizational Settings.* New York: Free Press of Glencoe, 1972.

Berger, P., and Luckman, T. *The Social Construction of Reality: A Treatise in the Sociology of Knowledge.* Garden City, N.Y.: Doubleday, 1966.

Breer, P., and Locke, E. *Task Experience as a Source of Attitudes.* Homewood, Ill.: Dorsey Press, 1965.

Crockett, W. "Introducing Change to a Government Agency." In P. Mirvis and D. Berg (Eds.), *Failures in Organizational Development: Cases and Essays for Learning.* New York: Wiley-Interscience, 1977.

Frank, L. L., and Hackman, J. R. "A Failure of Job Enrichment: The Case of the Change that Wasn't." *Journal of Applied Behavioral Science,* 1975, *11*(4), 413–436.

Golembiewski, R. T., and Carrigan, S. B. "The Persistence of Laboratory-Induced Changes in Organizational Styles." *Administrative Science Quarterly,* 1970, *15*, 330–340.

Goodman, P. S. "Social Comparison Processes in Organizations." In B. M. Staw and G. R. Salancik (Eds.), *New Directions in Organizational Behavior.* Chicago: St. Clair Press, 1977.

Goodman, P. S. *Assessing Organizational Change: The Rushton Quality of Work Experiment.* New York: Wiley-Interscience, 1979.

Goodman, P. S. "Quality of Work Life Projects in the 1980s." *Labor Law Journal,* 1980, *31*, 487–494.

Goodman, P. S., Atkin, R. A., and Schoorman, F. D. "On the Demise of Organizational Effectiveness Studies." In M. K. Cameron and D. Whetten (Eds.), *Organizational Effectiveness.* New York: Wiley-Interscience, 1982.

Goodman, P. S., Bazerman, M., and Conlon, E. "Institutionalization of Planned Organizational Change." In B. M. Staw and L. L. Cummings (Eds.), *Research in Organizational Behavior.* (Vol. 2) Greenwich, Conn.: JAI Press, 1979.

Goodman, P. S., and Lawler, E. E. *New Forms of Work Organization in the United States.* Monograph prepared for the International Labor Organization, Geneva, Switzerland, 1977.

Goodman, P. S. and Moore, B. "The Natural Controlled Experiment in Organizational Research." *Human Organization,* 1970, *29,* 197-203.

Goodman, P. S., and Moore, B. "Factors Affecting the Acquisition of Beliefs about a New Reward System." *Human Relations,* 1976, *29,* 571-588.

Granovetter, M. "Threshold Models of Collective Behavior." *American Journal of Sociology,* 1978, *83,* 1420-1443.

Hall, R. I. "A System Pathology of an Organization: The Rise and Fall of the 'Old Saturday Evening Post.' " *Administrative Science Quarterly,* 1976, *21,* 185-211.

Hinrichs, J. R. *Practical Management for Productivity.* New York: Van Nostrand Reinhold, 1978.

Ivancevich, J. M. "Changes in Performance in a Management by Objectives Program." *Administrative Science Quarterly,* 1972, *17,* 126-138.

Ivancevich, J. M. "A Longitudinal Assessment of Management by Objectives." *Administrative Science Quarterly,* 1974, *19,* 563-574.

Jacobs, R. C., and Campbell, D. T. "The Perpetuation of an Arbitrary Tradition through Several Generations of a Laboratory Microculture." *Journal of Abnormal and Social Psychology,* 1961, *62,* 649-658.

Jones, E., and others (Eds.). *Attribution: Perceiving the Causes of Behavior.* Morristown, N.J.: General Learning Press, 1972.

Keen, P. G. W. "Information Systems and Organizational Change." *Communications of the Association for Computing Machinery,* 1981, *24,* 24-33.

Kelman, H. "Compliance, Identification and Internalization: Three Processes of Attitude Change." *Journal of Conflict Resolution,* 1958, *2,* 51-60.

Kiesler, C. A. *The Psychology of Commitment: Experiments Linking Behavior to Belief.* New York: Academic Press, 1971.

Kiesler, C. A., and Kiesler, S. B. *Conformity.* Reading, Mass.: Addison-Wesley, 1969.

Lawler, E. E. *Pay and Organizational Effectiveness.* New York: McGraw-Hill, 1971.

Levine, A. *Why Innovation Fails.* Albany: State University of New York Press, 1980.

Lewin, K. *Field Theory in Social Science.* New York: Harper, 1951.

Locke, E. A., Sirota, D., and Wolfson, A. D. "An Experimental Case Study of the Successes and Failures of Job Enrichment in a Government Agency." *Journal of Applied Psychology,* 1976, *61,* 701-711.

MacNeil, M. K., and Sherif, M. "Norm Change over Subject Generations as a Function of Arbitrariness of Prescribed Norms." *Journal of Personality and Social Psychology,* 1976, *33,* 698-708.

March, J., and Simon, H. *Organizations.* New York: Wiley, 1958.

Meyer, J. W., and Rowan, B. "Institutionalized Organizations: Formal Structure as Myth and Ceremony." *American Journal of Sociology,* 1977, *83,* 340-363.

Miller, E. J. "Socio-Technical Systems in Weaving, 1953-1970: A Follow-Up Study." *Human Relations,* 1975, *28*(4), 349-386.

Mirvis, P. H., and Berg, D. N. *Failures in Organization Development and Change.* New York: Wiley-Interscience, 1977.

Moore, B. E., and Ross, T. L. *The Scanlon Way to Improved Productivity: A Practical Guide.* New York: Wiley-Interscience, 1978.

Oskamp, S. *Attitudes and Opinions.* Englewood Cliffs, N.J.: Prentice-Hall, 1977.

Rogers, E. M., and Shoemaker, F. F. *Communication of Innovations.* New York: Free Press, 1971.

Salancik, G. "Commitment and the Control of Organizational Behavior and Belief." In B. Staw and G. Salancik (Eds.), *New Directions in Organizational Behavior.* Chicago: St. Clair Press, 1977.

Scheflen, K., Lawler, E., and Hackman, J. "Long Term Impact of Employee Participation in the Development of Pay Incentive Plans." *Journal of Applied Psychology,* 1971, *55,* 182-186.

Vroom, V. A. *Work and Motivation.* New York: Wiley-Interscience, 1964.

Walton, R. E. "The Diffusion of New Work Structures: Explaining Why Success Didn't Take." *Organizational Dynamics,* Winter 1975, pp. 3-21.

Walton, R. E. "Teaching an Old Dog Food New Tricks." *Wharton Magazine*, Winter 1978, pp. 38–47.

Walton, R. E. "Establishing and Maintaining High Commitment Work Systems." In J. R. Kimberly, R. H. Miles, and Associates (Eds.), *The Organizational Life Cycle: Issues in the Creation, Transformation, and Decline of Organizations*. San Francisco: Jossey-Bass, 1980.

Warwick, D. P. *A Theory of Public Bureaucracy*. Cambridge, Mass.: Harvard University Press, 1975.

Weick, K. E., and Gilfillan, D. P. "Fate of Arbitrary Traditions in a Laboratory Microculture." *Journal of Personality and Social Psychology*, 1971, *17*, 179–191.

Zucker, L. G. "The Role of Institutionalization in Cultural Persistence." *American Sociological Review*, 1977, *42*, 726–743.

Increasing Worker Involvement to Enhance Organizational Effectiveness

□ □ □ □ □ □ □ □ □ □ □ □ □ □ □ □ □

Edward E. Lawler III

Much of the early literature on organizational change presented utopian models of participative organizations. The early seminal writings of Argyris (1957), Likert (1961), and McGregor (1960), for example, talked about the many advantages of such things as theory management, system 4 management, enlarged jobs, and participative decision making. The normative models they presented were lacking in some respects, but they were, nevertheless, very important statements. They provided models against which organizations could be compared to determine how far they had progressed toward an ideal participative organization. They also helped refine many details of just what a participative organization should look like.

Finally, they provided a number of arguments favoring a widespread movement toward participative management.

The early normative writings are also notable for what they did not say. They generally failed to provide significant guidance in two key areas: how participative organizations can be created and what kinds of organization structures, reward systems, information systems, policies, and designs are congruent with participative management. With respect to the first issue, generally missing was material on how existing organizations could be changed and on how new organizations could be created so that they would be managed in a participative manner from their beginning. Such issues as where and how to start, what type of diagnosis is needed, how long should a change project take, how can change be institutionalized, what type of developmental stages do new organizations go through, what type of resistance can be expected, and how should new organizations begin to introduce participative management were given little attention. With respect to the second issue, the theories eloquently described the type of climate and employee-organization relationships that should exist. They talked of employees being highly involved, a climate of trust, open communication, and consensus or participatory decision making. Much less time was spent talking about what types of pay systems, selection practices, career tracks, training programs, organization structures, and information systems are needed to produce the desired climate and motivation.

These omissions are hardly surprising, given the groundbreaking nature of the early writings and the lack of research knowledge at that time on such issues as organization change and systems theory. Indeed, it is remarkable that some of the early writings are as complete as they are. In any case, it is not surprising that the 1960s and 1970s theory building and experimentation has helped fill in these two voids in the empirical and theoretical knowledge concerning participative management and high involvement work systems. As a result, we are now in a much better position to comment on how high involvement systems can be created and on what the design, structure, and policies of a high involvement organization should look like. This chapter focuses on both these issues. First I present a normative view of what features need to be built into an organization in order for it to operate effectively in a high involvement mode. Next I speculate about the creation of organizations with these features.

Features of Effective High Involvement Systems

An effective organization provides its employees with a high quality of working life (QWL) and above average operating results. This definition recognizes that employees are legitimate stakeholders in the organization, as are investors and others concerned with operating results. This is not to suggest that operating results are not of interest to employees; indeed, good operating results can contribute to a high QWL and satisfactory ones are necessary for there to be a work life in most organizations. I begin by considering how above average operation results can be considered and then turn to QWL considerations.

Operating Performance

There are three important ways organization design and management style can affect organizational performance or operating results. As Figure 1 shows, motivation, performance capability, and communication/coordination all directly affect the operating effectiveness of an organization. These in turn can be affected by the way organizations are designed, structured, and staffed. These design features also determine how well employees' needs are met, that is, their QWL. If participative work structures are to be effective, they must impact favorably on these three factors, as well as on QWL. If they are to be more effective than traditional ones, they must have a more favorable impact. Although I consider motivation, performance capability, and coordination separately, they are very closely related, first, because some features contribute to more than one and, second, because, to be effective, an organization needs to be high on all three.

Motivation for Organizational Performance. A great deal has been written about the determinants of individual performance motivation. The key feature of most theories concerned with motivation is the relationship between performance and rewards (see, for exam-

Figure 1. Human System Determinants of Organizational Effectiveness.

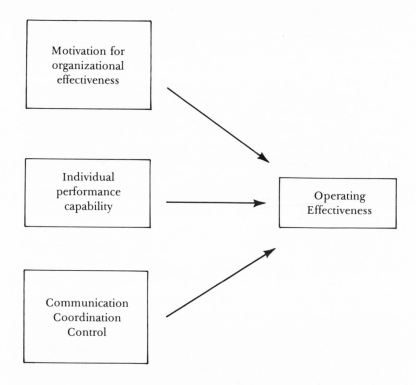

ple, Lawler, 1973). It is one thing, however, to specify that this is a key feature in creating motivation; it is another to specify how the perception of a close connection between performance and rewards can be produced. The problem becomes even more difficult when the concern is one of motivating people to maximize organizational performance rather than individual performance. Most of the writing concerned with motivation in work organizations stresses how to increase individual performance. Implicit in this is the assumption that if individual performance increases, so will organizational performance. This is a generally valid but distinctly different perspective than one that focuses on how people can be directly motivated to increase organizational performance (Lawler, 1981). One of the things that have always intrigued me about the idea of high involvement systems is the idea that people might be motivated not to maximize individual performance, but to maximize organizational performance. If motivation theory is any guide to practice, then in order to have people motivated to maximize organizational performance, they need to see their individual rewards tied to organizational performance. This is a simple idea but experience has shown that it is not easy to accomplish.

Figure 2 presents a model that details some of the design features hypothesized to lead to a high level of motivation for organizational performance. The model also specifies the psychological states that need to exist between the organizational design features and the motivational determinants of organizational performance. It distinguishes between extrinsic and intrinsic rewards and the different psychological states necessary for both types of motivation to exist. Briefly, it shows that extrinsic rewards will be seen to be tied to performance when people understand a pay system that actually rewards them for increases in organizational performance and when they have knowledge of organizational performance. It also specifies that intrinsic rewards will be tied to organizational performance when knowledge of organizational performance is present, when people feel responsible for organizational performance, and when organizational performance is meaningful to them. This feature of the model is based on what has been learned about intrinsic motivation and its relationship to job design (Hackman and Lawler, 1971; Hackman and Oldham, 1980).

A number of design features are shown as contributing to the desirable psychological states. In terms of extrinsic rewards, the key feature is shown to be the existence of a gain-sharing system that is developed and managed along participative lines and that ties extrinsic rewards to organizational performance (Lawler, 1981). The Scanlon Plan is a well-known gain-sharing plan; it usually pays monthly bonuses to employees when cost reductions are achieved. This kind of system can produce a good understanding of how extrinsic rewards and performance are related and can increase people's knowledge or organizational performance because it typically has a reporting system built into it.

A gain-sharing plan is one way to accomplish another key design feature, that of an open public information system about operating results. If people are to relate to and feel good about

Figure 2. Determinants of Organizational Motivation.

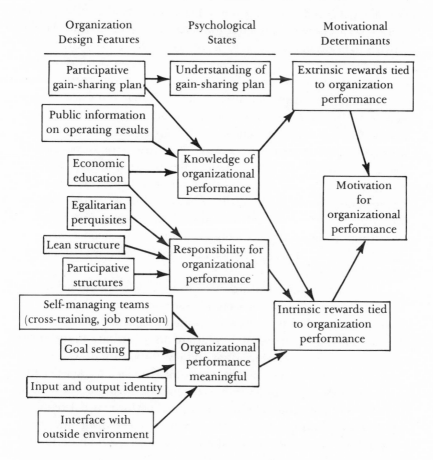

organizational performance, they have to know what it is, how it is measured, and receive regular information about operating results. In the absence of a gain-sharing plan, this feature can be created by regular meetings, labor-management committees, goal-setting structures, and other means.

A third design feature, economic education, also relates to people receiving meaningful feedback. Without it, people often cannot relate to the kind of measures used to assess organizational performance. Thus, although they get the information, they are in no position to understand its meaning and to evaluate performance based upon it. Economic education for this purpose needs to include the basics of cost accounting, and it needs to focus on specific information about how the organization measures itself. In other words, it needs to be organization-specific, not general economic education.

Along with economic education, egalitarian perquisites, the existence of a lean flat organization structure, various participative structures (such as works councils), and self-managing teams lead people to feel responsible for organizational performance. These design features all contribute to a felt sense of responsibility for organizational performance because they create conditions where the individual can actually influence the direction an organization takes, the choices it makes, and the kind of strategies and tactics it implements. The model suggests that only if these design features are in place will individuals throughout the organization feel they have some responsibility for organizational performance. Only if they feel this will they be motivated to increase organizational effectiveness.

Several of these features need to be briefly elaborated upon. Egalitarian perquisites, for example, are not as crucial as some of the others, but they do have a symbolic importance. When highly differentiated perquisites are in place in an organization, they tend to distinguish between important and less important decision makers. The message communicated to people who lack the key perquisites is that they are not an important part of the organization and therefore not responsible for organizational performance. Even with egalitarian perquisites, some people will be more influential than others, but this should be based more on expertise than on formal position.

Self-managing teams can contribute strongly to a felt sense of responsibility for several reasons. First, through cross-training and job rotating mechanisms, they give people a chance to learn about many of the functions that are necessary in order for the organization to perform well. In addition, because they operate on a participative basis, they provide the individual a chance to influence many of the day-to-day work place decisions. This is essential if the individual is to feel responsible for these decisions and for the success of the organization.

Participative structures, such as works councils and task forces, are, perhaps, less crucial but nevertheless positive forces because they provide individuals a chance to influence different kinds of organizational decisions—those concerned with broad policy and major strategies.

Finally, lean structures are important because with them much of the planning, scheduling, and managing of work tends to gravitate toward the shop floor and away from management support or staff groups. When substantial staff groups exist, they do much of the thinking work. As a result, the production people feel little sense of responsibility for the operating results of the organization because they are merely carrying out someone else's ideas.

Self-managing teams, along with goal setting, clearly identifiable product input and output, and interface with the outside work environment, all help make the performance of the organization meaningful to individuals. Self-managing teams contribute to the understanding of what organizational performance consists of, the kinds of problems involved, and the kinds of issues inherent in producing good performance. They also often allow individuals to influence the performance of many different parts of the organization because they allow people to rotate and do different jobs.

Goal setting, when done effectively, helps make organizational performance meaningful because it helps people recognize what good performance is and can produce a commitment on their part to high levels of performance. Input and output identity are crucial because they contribute to individuals being able to see a raw material turned into a product or service. The clearer the output, the more an individual can understand what the organization is all about and relate his or her own activities to that output. Finally, interface with the outside environment helps the individual understand what the consumer is looking for and how he or she utilizes the product or service offered. In some cases, it can help the individual understand the input side of the input-out process. This interface can often be produced by having employee task forces visit suppliers or by other vehicles that highlight the input feature of the organization.

Figure 2 outlines a number of conditions that, when in place, contribute to motivating individuals to increase organizational performance. An important point about these design features is that they are in many ways congruent with and complementary to each other. Putting one or two of these features in place is probably not enough to create an overall sense of motivation for organizational performance. Indeed, as is true with the work on individual job design, it is probably necessary for knowledge of performance, felt responsibility, and meaningful organizational performance to be in place in order for intrinsic motivation to exist. In short, the three psychological states outlined here as influencing intrinsic motivation are not so much summative in producing motivation as they are multiplicative, such that if any of them is missing, it is unlikely that motivation for organizational performance will be present. In this case of extrinsic motivation, both knowledge of results and an understanding of the key performance relationship are needed for it to exist. Overall, knowledge of the relation of rewards to organizational performance is crucial, for without it there can be neither extrinsic nor intrinsic motivation.

Performance Capability. High involvement systems, by their very nature, require greater individual performance capability on the part of employees than do traditional systems because the design features in these systems call for individuals to influence decisions, exercise a broader range of skills on the job, and interact with people in groups and other settings that are not part of traditional organizational activities.

Figure 3 outlines some of the organizational design features that can be expected to increase individual performance capabilities. It also shows that a key for having high individual performance capabilities is having preemployment skills, learning opportunities, and motivation for skill building. It hypothesizes that an individual's performance capabilities are a function of the degree to which people are motivated to build their skills, the learning opportunities they are provided with, and the relevant skills with which they enter the work place. Multiple design features can influence the degree to which motivation, learning opportunities, and preemployment skills are likely to be present.

Motivation for skill building is likely to be particularly high when three design features are incorporated into the organization. First, employment stability can help increase motivation because it

Figure 3. Organizational Determinants of Performance Capability.

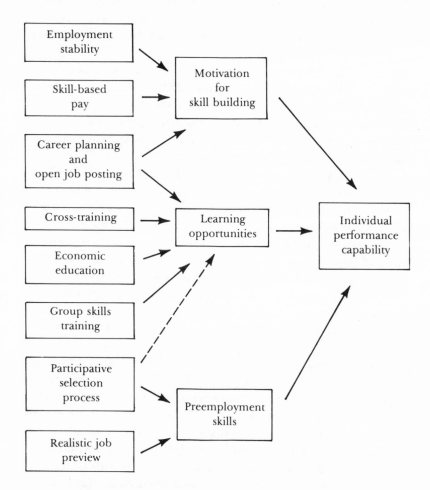

assures individuals that if they build situation-specific skills, they will be around long enough to utilize them. In addition, it aids in retaining people with the necessary skills.

A more direct influence on motivation for skill building is the use of skill-based pay systems. These systems pay people for the number of skills they have, not for the job they do at a particular time. There is therefore a direct connection between acquiring skills and higher pay (Lawler, 1981). Finally, a good career-planning system and open job posting can increase the motivation for skill building because they help make it clear that there is an opportunity to move up in the organization if a person has the necessary skills. Thus, they help establish a clear connection between extrinsic rewards and skill acquisition.

Career-planning and job-posting systems can also help provide good learning opportunities for individuals. They can, for example, help people be aware of the availability of jobs that can aid their further development and can also help them see formal training opportunities, both inside and outside the organization, that can aid their personal development.

The type of cross-training typically built into self-managing teams can provide a key learning opportunity for individuals in participative systems. This is the best way for individuals to understand how the operating area in which they work functions. Other learning opportunities also need to be provided for individuals, including opportunities for training in the technical skills necessary to do the job, group skills, and economic education.

Figure 3 includes economic education and group skills training because these are so often overlooked in traditional work organizations. This may be appropriate in traditional organizations because there is little need for individuals to exercise group skills. Economic education may be less useful because individuals do not see the data and make the kind of decisions that directly affect it. The opposite is true in high involvement systems. In order to understand feedback and participate in decision-making and operating groups, people need economic education and group skills training.

The selection and recruiting process can be an important determinant of the kind of preemployment skills with which individuals enter the organization. Participative selection (that is, allowing potential peers to influence the selection decision) seems to be crucial because it gives the members of work teams an opportunity to assess whether the team needs the applicants' skills. It also aids entry by creating a commitment on the part of the existing employees to seeing that the new hire is successful. To this extent, this process indirectly influences the kind of learning opportunities available to the new hire. In high involvement systems, it seems to be particularly appropriate to give individuals a realistic job preview so that people who are interested in this type of work situation will be attracted and those who are not will have the opportunity to select themselves out.

Figure 3 shows that there are a number of organizational design features that can contribute to a high level of the kind of performance capability that supports a high involvement management system. Again, as was true with the conditions that lead to a high level of motivation, many of these practices are complementary or congruent with each other. These practices are not likely to be effective if asked to stand alone. Simply providing employment stability or skill-based pay so that people will be motivated is not likely to be enough to produce high levels of individual capability. What is needed is good preemployment skills, good learning opportunities, and a high level of motivation. In the absence of all three of these, participative systems are not likely to be effective in producing individuals with the needed capabilities. In turn, it takes a number of appropriate organizational design features to produce motivation, learning opportunities, and preemployment skills. The absence of only a few of these is likely to assure poor performance capabilities.

Determinants of Communication, Coordination, and Control. A necessary condition for organizational effectiveness is the existence of organizational communication, coordination, and control mechanisms that allow individuals' performances to come together in ways that produce an effective organization. As is so often stressed, good performance on the part of a number of individuals is not enough to assure good organizational performance. Individuals' performances must come together in a synergistic manner.

Communication, coordination, and control can be influenced by a number of structural mechanisms. Figure 4 highlights some of those that are particularly congruent with a participative type system. It also shows that if they are to be effective, they need to influence the motivation for coordination, communication, and control and to provide the structures to allow for them. Figure 4 suggests that when intrinsic rewards are tied to organizational performance and when gain sharing exists, motivation for coordination will be high. As was pointed out in Figure 2, a number of conditions

Figure 4. Determinants of Communication and Coordination.

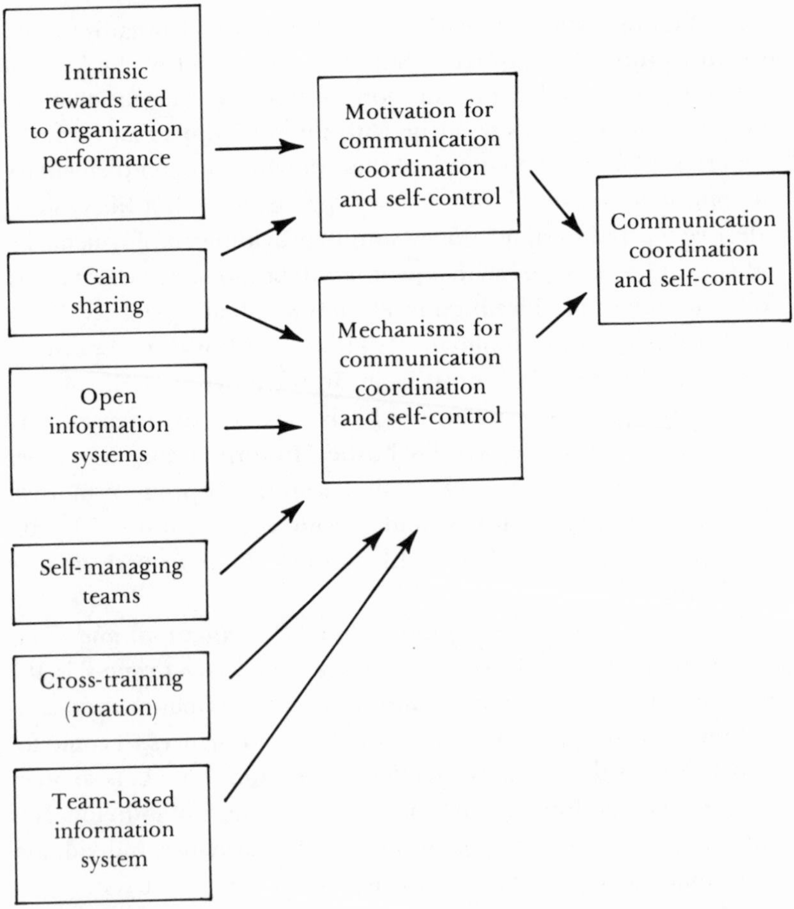

need to exist in order for intrinsic and extrinsic rewards to be tied to organizational performance.

Mechanisms that are useful for communication, coordination, and self-control include a number I have already mentioned as contributing to motivation: gain sharing, open informations systems, self-managing teams, and cross-training. These all contribute to the former because they encourage people to learn and understand what is going on in other parts of the organization and they provide individuals with information about how other parts of the organization and the total organization operate. Figure 4 also shows that team-based information systems are needed. Teams need information on their performance for self-management and interface with other teams.

Figure 4 shows different coordination vehicles than those traditionally used in organizations. Traditional organizations try to accomplish the goals of communication and coordination through a management hierarchy. They also structure tasks in such a way that the coordination is handled by an individual carrying out the task in the prescribed manner. Communication is handled through formal, often secret information systems that allow people at the top to manage many of the coordination and control issues.

Figure 4 emphasizes that both motivation and mechanisms for communication, coordination, and self-control need to be in place for them to exist in an organization. In turn, motivation and the mechanisms are likely to come into existence only if a whole pattern or congruent set of design features is built into an organization. Figure 4 is not an exhaustive list, but the features included illustrate those that can facilitate coordination, communication, and self-control.

Quality of Working Life and Design

Many of the design features I have listed can contribute in important ways to providing people with a high quality of working life. A high QWL exists when people's important needs are met. Figure 5 illustrates this point using a three-level system of needs similar to that discussed by Alderfer (1969). At the lowest level are such existence needs as food, safety, and security. At the next level are the social needs of affection and respect. At the highest level are the needs for growth, development, achievement, and control.

Figure 6 shows what practices can have a strong positive effect on satisfying existence needs. Except for flexible benefits, I have mentioned them before. Flexible benefits refers to fringe benefit programs that allow individuals to choose the type of benefits they need most.

Figure 5. Needs and QWL.

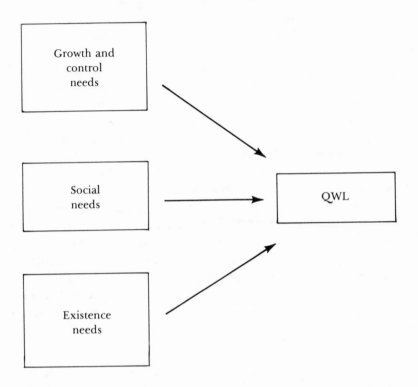

Figure 7 shows the practices that are particularly effective in satisfying social and esteem needs. Selection is included because of the kind of individual differences that exist in social needs. People who do not have strong social needs may see teams and interpersonal skill training as a negative contribution to QWL. Thus, some provision must be made for selecting people who have needs that are compatible with a high involvement approach. The use of egalitarian perquisites also can be seen as a negative by some higher-level managers who feel they have had something taken away from them. For most people, however, they are a positive in that they break down social barriers and lead them to have relatively higher status.

Figure 8 shows the relationship between organizational design issues and growth needs. Many more practices could be listed in the figure because most of the ones discussed so far are designed to

Figure 6. Design Features and Existence Needs.

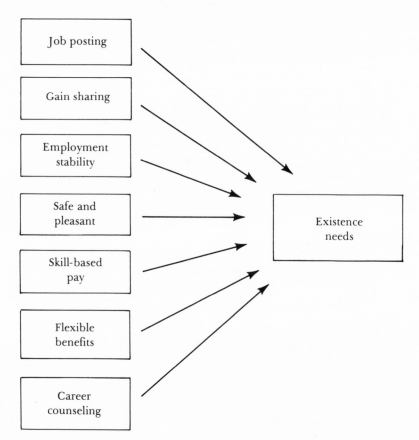

affect these needs. I included those predicted to affect this type of satisfaction most strongly. Again, selection is included because of the importance of considering individual differences and the fact that not everyone considers growth need satisfaction part of a high QWL.

Congruence of Design Features

In discussing design features that contribute to effective high involvement systems, two points have been stressed: (1) congruent

Figure 7. Design Features and Social Needs.

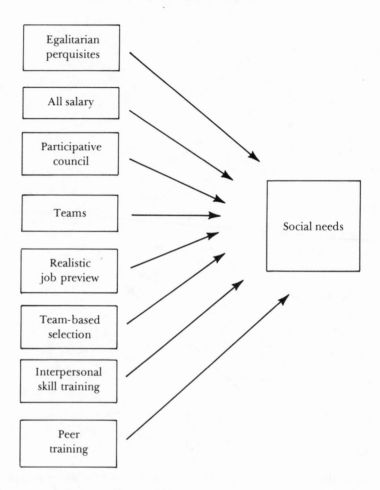

design features need to be selected, and (2) many of the design features I have discussed do not stand alone, that is, they become positive influences only when they are combined with other design features so that a total pattern exists that contributes to a desirable organizational condition. None of the three conditions specified in Figure 1 as leading to organizational effectiveness are likely to be effective if the others are not present. Motivation without capability is unlikely to lead to good organizational effectiveness, just as capa-

Figure 8. Design Features and Growth Needs.

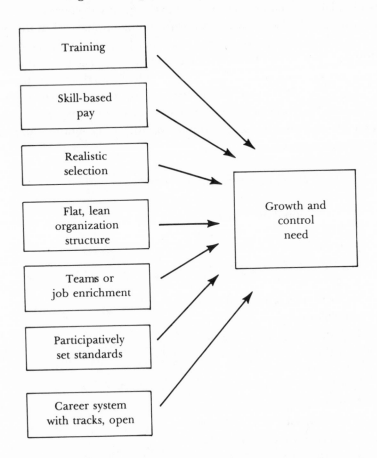

bility without communication, motivation, and so forth is unlikely to lead to effectiveness. All three of these conditions are needed in order for an effective high involvement system to develop or, indeed, for any effective organizational system to exist.

Motivation, capability, and communication in turn are not produced by a single design feature. As Figures 2, 3, and 4 illustrate, it takes a rather complex set of interrelated conditions for them to be produced. Perhaps the best way to summarize this point is to specify a congruent set of design features that are likely, in totality, to describe an organization as an effective high involvement system.

The following list of design features, drawn from the figures, is predicted to characterize an effective high involvement work organization. It adds a few design features not emphasized in the figures. For example, it stresses a reward system that is open, skill-based, includes flexible fringe benefits, and has minimum distinctions between people based on their horizontal level in the organization. It also stresses a physical layout that is congruent with team structures and is egalitarian in nature. Training is given prominence and includes nontraditional training in economics and interpersonal skills.

Design Features for a Participative System

- Organizational Structure
  1. Flat
  2. Lean
  3. Minienterprise oriented
  4. Team based
  5. Participative council or structure
- Job Design
  1. Individually enriched or
  2. Self-managing teams
- Information System
  1. Open
  2. Inclusive
  3. Tied to jobs
  4. Decentralized—team based
  5. Participatively set goals and standards
- Career System
  1. Tracks and counseling available
  2. Open job posting
- Selection
  1. Realistic job preview
  2. Team based
  3. Potential and process skill oriented
- Training
  1. Heavy commitment
  2. Peer training

3. Economic education
4. Interpersonal skills
- Reward System
  1. Open
  2. Skill based
  3. Gain sharing or ownership
  4. Flexible benefits
  5. All salary
  6. Egalitarian perquisites
- Personnel Policies
  1. Stability of employment
  2. Participatively established through representative group
- Physical Layout
  1. Around organizational structure
  2. Egalitarian
  3. Safe and pleasant

In many respects, the design features listed seem to be congruent with each other and to be mutually reinforcing. They all send a message to people in the organization that says they are important, respected, valued, capable of growing, and trusted and that their understanding of and involvement in the total organization is desirable and expected.

The list of design features should be viewed as ideal. It is not one that is characteristic of any existing organization to the best of my knowledge; nevertheless I believe it can be put into effect. The features listed are not completely untested and untried in today's work environment. Some organizations incorporate many if not all of them. The organizations that come closest to incorporating them all are the several hundred or more high involvement new plants that have sprung up around the United States during the last ten years. They contain a number of innovative features and, interestingly, seem to be proliferating at a rapid rate in the United States (Lawler, 1978). These features are also built into many of the more mature gain-sharing companies in the United States (Lawler, 1981). As Ouchi and Jaeger (1978) have pointed out, some very successful U.S. corporations (such as IBM) incorporate quite a few of the practices. They, however, do not go as far as the new plants do in incorporating all these design features.

Effectiveness of High Involvement Systems

Although there is a general lack of research, some positive assessments have appeared, and there is a certain consistency to the findings (see Davis and Cherns, 1975; Hackman and Suttle, 1977). In general, participative systems seem to be characterized by low turnover, low tardiness, low absenteeism, low material and supply costs, low labor costs, and high quality. In many ways, this is not a surprising pattern of positive results. When these systems are operating effectively, they are designed to have people more involved in and more informed about a variety of organizational decisions. This leads to people being more committed to the system, hence lower turnover, lower tardiness, and lower absenteeism. It also leads to their caring more about effectiveness and to their knowing more, hence lower material, supply, and labor costs. The finding of higher quality seems to be relatively similar to the finding with respect to job design (Hackman and Oldham, 1980). Here the data show that when individuals feel responsibility for a task, they are particularly motivated to improve the quality because they feel personally identified with the product and do not wish to be associated with a low quality product.

Not all existing high involvement systems that include many of the design features I have identified have produced all the favorable results I have enumerated. Indeed, at this point, it would be premature to say these systems are always more effective than traditional ones. Situational conditions may cause a participative organization to produce more favorable results in only a few of these areas. For example, when compared to traditional structures, a participative one may not produce lower labor costs if the technology and work flow is of a highly repetitive nature (for example, auto assembly or fast food sales). It may not produce high quality if quality is difficult to control. Perhaps the most reliable finding with respect to high involvement systems is that they do tend to produce good absenteeism and turnover records, although even this may be influenced by situational factors.

Overall, it seems that certain situational factors that favor creating organizations with high involvement management systems can be identified. Interdependent technologies, small organization size, situations where product quality or service quality is a key determinant of operating effectiveness, and situations that involve new start-ups seem to favor high involvement systems. The reasons for this seem to follow rather directly from the design features listed earlier.

Small size makes it easier for individuals to identify with organizational inputs and results. Interdependent technologies create conditions where there is a substantial performance advantage to having good communication, coordination, and control mechanisms in an organization. Because this is something that high involvement systems usually handle quite well, it gives them a competitive advantage over traditional organizations. Similarly, because the motivational climate produced by high involvement systems seems to be particularly favorable to getting high quality products, when this is a key results area for an organization, they do rather well. Finally, new start-ups provide the opportunity to put a complete design in place at once and thus create an internally congruent system from the beginning. Hence, this is a particularly favorable circumstance for high involvement systems, and as a result, new plants seem to enjoy a much higher success rate with participative management than do efforts that involve changing traditional systems to participative ones. When change from a traditional to a high involvement one is done, substantial problems involving the scheduling of different changes, and interface congruence between traditional and new systems always develop. It becomes hard, for example, to know where to begin change, how rapidly to move different design features to a more participative mode, and to get most of the design features into a participative mode.

Problem Areas

Problem areas are not necessarily fatal to the concept, but they are important to note because they provide some insight as to how high involvement systems work and because many of them can be prevented or contained when they are anticipated.

Individual Differences. Despite the growing orientation in our society toward democratic or participative management and an increased rejection of authoritarian decision making, not everyone prefers to work in a high involvement work setting. Thus, misfits occur and not everyone works well in these systems.

First-Level Supervisors. Most organizations that have tried participative management have had great difficulty in finding adequate first-level supervisors (see Walton and Schlesinger, 1979). Supervising a self-managing team is a very different function than supervising in a traditional work group. As a result, the supervisors often do not adapt and are not effective in new systems. Training can help some, but it still turns out to be a difficult position to fill and perform.

Permissiveness versus Participation. The difference between permissiveness and participation often becomes muddy in the eyes of management, as does the distinction between those issues on which participation is appropriate and those on which it is not. Examples have occurred of employees being given practically anything they wanted because there is a "consensus" that this is the way things should be. In other cases, participative decision making has been used on technical matters where it is totally inappropriate. The key to preventing problems seems to be for management to be clear as to what the boundaries are for participation and what kind of decisions are appropriately made participatively.

Office Personnel and Staff Functions. In most high involvement systems the office personnel and staff feel somewhat disadvantaged relative to the production people. They often comment that their jobs are pretty much the same as they would be elsewhere and that, despite all the talk about a different kind of work climate, they are in a very similar kind of situation that they would be in elsewhere. There undoubtedly is validity in this, although part of the problem may be that the relative advantage they once enjoyed over the production people has dramatically decreased, and, as a result, they feel relatively disadvantaged in comparison to traditional work settings. This is almost an inevitable consequence of making the shop floor jobs more like the office jobs. Still, it would seem that more innovation is needed and is possible in the design and management of office jobs.

Regression Under Pressure. In some high involvement systems, there has been a tendency to discard participation when a crisis has appeared in the organization. The feeling in some situations has been that participation is fine when things are going well but that strong, centralized decision making and control is needed when a crisis develops. Where participation has been abandoned in times of crisis, it has had a tendency to harm the high involvement system because it has communicated to people that participation is not a serious, permanent feature of the organization.

Interface with the Rest of the Corporation. Many of the high involvement systems that have been tried in the United States exist in plants that are part of a larger corporation. Because these new plants are not understood by people in the rest of the corporation, this has caused a number of problems. Key among these are suspicion and mistrust of the high involvement system, unwillingness to change corporate rules to allow the system to do things that it needs to do to be effective, and financial measures of the system that are not appropriate to the way the organization is being managed. All these problems are solvable and probably will lessen as broader acceptance and understanding of high involvement systems develops. In the meantime, however, it can cause conflict and jealousy and in some cases has led to the dismissal of managers in high involvement systems because they were "causing too many problems" for the rest of the organization.

Creating Participative Systems

In a number of respects, it is easier to specify the characteristic that should be present in a high involvement system than it is to specify how one can be created. The actual implementation of these characteristics is a complex and often situation-specific process that at times defies prescription. In addition, little research addresses such issues as where to start a change effort in an old organization, how many features are needed for a high involvement system to be operational, and how long it takes to install a high involvement system. I have studied some of these issues in the context of doing research on three types of planned organizational change efforts: gain-sharing plans, new high involvement work settings, and union/management QWL projects. In summarizing the conclusions suggested by these studies, I will focus on results concerning installing high involvement approaches to management, since this is a common theme in all the projects that have been studied. The conclusions that follow are not all original, nor do they represent a comprehensive list. They are a summary of thoughts concerning change in organizations that are data driven, but not necessarily supported by statistically significant tests on hard data.

Planning Change. Most of the planned change efforts I have studied began with rather detailed plans concerning the nature of the changes that were to be instituted. In most cases, the original plan had been abandoned within a year, and in some cases, the change project had taken on an entirely different nature. For example, in one site a program that began with a plan to get people more involved in their work through creating self-managing work groups ended up giving them the chance to go home early when they increased their productivity. In another case, an experiment in introducing a gain-sharing plan in one part of a company ended up changing the base pay of everyone in the company. These and many other examples suggest it is difficult to plan change, particularly when the implementation process has a high degree of participation built into it. Indeed, the only thing that can be planned is certain parts of its process.

This point has a number of implications, not the least of which is for how we do research. It strongly suggests that if researchers want to survive in this environment, they need to adopt a very adaptive stance to what they study. That is, they need to be able to change the measurement and theoretical emphasis to fit what is happening in the change effort. Failure to do this will likely result in the study of something that did not happen.

For the implementers of change, it suggests that the adoption of an adaptive stance is crucial. If they rigidly insist on sticking to the original plan, they, like the researcher, may find themselves expendable, as several of the "change agents" studied found themselves.

Organizations do not lend themselves to rigidly imposed change programs. There are a number of reasons for this, including the fact that they are constantly being buffeted by a changing environment that demands they change in order to survive. Thus, a plan that looks good at the beginning may not look good later in the implementation process. In addition, organizations are made up of individuals with different values, preferences, and power positions. It is almost impossible to take all of these into account in designing a change. However, once a change starts unfolding, it is almost impossible not to take many of these into account. Thus, the change must be altered and adapted to fit many of these interests.

Planned change is not impossible, but it often is difficult to implement such that it results in the original change. Change is an ongoing process. An end state cannot be reached, studied, and assessed.

Congruence and/or Ineffectiveness. A great deal of the writing on open systems theory stresses that organizations are interrelated systems. Because they are systems, issues of congruence and fit are paramount. A key to understanding the effectiveness of an organization is an analysis of how its different features go together (Nadler and Tushman, 1977). Lawler (1978) suggests that one reason for the effectiveness of new high involvement plants is their congruence with respect to their subsystems. That is, their pay plan fits their job design and so on. When fit does not exist, organizations tend to suffer a number of problems, including employees who are dissatisfied because they suffer from role ambiguity and role conflict. The organization also tends to be ineffective because the employees suffer from poor motivation, poor communication, and poor coordination. Because of the problems associated with incongruous subsystems, pressure builds to create congruence. This can result in those elements in the system that are deviant being altered and, as a result, can cause organizational change. It may not, however, result in the kind of change that a planned change effort is designed to produce. Indeed, it may lead to the elimination of changes that were put in place as part of the change effort. This can occur because congruence is easiest to produce by moving toward a system that fits the majority of the elements already in place. Often the majority of the elements are not consistent with the planned change effort and, as a result, the change effort is rejected.

Congruence does not assure organizational effectiveness. It is likely to occur only if the congruent internal system fits the external environment in which it must operate. This point follows directly from contingency theory and is consistent with points made earlier about when we can expect high involvement organizations to be successful. It is not accidental that they seem to be most effective when they, in turn, fit the types of people who are attracted to them and the type of production technology they employ, to mention two critical issues.

One important implication of the crucial role that congruence seems to play in organizations is that more research effort needs to be devoted to this issue. Research on the topic probably needs to be longitudinal in nature so that it is possible to test ideas about systems moving toward congruence. Finally, theoretical work that focuses on what constitutes congruence and how systems move toward it is needed.

Roads to Participative Systems. The organization development literature is full of suggestions about how to start change efforts designed to move from traditional systems to participative ones. Survey feedback, job enrichment programs, self-managing teams, and team building are among the approaches frequently suggested. If the views suggested so far are correct, any one of these can be a good place to start. The first key is to start with an issue that is of concern to people and where change can be introduced. This point comes directly from change theory and is based on the arguments that the change is meaningful only if it deals with important issues and that initial change efforts need to result in actual changes in order to produce a climate of success.

The second and perhaps most important key is that the initial changes must be followed and supported by other changes that are congruent with the original changes. This point follows directly from what was said earlier about the importance of congruence. I stressed that systems tend to congruence and that, as a result, there is a good chance that a deviant practice will be rejected unless other features of the organization are changed to be supportive of it. Thus, any single feature change effort needs to anticipate that to be successful it must rapidly move on to deal with other aspects of the organization (unless, of course, it is simply changing one feature to be congruent with the rest of the system).

The fact that it is possible to start successful change efforts with different approaches raises some interesting theoretical and research questions. It is common to stress the importance of diagnosis when starting a change project, and indeed this probably is appropriate. Missing, however, is theoretical and empirical work that specifies in any detail just what kind of diagnostic results indicate which type of start point for a change project. Perhaps the best we can do is to say that the change should deal with an important issue, but I do not think so. It should be possible to specify in much greater detail what type of diagnostic result suggests what change sequence.

Resurrection and Creation. The success rate of high involvement new plants seems to be very high. No one knows exactly what percentage of the high involvement new plant efforts that have been attempted have actually resulted in new plants that are more effective than traditional ones. Nevertheless, I estimate that about 90 percent are (I know of three "failures" and more than twenty successes). The success rate of change efforts in existing organizations seems much lower than this, regardless of whether they have focused on gain sharing, job redesign, or union-management cooperation, to mention just a few approaches to changing existing organizations. In most of these failures, implementation of a complete high involvement system has never occurred.

If we grant that creating new high involvement organizations is easier than changing old ones, we need to deal with the question of why. In a number of respects, this point follows directly from much of what has been said already about change. New organizations simply have a number of advantages when it comes to creating high involvement systems. They can start with a congruent total system; they can select people who are compatible; no one has a vested interest in the status quo; and it is possible to do the whole organization at once so the participative island disease is avoided. Given these advantages, it is hardly surprising that new situations have a higher success rate. Indeed, even though we learn a lot more about how to change existing organizations, it is unlikely that it can ever be as easy to change them as it is to establish new ones. Theoretically, a situation could exist in which change would be as easy, but it would have to have a number of conditions that are not typically present (for example, no resistance to change, the resources to install a congruent organizationwide approach at once).

Participate Islands. Frequently, organizations will begin change projects by starting with small "experimental" groups. The reasons usually given for the approach make good sense. It provides a chance for the organization to learn how to do it; they can "test" out the approach and see if it works; and it does not require a large amount of resources to start. There are two major problems with this approach, however. First, having an experimental group is of limited value both as a learning experience and as a test because having an experimental group is qualitatively and quantitatively different than having a high involvement organization. Second, experimental groups rarely survive for very long when standing by themselves in the middle of a "hostile" environment.

Having a single participative group is clearly quantitatively different than having all groups operating in this mode. It is often also qualitatively different because the surrounding circumstances are so radically different when a group is embedded in a participative situation. It means that social support is present, learnings from others are available, and organization policies and practices are supportive. As a result, groups in high involvement systems are much more likely to succeed than are experimental groups, and managing them is different because the key issues are less ones of protecting the groups against hostile forces.

Little research has been done on the issue of institutionalizing experimental groups, but there is some that suggests it often fails to happen (Goodman, 1979; Mirvis and Berg, 1977). One company, for example, studied the fate of fifty experimental self-managing teams it started in manufacturing facilities. Although many enjoyed short-term success, none were institutionalized. This is hardly surprising, given the importance of total system congruence and what is known in social psychology about the treatment of deviants. Unless the experimental areas are decoupled from the rest of the organization, there is every reason to believe that many pressures will build up toward congruence. Often experimental groups are granted waivers from certain policies, and after a while the people responsible from the areas try to get things back in order. In addition, surrounding groups often resent the treatment accorded to the experimental group, and they create pressure for everyone to be treated the same.

The experimental group should be used cautiously and with full knowledge of its limitations. In general, it probably should be used only when the organization is willing to establish several groups and where the groups are not experimental but merely the first areas to be changed as part of a total system change effort. Only if these two conditions are met are the groups likely to be successful enough and to survive long enough so that they lead to other groups being formed.

Changing Back to Traditional Systems. Most of the change literature on high involvement systems is concerned with the issues and problems involved in changing to this management system, an important issue because most planned change efforts are concerned with doing just this. There is, however, a second kind of change effort that is of considerable theoretical and practical interest: ones that are directed toward changing participative systems to more traditional ones. At first glance, it might seem that this would be very easy to do because democratic systems have often proved easy victims for autocratic leaders. Nevertheless, there are reasons for believing that, under certain conditions, it can be difficult to dislodge high involvement systems once they have become fully established.

If theory is correct, people will become comfortable with the high involvement practices and can be expected to resist any change. In addition, any change effort that deals with only a limited number of factors is likely to fail because the weight of the case will be on the side of high involvement management and the systems will tend to seek congruence. In this case, congruence will mean reversing the movement away from high involvement management.

Basic to the argument that high involvement systems are hard to eliminate is the view that even lower level participants in work organizations and, thus, their desires, can make a difference. They have power in a number of respects, including the ability to unionize, quit, slow production, and file court cases. It is precisely because they have power that the destruction of an attractive approach to management is likely to be difficult to accomplish.

There is little evidence on just how difficult it is to change high involvement work systems. There is one widely reported "successful" case. The press has carried a number of reports concerning the "failure" of participative management at the General Foods Toppers plant. According to the reports, after great initial fanfare, this new plant was changed to a more traditional approach to management. These reports make good reading but, to the best of my knowledge, they are wrong. It is true that several key managers were replaced with an eye toward making the plant more like other G.F. plants. Several traditional managers were put into place, but according to recent reports, the high involvement system still operates effectively because the employees were successful in resisting most changes to it.

The experience at Topeka is similar to ones that I have had in two other plants. In both cases, "traditional" plant managers were put in charge of high involvement plants. The result in both cases was the same—the systems survived and the new managers became strong supporters of them. Overall, there is not enough evidence to establish that high involvement approaches are difficult to eliminate; still, at this point some experience is consistent with the view that they may be difficult to eliminate once they are established as congruent systems if they are loosely coupled to nonparticipative systems.

Vision Is Critical. One characteristic that frequently separates successful from unsuccessful change projects is the existence of a vision or metaphor. In the successful projects, key participants typically share a vision of the desired end state. In the unsuccessful projects, the participants rarely have a clear idea of where they would like to take the organization, and they tend to lack a clear overview of how all the pieces fit together. In short, they tend to see the trees, not the forest.

When individuals have a good overview, they develop heuristics, which allow them to make ongoing decisions about the details of implementing particular changes. It allows them to reject or accept specific policies and practices and to deal with people in a consistent way. When they lack a vision, metaphor, or overall philosophy of what they are trying to accomplish, each decision cannot be tested against a set of overarching principles. The result is that decisions tend to be haphazard and a lack of consistency and congruence develops in the change effort. A poorly designed change develops, and the system tends to bog down in details and minutiae.

The implication of this observation is clear. Organizational change projects, in order to be successful, need to install within the organization a collective vision of what the desired end state looks like. It is not a simple matter to develop such a shared vision. In our change projects, we have tried a number of approaches to this, including readings, visits to other projects, long discussions with key management groups in the organizations, and exercises designed to help the people identify their ideal model. All this can help, but in my experience, it is difficult to move some people in this direction. It requires thinking at a rather abstract level and some people simply find this very difficult to do. You can help people develop a conceptual model or concept of what they are trying to do with the organization, but certain inclinations and natural abilities are needed. Thus, no guarantee is possible upon entry into an organization that the capability to develop the kind of conceptual model that is needed will be present in the organization. In many of the successful change projects that I have studied, these skills and partially developed conceptual models were present in people's heads before the change agent ever entered the scene. All the change agent did was provide a little flesh to the existing bones.

Relation of Values to Energy. The scientific literature on organizational change often presents the change process as a rather antiseptic one in which a description of a new method and its possible outcomes are presented to a site and the site then decides whether to adopt or reject the approach. The energy for the change is assumed to come from the presumed advantages to the organization and to the individuals of the change. The participants' values and their impact on the change process are often ignored.

In several of the projects studied, the key source of energy for the projects was not expected improved organizational effectiveness or greater economic gain for the employees, but a successful appeal to the employee's values. In these cases, the change agent or other leaders of the change program talked about the underlying values that were guiding the project, such things as democracy, equity, and individualization. They used these to support the specific changes that were implemented. In many respects, this proved to be an effective strategy because the values stated were strongly held by the participants and they wished to see them forwarded. A clear implication of this outcome is that change can be stimulated by values, as political scientists and others interested in social reform and revolution have often noted. Apparently, work organizations are no different, and change can come about based on the skillful appeal to values. How this can best be done and details of the impact need to be the subject of a great deal more research and theory.

Types, Sources, and Importance of Data. Most writings on how to do organization change projects stress the importance of evaluating the success of change efforts. They talk about the kind of financial, attitudinal, and behavioral data that can be collected to support the overall evaluation of the success or failure of the project. In all the change projects I have been involved in, a conscientious effort has been made to gather this kind of "objective" data. One problem has consistently developed, however. The people in the organization tend not to use these data when they evaluate project success or failure. They often express interest in the data, but for a number of reasons evaluate the project based on other factors.

In many cases, the evaluations the participants and the organizational decision makers involved in the change projects reach are based on odd pieces of circumstantial or happenstance data. For example, at one site a decision maker walked into the plant and casually bumped into a worker. He asked the worker how he liked the project. The worker said that not much was happening. The executive turned to me and said, "See, I told you it wouldn't work." From then on he was very resistant to any data that suggested the project was going well. In another case, the reverse happened. The key decision maker encountered several workers who raved about the project. From then on he was strongly committed to the project, despite the fact that the economic data showed no financial effect of the project. Ironically, the same individual had stressed at the beginning of the project that he would be convinced only if we could show strong financial changes as a result of the project.

What seems to be going on in these two cases and in many others is that people in decision-making positions in an organization tend to make ongoing real-time evaluations of projects. Because they are unschooled in data and data collection, they are often strongly influenced in these evaluations by haphazardly collected and often misleading data. Our data are not their data, and often by the time we get around to a thorough evaluation of a project, it has been either written off as a failure or declared a large success in the organization.

This is a troubling tendency, one that is very hard to overcome when a change project is being done. Perhaps the only way is to try to simplify the data that we collect, have more involvement in it so that it will be more broadly owned, and be more timely in reporting it back. In addition, perhaps more time spent on training the managers to interpret and react to data would help. These points have some important implications for both theory and research. We need to know a great deal more about how managers judge the success to change projects. For some reason, research and theory on this topic have been lacking.

Effects of Declaring a Success. Several projects that were studied developed a very high profile in the popular press. The participants in these projects frequently appeared on panels at meetings and in some cases on TV and radio shows. Interestingly enough, these appearances came very early in the history of the projects, sometimes so early that little data were available to indicate whether the project was successful. This, however, did not stop the change agents and the project sponsors from declaring publicly that the projects were already successful. Participants from the projects themselves seemed to fall into a similar mode when they appeared in public to describe their projects. These premature declarations of success seemed to energize the participants to make the projects successful. In essence, it seemed to lead to them being more committed to seeing that the projects were successful because they had become publicly committed to the fact that the projects were successful. Of course, this public declaration of success did not prevent them from privately talking about the project limitations and shortcomings. Nevertheless, overall it seemed that premature declaration of success was more helpful than harmful in the long term because the projects did later enjoy some meaningful success.

Conclusion

Quite a bit has been learned since the early writings on participative management systems. A considerable amount of theory has been developed and there is a slowly increasing body of empirical results, but perhaps the most interesting developments have taken place within organizations. The willingness of some organizations and managers to experiment has produced knowledge about how to change organizations and design high involvement systems. They have converted the theoretical ideas into a reality-based management system. Because of this, it is possible to specify in some detail the characteristics of systems. In essence, they have done much of the development engineering work in the field of participative management.

I think the future will bring an increasing rate of adoption of participative management and high involvement work systems. Now that some of the development work is done, it seems ready for broader dissemination. Predictions of dissemination are not new; they were made decades ago and typically proved to be too optimistic. Nevertheless, the situation is sufficiently different now to warrant limited optimism. There remains a large number of theoretically and empirically interesting issues to be resolved. We need to know more about how, when, and where to initiate change and we need to know more about what constitutes congruence and how systems move toward it. Finally, there is the question of how best to do research on these issues.

References

Alderfer, C. P. "An Empirical Test of a New Theory of Human Needs." *Organizational Behavior and Human Performance,* 1969, *4,* 142-175.

Argyris, C. *Personality and Organization.* New York: Harper & Row, 1957.

Davis, L. E., and Cherns, A. B. (Eds.). *The Quality of Working Life.* Vols. 1 and 2. New York: Free Press, 1975.

Goodman, P. S. *Assessing Organizational Change: The Rushton Quality of Work Experiment.* New York: Wiley-Interscience, 1979.

Hackman, J. R., and Lawler, E. E. "Employee Reactions to Job Characteristics." *Journal of Applied Psychology,* 1971, *55,* 259-286.

Hackman, J. R., and Oldham, G. R. *Work Redesign.* Reading, Mass.: Addison-Wesley, 1980.

Hackman, J. R., and Suttle, J. L. (Eds.). *Improving Life at Work.* Santa Monica, Calif.: Goodyear, 1977.

Lawler, E. E. *Motivation in Work Organizations.* Monterey, Calif.: Brooks/Cole, 1973.

Lawler, E. E. "The New Plant Revolution." *Organizational Dynamics,* 1978, *6*(3), 2–12.

Lawler, E. E. "Motivation: Closing the Gap Between Theory and Practice." In K. D. Duncan, M. M. Gruneberg, and D. Wallis (Eds.), *Changes in Working Life.* New York: Wiley-Interscience, 1980.

Lawler, E. E. *Pay and Organization Development.* Reading, Mass.: Addison-Wesley, 1981.

Likert, R. *New Patterns of Management.* New York: McGraw-Hill, 1961.

Likert, R. *The Human Organization.* New York: McGraw-Hill, 1967.

McGregor, D. *The Human Side of Enterprise.* New York: McGraw-Hill, 1960.

Mirvis, P. H., and Berg, D. *Failures in Organizational Development and Change: Cases and Essays For Learning.* New York: Wiley-Interscience, 1977.

Nadler, D. A., and Tushman, M. L. "A Diagnostic Model for Organizational Behavior." In J. R. Hackman, E. Lawler, and L. W. Porter (Eds.), *Perspectives on Organizational Behavior.* New York: McGraw-Hill, 1977.

Ouchi, W. G., and Jaeger, A. M. "Type Z Organization: Stability in the Midst of Mobility." *Academy of Management Review,* 1978, *3,* 305–314.

Walton, R. E., and Schlesinger, L. A. "Do Supervisors Thrive in Participative Work Systems?" *Organizational Dynamics,* 1979, *8*(3), 25–38.

▣ ▣ ▣ ▣ ▣ ▣ ▣ **8**

Philosophical Problems in Thinking About Organizational Change

▣ ▣ ▣ ▣ ▣ ▣ ▣ ▣ ▣ ▣ ▣ ▣ ▣ ▣ ▣ ▣ ▣ ▣

Kenwyn K. Smith

In this chapter I want to explore the idea that we might need to change the organization of our thinking in order to think about how we change our organizing.

Many of the planned changes we attempt to make in our organizations seem to fly in the face of naturally occurring changes—the seasonality, if you will—of an organization's life. As organizational actors, be we managers, workers, investors, or interventionists, we often observe that things need to be different than they are: Productivity is low; morale is poor; the economy is sagging; the quality of our work lives is inferior to the Japanese or Tongans or some newly chosen referent group. These signs lead us to believe that we should take action to produce changes. That is understandable; the problem is what we think these signs are telling us and how our interpretations shape our actions. Do we interpret the signs through a technological/medical mindset, viewing low productivity and such as diseases for which some magical medicine or technological innovation may be found? Or are they symptoms of some deeper ill, some social cancer that must be exorcised? Or do we interpret these signs from a more organic perspective, viewing them as the organizational and social equivalent of something we all know about ourselves: When we are tired, we must rest; if we over-stress our bodies, it takes time to recover; if we go beyond the break-ing point, we might not make it back; if we go to the mountaintop, our next journey will be into the valley.

Most organizations seem to be constantly dealing with either some major organizational transition, such as a strike or budget cutbacks, or the problems of being stuck in some developmental plateau. Hence, rather than thinking of change as something we do to our organizations, I treat change as a natural part of a larger organizational life cycle perspective.

As a starting point for reorienting my thinking, I turned initially to Sarason (1972), who for more than a decade had been calling for a developmental perspective on organizations. I looked to the rich set of metaphors that development theorists have of-fered us (Erikson, 1950; Freud, 1953; Kline, 1932; Levinson, 1978; Levi-Strauss, 1958; Piaget, 1968) and attempted to map these onto the transitional phenomena I had been encountering in organiza-tions. I patiently struggled with what Campbell and Mickelson (1975) described as the life cycle stages of communication systems—chaos, increasing coherence, purpose, and decision bias. No matter which way I turned, however, I kept running into a number of epistemological roadblocks, some of which were easy enough to blast a way through, others to circumvent. But most of them were stopping me cold.

By the time I had finished reading my colleagues' chapters for this book, I realized that the epistemological problems I was en-countering lay latent and unexplored in their work also. Hence, it felt time to stop, take stock, and reexamine how we think about change. That is what I wish to do here. In this chapter I do not explicate a theory of change. Nor do I theorize specifically about organizational life cycles. Rather, I have chosen to enter into some of those epistemological knots that I believe we must untangle before we can make further significant advances in our understanding about change processes in organizations.

First I look at some of the other chapters in this book for examples of the epistemological problems I think we must examine more closely. Then I ask what is organization. I end up defining organization as relations among parts and relations among relations and hence come to realize the only way organizations can be understood is metaphorically. This leads me first into discussing the theme of metaphor and metonymy as a way of setting the foundation for the rest of the chapter, which is organized around three further topics: the boundary *"not,"* sense making of collectivities, and morphostasis and morphogenesis. Although I am discussing these topics under four different headings, the ideas of each section contain the concepts of each other section within it.

Sketching the Terrain

Argyris and Staw (Chapters Two and Three) both discuss whether organizations and organizational actors can and do learn how to change and, in particular, whether these changes alter the very core of things, such as the governing values and master programs that shape actions—or whether they merely change appearances, the domain of the superficial. This is a deeply complex question and is at the heart of the topic cybernetics theory calls the morphostasis/morphogenesis issue.

Morphogenesis is applied to changes similar to those that occur in natural evolution. Here change is of a form that penetrates so deeply into the "genetic code" that all future generations acquire and reflect those changes. In morphogenesis the change has occurred in the very essence, in the core, and nothing special needs to be done to keep the change changed.

Morphostasis encompasses two types of changes. First there are those that enable things to look different while remaining basically as they have always been. This is captured cryptically in the old French proverb "the more things change, the more they stay the same" (Sarason, 1971; Watzlawick, Weakland, and Fisch, 1974). These changes are not very enduring and have the propensity to disappear unless change effort is continually applied. The second kind of morphostatic change occurs as a natural expression of the developmental sequence. These are the changes embedded in the natural maturation processes. Here the boundaries on the possibilities of change are contained *within* the instructions coded into the system. For example, as a kitten or duckling matures, it becomes a cat and duck, respectively. The duckling will not become a cat. Such developmental/maturational changes are called morphostatic by cybernetics theory, in contrast to morphogenic, which is preserved for changes in the actual instructions that shape the unfolding of the system.

We can see in Chapter Two by Argyris the philosophical problem of morphostasis/morphogenesis that plagues all our attempts at planned change. Although I am convinced Argyris is correct in his assertion that one's governing values must be changed to alter human action significantly and I have great respect for the enormous energy and insight he has brought to understanding change processes, I am concerned about the philosophical issues embedded in whether and how governing values can be altered. Argyris, like the rest of us, appears to be struggling with how to produce morphogenesis, but our tools, our technologies, are of a fundamentally morphostatic type. This is the functional equivalent of attempting to create some genetic mutation in an animal with the expectations it will be passed on to its progeny by simply working to change its behavior through operant conditioning. I address morphostasis/morphogenesis in some detail because it is central to any coherent attempts to produce organizational change.

Staw (Chapter Three) talks about the rigidity of an organization's behavior and how problematic this can be, especially when ecological conditions call for flexible and adaptive behavior. One problem latent in the whole of his discussion is that he talks about the rigidity as being an aspect of the system he is studying. He does not treat it as a characteristic of the relationship between that system and its environment. The question must always be how we are going to formulate the topic of inquiry. It may be that from the point of view of the acting organization, rigid behavior is dysfunctional because it leads to its extinction. However, from an ecological perspective, the death of that particular organization may be the source of renewal. Rigidity and pathology at one level of analysis may be adaptive and regenerative at the next. Staw ignores the philosophical implications of this and provides an example of the domain of sense making, where we need to do some major rethinking.

This topic has been reflected on in other scholarly domains, both as an issue in the problems of logical typing and in cybernetics through the often discussed example of the ecological relationship between rabbits and lynxes (Tustin, 1952). Consider a territory inhabited by rabbits, which are the prey for the predatory lynxes. Where rabbits are abundant, the lynx population increases, but if the lynxes become abundant, the rabbit population falls because more rabbits are caught. Then as the rabbits diminish, the lynxes go hungry and likewise decline, and so forth. The system goes into oscillation. Imagine, however, if while the rabbits are in decline, the only ones to escape and survive are the ones who have evolved a few extra IQ points that make them bright enough to know when and how to hide from the lynxes. Then the fact that the lynxes were doing well getting all the rabbits they needed was sufficient to trigger this special evolutionary act of the rabbits, thereby enabling the rabbits to survive but in turn threatening the survival of the lynxes. The short-term success of the lynxes leads to the longer term threat to their own survival. Imagine, however, if the lynxes can also evolve intelligence; then those that will survive the shortage of rabbits will be those who fall in the range of being smart enough to "outfox" the rabbits' new hiding techniques and stability at a new level will be developed. If, however, the only lynxes that are surviving are those with a higher "intelligence" and this happens to be superior to that of all the rabbits, the lynxes will begin to flourish again. Only short-term, though, for as they increase and proceed to catch all the rabbits, they do so well that they kill off all the rabbits and in turn extinguish themselves.

The system is in oscillation. If we look only at the behavior of the lynxes, ignoring the oscillatory nature of the larger ecological set of relationships, the same behavior—namely, catching and eating rabbits—is highly flexible, adaptive behavior at one point and rigid and maladaptive at another. The behavior itself is not really adaptive or rigid; it is just behavior. It is the nature of the larger system that makes it appear as adaptive or rigid from the lynx perspective. On the larger scale, however, the very rigidity of the lynxes' behavior, leading at certain times to a fall in their own population, is very adaptive at the ecological level, for it preserves the oscillation pattern, which in fact guarantees the long-term survival of both lynxes and rabbits.

The problem in thinking raised by Staw's discussion of rigidity/perseverance may be expressed as "adaptation at one level may be rigidity at another." This level-of-analysis problem spans most of our writings about organizational issues. For example, when Weick (Chapter Nine) uses the term "loosely coupled," we must immediately ask loosely coupled from what point of view. Tightly coupled activity from a within-system perspective may appear very loosely coupled from the vantage point of the suprastructure or vice versa. Simmel (1955) and Coser (1956) highlighted this nicely for us in their exposition that social and industrial unrest, which may be too tightly coupled behavior for the infrastructure, may in fact help preserve the order of the larger system just perfectly.

An attendant issue in the previous examples of the level of analysis/level of abstraction problem is how meanings get attached to behavior and experience. The meaning "rigid" or "adaptive" does not lie within the behavior itself—otherwise its meaning would remain constant across times, situations, and levels of analysis. The meanings change, depending on context and on whose system of attributions we are talking about. To understand the meanings attached to behaviors, we must look at the relationships between events and the contexts in which they occur.

This is a philosophical issue that we could approach through several different theoretical frameworks, for how meanings get attached to events and experience is at the heart of all attempts to understand knowledge. I am choosing the framework of linguistics to discuss this issue, mainly because it provides a language that enables us to link it to two other major topics relevant to thinking about changing thinking, namely, the analog/digital distinction in communications theory and morphostasis/morphogenesis. I will discuss the question of attaching meanings to experience under the broad heading of metaphor/metonymy. Linked directly to this theme is how groups, people, and systems make sense of their own experience and the experiences of other related groups, people, and systems in their environment. Hence, I explore the relationship between metaphor/metonymy and sense making (Weick, 1979) at the level of the collectivity.

This topic is especially important to understanding change because when we are dealing with human experience, be it individual or collective, the meanings that get attached to experience are an integral part of that experience. Hence, to change the systems of meanings and attributions tied to experience is, in fact, to change the experience, at least in *how* it is experienced. If we wish to change the ways meanings are linked to events/objects/experiences, the place to focus our change efforts is not on the events/objects/experiences themselves, but on the *relationships* between those events/objects/experiences and the context in which they are embedded.

Rigidity/perseverance/flexibility or whatever is not a characteristic of the entity itself. It is a characteristic of the relationship between the entity and its context, even though it may be expressed or made visible in the actual behavior of the entity. Social science discourse is filled with theory built on the faulty premise of inappropriately attributing to an entity itself characteristics of the relationships among entities or between an entity and its ecosystem.

This misattribution emanates largely from our failure to understand the relationship between a social entity and what it is not. This is very critical to untangle for "not" is at the center of all change. Anything that is changing is in the process of becoming something it previously was *not*. As it matures, it *is* now no longer as it *was*. The very idea of an entity as being something separate from and identifiable within its environment or ecosystem means the entity is *not* like the rest of the environment in some critical ways. It is over and against, definable against the backdrop of the environment. Any new construction involves the destruction of something else (Burke, 1966). Any change means the status quo is *not* any longer as it was (Thayer, 1968). "Not" is central to all change.

"Not," however, is *not* a thing; it is a boundary that summarizes a relationship. It "belongs" neither to the entity nor to what it is not. It is a meta statement, a characteristic of the relationship between an entity and what it is not. Many social scientists fail to recognize this. For example, Piaget (1968) tends to see the boundary *between* an entity and its environment, what it is not, as somehow belonging to the structure of the entity itself. Borrowing from gestalt metaphors, this is like separating figure from ground by a boundary delineation and then attributing the boundary between them to the figure. This is a logical error. The boundary "belongs" neither to the figure nor to the ground. In fact, this boundary is not a thing; it is a rule about how ground and figure relate to each other and as such is of a different logical type than both the figure and the ground. This error in Piaget's thinking is most evident when he wishes to change an entity. He rightly goes to the boundary, the place where changes occur, but he inappropriately attempts to alter the structure of the entity because he has located the boundary within the entity instead of working on changing the relationship between the entity and its environment.

These four epistemological issues provide a sketch of the problem terrain I feel we must understand more fully if we are ever to advance our thinking about change in organizations. Unfortunately, there seems no clear, easy, or logical way to explore these epistemological themes, for they are all intertwined. The loose threads in one domain, when followed, seem to end up at the core of another. Hence, I simply plunge headlong into them and see what different theoretical strands are available to be grasped.

An Organizational Example

In order to ground this exploration, I shall provide examples from a lengthy involvement we have had with the Design and Engineering unit of a large Buildings and Maintenance operation at Weymouth State Hospital. (This work is reported in detail in Smith, Simmons, and Thames, 1982.) Buildings and Maintenance consists of approximately six hundred employees who are engaged in all types of work, including cleaning, maintaining the grounds, fixing plumbing, painting, and providing air conditioning and heating. Within Buildings and Maintenance there are two units: Operations and Design and Engineering. Design and Engineering consists of three sections: Architecture, Engineering, and Construction supervision. It employs thirty personnel, directed by Peter Lumsford. Our involvement commenced after a series of turbulent events had occurred. Lumsford had been accused of "being racist," and, without any investigation by the hospital management board, the superintendent had ordered the director of Buildings and Maintenance, Ernie Catucci, to fire him. Catucci had refused, arguing that due process had not been followed. The superintendent backed down but passed the strong message, through Catucci, "We're keeping a close watch on Lumsford; another wrong step and he's gone."

In addition to the racial tensions within Design and Engineering, there was a severe problem in the relationship between three key women, and Lumsford felt it was almost impossible to keep the lid on it any longer. Tania and Gwen, with Dianne caught in the middle, had become so volatile about their fights with each other that many people unrelated to Buildings and Maintenance in the hospital were aware of what was going on. Gwen was the hospital's interior decorator and she had friends in very high places; so a little complaining in the right ears at the right time could create many waves. She had Peter Lumsford somewhat intimidated; so he was ready to receive us when Catucci suggested to him the involvement of a group of outside psychology action researchers who could help him work on the problems of sexism within his Design and Engineering unit.

A full organizational diagnosis using the methodologies of Alderfer, Brown, Kaplan, and Smith (forthcoming) revealed three powerful covert cliques. One revolved around the chief architect and assistant director of Design and Engineering, who had been a candidate for the director's job when Lumsford was appointed. The other revolved around the chief engineer, who was a sharp, forceful, ambitious man who saw himself as Lumsford's successor if Peter were forced to leave. The other revolved around the director himself. Each of these informal cliques of four or five people consisted of men, except that Gwen belonged to one of them, Tania another, and Dianne the third. There were many deeply felt tensions between these cliques, but none of them ever surfaced. Instead, the three women fought and the members of the three cliques expressed their disgust at the fact that the women's relationship with each other was so poor.

It became evident to us very early that we could choose to deal with the women's relationship as a triangle of interpersonal issues or we could jump to a higher level and make the intergroup tensions between the three cliques explicit and work with these. We chose the latter path, which led to the surfacing of an enormous amount of conflict among the men and a recognition by the women that their fighting served as an effective smokescreen to other conflicts in the unit that the men seemed invested in avoiding.

This is a brief introduction to the Design and Engineering unit of Weymouth State Hospital, which I want to use as a source of practical examples and illustrations of theoretical material. I wish it were possible at this time to make explicit a whole theory of change but that would be premature. Nevertheless there are insights into the major domains of changing that should be noted. I indicate these and comment on them in asides I call "change hints," that occur throughout this chapter.

Organization Defined

Organization has been defined in a variety of ways. At one end of the spectrum are the structural approaches of Scott (1964), Schein (1970), and Thompson (1967), which Porter and others (1975, p. 69) summarize as follows: "Organizations are composed of individuals and groups in order to achieve certain goals and objectives by means of differentiated functions that are intended to be rationally coordinated and directed through time on a continuous basis." At the other end we can find the process perspective of Weick (1979, p. 3) who discusses organizing as "a consensually validated grammar for reducing equivocality by means of sensibly interlocked behaviors."

Although in a general sense we all know what we mean when we talk about the Weymouth State Hospital, what we mean by the *organization* of this particular entity is hard to pinpoint because the organization itself does not exist in any physically verifiable way. It is impossible to point to it as we can a tree, for the only *things* our eyes will settle on are the parts of which the entity appears to be made, such as the buildings, the people, the ambulances, respirators, and so forth. However, the buildings, the people, and the machinery, even when aggregated, do not individually or collectively constitute organization. They are merely the parts. The organization I am actually referring to here is the set of relationships that exist among these parts, which bind them together into a collectivity that makes the entity-as-a-whole something that is different from and more than the mere sum of its parts (Laszlo, 1972; Watzlawick, Weakland, and Fisch, 1974). It is the system of relations that makes the whole, which constitutes the essence of what we mean by the term *organization*. Without a system of relations to draw the parts together into a whole, there is no organization, just free-floating parts. Hence, to talk about organization is to talk about relationship, relations among parts and relations among relations.

I preserve the use of *organization* for those dimensions of entities like General Motors, the state government, or the local church, that constitute the essence of organizational phenomena, namely, the relations among the parts and the relations among the relations. In doing this, I am eager to keep the same global definition of organization, at least at a theoretical level, when it is applied to entities as different as an individual and a culture. I will use the term *entity* to represent the collectivity-as-a-whole, which is made up of the parts bound together by the relationships that we call organization. For example, the Design and Engineering unit of the Buildings and Maintenance Division of Weymouth State Hospital may be viewed as an entity made up of a series of parts such as people, offices, and small work groups, together with the relationships that exist among those people, work groups, materials, and so forth. It is important, however, to recognize that the entity-as-a-whole is different from and in fact more than the organization that is the pattern of internal relationships. The entity, Design and Engineering, exists within a context that I term the *ecosystem* for that particular entity.

Using the definitional perspective, the entity Design and Engineering may also be viewed merely as a part of a larger entity, namely, the Buildings and Maintenance Division that is embedded in turn in the larger ecosystem of the hospital. Shifting levels of analysis in the other direction, the parts of Design and Engineering, such as the work groups, may likewise be treated as entities in their own right, existing in the ecosystem of the Design and Engineering unit. Hence Design and Engineering may be treated as a part of an entity at one level of analysis, as an entity in its own right at another level, and as an ecosystem at yet another level.

In using the term *entity,* I am easing into difficult philosophical waters, for a question debated at length in the social sciences is whether it is appropriate to view entities such as a social group as capable of collective action or whether the only "real" actions are those of the individual members whose aggregated individual behaviors constitute the apparent group behavior (Buckley, 1967). I am choosing to take a definitional stand on this topic in this chapter. I think it is appropriate to talk about an entity-as-a-whole when three conditions are met: (1) when the relations among a set of elements on the critical issues being examined are of a different logical type than the relations between that set and other sets with which it interacts (this is like the similarity definition of Campbell, 1958); (2) when other entities in the ecosystem hold the entity-as-a-whole accountable for the actions of its elements; and (3) when the actions of the elements of the entity may be meaningfully attributed to the patterns of relationships within the entity and not to the unique characteristics of the acting parts. If we replace individuals or groups with other individuals or groups that have very different characteristics and they end up behaving just like those who had been replaced, the behaviors of both the replaced and replacing people may be viewed as expressing the character of the entity-as-a-whole and not merely the character of the elements displaying the behavior.

If we view the essence of the organizing phenomenon to be relationships, we immediately encounter an epistemological problem, for we cannot actually see relationships; we can only infer them. When we look at the behaviors of two parts, such as two people interrelating, the interactors' behaviors are visible; the interactions themselves are not (Smith, 1982). We must derive or infer them from what is visible. When the mime Marcel Marceau takes his invisible dog for a walk on stage, as Marceau's arm jerks back and forth, everyone "sees" the dog straining on the leash even though there is no dog and no leash (May, 1975). We "see" something that does not exist. We "look" into the gaps, into the space between actor (text) and context, and there we find (infer or impute) relationships.

This is conceptually analogous to focusing on the wind as it blows through trees. The wind is recognizable primarily by its impact on objects, which move and behave within the realm of the wind's presence. We could observe the rippling of the leaves and the bending of the trees and describe these behaviors as an expression of the tree's inner nature. Or we could talk about the wind. We do the latter. We all "see" the wind, even though it is invisible. Just as the trees express the existence of the invisible wind, so the behaviors of the parts carry in their actions the invisible relationships between them (Smith, 1982). We "see" relationship even though the only things we can look at are the behavior of the parts, the elements through which the relationships are expressed. Hence, we see organization, even though it does not "exist" in any physically verifiable form.

If organization does not exist in a concrete form, then the only way we can talk about it is metaphorically, just like talking about ego or God or ghosts (Pirsig, 1974). And then the nature of our understanding of organization will depend on the metaphors we use, just as our understanding of God depends on the system of religious beliefs that undergird our experience. This means that how we experience, see, and infer organization, relations between parts, and relations between relations will depend primarily on the characteristics of the metaphors we choose to use and on the relationships (organization) among the metaphors themselves, for how we talk shapes what we talk about.

Taking this a step further, if we are to study organization as the system of relationships and these do not exist in any physically verifiable way, then we must also examine how we think and talk about relations, for our system of talking and what we are talking about are intertwined (Pondy, 1978). Because the structure of language has constraints that limit our thinking to particular contours (Feyerabend, 1975; Whorf, 1956), those linguistic limits will also shape our level of knowing about organization.

This thought can be extended a little further to generate a classical Laingian Knot (Laing, 1970). Because all behavior is language (Bateson, 1972), how we talk (behave) shapes our relations (organizing), and our relating (organizing) is our language (behavior). Rather than get buried in the paradox of this issue, I simply want to highlight here that we cannot think of organization separate from the language we use nor can we think of language separate from the organization that makes it a language. Organization and language are integrally entwined in each other's existence. This leads us to the theme of metaphor and metonymy.

Metaphor and Metonymy. If understanding organization involves understanding how we talk about organization, then it is important to focus on how language changes if we want to map out the underlying processes involved in organizational change. To explore this, let us start by looking at metaphor, which Jaynes (1976) indicates is the most fundamental component of language. In its broadest sense, a metaphor is a term for one object or relationship applied to another on the basis of some kind of similarity between them. In using a metaphor, two aspects must be attended to: that which is to be described and the object or relation being used to elucidate it. Jaynes (1976) points out that to talk about anything demands the mapping of the familiar upon the unfamiliar. The adequacy of the map depends upon the degree of similarity between the map and the terrain it represents. He calls this relationship an *analog,* and the relation between the analog map and its land is a *metaphor.* One critical aspect of the analog is that how it is generated is not how it is used. The mapmaker knows the land and tries to represent it on a blank piece of paper. Map users, however, do not know the terrain. They have only what is on the paper and wish to use this as a guide for their exploration of the unfamiliar.

To understand relationships demands that we explore both the properties of the metaphor and the degree of alignment between what is being mapped and what the map conveys. Consider Jaynes' (1976) example of the metaphor of the snow *blanketing* the ground. The metaphor conjures images of a blanket on a bed, with the attendant associations of warmth, protection, and slumber until some period of awakening. All this is contained in the metaphor, which captures the relationship between snow and earth as being one of sleeping under the protective snow cover. Had the metaphor been the snow *sits* on the ground, this would have spoken about the same thing (namely, there is snow on the ground), but it would have captured the relationship as one of dominating and overpowering, as opposed to protecting and caring. The key to the difference in the relationship between snow and earth in these two examples may be found entirely in the difference between the metaphors "sit" and "blanket."

Metaphor operates on the principles of *selection* and *substitution*. I selected "blanket" from a set of possible metaphors and substituted it into the content of the thought about snow on the ground. Its meaning however, snugly protecting, depended on the context into which it was placed. Before it was added to the context, it did not have meaning (semantics). This context into which the metaphor is placed is referred to as *metonymy* (Jacobson and Halle, 1956). Together, metaphor and metonymy make up the basis of syntax or structure of a language, and its semantics, its meanings, emerge from the relations between them.

To illustrate what is meant by metonymy, consider again the metaphor of the blanket. If we placed it in the context of "The thick fog blanketed the city," no longer would we think of protection, slumber, and warmth. Now the metaphor carries images of stifling and suffocation. However, the metaphor has not changed. What has been altered is the context, the metonymy. If we put "sit" in a metonymy (context), such as "The thin wisp of smoke sits playfully above the chimney," we would no longer experience the metaphor sit as a term of domination. Having changed metonymies, I have changed the meaning of the metaphor. In other words, the meaning of the metaphor depends on how it is combined with other metaphors in a context. This context is what I mean by the term *metonymy*.

Metaphor is the major vehicle for describing a relationship. However, the meanings attached to the metaphors depend on the relationship between the metaphor and its metonymy, the context in which it is embedded.

> Change Hint: If we want to change relationships, we can do this by changing the metaphors used to describe those relationships or by altering the metonymy in which the metaphor is embedded. By changing metaphor, we alter the descriptive elements of the relationship. By changing metonymy, we alter the meanings attached to those descriptive elements of the relationship.

As applied to organizational phenomena, the range of metaphors is wide, from machines to galaxies (Hayek, 1967; Weick,

1979). It is self-evident that some metaphors fit better than others. Machine analogies do not work very effectively for capturing the meaning of a lovemaking relationship. Here cosmic images are easier to handle. However, it strains the mind to think of the relationship between an army captain and a corporal in cosmic terms. Here machines seem more appropriate.

We tend to take our metaphors from those things that are most familiar to us. For example, our bodies are a rich source (Jaynes, 1976)—*head* of an army, *face* of a clock, *leg* of a table, and so forth. Once we have developed a source of familiar metaphors, we use them by mapping them onto that which is unfamiliar. What we then "know" about the unfamiliar is stored in the known aspects of the metaphor we use and in the context in which we place it. It may well be that the unfamiliar phenomenon we are attempting to represent is very much richer and more complex than is able to be captured by the metaphors we have chosen to use for talking about it. Or the metaphor may be rather loose in that the phenomenon being represented does not fit very well with the term being used to describe it. Hence, the appropriateness of the metaphor is critical, as is the question of how well it fits.

One problem with how we think about phenomena is that once we have chosen a set of metaphors and applied them to a particular context, they slowly become reified and it is hard to think of that phenomenon independent of the metaphors and metonymies we have been using as the vehicle of our thinking. To generate an alternative set of metaphor/metonymies is hard, for the earlier set has become established as the major indicators of the phenomenon. For example, once Weick (1979) has labeled something a "loosely coupled system," if we want to generate a new term, such as "faintly linked connections," it is easy to point to the first set of metaphors as the referent for the second. This means that when one set of maps has been drawn via the metaphoric/metonymic process, if I find a more appropriate metaphor/metonymy, it is most likely that they will be mapped not onto the original terrain but upon the first set of metaphors/metonymies. Accordingly, they become second-level maps as opposed to a genuinely alternate map of the terrain, although it is hoped that the second map will reflect the terrain better than the original.

Organizational phenomena have become very much trapped by this dynamic. Take, for example, the standard authority relations of most work organizations. Most metaphors have been taken from those developed and reified within the military. Authority relations are couched in hierarchical terms, with the center piece being the superior-subordinate dyad. Everything gets totally muddled if Peter and Lemar are both each other's boss and subordinate at the same time. Likewise, we have observed a particular set of relationships between hens that we have labeled a pecking order. We have fused this pecking order metaphor with the military structure of hierarchical superior-subordinate relations in such a way that we all know what is meant by a statement such as "In Design and Engineering, the pecking order is Peter, Lemar, and Gwen." It may be, of course, that such a set of metaphors is very appropriate for authority relations of the military but very inappropriate for a hospital.

A second difficulty arises once our metaphors have become fixed. If the fit between the metaphor and the phenomenon is inadequate, the obvious thing to do is to change the metaphor. But that is often very hard to do, for the metaphor may have become a central part of a much larger reality structure that could be fractured or disequilibrated if it were significantly altered. The alternative often is to try to make the phenomenon fit the metaphor. Ludicrous though this may seem, it is very easy for this to happen. If we talk about an organic phenomenon, such as organization, using machine-like metaphors, when the fit breaks down, we may choose to get organization more mechanized and controlled rather than searching for a richer set of metaphors. This may be as problematic as working to increase the accuracy of a map by trying to shift the valleys, mountains, and rivers instead of the other way around.

Consider again the example of authority relations. When the hierarchical, supervisor-subordinate structure begins to fail in that subordinates are less inclined to follow orders, it may be time to develop a different conception of how those relations operate. Perhaps the boss/worker, owner/slave metaphor no longer fits. However, if it is retained, any disturbance stirred by the less powerful will be viewed as something like insubordination while those stimulated by the superior are viewed as basic managerial/owner's rights. In this sense there are severe limits on the growth of understanding of the authority relations that can develop within this particular metaphor. When this occurs, there are two broad options. The first and most common is to force the behaviors to fit the metaphor either by coercing the wayward individuals or groups or whatever or replacing them with people or groups who will comply with the parameters of the metaphor. The second choice is to change the metaphors to ones that capture the domain of the authority relations more adequately.

A third problem that must be understood is that if the terrain is going through changes, then the map chosen to represent it must be capable of representing those changes within its basic format. If, for example, valleys and mountains and rivers were to change their relative positions with respect to each other whenever the seasons changed, it would be important that the metaphor chosen to represent this terrain in map form contain within it similar processes of change. If there is not a similar alignment between the changing elements of the map and the changing elements of the terrain, then either changes in the terrain will not be detectable within the structure of the map or the map will be changing in ways that do not capture what is happening in the terrain. Such a problem could generate significant "epistemological blind spots" (MacKay, 1969).

If a relationship is changing, the metaphor being used to capture that relationship must also have the capacity to change in ways similar to the dynamic properties of the phenomenon. Otherwise, because the relationship and the metaphor used to discuss the relationship are in a mutually causal relationship with each other, the development or growth of the relationship may be stunted by the limitations of the metaphor. Or for that matter the looseness of the metaphor may "encourage" a development of the relation (organization) that is more chaotic or unbounded than if another metaphor had been selected.

In examining the appropriateness of a metaphor, it is important to ask two questions. The first is whether the internal properties of the metaphor being used have a similar configuration to the internal properties of the terrain it is representing. Second, we must ask whether the internal aspects of the metaphor can change in concert with the internal changes in the phenomenon it is being applied to. We need a broader array of metaphors and different ways of understanding our linguistics than we currently have to capture how relations change and how organization evolves.

To summarize the discussion thus far, I have indicated that the essence of organization is the system of relations that draw the parts of an entity into a whole that is conceptually much more than the mere aggregation of its parts. Also I have suggested that since these relations, which constitute the building blocks of the concept of organization, do not exist in any physically verifiable way the only vehicles available for our exploring them are the linguistic tools of metaphor and metonymy, which provide a syntactical, semantic framework that shapes the ways "organization" is knowable to us as social actors. I have also argued that the central dimension of changing the organization of any entity must be in its relationships, for those relationships—and not the entity itself—are what we mean by organization. In addition, I have indicated that because the relationships and the metaphors used to capture them are phenomenologically intertwined, we must look at the metaphoric/metonymic domain as a significant place for seeing and producing changes. If you alter the metaphor you in fact alter one of the basic building blocks of the relationship. If you alter the metonymy, you alter the meanings attached to those relationships.

I now want to turn to another domain that is important to understand if we are to change our ways of thinking about change. This is to the concept of the boundary "not."

The Boundary "Not". There are four preliminary comments I must make to set the stage for exploring the theoretical and philosophical underpinnings of the concept "not" and "negation."

1. "Not" forms a boundary, a boundary between what "is" and "what is not." To use "not" as in the phrase "I am not happy" means to draw lines between, to make distinctions between, a condition labeled "happy" and one labeled "not happy."
2. The boundary "not" is always being evoked and used even when it is not being explicitly referred to. Every time we create or define an entity, we draw a "line" to distinguish it from what it is not. Defining "A" as "A" also defines what is "not A." (Saying "thou shalt love thy neighbor" also says "not loving thy neighbor is a possibility.") The delineation of A involves a

separation that is both an affirmation (this is "A") and a negation (this is "not A").

3. Although "A" and "not A" are different, they are part of the same unity, for without "not A," there can be no "A." "A" and "not A" belong as parts of a whole. Each contains the other within it. All things are rooted in a yes and a no (Tillich, 1952), which is the basis of the existentialists (Heidegger [1927], 1962; Sartre, 1966; Tillich, 1952) placing nonbeing at the center of their ontologies. Being itself can be thought of only in its totality with nonbeing. To the question, how are being and nonbeing related to each other, Tillich (1952) replies that it can be understood only metaphorically. "Being has nonbeing *within* itself." Affirmation and negation contain each other in what Jung (1958) calls the antinomy, the totality of inner opposites. In this sense, in order for any entity to have an identity, it must involve negation within the identity. By an entity's affirmation "This is me," it is also affirming that "it is not me" by an act of negation. Negation is thus not exclusively a part of "not me." It is as much a part of "me." A more accurate way to say this is to indicate that *not* "belongs" neither to the entity "A" nor to its negation "non A." It is both neither and nowhere. We cannot find something in the real world to which it corresponds. It is a rule about relations. In terms of the sets "A" and "non A" that it divides, it is a metaset containing no elements. It is a boundary that distinguishes, enabling either/or distinctions to be made.

4. Because "not" is a boundary that distinguishes between things, objects, entities, and what they are not, it can be found lurking in the foundation of every relationship. In fact, the presence of the boundary "not" is a precondition of all relationships, for the most basic element of relating is that the components of the relationship can be distinguished from each other.

"Not" is not an entity. It is a boundary that hovers above, beneath, and within every relationship. As such it can be understood only metaphorically. It cannot be represented concretely. This can be illustrated by trying to draw a picture that contains the concept "not" within it. It is easy to produce a picture of the statement "The man plants a tree," but try to do one of "The man does not plant a tree." However this is done, it cannot be presented unambiguously, for a painting lacks the highly developed logical syntax that is necessary for capturing "not" (Watzlawick, 1978). This flows as a natural consequence from the fact that there is only really one way for something to be organized. If it were organized differently, it would be something else. However, there are many ways for something not to be organized (Bateson, 1972).

In order to lay out the central issues that link the boundary "not" theme to organizational change, I turn to Bateson's (1955) theory of play. He raises the question of how an animal communicates "not" when it has very limited consciousness. Bateson illustrates the issue by indicating that if an animal wants to say "I don't want to fight," it can communicate this behaviorally by merely refusing to fight. However, for the animal to say "I'm not fighting," what it does is to fight and then stop. In the process it is saying "it's fighting I'm now not doing." In this sense, the animal who has had to fight to say it is not fighting has said the opposite of what it meant in order to mean the opposite of what it said (Bateson, Jackson, Haley, and Weakland, 1956). This is just like a schizophrenic (Watzlawick, 1978). In technical communications theory jargon, we can say the animal is not yet able to digitalize its experience, for it has no concept of "not." Thus, to communicate "not," it must make two contradictory analog statements.

Bateson elaborates the complexity of this theme in his analysis of play in animals where the playful nip stands for a bite, something it is not. Whereas the bite is what it is, the nip is not. The nip signifies both the absence *and* the presence of the bite. In this sense it is a metacommunication. It contains both a negative statement and an implicit negative metastatement folded inside it (Bateson, 1955). The playful "nip" is a phenomenon in which the actions of "play" are used to denote actions other than what it is, namely "nonplay." Hence, "nip" is a metaphor. It stands for something concrete and something abstract at the same time. Concretely it says "this is a nip." Here the symbol "nip" stands for what it denotes. However, it also says "this is not a bite." Here the symbol does not consist of what it denotes. It has been made into a second-level metaphor and in this sense it is a metacommunication. Hence, the "nip" in its concrete form is a direct communication and in its abstract form of standing for "this is not a bite" it is a metacommunication.

This example can be tied back to my earlier discussion of metaphor and metonymy. The meaning of the nip was originally established on the basis of how it was used in a particular context. Then that context or metonymy became incorporated into the second-level metaphor. Hence, the nip has become simultaneously a statement in a "language" and a statement in a "metalanguage" about relationships in a "referent language" from which it emerged and with which it coexists (Wilden, 1972). ("I'm not biting you, I'm just nipping, but be warned, I just might bite you.")

One problem with the concept of "not" is that it can be used in two totally different ways, and each is a different logical type. There is a logical difference between the syntactical "not" of negation and the commonsense way we use "not" to mean the absence (nonpresence) of something. In saying "A is *not* present," we use "not" differently than we do when we assert "A" is *not* "not A." In the latter case "A" and "not A" are in a structural relationship of negation with each other. To say "A" is not present (absent) in the particular context is describing a relationship of exclusion rather than negation. "Houseness" is simply not present in the context of "tree." "Houseness" is absent from "treeness." It simply does not belong there. However, the light and the shadow exist in negative relationship with each other. Negate light and you have shadow. Negate tree and you do not have house. You get nontreeness. House may belong to the class of nontreeness, but it does not define "nontreeness."

The problem of logical typing is very complicated, but it must be recognized and dealt with, for it is all pervasive in the domains of social reality. Stated succinctly (in Bateson, 1972, p. 202), the theory of logical types asserts that "a class cannot be a member of itself, nor can one of the members *be* the class, since the term used for class is of a *different level of abstraction*—a different logical type—from terms used for members." Less obviously, but just as important, "a class cannot be one of those items which are correctly classified as its non members" (p. 280). Bateson expands this point by illustrating that if we classify chairs together to constitute the class of chairs, we can note that objects like tables and lampshades are members of a large class of "nonchairs." The class of chairs does not belong to the class of "nonchairs." In addition, in the same way the class of chairs is not a chair, the class of "nonchairs" is not a "nonchair."

One of the major problems with the issues of logical type is that there is no direct path for moving from one logical type to the other. The punch line in the old joke "How do you get to Thompsonville?" applies here: *"There's no way to get there from here!"* This is very central to the logical typing issue and hence is critical for all activity dealing with the boundary "not." Compare, for example, the difference between the boundary "not" in a syntactical structure of negation and the "not" in the concept of absence. The mere placement of "not" in front of a word (I am not happy) can generate statements of different logical types, depending on syntax and whether it is the operation of negation or absence that gets so activated. Consider I am happy; I am not happy; I am unhappy; I am not unhappy. Happy and not happy are in a relation of negation with each other. Unhappy and not unhappy are not, however. "Not" in this case is a statement of absence. Unhappiness is not in my current experience. This does not mean happiness is. In fact, I could be a lot of things other than happy in my condition of "not unhappiness." "Not" can get ambiguous because of this logical typing problem. To say "I am not organized" may mean "I am organized and this is the nonorganized (messy) side of my organization." Or it may mean organization is currently absent from, not yet developed, in my existential condition. In this case the meaning of "not" is confusing because, without more context or more sharply delineated syntax, we cannot determine which "not" is being discussed—negation or absence. If I am unhappy, I am very unlikely to become happy just by negating unhappiness. There is no sure path from unhappiness to happiness; they are of different logical types. You cannot necessarily get there from here—although, interestingly enough, most of us assume we can because it is so easy to get from happiness to unhappiness, a very different kind of path.

These nuances are forever overlooked when we try to change something into what it is not. They are also grossly overlooked (violated) when questionnaire makers develop items that are positively worded and then want to balance them for positiveness and negativeness and accordingly place a "not" in front of half of them, assuming that they will then be opposites of each other in some simplistic way. If we make an assertion or affirmation and then place a negative word in front of it, we are in fact creating two statements of logically different types. Disagreeing with a negative statement is in no way logically the same as agreeing with the equivalent statement made in the affirmative.

There are two broad systems of mapping, analog and digital. One of them contains the concept of "not" within it; the other does not. Hence, one is very much better equipped to deal with the difficulties of the boundary "not" issues than the other. These are the digital and analog mapping processes. *Analog mapping* operates on the basis of real, continuous quantities, such as the ruler, clock, and thermometer. *Digital mapping* involves discrete elements and discontinuous scales. If we examine a thermostat, we can see it depends on continuous analog quantities until it reaches a particular threshold. Then it switches on or off. At this point it is digital. In this regard the thermostat is first analogic in its primary functioning; then it becomes digital when it reaches the threshold. Hence, it is digital at a secondary level (Wilden, 1972).

Wilden (1972), in a fascinating discourse, points out the basic difference between the analog and digital. I draw heavily on his explanations. The analog and the digital operate on two totally different principles. The analog is based on the principle of more/less and both/and; the digital is much more precise in that its basic mechanisms are either/or and on/off. In the analog map the representations are continuous, like the markings on a ruler. After two comes three and after three comes four, and so on. There is a flow from one element of the ruler to the next. In the digital map the representations are discrete, like a light switch. It is either on or off; one or the other is true. There is no degree of "onness" or "offness." It is light or dark. In this sense the digital is discontinuous. In fact, the basic element is the gap, whereas in the analog map there are no gaps. In the analog structure there is no true zero, for at the zero point the system is not functioning. It is off. When we are at zero with a ruler, we are not measuring. Only when we are into the positive numbers does the measuring process occur. Because there is no true zero, there also cannot be negative numbers, for the very idea of negative has no meaning in an analog system. We cannot talk about negative measuring. The opposite is true for the digital. It makes zero a central element, and all its mapping depends on combinations based on a series of on/off processes. The combinations all depend on the placing and ordering of the elements formed by the on/off mechanism.

In the analog form, the map consists of concrete representations. Hence, signs and symbols in the analog structure are used to make as explicit as possible the relationship of the map to the terrain it represents. Most important, we cannot represent "no-thing" in the analog system, for in the "no" position, it is off. Applying these concepts of analog and digital to my earlier discussion of animal play, the animal's inability to say directly "I am not fighting" arises because it is restricted to the analog structure. Not until it developed the capacity to digitalize could it say "not fighting" directly. It is, however, able to say "I am not fighting" indirectly by making two contradictory analog statements—that is, it fights and then stops.

In comparison with the analog, in the digital structure we cannot map a continuum precisely. The only things that can be represented precisely in the digital system are boundaries—which happens to be the major strength of digital mapping when compared with the analogic.

In each of the analog and digital forms, we can find a distinction in semantics and syntax. Because the digital deals with boundaries and because it is based on arbitrary combination, it has the necessary syntax (syn—with, taxis—order) to enable precision and unambiguity to be established. The analog is imprecise and ambiguous, though rich with meaning (semantics). It is virtually impossible to capture the semantic potence of an analog image (such as being in love) into a more precise syntactic digital form. Combinations of on/off switches do not work for such concepts as love. However, if we try to explain what being in love is like, the more precise we can be by saying what it is not, for which we must use the digital, the less meaning the concept will end up having. What can be gained with the digital in syntax gets lost in semantics; what can be lost with the analog in syntax gets gained in semantics. Hence, when we attempt to translate from the analog to the digital, we trade off a gain in information (organization) for a loss in meaning (Wilden, 1972).

Analog and digital may differ in *function,* as well as in form. The digital mode of language, when used to talk about things, operates in the language of facts, objects, and events. It objectifies. Overall it functions to transmit patterns and structures. The analog, however, has only the capacity to talk about relationships. Wilden (1972) illustrates these differences in function by considering how prosecutors or defenders in a court of law work on the jury. They play with facts and figures, using communications whose contents are digital. Yet all the time they are using the facts as a way of working on their relationship to the jury and their relationship with the defendant. These communications may be digital in form, but they are analogic in function.

The existence of both digital and analogic forms and functions are absolutely essential for the development and existence of identity for social entities and for an entity to be able to reflect on itself and its relations with others. To make the important distinction between what it is and what it is not, an entity must be able to digitalize. Entities may relate analogically, but in order *to talk about or be aware of that relating,* the digital is necessary. Without this digitalizing capacity, an entity can neither draw maps nor read maps, for it will be unable to draw distinctions and hence will not be able to distinguish between a symbol and what it stands for. This is classically illustrated by the schizophrenic who walks into a restaurant, reads a menu, concludes that the food is great, and proceeds to eat the menu card instead of the meal. He or she fails to distinguish the symbol from what it represents. Then afterwards the schizophrenic complains of the meal's bad taste (Bateson in Watzlawick, Weakland, and Fisch, 1974).

To illustrate the issue a little more pointedly, consider the communication system of the bee. It communicates analogically about where the pollen is by its dance (Hockett and Altman, 1968), but it cannot digitalize. It cannot say where the pollen is not. The bee can use its dance as an analogic statement about the relationship between the bee and the pollen, but without the digital it cannot say what the dance is not. Hence, it cannot communicate about its dance. It cannot metacommunicate.

To comprehend the analog as analog, we must be able to digitalize, to separate the analog from what it is not. The analog cannot do this for itself because it does not possess a "not" system within it. In other words, to be able to talk about relations (analog), we must be able to digitalize. We can relate analogically, but we cannot relate to our relations analogically. We cannot metacommunicate analogically; for that we need to be able to digitalize. Were it not for "not," we could not talk about "not." In fact, we could not make distinctions between a part and its whole and therefore metacommunication would be impossible. We could not talk *about* anything. We could talk (relate-analog) but we could not talk about (meta-relate). In this sense "not" is a metacommunicative boundary and constitutes a necessary precondition for an entity's having both consciousness of self and consciousness of other.

What relevance do Bateson's theory of play, the analog/digital mapping processes, and the issues of logical typing have to understanding the impact of the boundary "not" on the changing of relationships? The central issue is whether an entity such as the Design and Engineering unit at Weymouth Hospital could develop the syntactical sense-making structure such that it could untangle what it is from what it is not and whether it could reflect on its own behavior-as-a-whole, on the behavior of other entities in its ecosystem, and on how those entities relate to themselves and each other in their mutual ecosystem. If such sense-making apparatus does not exist, is it conceivable that when a social entity acts-as-a-whole, it will end up in the same binds of "consciouslessness" the animal did where it had to say or do the opposite of what it meant in order to mean the opposite of what it said or did? In other words, can an entity such as a social group say directly "I am not fighting" or does it have to fight and then stop in order to make such a statement? I find this a fascinating question when I think of how many groups I have seen engaging in fighting while they are saying that their actions are in peace. Perhaps this has relevance to the sense-making mechanisms of nation states who seem to need arms capable of blowing up the world a thousand times in order to say to themselves and the world that they are living in peace by not blowing up the

world. Might it be that such a social entity, given its level of consciousness, has to threaten to extinguish life to affirm the importance of life? Does it have to do and say the opposite of what it means
to mean the opposite of what it does and says?

I shall illustrate these issues by our experiences with Design
and Engineering. Major building maintenance problems at Weymouth resulted from the state contracting laws, which demanded
that the lowest bidder be employed when a new building was to be
constructed. Invariably, however, the lowest bidder beat out the
competition by taking short cuts that made maintenance almost
impossible because something like a whole engine had to be pulled
apart simply to tighten some loose screw. It was Design and
Engineering's job to make sure such things never happened. Hence,
when they did their job well, maintenance work was made much
easier. This meant they forever felt pressured from within Buildings
and Maintenance because whenever something required repairing,
design problems were evident. Even though many of the buildings
were thirty or more years old, current Design and Engineering personnel were assaulted for the faults of earlier generations of designers. Another source of pressure was that the Design and
Engineering unit was forever having to comply with a myriad of
state regulatory systems demanding reports on this and that. The
hospital in general also pressured them with severe budget limitations and by getting very upset with cost overruns even though the
state system had built in delays that made contractors' costs inevitably higher than the costs when the budgets were set. In short, Design
and Engineering was a unit permanently under siege.

Early in our contact with this unit, we found them pressured
beyond belief but seemingly unable to say "no." Whenever they
received an external request, even if it were unreasonable, they said
"yes." However, they acted out the "no" by hardly ever finishing the
jobs they undertook. In fact, no sooner did they say "yes" than they
started complaining about how overworked they were, so much so
that they exhausted themselves to the point where they had little
creative energy left for actually working. They seemed just like the
animal and the schizophrenic in doing the opposite of what they
meant. When we suggested that they might be selective and say

"yes" only to the things they could reasonably complete effectively, they were outraged, describing such an idea as irresponsible.

We pushed them in an attempt to get them to say "no" directly. Their response was to remain passive and to complain profusely about the fact that people used their open-spaced office area as a passage way to get to the time clock on the wall outside their building, to get to the bathrooms, or to take a short cut from one building to the next. They had made this complaint of others not respecting their physical boundaries into a *symbol* about how permeable their psychological and system boundaries were in general. As we worked to encourage them as a unit to take more control over their boundaries, their collective solution was actually to stop other people from walking through their office by keeping the doors locked. In so doing, they confused the symbol for what it represented. Their door-locking solution created more problems than it solved and led to the rest of Buildings and Maintenance being even more aggressive and adversarial with them. As Design and Engineering retreated, they used the failure of their door-locking attempts as proof that their bad feelings about everyone else were correct. They seemed unable to understand that simply working with their symbol of their excessively permeable boundaries was not the same as dealing directly with the system boundaries. This door locking was a start, however, because it meant that for one of the first times Design and Engineering actually took action instead of being passive.

This door-locking behavior also had contained within it another example of the "doing of the opposite of which you mean" problem. By locking the door, Design and Engineering tried to change what was outside itself. Instead of changing itself, it tried to alter others, as if by changing others it would be changed.

One critical issue concerning Design and Engineering is whether they actually possessed the epistemological equipment to be able to make sense of their relations. They clearly were able to relate; all they needed for that was the analog structure. However, to "talk" and "think" about their relations, they needed the digital at the collective level, which they lacked.

In summary, major changes in an entity take place on the boundaries. The most basic element of relationship is the boundary "not." These boundaries, however, do not actually belong to the entity. They are part of the relationship between an entity and other entities in its ecosystem. Because all relationships are predicated in part on boundary "nots," changing the location of "not" changes the entity's relationship with itself and what it is not. To be able to relate, entities need only to engage in analog mapping. However, for them to talk about their relating, they must be able to digitalize, that is, they must be able to include the distinctions generated by the boundary "nots." Hence, "not" is an essential element for an entity to have consciousness of how it relates.

Change occurs at both the concrete and meta levels and these are linked. The one cannot be changed without there being consequences for the other, although the concrete and the meta levels are of different logical types, hence, there is no way to know in advance how changes at the concrete level will influence the meta system or vice versa.

> Change Hint: In order for an entity to be able to change itself, it must first have a conception of itself as an entity-as-a-whole, separate from other entities in its ecosystem, and be able to draw coherent distinctions between what is its own behavior and what is the behavior of other entities in its ecosystem. To develop such a conception, the entity-as-a-whole must be able to say "no." This means it must be able to digitalize.

Sense Making of Entities at the Collectivity Level. How an entity-as-a-whole makes sense of itself, of its ecosystem, of its parts, and of all the relationships between and among the elements, entity, and ecosystem is critical to the arguments of every chapter in this book; yet the field of organizational change has left it basically unexplored. What I mean by sense making of an entity-as-a-whole could be seen in how Design and Engineering talked about itself as a collectivity having characteristics that were different from the larger hospital and state system of which it was a part. All members of Design and Engineering made statements such as "we all care about. . . ," "what we need is strong leadership," and "they don't have any idea of what it's like to have to work here." Although these words actually came out of the mouths of individuals who in definitional terms were parts of the Design and Engineering entity-as-a-whole, they were spoken as though read from a script that belonged to the collective entity, for all Design and Engineering members used the same words and produced the same statements under similar circumstances. They were not individual statements. They were statements made on behalf of the collective entity and concurred with by other members who were not actually speaking them or behaving them at that time.

This question of how an entity makes sense of itself and its world raises epistemological problems I really have no idea what to do with. Although I am going to address this as a topic in its own right, this is an artificial distinction I make just because of the problems of getting ideas onto paper. All of what comes before belongs within this theme and everything I say in this section belongs as much within each of the concepts I have discussed elsewhere.

Individuals do sense-making things in the Weick (1979) sense of this term. But individuals have minds; so it is not all that difficult to comprehend concepts like consciousness or the unconscious as they apply to individual organisms. The problem becomes how adequate these metaphors are for looking at how an entity such as a social group makes collective sense of itself and its relationship with its environment. Can a group think? Does organization have unconsciousness? Is there such a thing as systems memory? If so, what is it? The questions and difficulties can become unending, for if organization is simply metaphor, we cannot think of metaphors as having physical properties like the things from which we draw our metaphors, such as our mind. We seem to lack an adequate source of metaphors to provide a base for thinking about this topic.

Does such an entity as the Design and Engineering unit have a memory? If so, is it objective? Is it subjective? Does it work like human memory? Perhaps a moment's reflection on something we do know about individual memory might help as a starting point. The most primary and basic operation distinguishable about human memory is the emergence of difference. Only with differentiation can form emerge. It is the starting point of *in*formation. This difference, however, is not a place. As a distinction, it is nowhere, as we saw in our discussion of the boundary "not." It is a relation. The distinction, difference, is in-form(ation). The development of difference opens up the possibility of entities that have been distinguished as being signified in some way. And it is here in the properties of the signification of the relationship of difference that we can find the foundation of individual memory. It is on the basis of the relationship that gets developed between the separated and the whole from which it has been differentiated that identity is formulated (Hegel [1845], 1971) and the shape of this identity will depend greatly upon how the relationship between the differentiated and the whole is signified.

If we take this same image and apply it to a collective entity such as a social group, we can see the beginning stages of how to make sense of an entity's sense-making processes. We can look at *how* an entity inscribes its collective experience and *where* it "locates" that "storage." Jung (1964) helps significantly in his discussions about how the "memory" of a culture develops. He points to our symbols and myths, suggesting that we can find painted on our church ceilings and in our mosque mosaics stored representations of how we, as a collectivity, remember our experience—thousands of years collapsed into a painting, into a mythological figure. Jung also directs us to our rituals, our gladiatorial contests, our sadomasochistic football games, and suggests that if we look through the scripts of these exchanges, we can find latent in the texts of our collective behavior information about our collective past.

A superficial conversation with a group of people who are part of a collective entity reveals two obvious "locations" for the storage of "memory." One is external; the other is internal. The group of individuals may talk about the entity of which it is a part, making the attribution that the entity is like it is because of what others in its ecosystem are like. "We have to be competitive to survive in this economic jungle." "If you work for the state system, you'd know you just can't do that." Here we find the group's "memory" code inscribed elsewhere. Remember that this code is based on differentiations; so it is a code applied to a relationship between the entity and its context. However, it is given a "location" in the collective "not-I." The entity will tend to treat these externally located inscriptions as God-given and will describe its behaviors in terms that are a reaction to this code; that is, the entity internalizes and acts out the external code and continues to experience that code as being outside of and beyond itself.

On the other hand, the entity may write its code in itself. Here the behavior of the entity *is* the code. It is the text to be read. It is both itself and its memory. In this regard, the behavior of the entity can be treated as iconic. Rather than an alphabetic system of storage, the icons are not objects or patterns such as houses, the village grounds plan, and so forth, but are the actual behaviors of the entity and its parts (Wilden, 1972). Here the behavior of the entity represents its code, both what it is and what it is not.

Taking the perspective that all behavior is language, we can find in the behavior of an entity-as-a-whole, of its elements, and of its ecosystem and of all their interrelationships with each other, both the text and the context in which its memory, its collective experience, is stored. Like the painting on the church ceiling, where much history is collapsed into a single image, one piece of collective behavior may contain summarized in its text years of experience in much the same way as one moment of my relating to my therapist as father figure encapsulates the dynamics of years of experience with my own father. This idea may be hard to accept if we think of stored information as in a computer. However, if we switch to the language system of the right hemisphere of the brain, we can borrow the metaphors that have been developed for the language of dreams, fairy tales, and myths. These language systems are highly condensed and charged with meaning. For example, a dream may take only a paragraph to recount but may need many pages to interpret (Watzlawick, 1978). In right hemisphere symbology, a few brief seconds can be timeless, as has been reported by dying patients who on being brought back to life report seeing virtually the whole of their life rerun like in a film in perhaps a second or two (Moody, 1976). Using these images as a base, we can treat the behavior of an entity-as-a-whole simultaneously as behavior, as memory, and as myth. As such, we can read it like we read a book, poetry, music, dream, or any iconic system.

Consider the difference between a game of chess and a kinship ritual. In chess, the memory process is simple. We can look at the configuration of the pieces on the board and so long as we know the rules of relating, which in chess are fixed, the state of the board at each move contains all the memory that is necessary to understand its possible condition at the next move. All the next possible moves are determined by the current condition of the board and the fixed rules. This is not so, however, in a kinship system. If we want to understand, for example, the possible marriages that could take place in any generation, this would of necessity depend on the marriages that took place in the previous generation, those in the generation before that, and so forth (Levi-Strauss, 1958). In the kinship case, it is impossible to determine an initial state or origin on which to base the "memory" of the system. The marriage relationships between the actors will be shaped by changes that occur within each actor, by changes in the rules of relating (taboos and so forth), and the whole history of previous marriage relationships. This stands in stark contrast with the chess board, where all previous history collapses into the current configuration on the board.

The relevant "memory" of the chess game is stored in its *fixed* rules and in its board configuration at any point of time. To look into the memory of the kinship system, however, we must go not only to the current configurations, but also to the *changing* taboos, myths, and symbols, for they summarize the history, collapsed into a set of prescriptions and understandings for the present. Chess may be understood in Markov terms because its rules do not vary. This is not so in a kinship system.

There are so many different behaviors, so many different books to draw upon to retrieve the system's "memory" that, rather than thinking of it as a book, it seems more like a library, with books in many languages. And many of the languages have different grammatical structures, different rules of relationship, different metaphors. And different parts of the collectivity can speak in one language but not another; so they go to the shelves of their system's memory bank and pull out the "books" written in the languages and metaphors they understand. "Top management doesn't care." "The workers aren't motivated." "It's all because of the economy." "Those radicals are communists." Those who speak exclusively in French cannot read the German books and vice versa. And when they speak to each other via a translator, because they draw on different parts of the library, retrieving different parts of the system's memory, they do not understand each other. To make things worse, a part of any system cannot comprehend how its behavior captures the scripts for the system in general.

The relationship between the three internal cliques in Design and Engineering became the source of much social tension with the unit-as-a-whole. However, it was kept very much underground. This tension became located in the relationships among the three principal women (Gwen, Tania, and Dianne) and in the relationship between Design and Engineering and the office of the director of Buildings and Maintenance. Each organizational actor was able to see events such as the explicit clash beween Tania and Gwen or hear the loudness of their silence with one another, but these behaviors were read in radically different ways. For some they indicated "there go the women again, bitching relentlessly with each other." For others, such as the director of Buildings and Maintenance, it meant that Tania had been given yet another favor by Design and Engineering director, Peter Lumsford, and Gwen was feeling resentful. For others it was interpreted as evidence that one of them was having an affair with one of the men in the office and the other had found out, or was jealous, or angry. The same event would be read in many different ways. *How* it was read could be interpreted as a summary of many of the experiences, literal and fanciful, of those doing the reading. They used the women's relationship as a screen upon which to project their own encoded experiences and then treat them as though they belonged to those upon whom the projections were being placed.

My purpose here is to raise an issue that can be summarized as follows: (1) How an entity-as-a-whole makes sense of itself and its relationship to its ecosystem is important for us to study in understanding the evolution of human systems. (2) The place for us to look for those sense-making processes is how the entity encodes its memory into its behavior (of its parts and of its totality) and that of its ecosystem. (3) The entry into the encoding is via the metaphors, metonymies, myths, and rituals written in a wide variety of behavioral languages. (4) Subentities within the entity-as-a-whole will read differential portions of these texts and in different ways, using the "linguistic" structures of their own particular experiences. (5) Contained within these behavioral scripts may be found the evolution of the scripts themselves, based on the principles of all I have discussed so far.

If the behavior of an entity-as-a-whole can be viewed as a language, how does its code develop? I touched this topic indirectly earlier in discussing metaphor and metonymy. To sharpen the issue, let me formulate the question as follows: How do metaphors change, and in particular how does a metaphor come to incorporate within itself its historically antecedent conditions? In the final analysis, this question is the central issue in the evolutionary process we call morphogenesis.

I can best provide a simple answer by an illustration at the individual/interpersonal level of analysis. We were talking with Lemar about how he related to his boss, Peter Lumsford, at Design and Engineering. Lemar was angry that Peter was a boss who meddled in everyone's affairs. Lemar summarized his complaint as "Peter is a real meddler." We may think of this as a first-order metaphor applied in the metonymic context of the boss-subordinate relationship of Peter and Lemar. We then talked with Lemar's subordinate, Ling, and asked him to describe his boss. Ling wanted to say "Lemar is a boss who is very much like his own boss, Peter. They're both meddlers in the same way." To do this, Ling simply said "Lemar's a real Peter." In this sense he created a second-order metaphor by making Peter into a metaphor that contained both the first-level metaphor, meddler, and the first-level metonymy of the boss-subordinate relationship in which the metaphor, meddler, was initially given its meaning. Everyone in Design and Engineering knew what Ling meant when he said "Lemar's a real Peter." We asked Ling what he was like with his subordinates. He replied "I'm *not* a Peter." In his response Ling indicated that he had an operative concept of both the first- and second-level metaphors and metonymies of meddler and Peter and was able to talk about "non-Peterness." In other words, the metaphor Peter had been developed in such a way that the digital had been folded into it. "Meddling" and "nonmeddling," "Peterness" and "non-Peterness" had become incorporated into this entity's communicating code.

This process can be thought of as incorporation into the metaphoric process at the secondary level of those elements of the message that were embedded in the metonymic structure at the first level of the metaphor. What was originally a metonymic message is now part of the metaphoric code and involves the elaboration of new structures within the system (Wilden, 1972).

This topic of incorporating the metonymic into the metaphor brings us teasingly toward the edge of the dialectic and contradiction. Perhaps I can illustrate this best by discussing it at the more familiar individual level of analysis and by using just one concept. For illustrative purposes I shall use the notion of goal because it is central to all our writings on organizational phenomena. By way of introduction, consider "that great sense of void or meaninglessness" any of us can feel as we contemplate existential matters of ultimate concern, such as death (Becker, 1973). When faced with emptiness, our goal becomes one of feeling full. We want a lot. Our goals and our desires may be viewed as a very direct communication about our internal conditions. However, they may also be treated as a metastatement about our relationship with the void. As a metaphor, "our desire for fullness" is a second-order statement about a first-order metaphoric/metonymic relationship between our condition of hopelessness/emptiness in the context of an ultimate concern (death). In this sense, our goal/desire/wish/want is in a dialectical relationship to our void. It tells us about our void, about our wish, our goal, and about the contradictory/opposite/dialectical relationship between them. We must be careful here not to think, however, of this dialectic in either/or terms. It's both/and. Void and want can be understood only in terms of each other. Paradoxically, if one feels hopeless, a sure cure is to give up hope. Without hope, there can be no hopelessness.

This development of a goal to be full as a way of dealing with one's inner condition of void, however, involves a code-switching quantum leap across different levels of logical typing, for a goal is at a metalevel when compared with the void. Thus, the concept goal contains two levels of coding within it. One level deals with the goal to be full, for example, as a contradictory counterpoint to the condition of void. The other level deals with goal as a metastatement about the relationship between the void and the desire to be full. This level of goal stands in paradoxical relationship to the lower level. Further, the concept goal will contain within it both the metalevel codes and the more rudimentary codes that exist at the basic contradictory level of void and full as being opposites of each other. In this sense the goal-seeking behavior of an entity may be looked at simultaneously as a specific activity of an entity and as a metastatement about the relationship between that entity, what it is not and of the entity's relationship to its ecosystem.

Any entity that develops a goal is "driven" as much by what it is not—its void—as by what it is, for no entity "strives" to become or do something if it has already reached that level of becoming or is already doing those things. It is primarily what an entity is not that shapes its goals. Then to talk about the goals of an entity is in reality a discussion both of what it is "not" and how what it "is" relates to what "it is not." In this sense we can think of goal as both a communication and a metacommunication. Goals, accordingly, reveal the way the system is "driven," "propelled," by the dialectical interplay between the state it is "in" and the state it is "not in." For this reason, the constructs of identity of an entity and its goals cannot be separated from each other. Each is grounded in the other, and both are entangled in the analog/digital and boundary "not" conditions I discussed earlier.

At Design and Engineering we observed repeatedly the total confusion generated by that entity's inability to recognize how its goals and its ongoing commitment always to do the right thing were a statement about how hopeless a situation it really found itself in and how much as an entity it was inclined to simply give up. As an entity, Design and Engineering experienced itself as undersupported and undernourished, and instead of doing what it could with what it had, it poured most of its energy into obtaining what it lacked. By so doing, it made focal the "other," in this case the directorate of the Buildings and Maintenance department, and attempted to draw from "other" (what it was not) the very things it itself was not. Of course, this was impossible, for the things it was not were so because of what it was, and hence the unit returned to inaction and bitter complaining about how the "other" was *making* it impossible for them to do their tasks by not being cooperative.

From an external point of view, we could look at these goal directed activities of Design and Engineering as a metacommunication about this entity's relationship with its ecosystem. As information, it told us about certain patterns of relating. The entity, however, did not experience it as relating. Instead of treating it in the relational format, the entity made central what the "other" had and focused on how hard the "other" made it for the entity to become what it was not, to obtain what it lacked. In the meantime, this goal and the way Design and Engineering used this goal to "get" or to "become" what it lacked or was not served as a powerful tool to deny its own very existence. The goal became used as a way to negate the entity's own negative side. And here the problem became just like the struggle of the alcoholic, as described by Bateson (1972).

Bateson describes the epistemological binds an alcoholic engages in as he struggles for mastery over the bottle. He sets this battle in the split between the heroic and submissive figures that we all have within us, the will to be master and the will to be dependent (May, 1971). For the alcoholic, drinking mediates this struggle. He takes drinking, the bottle, and makes it a problem outside of himself. Then, instead of "being" a problem (an inner struggle), the alcoholic "possesses" a problem, a thing. No longer is it a relationship. In so doing, the alcoholic casts (frames) himself into an either/or battle, oscillating between the bottle and the wagon.

Bateson places this oscillation in the socially generated need to perform in order to establish self-worth. The alcoholic comes to play out his performance struggles around demonstrating he has the strength with which to meet the challenge, namely, to conquer the bottle, his drinking problem. It is precisely because he makes this the battleground that the bottle is destined to defeat him. As Wilden (1972) puts it, it ends up being a confusion of process and goal, thereby creating an *obstacle*. The alcoholic is faced with the monumental struggle of desiring to abolish desire itself. That becomes the obstacle. He becomes addicted to testing himself against the obstacle. The problem for the alcoholic becomes transformed into the bind that if he stops drinking, he will take away the very challenge that made him want to stop drinking in the first place. To drink or not to drink. To be or not to be. We can never escape from the oscillation between these two impossible poles while we embed them in the dualistic struggle by trying to prove ourselves according to the standards of the "other," what one is not, for we are trying to relate across different logical types, a relationship impossible to explicate or resolve. Driving ourselves into a relationship of rivalry with "others" is a way of covering up, of denying, of hiding from the simple reality that as well as "being," we are also "nonbeing"

(Tillich, 1952). This reality is so, not because of any lack in us, but because it is in the nature of things.

Design and Engineering's attempts to change came in the form of Bateson's alcoholic. Rather than focus on the relationship between their unit and the Buildings and Maintenance department in general, they located their change efforts in the "other," and in so doing externalized and objectified their own internal dialectical processes. They made the other into an obstacle, like the alcoholic's bottle, thereby ensuring that the fundamental structure of their experience remained essentially unaltered by their enormous change efforts.

> Change Hint: If an entity develops goals that involve change and if it tries to achieve these by focusing its efforts on others, it is certain to be building for itself a reality structure that is resistant to authentic change and that keeps the entity unaltered in its essence (in a morphostatic state). To overcome this paradox, the entity should be encouraged to abandon its goals, to affirm its own negative side, and simply to work at being what it is, for no entity can produce genuine change (morphogenesis) in itself from within.

The specific importance of these thoughts about sense making to this chapter is that if we read the goal-seeking behavior of human entities from multiple "language structures," we can find within its text a great deal about the current state of the entity and of its relationship to its ecosystem and its nonentity.

First, it is probably the most direct way we can find out how an entity conceives of what it is not. Its goal will contain its confession of its own limitations, for what it tries to achieve is ruled as much by what it is "not" and by what it "may be" as by what it "is." Second, it will reveal how the entity takes its relationships with its environment and transforms these relationships into a thing, which is similar to how the metaphors of one logical type contain both the metaphors and the metonymies at lower logical levels. It will tell us about how an entity objectifies and externalizes its own inner dialectical processes. Third, it will suggest the ways current patterns will shape future relationships. Like the alcoholic locked forever in the heroic struggle between the bottle and the wagon, an entity's goals can inform us of the issues around which it is addictively revolving. Fourth, it will point to ways the system's mapping of its environment both reflects and influences the way it understands its own existence, its goal seeking, adaptations, and information processes.

The way the text became developed was that a set of metaphors was mapped into a context (metonymy), thereby creating a basic unit of meaning—in the relationship of the metaphor with its metonymy. Then a second-level metaphor was selected to represent the first-level metaphoric-metonymic relationships, thereby creating a second level of meaning. This was repeated at several more levels until the text became crystallized as a map of a map of a map of a map of. . . . At each level the map represents a metamap for the level below. In this system of map drawing and classification, meanings were attached to events according to some basic rules—not rules that could be expressed as logical equations, but rules that operated like the grammar of language. These rules control and circumscribe by providing a general scheme—"pattern of grooves"—that limits the range of possibilities. These rules shape how certain metaphors are selected and how they are placed in particular contexts. Thus, the linguistic rules play a powerful role in the creation of meaning.

Two things about these rules stand out. First, knowing them will not help in predicting action. They will help, however, in understanding the meaning of action as it occurs. For example, if I know the rules of grammar, this will be of no help in predicting what a person is about to say. However, as that person speaks, knowing those rules of grammar helps inordinately in making meaning of what otherwise would be a list of nonsense syllables. Second, we all use rules of grammar when we speak. When our language is verbal, those grammatical rules are linguistic in form. When our language is behavior, those rules may be thought of as a grammar of situations. Although we all use rules of grammar, we may not be directly aware of them while we are actually using them in our speech. We all perceive the rules of grammar and abide by them even though we are not specifically paying attention to them while we are speaking or behaving. For example, young children, even before they can be taught grammar, perceive a grammatical structure of language and conform to it, unknowingly, as they begin to become verbal.

I have spoken previously about developing metaphors and mapping one set of images upon another—classifying, if you will. These acts of classification, or metaphor application, are themselves an unexplicated application of unreflected-upon-rules. Meanings get attached to events in acts of classification, as an expression of further perceived rules or patterns—*not because there is a reason these meanings fit, but simply because the entity using them perceives them to fit.* Only when, after the event, an entity is asked what processes it used in making its classifications is it likely to examine how the underlying rules were unknowingly influencing that entity's reality. The original classificatory work was done on the basis of perceived meaningful wholes and was experienced as self-evident by the classifying entity. Such an entity would probably not even ask whether those rules were appropriate unless confronted by another actor who, perceiving the same events or objects, saw a different meaningful whole and therefore applied a different set of latent, unexplicated rules of social discourse. Only then, when realities clash, do post hoc questions get raised about how rules of grammar were applied. It is precisely because all social entities do not have the same kind of experience, the same perception of the rules or regularities, that multiple realities become created. When two sets of realities clash because different rules were used by two entities to give meaning to events (by mapping metaphors into metonymies), a set of metarules has to be created or drawn upon to provide a framework for looking at how the rules each entity used shaped its respective reality. There is no precise logic for the selection or creation of these metarules. Like the rules at the lower level, the metarules are chosen simply because the entities choosing/creating them perceive them to fit.

The major issue here is that when entities communicate through their behavior, their language is constrained by metarules to which they pay no attention while they are communicating. When they do move to the metalevel and attempt to metacommunicate, their language is again constrained by meta-meta rules and so forth.

This theoretical problem can get very complex; yet the basic issue can be put simply: Social entities know more, depend on more, and are attentive to more than they are able either to state or reflect on. Hayek (1967, p. 61) expresses it as follows: "If 'to have meaning' is to have a place in an order which we share with other people, this order itself cannot have meaning, because it cannot have a place in itself. A complex structure of relationships may be distinguished from all other similar structures by a place in the more comprehensive structure which gives each element of the first structure and its relations a distinct 'place within place.' But the distinguishing character of such an order could never be defined by its place in itself." Putting it differently, there is no ultimate metasystem with a metalanguage based on metarules that are able to comment on the system of relationships upon which that metasystem, metalanguage, and metarules are based because the means of analysis is part of the system being analyzed (Wilden, 1972). This is the heart of the paradox the mathematician, Gödel, unraveled. A brilliant exposition of Gödel's work and its relevance to the construction of reality can be found in Hofstadter (1980).

There are several critical consequences of this paradox. First, any attempt to talk about anything presupposes the existence of a framework that determines its meanings. The meanings, however, will be latent in the relationship between the contextual framework and the entity. If we wish to change the entity, we need to change the meanings the entity attaches to its and others' experiences. To do this, we should focus on the relationship between that entity and its context. The most potent way to do this is to alter contexts, for this in turn will alter the relationship from whence meanings emerge.

Second, the framework or the governing procedures at the metalevel may be thought of as "the system of rules which operate us but which we can neither state nor form an image of and which we can merely evoke in others insofar as they already possess them" (Hayek, 1967, p. 62). This means that if we want these metalevel governing rules evident, they cannot be explicated just through logic. Knowing them is mainly a matter of perception. We stumble on them as we say "oh, I *see* how that's happening," as in emotional insight when a patient says to the therapist "I see how I'm treating you as though you were my father." Comprehending these governing rules is not a matter of reassessing; it is a matter of perception. Hence, it is possible to perceive and comprehend much more than we know or are able to make explicit in logical ways. This theme has been discussed at great length in the split brain research (see Jaynes, 1976; Ornstein, 1972; Watzlawick, 1978).

Third, the more precise and theoretically tight and closed we make the framework for exploring metaissues and the more we attempt to ground meta-level issues in illustrations and metaphors that make sense at the micro level, the sooner the metaframework will be paradoxically double-bound by being, in effect, outside itself (Wilden, 1972) in that it will treat as context that which essentially is text.

> Change Hint: An entity will not be changed in its essence if the metarules that shape that entity's actions are left unaltered. These metarules are themselves shaped by meta-meta rules. To understand the impact of metarules, an entity must be able to enter a metareality framework. To do this, it must be able to digitalize at that level. This is a problem of infinite regression, however, for no matter what level an entity is able to raise its awareness to, there will always be yet another meta-meta-meta level that is unknowable to the entity and that imposes constraints the entity is unable to comprehend while they are actually in operation.

Morphostasis and Morphogenesis. When an entity switches to a metalevel in order to talk *about* its experience, it begins to operate on a set of rules that are of a different logical type than those used when it simply functions *within* its experience. Then if it begins to incorporate the metalevels used for talking about its experience into its experience itself, in effect what happens is that contexts that were once external to the entity are made internal and in so doing are transformed into texts. This is what happens when second-level metaphors are developed out of melding first-level metaphors with the metonymies that frame them, as illustrated in my earlier discussion about goals. In a very basic sense the entity is taking those things that are characteristics of what is external to itself and making them internal by embedding them in the entity's basic structures. Another way to say this, in summary form, is that the metaphor/metonymy switching involves transformation of structure into system and system into structure at increasing levels of logical typing. This is the heart of the morphogenesis process.

Virtually every significant writer on organization uses the term *structure* in one way or another (Meyer, 1971), and those who wish to alter organizations invariably talk about structure as one of the available levers to catalyze change (see Alderfer, 1977; Beer and Driscoll, 1977; Friedlander and Brown, 1974, for appropriate reviews). However, social scientists often seem to talk about it in the simplest of ways. Ranson, Hinings, and Greenwood (1980) indicate that structure has usually been understood as patterned regularity and has been treated either as a framework that prescribes a formal configuration of roles and procedures or as an interactionist perspective of symbolic mediation and negotiated processes. Breaking out of the either/or definitions provided by the structuralists and the interactionists, Ranson, Hinings, and Greenwood (p. 1) emphasize that structures are continually produced and recreated by members so that "the structures embody and become constitutive of their provinces of meaning."

Following the lead provided by Ranson, Hinings, and Greenwood, I think of structure as the socially mediated patterns among the parts of an entity in which meanings are placed and constantly recreated through the internal interactions of the parts of the entity in the light of the contextual constraints provided by the ecosystem. These structural patterns are regulated by rules to which the parts adhere, to varying degrees, despite the fact the parts may not "understand" that is what they are doing, as in my earlier example of young children using the rules of grammar in speech even before they "know" anything about the rules of grammar.

For Piaget (1968), perhaps the greatest structural theorist, structure is the system of transformations that preserves the whole, the whole being the organization, the cohering relations between the parts as compared to the aggregation of the parts, which is how some social scientists naively treat structure.

In this sense Piaget makes the referent for wholeness the relations *within it*, the processes of repetition, ordering, and associative connecting by which the whole is formed, rather than the wholeness itself. He argues that to understand the whole, we must focus on the dynamic structural laws or rules by which it became composed. He would have us believe that to understand the character of the wholeness of a collective entity, we should look *within* that collectivity and examine the way the rules regulating and transforming the relationships between the parts develop. For Piaget, then, structure is a property of the collectivity, though it may be "found" in the relationships between the parts of the whole. Although the structure of an entity might be expressed in the patterns among the elements of the entity, the forces that truly shape structure emerge from the relationship of the entity with other entities in its ecosystem. Hence, if we want to understand the character of wholeness of an entity, we should look to the relations *between* that entity and other entities in its ecosystem and examine the way the rules regulating and transforming the relationships between the entities in the ecosystem develop.

To illustrate the import of this idea, let us return to our cybernetic example of the rabbits and the lynxes and the general relationship between territoriality and the survival of the species. The question can be posed in the following way: Do the actions of defending its territory lead to increased or decreased probability of the species' survival? The answer to this is not immediately knowable, especially to the animals involved in the predatorial-prey relationship. We know that the system is in oscillation, hence at certain times successful territoriality, an action at the micro level, will lead to the survival of the species at the macro level; at other times this same behavior contributes to extinction. The problem can be seen most sharply if the situation is reversed. If an animal concluded that its own species was being threatened with extinction and that it should do something to counteract this, unless it could move itself to the macro level and understand the metarules that were regulating the particular configurations of oscillations on which the survival of its species were operating, it would not know what individual action to take. Intuitively, it would probably deduce that to defend its own territory more vigorously would help. However, that may be the exact opposite of what is needed. Maybe letting itself get caught and eaten would contribute more to the survival of its species than if it itself tried to survive.

In this example, the patterns of oscillation in the ecosystem, a macro issue, shape whether the micro-level act of defending one's territory leads to increased likelihood of survival or extinction at the species level. In fact, an organism's conforming more tightly to the internal rules of the little system of which it is a part, such as "defend your territory at all costs," an act designed to preserve order, may in fact increase the level of disorder of that system. Putting this in a more general form, increasing the degree of structure, that is, the orderedness in the internal relations of the elements of an entity, may in fact increase the amount of disorder at the level of the collectivity, depending on what is occurring in the relations among the entities within the ecosystem.

Piaget's view of structure is probably fine for some purposes, but in general, this approach gets us into a lot of trouble when we try to understand change. To generate order, he would have us look to the *internal* relations. I would argue that to generate order we must look to the *external* relations and see how the internal and external interrelate. For Piaget, increasing structure, that is, the internal orderedness of elements, creates *order*. However, increasing structure may create *disorder*. It all depends. Making this type of distinction reveals another problem that rarely gets exposed: Order and structure are concepts of logically different types. Hence, it is not possible to argue logically that if we produce particular changes in the structure, it will lead to particular changes in order, for such causal maps cannot be drawn across logical types, neither theoretically nor empirically.

Throughout the sections on metaphor/metonymy, boundary "not," and sense making, I have been lightly sketching how I understand change to occur within these processes. Now I want to look, at a more general theoretical level, at the similarity of change processes that cut across multiple systems of thought, be they the development of linguistics, communication systems, or the sense making of collectivities.

The potentiality for change exists whenever there is turbulence or chaos within an entity, between it and other entities in its ecosystem, or within the elements of which the entity is made. Cybernetics uses the term *noise* for this turbulence, which might be due to some specific event or merely to random variations that trigger novel tensions to surface, demanding a reaction.

"Noise" is a natural part of organizing. The very act of bringing objects and events into relationship with each other brings tension of some form. There are tensions that belong *within* the entity and those that exist in the relationship *between* an entity and its ecosystem. There are tensions that exist in some form of opposition or contradiction, as I discussed in my boundary "not" selection, and there are tensions of paradoxical form that become triggered whenever we attempt to jump across logical types.

Paradox is the tension that can be generated by self-reference, as can be seen in the old Cretan statement "I am lying." "I am lying" is both a statement and a metastatement, and the relation between the two levels of statement is paradoxical, for it is jumping across levels of logical typing.

Hofstadter (1980) discusses paradox most eloquently. He invites us to consider the following statements: The following sentence is false. The preceding sentence is true. Taken separately, these sentences are harmless enough. Yet when put together, they generate paradox because they become double bound by the problems of self-reference. When taken separately, each sentence has no self-referential problem. When put together and a whole is made out of the two parts, the self-referential difficulty becomes created. However, the paradox does not lie within the statements. It is located, as it were, in the space between the sentences, in the intangible relationship that binds the two statements to create a whole.

Tension, contradiction, conflict, and paradox all create noise, and noise stimulates change. Three types of response are identifiable when noise occurs. (1) An entity can protect itself by dealing with the tensions as though they were external, environmental intrusions, noise from the ecosystem. Such a response has the entity attempting to maintain itself, and as such it can be described as homeostatic. It operates on the basis of repetition. (2) The entity may deal with the situation by responding with behaviors that are inherent within its own infrastructure. This may involve change, but any changes will be within the limits defined by the essential nature of the entity. Such a response may be thought of as the purely developmental (homeorhesis). (3) The entity may deal with the tensions as if they were the results of the structure of the entity being out of alignment with other parts of the ecosystem and be jolted into a new level of order to cope with the tensions inherent between the levels. This is morphogenic change and is the basis of dialectical evolution in the Marxian sense (Marx [1894], 1962).

Although development and repetition may involve changes, they operate to keep the core of the entity unaltered. Hence, they are morphostatic (that is, form preserving). Changes that actually alter the order of an entity may be thought of as evolutionary (morphogenic).

These systems of change/stability are metaphors, not entities in and of themselves. They are ways to think and as such are elements of a meta language. However, they each contain the other within it. Consider, for example, the theories of Freud or Hegel. Despite the fact that their work is radically different, we can find in each the developmental metaphor operative at the level of material, the repetition metaphor in the realm of human conditions, and the evolutionary metaphor when discussing the level of consciousness (Wilden, 1972).

Typically, structural theories (Levi-Strauss, 1958; Parsons, 1949; Piaget, 1968) are morphostatic. They are structure maintaining in that they operate on principles of equilibrium, viewing tensions, problems, deviations, and conflicts as intrusions into the entity from the ecosystem and not as properties of the entity itself (Ashby, 1961). A typical structuralist treats such random variations and disturbances as "pathological" or system-disrupting interferences from the outside, making the epistemological error of automatically separating the entity from its ecosystem. This leads them inevitably to limiting their developmental perspectives merely to within the entity, thereby providing no framework for contemplating ideas such as evolution. For these theoreticians, any development is restricted to the potentialities contained in the pathways delineated by the "genetic" code of the entity's infrastructure (Waddington, 1968).

Within the homeostatic image, there is no room for entertaining the idea of tension being the product of and therefore inherent in organization itself (Coser, 1956). For this we need concepts that allow for the elaboration of new structures, which is the basis of morphogenesis (Maruyama, 1963).

In morphogenesis we find the evolutionary or historical changes in the messages and the code that the developmental and repetition systems operate on. Evolution involves a discontinuous, digital jump in level of structuring and includes a reshaping of goals. Maruyama (1963) discusses this jump as those processes of mutually causal relations that "amplify an insignificant or accidental initial kick" into enough of a deviation to enable a diverging from the initial conditions, demanding more complex mediating processes to intervene between external and internal forces. These mediating processes perform the operations of (1) reorienting the entity to changing external contingencies, (2) directing the entity toward more congenial locations in the ecosystem, and (3) readjusting its internal contours to more effectively cope with the tensions from the ecosystem. In morphogenic change these mediating processes become more elaborate, more independent, more autonomous, and more determinative of the entity's behavior (Buckley, 1967).

This concept of morphogenesis is basically the same as I discussed previously under metaphor/metonymy and boundary "not." In Batesonian terms, when the context of a communication is incorporated into the communication itself at a higher level, an entity is able to communicate and metacommunicate at the same time. This is similar to the creation of higher order linguistic structures where a metaphor at one level contains both the metaphor and the metonymy at a lower level. By taking the messages embedded in the metonymic structure and incorporating them into the metaphor, we have a jump in level and the elaboration of a new internal structure that contains within it the old, lower order internal *and* external relationships. This process was also evident in the digital/analog material. Consider the example of the animal "nip." When the statement matured to the level of "I want you to know I could bite you, but at this moment I'm not going to," as opposed to actually biting and stopping, we have witnessed the previous "this is *not* a bite," which has the "not" embedded in the metonymy incorporated into the metaphor. The same process is found when the animal comes to incorporate negation (the digital) into the codes of his messages such that he says, "I am not fighting you" instead of having to fight and then stop in order to communicate "not fighting." Using this example, we can think of morphogenesis as a metaphor for that process wherein the metonymic principles of combination and contexture are incorporated *within* relations of similarity where the basic operations are selection and substitution (metaphoric) (Wilden, 1972).

In morphostasis, however, according to Waddington (1968), developments that come through maturation and learning occur according to the possibilities contained *within* the instructions or the code of the system. Although it involves an ongoing metacommunication about prior and antecedent states, the actual processes of adjustment, which are selection (metaphoric) and combination (metonymic) activities, occur *within* the given norms of the system. This means that *within* its code it is both metaphoric and metonymic. Or we could say it involves both the analogic and the digital in its most basic operation, but it exists within an analogic structure.

Kim (1975) cautions us strongly not to think of development, repetition, and evolution as alternatives. He points out that human interactions must be thought of as dynamic wholes. Hence, evolutionary activity at one level of the system may be homeostatic at another and vice versa. Kim (1975) argues that it is possible for morphostatic systems, in their very attempts to remain the same, to end up decreasing in structure. This he calls downward morphogenesis. He presents it as a concept linked to but different from the traditional system theory notion of entropy. In downward morphogenesis (or devolution) it is not that the system is moving to a state of disorganization, though that can happen as well, but that it is moving to a level of structuredness of a lower logical type. None of these concepts has any real meaning without clear referents, as noted earlier in my discussion of the counteradaptive consequences of adaptive change in the example of the rabbits and the lynxes. Because morphostasis can be thought of as the process of maintaining the structuredness of structure (Maruyama, 1963), everything will eventually depend on the frame in which the entity is being conceived at that time.

Although I am talking about the development, maintenance, or evolution of the structure of an entity, morphostasis and morphogenesis are *not* properties of the entity as such. They "belong" to the relationship of the entity and the ecosystem and cannot be understood separate from this relationship. This can be confusing, for the action of morphostasis and morphogenesis is on the structure of the system. This is where it can be seen operating. Nevertheless, they are not within-system concepts. They are concepts addressing the relationship of the order of an entity with the order of its ecosystem. Hence, they are themselves concepts relevant to the relationships between different logical types. For this reason, if we wish to study the morphostatic and morphogenetic properties of an entity, the focus of the study cannot be on the entity itself; it must be the relationship of entity and the ecosystem with each other. The implications of this morphostasis/morphogenesis material for the ways organization change are too extensive to elaborate here, but I offer the following four points for consideration.

> Change Hints:
> 1. If we wish to change the order of an entity, we must focus these changes at the abstract rules that shape and limit the activities of that entity-as-a-whole, that is, in the relationships with other entities in the ecosystem. It will not make sense to work on the internal rules. This will alter the structure of the entity-as-a-whole but will not influence the order in any predictable way.
> 2. We must work with the boundaries, for it is here that change takes place. However, we must not treat the boundary as a thing; and certainly we must not make the mistake structuralists do of seeing the boundary as part of the structure of the entity. The boundary is a relation, and it can be really understood only in relational terms. Failure to keep this image paramount is as problematic as treating a symbol as though it were the object it represents, like Bateson's schizophrenic who eats the menu card instead of the meal.
> 3. Change demands that we keep logically different orders separate. To mix them or treat one as the other creates a great deal of confusion.
> 4. Changing organization, that is, the relations among parts and relations among relations, necessarily involves changing the metaphors used for conceiving of those relations. Because the metaphor derives its meaning from the context (metonymy) in which it is embedded, new meanings can be generated by altering the frame in which the metaphor exists. Watzlawick, Weakland, and Fisch (1974) point out that such reframing operates at a level of metareality. Hence, the process of reframing may be viewed as developing in metaphoric (or analogic) form metaphors (or analogs) at one level of analysis that contain both the metaphoric and metonymic (analog and digital) elements at the lower logical levels. This is tan-

tamount to taking elements of the context in which something exists and incorporating them into itself—transforming system into structure or structure into system.

Conclusion

This chapter opens up more themes than it resolves in terms of how we change the organization of our thinking about changing organization. We have to incorporate the following major topics and concepts into our thinking to expand the horizons of how we deal with change and then how we formulate developmental theories of organization.

An organization does not exist in any physically verifiable way. It is a system of relationships and, like all relationships, is both invisible and knowable only in an abstract, derivative way, as with any other construct such as ego or God.

Hence, we can talk about organizations only metaphorically. This means that the quality of our thought and, in turn, the nature of our organization will be powerfully shaped by the metaphors and metonymies we use in our talking.

The specific value of each metaphor and metonymy is how adequately the map-drawing process (metaphor/metonymy creation) enables a map reader to conjure up images of the terrain such that it can be explored in ways similar to and congruent with other map drawers and users.

Because organization can be re-presented only metaphorically, what is known about organization (relationships) must be stored latently in the metaphors (or symbols, myths, or whatever).

Change involves creating something that is "not." "Not," however, is a boundary. It belongs neither to the entity nor to what "it is not."

"Not" becomes all tangled up in the problems of logical typing.

There are two fundamental processes in mapping that create information (give form to the unformed): the analog and the digital. The analog operates on a real, continuous basis and is undergirded by the processes of more/less and both/and. The digital involves the discrete and discontinuous and operates on/off, either/or forms.

The analog cannot represent "not." It lacks the syntax to negate. It is imprecise and ambiguous.

The digital is based on boundaries, on gaps, on the principles of yes/no. It possesses the necessary syntax to be precise, unambiguous, and to negate.

What the digital gains in syntax it loses in semantics. What the analog loses in syntax it gains in semantics.

To relate, we need only the analogic. To talk about relating (metacommunicate) demands the digital as well.

Communication and metacommunication are of logically different types.

Systems store their information about themselves, about their ecosystem, and about their relating and their history in behaviors. Behavior is communication. It is iconic and contains a lexicon. It can be read like any text, and each reading may reveal multiple texts—multiple levels of reality.

All behavior is communication. Hence, when organisms behave, they do so according to rules similar to those of any linguistic structure and are trapped by Gödel's paradox in the same way that all relations are.

All communication is conducted according to rules that cannot be discussed while the communication is in process. To do so involves metacommunicating, which in turn is governed by another set of rules, which cannot be attended to while the metacommunication proceeds, and so forth (Gödel's paradox).

All metacommunication requires distinctions, and all distinctions require the boundary "not." "Not" is a necessary precondition for identity. Without the digital, identity is a logical impossibility.

Every "not" digitalizes the analog and as such creates the conditions for new relationships, demanding analogs of a higher logical type than those that the "not" digitalized.

Organization has structure and order, but structure and order are of different logical types.

There may be no one-to-one direct relation between order and structure. In order to counter disorder at the level of the collectivity, creating more structure in the light of internal disorder may lead to more disorder at the level of the collectivity.

Change, development, and evolution may be adaptive or maladaptive, depending on what level of system it is examined from.

Organization is the source of tension. The tension of organization may be (1) within the entity or (2) between the entity and its ecosystem. The tensions, which may be contradictory or paradoxical, are system disturbing.

Organizations may be morphostatic (preserving their order) or morphogenic (changing in their order).

Morphostatic systems treat disturbance as external noise to be blocked out or adjusted to.

Morphogenetic systems treat disturbance as information about internal conditions of the system and respond by altering their orders.

Morphogenesis is like a metaphoric change in code such that the subsequent code is of a logically different order than that which preceded it.

Morphogenesis is analogous to a metaphor taking its metonymy into itself. It involves the transformation of structure into system and system into structure at increasing levels of logical typing.

A system may be morphostatic and morphogenic at the same time.

Morphostasis, morphogenesis, contradiction, paradox, and so forth, are not properties of a system. They belong to relationships, to the spaces in between. Thus, they cannot be found. They are principles of relating.

References

Alderfer, C. P. "Organization Development." *Annual Review of Psychology*, 1977, *28*, 197–225.

Alderfer, C. P., Brown, L. D., Kaplan, R. E., and Smith, K. K. *Group Relations and Organizational Diagnosis*. New York: Wiley, forthcoming.

Ashby, W. R. *An Introduction to Cybernetics*. New York: Wiley, 1961.

Bateson, G. "A Theory of Play and Fantasy." *A.P.A. Psychiatric Research Reports*, 1955, *11*, 39–51.

Bateson, G. *Steps to an Ecology of Mind.* New York: Ballantine, 1972.

Bateson, G., Jackson, D. D., Haley, J., and Weakland, J. H. "Towards a Theory of Schizophrenia." *Behavioral Science,* 1956, *1,* 251-264.

Becker, E. *The Denial of Death.* New York: Free Press, 1973.

Beer, M., and Driscoll, J. W. "Strategies for Change." In J. R. Hackman and J. L. Suttle (Eds.), *Improving Life at Work.* Santa Monica, Calif.: Goodyear, 1977.

Buckley, W. *Sociology and Modern Systems Theory.* Englewood Cliffs, N.J.: Prentice-Hall, 1967.

Burke, K. *Language as Symbolic Action: Essays on Life, Literature and Method.* Berkeley: University of California Press, 1966.

Campbell, D. T. "Common Fate, Similarity, and Other Indices of the Status of Aggregates of Persons as Social Entities." *Behavioral Science,* 1958, *3,* 14-25.

Campbell, J. H., and Mickelson, J. S. "Organic Communication Systems: Speculations on the Study, Birth, Life, and Death of Communications Systems." In B. D. Ruben and J. Y. Kim (Eds.), *General Systems Theory and Human Communication.* Rochelle Park, N.J.: Hayden, 1975.

Coser, L. A. *The Functions of Social Conflict.* New York: Free Press, 1956.

Erikson, E. H. *Childhood and Society.* New York: Norton, 1950.

Feyerabend, P. *Against Method.* London: Verso, 1975.

Freud, S. *The Complete Psychological Works of Sigmund Freud.* (J. Strachey, Ed.) London: Hogarth Press, 1953.

Friedlander, F., and Brown, L. D. "Organization Development." *Annual Review of Psychology,* 1974, *25,* 313-341.

Hayek, F. A. *Studies in Philosophy, Politics and Economics.* London: Routledge & Kegan Paul, 1967.

Hegel, G.W.F. *Hegel's Philosophy of Mind.* Oxford, England: Oxford University Press, 1971. (Originally published 1845.)

Heidegger, M. *Being and Time.* (J. Macquarrie and E. Robinson, Trans.) London: SCM, 1962. (Originally published 1927.)

Hockett, C. F., and Altman, S. A. "A Note on Design Features." In

T. A. Sebeok (Ed.), *Animal Communication*. Bloomington: Indiana University Press, 1968.

Hofstadter, D. R. *Gödel, Escher, Bach: An Eternal Golden Braid*. New York: Vintage, 1980.

Jacobson, R., and Halle, M. *Fundamentals of Language*. The Hague: Mouton, 1956.

Jaynes, J. *The Origin of Consciousness and the Breakdown of the Bicameral Mind*. Boston: Houghton Mifflin, 1976.

Jung, C. G. *Answer to Job*. Princeton, N.J.: Princeton University Press, 1958.

Jung, C. G. *Man and His Symbols*. Garden City, N.Y.: Doubleday, 1964.

Kim, J. Y. "Feedback in Social Sciences: Toward a Reconceptualization of Morphogenesis." In B. D. Ruben and J. Y. Kim (Eds.), *General Systems Theory and Human Communication*. Rochelle Park, N.J.: Hayden, 1975.

Kline, M. *The Psychoanalysis of Children*. London: Hogarth, 1932.

Laing, R. D. *Knots*. New York: Pantheon, 1970.

Laszlo, L. *Introduction to Systems Philosophy*. New York: Gordon and Breach, 1972.

Levinson, D. J. *The Seasons of a Man's Life*. New York: Ballantine, 1978.

Levi-Strauss, C. *Structural Anthropology*. (C. Jacobson and B. G. Schoeff, Trans.) New York: Basic Books, 1963. (Originally published, 1958.)

MacKay, D. M. *Information Mechanism and Meaning*. Cambridge, Mass.: M.I.T. Press, 1969.

Maruyama, M. "The Second Cybernetics: Deviation-Amplifying Mutual Causal Processes." *American Scientist*, 1963, *51*, 164–179.

Marx, K. *Capital*. (F. Engels, Ed.) London: Lawrence and Wishart, 1962. (Originally published 1894.)

May, R. *Love and Will*. New York: Norton, 1971.

May, R. *The Courage to Create*. New York: Bantam, 1975.

Meyer, M. W. (Ed.). *Structures, Symbols and Systems*. Boston: Little, Brown, 1971.

Moody, R. *Life After Life*. New York: Bantam, 1976.

Ornstein, R. E. *The Psychology of Consciousness*. San Francisco: Freeman, 1972.

Parsons, T. *The Structure of Social Action.* New York: Free Press, 1949.

Piaget, J. *Structuralism.* (C. Machler, Trans.) New York: Basic Books, 1970. (Originally published 1968.)

Pirsig, R. M. *Zen and the Art of Motorcycle Maintenance.* London: Corgi, 1974.

Pondy, L. R. "Leadership is a Language Game." In M. W. McCall and M. M. Lombardo (Eds.), *Leadership: Where Else Can We Go?* Durham, N.C.: Duke University Press, 1978.

Porter, L. W., Lawler, E. E. III, and Hackman, J. R. *Behavior in Organizations.* New York: McGraw-Hill, 1975.

Ranson, S., Hinings, B., and Greenwood, R. "The Structuring of Organizational Structures." *Administrative Science Quarterly,* 1980, *25*, 1–17.

Sarason, S. B. *The Culture of the School and the Problem of Change.* Boston: Allyn & Bacon, 1971.

Sarason, S. B. *The Creation of Settings and the Future Societies.* San Francisco: Jossey-Bass, 1972.

Sartre, J. P. *Of Human Freedom.* (W. Bookin, Ed.) New York: Philosophical Library, 1966.

Schein, E. H. *Organizational Psychology.* (2nd ed.) Englewood Cliffs, N.J.: Prentice-Hall, 1970.

Scott, W. R. "Theory of Organizations." In R. E. L. Faris (Ed.), *Handbook of Modern Sociology.* Chicago: Rand McNally, 1964.

Simmel, C. *Conflict and the Web of Groups—Affiliations.* (K. H. Wolff and R. Bendix, Trans.) New York: Free Press, 1955.

Smith, K. K. *Groups in Conflict: Prisons in Disguise.* Dubuque, Iowa: Kendall/Hunt, 1982.

Smith, K. K., Simmons, V. M., and Thames, T. B. "Organizational Transitions." Unpublished manuscript. University of Maryland, 1982.

Thayer, L. *Communication and Communication Systems.* Homewood, Ill.: Irwin, 1968.

Thompson, J. D. *Organizations in Action.* New York: McGraw-Hill, 1967.

Tillich, P. *The Courage to Be.* New Haven, Conn.: Yale University Press, 1952.

Tustin, A. "Feedback." *Scientific American,* 1952, *187*, 48–55.

Waddington, C. H. (Ed.) *Towards a Theoretical Biology.* Hawthorne, N.Y.: Aldine, 1968.

Watzlawick, P. *The Language of Change.* New York: Basic Books, 1978.

Watzlawick, P., Weakland, J., and Fisch, R. *Change.* New York: Norton, 1974.

Weick, K. E. *The Social Psychology of Organizing.* Reading, Mass.: Addison-Wesley, 1979.

Whorff, B. L. *Language, Thought and Reality.* Cambridge, Mass.: M.I.T. Press, 1956.

Wilden, A. *System and Structure.* London: Tavistock, 1972.

⊡ ⊡ ⊡ ⊡ ⊡ ⊡ **9**

Management of Organizational Change Among Loosely Coupled Elements

⊡ ⊡ ⊡ ⊡ ⊡ ⊡ ⊡ ⊡ ⊡ ⊡ ⊡ ⊡ ⊡ ⊡ ⊡ ⊡ ⊡ ⊡

Karl E. Weick

Organizational theory is beginning to move away from a preoccupation with rational systems toward equivalent development of ideas about natural systems and open systems (Scott, 1981). I suggest how traditional ideas about organizational change, many of them grounded in theories of rational systems, may need to be altered when they are fitted to one distinctive property of open systems, loose coupling among their elements (Weick, 1976).

The image of rational systems contains assumptions such as the following: "In the rational system perspective, structural arrangements within organizations are conceived as tools deliberately

I am grateful to Lee Sproull, Charles Perrow, Barry Staw, David Clark, Randy Bobbitt, and Paul Goodman for comments on a preliminary draft of this chapter.

designed for the efficient realization of ends. . . . Rationality resides
in the structure itself, not in the individual participants—in rules
that assure participants will behave in ways calculated to achieve
desired objectives, in control arrangements that evaluate performance and detect deviance, in reward systems that motivate participants to carry out prescribed tasks, and in the set of criteria by which
participants are selected, replaced, or promoted. . . . We have noted
the great emphasis placed in the rational system perspective on
control—the determination of the behavior of one subset of participants by the other. Decision making tends to be centralized, and
most participants are excluded from discretion or from exercising
control over their own behavior. Most rational system theorists justify these arrangements as being in the service of rationality: control
is the means of channeling and coordinating behavior so as to
achieve specified goals" (Scott, 1981, pp. 77-78).

To manage change in a rational system "is to find goals
and/or means that can be evaluated easily and to which the participants can commit themselves. It is assumed that if relevant information is gathered to define the problem properly and if the resistance
of recalcitrant parties is overcome, then a decision can be made that
will correct any problems. In this view, a fairly stable group of
decision makers who agree on goals and technology is managing
change" (Berger, 1981, p. 135).

The image of organizations as open systems contains assumptions that differ substantially from rational assumptions. "The
open systems view of organizational structure stresses the complexity and variability of the individual component parts—both individual participants and subgroups—as well as the looseness of
connections among them. Parts are viewed as capable of semiautonomous action; many parts are viewed as, at best, loosely coupled to
other parts. Further, in human organizations, the system is multice-
phalous: many heads are present to receive information, make decisions, direct performance. Individuals and subgroups form and
leave coalitions. Coordination and control become problematic.
Also system boundaries are seen as amorphous; the assignment of
actors or actions to either the organization or the environment often
seems arbitrary and varies depending on what aspect of system functioning is under consideration. Open systems imagery does not

simply blur the more conventional views of the structural features of organizations: it shifts attention from structure to process" (Scott, 1981, p. 119).

To manage change in an open system is to adopt strategies such as these:

1. Concentrate efforts on one or two critical problems.
2. Learn the history of an issue, including when it came up, who took what positions, who won, and who lost.
3. Build coalitions to mobilize support.
4. Use the formal system of committee memberships and the informal system of discussions and mediation (Berger, 1981, p. 136).

These four guidelines for change are cryptic, incomplete, and tentative, as are March's (1981) five footnotes to change, Cohen and March's (1974) eight administrative tactics, and Peters's (1980) signals, phases, and tools by which attention of organizational members can be redirected. All these sources do little more than hint at subtleties and complications that follow when assumptions about rationality are relaxed and assumptions about indeterminacy are substituted for them. The purpose of this chapter is to add substance to the few commentaries available concerning change and loosely coupled systems. The discussion focuses on characteristics of loosely coupled systems, characteristics of change in loosely coupled systems, and targets for change in loosely coupled systems.

A microcosm of the themes to be developed in all three sections is contained in the following demonstration.

> If you place in a bottle half a dozen bees and the same number of flies, and lay the bottle down horizontally, with its base to the window, you will find that the bees will persist, till they die of exhaustion or hunger, in their endeavor to discover an issue through the glass; while the flies, in less than two minutes, will all have sallied forth through the neck on the opposite side. . . . It is their (the bees') love of light, it is their very intelligence, that is their undoing in this experiment. They evidently imagine that the issue from every prison must be there where the light shines clearest; and they act

in accordance, and persist in too logical action. To them glass is a supernatural mystery they never have met in nature; they have had no experience of this suddenly impenetrable atmosphere; and the greater their intelligence, the more inadmissible, more incomprehensible, will the strange obstacle appear. Whereas the feather-brained flies, careless of logic as of the enigma of crystal, disregarding the call of the light, flutter wildly hither and thither, and meeting here the good fortune that often waits on the simple, who find salvation there where the wiser will perish, necessarily end by discovering the friendly opening that restores their liberty to them. (Maurice Maeterlinck, Belgian, 1862–1949) [Siu, 1968, p. 189].

This episode speaks of experimentation, persistence, trial and error, risks, improvisation, the one best way, detours, confusion, rigidity, and randomness all in the service of coping with change. Among the most striking contrasts are those between tightness and looseness. There are differences in the degree to which means are tied to ends, actions are controlled by intentions, solutions are guided by imitation of one's neighbor, feedback controls search, prior acts determine subsequent acts, past experience constrains present activity, logic dominates exploration, and wisdom and intelligence affect coping behavior.

In this example loose ties provide the means for some actors to cope successfully with a serious change in their environment. Each individual fly, being loosely tied to its neighbor and its own past, makes numerous idiosyncratic adaptations that eventually solve the problem of escape. Looseness is an asset in this particular instance, but precisely how and when looseness contributes to successful change and how change interventions must be modified to cope with the reality of looseness is not obvious.

Our understanding of change against the backdrop of loose ties is underdeveloped because most models people use to think about change rely heavily on connections, networks, support systems, diffusion, imitation, and social comparison, none of which are plentiful in loosely coupled systems.

The Nature of Loosely Coupled Systems

Here is an example of a loosely coupled system:

A bizarre case of segregation of parts of an organization concerns the Butterfield Division of UTD Corporation, which makes precision cutting instruments. This factory straddles the international border between Vermont and Quebec, with its front door in Canada and its back door in the United States. As a result of a treaty made in 1842, the Canadian-American border was fixed through a number of existing communities, sometimes even dividing buildings. One of these was this precision instrument factory. Both matter-energy and information processes are affected by this split. An imaginary line, which only top executives cross, is drawn through the plant. On the American side the plant buys raw steel from producers in the United States, maintains a separate stock room and machine shop, and hires citizens of the United States, who are paid in United States dollars. On the Canadian side the plant buys from Canadian producers, also maintains a separate stock room and machine shop, and hires workers from Canada, who are paid in the currency of that country. Since moving steel from one side of the shop to the other would constitute smuggling, steel on one side of the factory is "exported," driven across the international border, and "imported" through customs, where forms are filled out and duty is paid. At regular intervals taxes are paid to each government based upon the profit made on that part of the operation which is inside its borders [Miller, 1978, p. 702].

Here is an example of a tightly coupled system: "Martin Coyle, the head of Chevrolet, always preached with great unction. Once when I [Peter Drucker] was sitting in his office listening to his favorite sermon on the beatitudes of decentralization, the teleprinter in the corner of the office next to a big brass spitoon began to yammer. 'Pay no attention,' Coyle said. 'It's only the Kansas City plant manager letting me know he's going out to lunch,' and continued the sermon on complete freedom by local managers" (Peters, 1979, p. 54). The contrasts implicit in these two examples will be discussed in terms of their differences in determinacy, system integration, levels of analysis, and bounded rationality.

Loose Coupling and Indeterminacy. Miller's (1978, p. 16) description of systems provides the context within which I can specify the property of organizations on which this chapter is focused: "A *system* is a set of interacting units with relationships among them. The word 'set' implies that the units have some common properties. These common properties are essential if the units are to interact or have relationships. The state of each unit is constrained by, conditioned by, or dependent on the state of other units. The units are coupled." When people make theoretical verbal statements about the units and relationships in systems, "nouns, pronouns, and their modifiers typically refer to concrete systems, subsystems, or components; verbs and their modifiers usually refer to the relationships among them" (Miller, 1978, p. 17).

This chapter is grounded in five adverbs that modify the relationship between any two components in a system. Loose coupling exists if A affects B (1) suddenly (rather than continuously), (2) occasionally (rather than constantly), (3) negligibly (rather than significantly), (4) indirectly (rather than directly), and (5) eventually (rather than immediately). Connections may appear *suddenly*, as in the case of a threshold function; may occur *occasionally*, as in the case of partial reinforcement; may be *negligible*, as when there is a damping down of response between A and B due to a constant variable; may be *indirect*, as when a superintendent can affect a teacher only by first affecting a principal; and may occur *eventually*, as when there is a lag between legislator voting behavior and response by his or her electorate.

The Canadian side of the Butterfield Division affects the American side occasionally, negligibly, and often indirectly. Relations *among* the Canadian components are more continuous, constant, significant, direct, and immediate. The plant manager in Kansas City is in fact tied to Martin Coyle constantly, directly, and immediately, even though Coyle prefers to see these ties as occasional, indirect, and slow.

The five adverbs provide a guideline for inquiry because they advise investigators to pool all organizational episodes of the variety "if A, then B, maybe" and see what they have in common. These episodes are not treated as errors, as testimonials to poor measurement, as sloppiness, or as randomness. Instead, they are episodes from which we induce a picture of normal functioning in the face of indeterminate relationships.

The adverbs index loose coupling in terms of the reliability with which B can be predicted given the behavior of A (Glassman, 1973). The concept of loose coupling indicates why people cannot predict much of what happens in organizations. In this sense, the concept has some parallel with meteorology. The science of meteorology often explains conditions under which it is impossible to forecast the weather. To gain a better understanding of weather is to understand more clearly why accurate forecasting is sometimes impossible. Understanding does not necessarily lead to more accurate predictions; rather, it leads to better predictions about those times when predicting will not work. Loose coupling operates the same way. To understand a loosely coupled system is to understand more clearly why predictions about that system may fail. To talk about a loosely coupled system is not to talk about structural looseness, but about process looseness. The image is that of a sequence of events that unfolds unevenly, discontinuously, sporadically, or unpredictably, if it unfolds at all.

The concept of a loosely coupled system is an attempt to reintroduce some indeterminacy into conventional portraits of systems. To describe an organization as a system is to imply that connections are tight and responsive and that effects are large and ramify swiftly.

To affirm that systems in organizations also have delays, lags, unpredictability, erratic guidance by feedback, unstable equilibria, and untrustworthy feedback, one can highlight the fact that components within the system are loosely coupled.

Loose Coupling and System Integration. Phenomena related to loose coupling in organizations appear most often in discussions of "integration." Lawrence and Lorsch (1969), for example, argue that greater differentiation among components is necessary to cope with complex environments, and this creates added problems of coordination. To cope with these problems, tighter coupling among units is required, and this is often accomplished through devices such as liaison roles. Thus, Lawrence and Lorsch are most interested in cases of high differentiation—high integration. My interest is in cases of high differentiation—low integration and in the possible ways in which such cases may trade off short-term adaptation for longer term adaptability. Systems with high differentiation—low integration may appear ineffective when assessed by criteria tied to efficiency, but may be more effective when assessed against criteria that index flexibility, ability to improvise, and capability for self-design (Weick, 1977).

Miller's (1978) discussion of integration provides an additional contrast to highlight the nature of loosely coupled systems. Miller argues that as size, number of units, and complexity increase, organizations reorganize into semiautonomous, decentralized components acting on information that is partly segregated. "As a system grows and adds more components, the components in general become increasingly independent in decision making" (Miller, 1978, p. 109). The point at which my interest diverges from Miller's is a proposition that resembles Lawrence and Lorsch's. Miller (1978, p. 109) predicts that "As a system's components become more numerous, they become more specialized, with resulting increased interdependence for critical processes among them." My disagreement is with "more specialized" and "increased interdependence." Differentiation can produce generalists as well as specialists, independence as well as interdependence. Differentiated systems can be self-contained and can carry out critical subsystem processes. If there is an emphasis on general competence rather than specific skills, people can replace one another and the unit can survive even if its ties to other units are infrequent and weak.

Decentralization, differentiation, segregation, and division of labor often are confounded with specialization. As a result, differentiation seems to increase dependence on those whose skills lie outside one's own specialty and special efforts must be made to tighten the relationships among the specialists. Differentiation, however, can produce either general, self-organizing, independent units that can remain loosely coupled to other units and still adapt or specialist, reactive-organizing, dependent units that maintain tight couplings with other units in order to adapt. A loosely coupled system need not be a vulnerable system.

Loose Coupling and Levels of Analysis. The property of loose coupling is pervasive, and all organizational theorists and change agents are affected by it, even if they choose to ignore it. The property is pervasive in at least two decisions: (1) the level of analysis used to conceptualize phenomena and (2) the choice of target at which change efforts are directed.

Simon's (1962) empty world hypothesis and concept of the nearly decomposable system asserts that in any set of systems ties *within* a subsystem are stronger than are ties *between* subsystems.

Investigators often say that the concept of loose coupling applies only to "higher" levels of analysis. What sometimes gets missed is that, pragmatically, a higher level of analysis is *anything* above the level at which the investigator concentrates. For example, if as a psychologist I study individuals, then dyads and small groups—both higher levels of analysis—will seem to be loosely coupled systems. Ties are stronger within individual actors than they are between actors. Notice that the small group, which seems like a loosely coupled system to me, may seem tightly coupled to the investigator who *starts* with that level of analysis. Notice also that all of us who study small sized units—individual, dyad, triad, small group, set of small groups—will agree that an organization is loosely coupled because organizations are a higher level of analysis than any of us works with. We will encounter disagreement from those people who talk about firms, industries, communities, occupations, societies, professions, and interorganizational networks. For these people, individual organizations are relatively tightly coupled.

It is not obvious what an investigator concludes about units of analysis *smaller* than the one being examined. For example, as a person who works with the individual level of analysis, I find it inconceivable to talk about systems of loosely coupled organs or loosely coupled cells; yet physiologists argue that indeed that is possible.

The moral is that you first have to specify what elements you are examining and then look *among* these elements to find instances of loose coupling. Disagreement about the presence or absence of loose coupling may reflect a confounding of different levels of analysis.

The choice of targets for change and the success of change efforts should also be affected by the pattern of tight within, loose between. The general rule is that it is easier to produce change within than change between. Change interventions within are more likely to diffuse quickly with less modification than is true for change interventions between. If I focus on individuals, then individuals are tight within and loose between. Thus, I should have more success changing one individual and less success changing a couple or a family. If I concentrate on the small group, then the group is tight within and there are loose ties among groups. Thus, I should have more success changing a nuclear family than an extended family. Between change will always be harder than within change, even though there is a certain amount of arbitrariness involved in the decision of where to draw the boundaries that separate units. To draw boundaries around people is to direct their attention and energy *inside* the box. Change efforts within are more successful simply because they capitalize on that occurrence.

Loose Coupling and Bounded Rationality. Systems may become more loosely coupled as organizational size increases or as environments become more complex, but cognitive processes on a much more micro level may also produce loose coupling.

Loosely coupled systems are often characterized as systems in which there is low agreement about preferences and cause—effect linkages (Thompson and Tuden, 1959). When people see things differently, their efforts will be only loosely coordinated and they will share few variables in their individual cause maps (Bougon, Weick, and Binkhorst, 1977) of the organization and its environment. Furthermore, those variables they do share will often be unimportant.

Disagreements about preferences and cause—effect linkages occur not simply because people have different perceptions, but also because they act and modify the environments they perceive. People wade into settings that puzzle them, rearrange those settings (often inadvertently), and when they finally ask the question, "what's up here," they *already* have had an effect on the answer (for example, Jones, 1977). When people examine environments, they often see the effects of their own actions emitted while positioning themselves for a better view. People implant a sizable portion of what they reify into *the* external reality but underestimate the extent to which different people implant different things.

The sequence of activity and sense making that produces loose coupling begins when individual actions produce individual realities that have only modest overlap. Having acted toward chaos differently, people arrange that chaos in different ways and, as a result, see different things when they inspect it. These unique "things" are the raw material from which multiple realities are built. Multiple realities, in turn, cause loosely coupled systems because individuals share few variables, share weak variables, and differ in their perceptions of covariation among these variables.

The existence of multiple realities is not just a byproduct of enactment; it is the major consequence of bounded rationality. People with limited information processing capabilities, memories that are loosely coupled to detail and uniqueness, and attention spans that are short individually will notice different things, will reflect at different times, and will process different segments at different speeds.

Steinbruner (1974) suggests the potential for loosely coupled systems that is implicit in bounded rationality. He argues that many cognitive processes, such as the search for cognitive consistency, simplify complex inputs. Cognitive processes transform problems into simple replicas that can be monitored by simple cybernetic processes. The important outcome of this process for students of loosely coupled systems is that massive typification and editing leave a great deal of variance unaccounted for. Even though it is unrecognized, this variance *does* influence processes, overdetermine phenomena, and introduce slippage between intention and outcome. What simplification procedures ignore remains to undo plans built on incomplete versions of "what's up."

A loosely coupled system is one consequence of bounded rationality, but the constraints on rationality *differ* across people and groups. Bounded rationality is not homogeneous. For example, when people search in the vicinity of the problem, it has been presumed that they will search in the same ways and in the same places. However, because people differ in their definitions of what a problem is, what constitutes search, and how much information they can store before they have to process it, they differ in what they find.

We have mistakenly thought that bounded rationality meant that people use similar simplifications. Similar simplifications are easy to coordinate because everybody sees the "same" world even though each is seeing very little of it. However, people bound rationality in different ways. They focus on small portions, but they focus on different small portions. As a result, the best they can do is have vague understandings of what to do next. They find it hard to agree either on explicit definitions of ends or on clear statements of what will lead to what. As a result, their actions are only moderately contingent on those of their neighbors or on their own personal intentions.

The propositions implicit in this analysis are the following: To the extent that rationality becomes less bounded, pressures toward cognitive consistency decline, attention spans lengthen, and cognitive complexity increases, people should share a greater number of important variables and become more tightly coupled. Furthermore, when enactment becomes less prominent as an input to the environment—a circumstance that is possible when tasks are specified, supervision is close, and sanctions for deviance are swift and harsh—there should be fewer realities, more shared variables, and tighter coupling among people.

The Nature of Change in Loosely Coupled Systems

A key dilemma in organizations involves the trade-off between adaptation to exploit present opportunities and adaptability to exploit future opportunities. Future opportunities may appear suddenly when the environment changes and may require a repertoire of responses that have been neglected because of their irrelevance to present demands. The trade-off between adaptation and adaptability is often described in the context of flexibility and stability.

Flexibility is required to modify current practices so that nontransient changes in the environment can be adapted to. This means that the organization must detect changes and retain a sufficient pool of novel responses to accommodate to these changes. But total flexibility makes it impossible for the organization to retain a sense of identity and continuity. Any social unit is defined in part by its history, by what it has done repeatedly and chosen repeatedly. Stability also provides an economical means to handle new contingencies; there are regularities that an organization can exploit if it has a memory and the capacity for repetition. But total adherence to past wisdom would be as disruptive as total flexibility because more economical ways of responding would never be discovered and new environmental features would seldom be noticed.

An organization can reconcile the need for flexibility with the need for stability in several ways: by some form of compromise response (a solution tried too often with much too disastrous results), by alternation between stability and flexibility, or by simultaneous expression of the two necessities in different portions of the system. Only in the last two cases is continued existence possible. A compromise response often accomplishes neither flexibility nor stability.

Adaptability in Loosely Coupled Systems. The dilemma involving adaptation and adaptability threads through loosely coupled systems in several ways. First, loose coupling is the source of adaptability in most organizations, whereas tight coupling is the source of most adaptation. Second, in a loosely coupled system there is less necessity for major change because change is continuous. Frequent local adjustments, unconstrained by centralized policy, keep small problems from amplifying. If major change becomes necessary, however, it is much harder to diffuse it among systems that are loosely coupled. Loosely coupled systems reduce the necessity for large-scale change but also make it more difficult to achieve if it is needed. Third, tight coupling can facilitate adaptability under certain conditions, and loose coupling may also produce adaptation under specific circumstances.

The ways in which loose coupling preserves adaptability and flexibility are straightforward. Loose coupling of structural elements "may be highly adaptive for the organization, particularly when confronting a diverse, segmented environment. To the extent that departmental units are free to vary independently, they may provide a more sensitive mechanism to detect environmental variation. Loose coupling also encourages opportunistic adaptation to local circumstances, and it allows simultaneous adaptation to conflicting demands. Should problems develop with one departmental unit, it can be more easily sealed off or severed from the rest of the system. Moreover, adjustment by individual departments to environmental perturbations allows the rest of the system to function with greater stability. Finally, allowing local units to adapt to local conditions without requiring changes in the larger system reduces coordination costs for the system as a whole" (Scott, 1981, p. 248). A loosely coupled system reduces the costs of trial and error, preserves variety because it allows innovations to be retained and cumulate (Ashby, 1960), and can improve the accuracy with which situations are diagnosed.

The suggestion that loosened couplings improve the accuracy of perception (Campbell, 1979; Heider, 1959; Weick, 1978) introduces a productive tension into theorizing about change. When things are loosely coupled, sensing is improved, small deviations are sensed more quickly, and corrective actions are directed at those small deviations sooner. The result of this swifter response to smaller deviations is that potentially big problems are anticipated and solved before they become unmanageable and before they attract the attention of lots of other people. With loose coupling, diagnosis is more accurate, but interventions on the basis of this diagnosis have only minor, local effects. With tight couplings, diagnosis is less accurate, but interventions on the basis of the misdiagnosis have large effects.

The tidiness of the proposition that loosely coupled systems improve adaptability and tightly coupled systems improve adaptation is weakened by the possibility that tightly coupled organizations can sometimes communicate quickly that an environmental change has occurred and can retool with it. This sequence is not common because information about all changes, spurious as well as serious, flows through a tightly coupled system and overloads participants (for example, see Perrow, 1981a, 1981b). To cope with this overload, people ignore indiscriminately most data signifying environmental change and therefore miss the necessity for organizational change. Because they also have to do a more significant retooling to adapt to what may prove to be a spurious event, lags persist and escalation of current commitments is likely.

Nevertheless, a tightly coupled system may be slow to innovate yet retain "the privilege of historic backwardness" that allows it to benefit from the lessons of the more loosely coupled systems that made the first innovation. The efficiencies that accompany tight coupling may then allow those organizations that are second on the scene to grind up those who were first.

Problems with Local Adaptations. Lustick (1980), in an important critique of the strategy of disjointed incrementalism, suggests four conditions under which local adjustments, such as occur in loosely coupled systems, could lead to outcomes that are inferior to those that could be achieved by more synoptic, rational, centralized planning. Three of these conditions are relevant in the present context.

First, if the values of variables in the environment generate smooth continuous changes in values of causally connected variables, then local remedial actions are less harmful than if there are sharp discontinuities or thresholds in the values of the variables. Diverse local attempts to manage levels of sulphur dioxide pollution are plausible, but local experiments to manage radiation pollution by nuclear power plants are not. In the case of radiation, there are sharp discontinuities in the levels of damage that can be produced by incremental errors.

Second, if the complexity of an organization's environment can be decomposed into short causal chains so that consequences can be contained and monitored, then local remedial actions are less harmful than if causal chains were elongated. A society with many separate watersheds can experiment with diverse strategies to use and protect water resources because errors do not ramify the way they would if a society's watershed was a single large river with all pollution experiments being conducted upstream. Elongated causal chains are relatively nondecomposable and they conceal the significant consequences of discrete actions. This means that dependence on immediate feedback, a common feature of adjustments in loosely coupled systems, is misleading in complex environments where effects are delayed.

Lustick (1980, p. 347) summarizes the proposition concerning complexity and causal chains this way: "Complexity is commonly defined as some combination of differentiation, rate of change, and interdependence. Complex task environments are relatively more resistant to incrementalist coping techniques to the extent that their complexity derives from the interdependence of changing and differentiated components, rather than from the rate of change or extent of differentiation per se."

Third, incremental, local, disjointed accommodations are less harmful when an organization has redundant resources than when it lacks such redundancy. "For an organization with minimal slack in its budget, the sacrifice of some resources now for a little knowledge later may prevent it from surviving long enough to apply the knowledge gained" (Lustick, 1980, p. 349). A rich family can use its food budget to experiment with nutrition in food purchases and can discard the failures, but poor families cannot afford this hit-or-miss strategy. As resources diminish, a series of expensive partial successes from incremental changes made to collect insights may ensure total failure.

The relatively swift, relatively frequent adjustments to environmental changes made by loosely coupled systems may be detrimental when the variables affected are of different orders of magnitude or embedded in long causal chains or when scarce resources are used up so that the system dies. Organizational change should be centralized when subunit adjustments can have discontinuous, long-term effects at considerable expense and decentralized when adjustments have continuous, abbreviated, inexpensive effects.

One reason schools may persist as loosely coupled systems is that their local experiments with curricula, staffing, parent relations, and special programs have small, linear effects that do not ramify across time in obvious ways (for example, at age forty-five, I cannot see how I am better or worse off because I went to Lincoln Elementary School in Findlay, Ohio) and do not cost much. However, as resources become less plentiful, adult lethargy is traced to malnutrition in school lunches, and curricular decisions about creationism have discontinuous effects on the number of people who now monitor a school, loose coupling should be less satisfactory as a structure for adaptation and efforts should be made to recentralize strategy to avoid actions or commitments that become amplified.

In summary, change in loosely coupled systems is continuous rather than episodic, small scale rather than large, improvisational rather than planned, accommodative rather than constrained, and local rather than cosmopolitan. Furthermore, loosely coupled systems may store innovations that are not presently useful. Change diffuses slowly, if at all, through such systems, which means that components either invent their own solutions—which may be inefficient compared with other solutions available in the system—or they die. To construct a loosely coupled system is to design a system that updates itself and may never need the formal change interventions that sometimes are necessary to alter the hard-wired routines in tightly coupled systems.

Adaptability requires loosening; adaptation requires tightening. How a person manages this opposition over time will determine how well a component can both exploit an explicit niche and adapt to change in the niche. Simultaneous loose and tight coupling could represent "ambivalence as the optimal compromise." Simultaneous loose and tight coupling occurs, for example, when people simultaneously credit and discredit their past experience. Crediting of past experience is the equivalent of tight coupling in the sense that experience is used as a direct guide to future action. Discrediting is equivalent to loose coupling in the sense that people treat past knowledge as dated and no longer relevant to the environment that exists. Both conclusions are partially true in most settings. There has been some change but there has also been some continuity.

Targets for Change in Loosely Coupled Systems

There are several properties of loosely coupled systems that are crucial for their functioning and thus important objects of change. It is important to begin an inventory of such targets because they differ from targets such as goals, procedures, rules, controls, and design, which are targets in rational systems. The targets to be reviewed here include the following:

1. Presumptions of logic that tie loose events together (doubt produces change)
2. Socialization processes where common premises for dispersed decision making are implanted (resocialization produces change)
3. Differential participation rates that accelerate processes of loosening (equalization produces change)
4. Constant variables that disconnect parts of systems (distraction produces change)

5. Corruptions of feedback that obstruct contingent action (dependability produces change)

Presumptions of Logic. The introduction of doubt into a loosely coupled system is a much more severe change intervention than most people realize. Core beliefs, such as the presumption of logic and the logic of confidence, are crucial underpinnings that hold loose events together. If these beliefs are questioned, action stops, uncertainty is substantial, and receptiveness to change is high. The rationale for these expectations is this: Prevailing thinking about organizations places a disproportionate emphasis on interaction, interpersonal relations, and being together. Loose coupling imagery suggests that people can get by far longer, on less thick socializing, with less pathology, and more energy and creativity than we presumed. The loose coupling image has also suggested that people can be tied together by less tangible relationships than face-to-face contact. Meyer and Rowan (1977, p. 358) argue that weak ties can be sustained by a *"logic of confidence. . . .* Confidence in structural elements (in loosely coupled systems) is maintained through three practices—avoidance, discretion, and overlooking. . . . Assuring that individual participants maintain face sustains confidence in the organization, and ultimately reinforces confidence in the myths that rationalize the organization's existence. . . . The assumption that things are as they seem, that employees and managers are performing their roles properly, allows an organization to perform its daily routines with a decoupled structure."

In my own work the concept of the *presumption of logic* (Weick, 1979; Weick, Gilfillan, and Keith, 1973) has served the same purpose as the concept of logic of confidence. The presumption of logic resembles a self-fulfilling prophecy. A person about to confront an event presumes in advance that the event *will have* made sense. Sensibleness is treated as a closed issue a priori. Having made this presumption, the person then tries to make the event sensible as it unfolds, postpones premature judgments on whether it makes sense or not, and thereby makes his or her own contribution toward inventing a sensible, complete experience. Other persons are not central in this sense making.

The presumption of logic is a way to bridge weak connections among events. A cause map (Weick, 1979) can be thought of as a summary of the presumptions one makes about a structure that hold that structure together. People do not actually see causes and effects; they infer them. With that cause map in mind, people examine events and act as if those events are tied together in the ways displayed in the map. Acting toward those events as if they were tied together causally in fact makes those events cohere more tightly than they would if a person without those assumptions had encountered them.

A member of the Utrecht Jazz Orchestra (Bougon, Weick, and Binkhorst, 1977) basically says that this rehearsal will have made sense because the events here are all organized so as to produce more satisfaction for me with my performance. Having presumed that order in a rehearsal, the musician treats it as a sensible event and *transforms* the assortment of happenings into an orderly, predictable evening.

Presumptions fill in the gaps that are created when a loosely coupled system is built. People create loosely coupled systems so they can sense and adapt ɔ changes in the environment. In the face of that loose structure, which is finely tuned to accomplish adaptability, people simultaneously improve their present adaptation by presuming that any present niche in which they find themselves *does* make sense. To presume that it makes sense is to create that sense.

The question for change agents is how local perceptions of order break down. The answer would seem to be that the presumptions simply do not work. People make presumptions and act; yet nothing makes sense.

To change the presumption of logic is to weaken all presumptions by inducing the role of stranger, introduce novel logic systems either as presumptions or into the event being comprehended (Shapiro, 1978), make people self-conscious about their presumptions so that it is harder for them to invoke them, demonstrate that events are related randomly, discredit the rationality of the event to be observed, lower the self-esteem of the presumer, evoke contradictory sets of presumptions, demonstrate how much data are overlooked by the presumptions the observer is using and that the overlooked data contradict the presumption in force, and so forth. All these actions are nothing but variants on what happens when change agents try to unfreeze people. The difference is that all these variants share a common relevance to the "glue" presumed to hold loosely coupled systems together. To insert change into a loosely coupled system is to pay special attention to the nature and quality of those ties that do exist, namely, ties fashioned out of presumptions.

Socialization Processes. "An anecdote comes to mind. A friend recently said to me, 'You're damn right we're autonomous; for example, last year corporate didn't modify any of my 17 top management salary/bonus recommendations.' I responded, 'It sounds to me like the height of "centralization"; *you* didn't make any recommendations that were out of bounds.' We agreed that there was truth in both statements" (Peters, 1979, p. 22).

One way to explain the persistence and functioning of loosely coupled systems is to argue that some form of integration overlays the systems and binds members together. Two suggestions of such an integrative overlay have already been discussed: the logic of confidence and the presumption of logic. Explicit internal controls, which are the essence of tight coupling, can be relaxed if organizational members are homogeneous at the time they assume their jobs or if they mingle and know one another sufficiently so that they can anticipate the moves of one another and coordinate actions at a distance.

Prior homogeneity that constrains subsequent variability can occur through rigorous selection and training procedures, anticipatory socialization, recruitment from a common source, or socialization into independent functioning. In each case, individuals are stand-ins for one another and explicit tight coupling is unnecessary. Issues are defined in a similar fashion because alternative sets of premises simply are not recognized. District school administrators who have come up through the ranks "know" the small latitude of discretion present in local schools and turn this into a self-fulfilling prophecy by not making proposals to the principals that presumably would be rejected anyway. Patterns of succession serve to homogenize the premises, presumptions, and ideology of administrators and to allow for their coordination at a distance.

Thus, loosely coupled systems may have pseudolooseness because members are tightly coupled to a limited set of decision premises determined by top management and implanted during socialization experiences. If we assume that more intense indoctrination leads to tighter coupling of people and premises, then, using Van Maanen's (1978) eight strategies for socialization, we would predict that newcomers who were socialized formally, collectively, sequentially, in a closed manner, with divestiture rituals would be more tightly coupled, more interchangeable with their peers, better able to coordinate at a distance, and better able to predict one another's behavior than newcomers who were socialized informally, individually, nonsequentially, in an open manner, with investiture rituals.

However, loosely coupled systems of people, decision premises, and procedures may be much less integrated than the preceding case suggests, if socialization practices encourage individuality, independence, and improvisation and expose newcomers to inaccurate or incomplete versions of organizational practice. This happens when newcomers encounter unique training, develop restricted loyalties, gain experience in being self-contained, and see the organization in ways that are shared by few other people. These outcomes can result from socialization strategies that are informal, individual, nonsequential, variable, disjunctive, and open.

Consider the contrast between formal and informal processes. Formality refers to the degree to which the setting in which training takes place is set apart from the on-going work context and to the degree to which the individual's role as recruit is specified (Van Maanen, 1978). When the recruit's role is segregated and specified, the formal training processes focus on attitudes, rather than acts. (This happens of necessity because of the separation from the everyday work place.) As a result, there is inconsistency between what the person is taught and the realities of the job situation. The greater the separation of the newcomer from the work-a-day reality of the organization, the less the newcomer will be able to carry over or generalize any abilities or skills learned in the socialization setting.

Informal socialization also encourages loosely coupled systems, but through a different mechanism. Informal socialization increases the influence upon the individual of the specific group doing the socializing, a circumstance that is almost ideal to create stronger ties within than between groups. Left to their own devices, recruits drift toward those veterans who are most attractive. Whatever controls, this attraction also restricts the range of training and exposure recruits will get from the informal training.

Perhaps the most crucial contributor to loose coupling in informal socialization is the shielding of the recruit from mistakes. Mistakes happen, but learning on the job can be dangerous in the case, for example, of interdependent police work. The recruit's need and desire for real experiences may be ignored on the grounds that veterans cannot afford to take the chance of giving the new person sufficient discretion to put their own assignments and reputations in jeopardy.

In both formal and informal socialization, the causal linkages between A and B become more tenuous, but for different reasons. Formal socialization, with its cultural island, does produce homogeneity in attitudes and, to the extent that similar attitudes facilitate coordination at a distance, produces a tightly coupled system that may appear loose. Ironically, formality also can produce loose coupling directly because this very emphasis on attitudes ill prepares the similar recruits for what they will encounter once they graduate. When this discrepancy becomes apparent, the recruits begin to resocialize themselves in ways that are more idiosyncratic and more attuned to the specific situation in which they find themselves. The similar attitudes with which they have been prepared become less valuable as guides for action and are dropped in favor of more pragmatic beliefs that are locally appropriate.

Informal socialization promotes loose coupling because recruits align themselves with veterans who themselves have had a skewed sample of experience and who also are wary of allowing the recruit to make instructive errors in serious activities. The recruit gets exposed to a novel set of moderately safe aspects of the ongoing organization and is ill prepared to cope with worlds other than the one to which he or she was initiated.

Having considered just one of Van Maanen's eight distinctions, we find ourselves in the unusual position of arguing that no matter what happens during socialization, individuals will develop a loose coupling between their own beliefs and actions, between themselves and rules and procedures, and between themselves and both peers and predecessors. The socialized newcomer is unlike everyone else and therefore shares few variables and unimportant variables with them. The recruit is also like everyone else in the training cohort, and to the extent that recruits function among themselves after training as a separate organization, the recruits can coordinate actions through accurate anticipation of others' responses and assumptions. If people are trained similarly but then dispersed, there is still slippage between training and practice when each individual discovers different ways in which formal instruction is dated and idealized and tries to remedy the misinformation.

The preceding line of argument suggests a curvilinear relationship. Both relatively pure formal socialization and relatively pure informal socialization have identical outcomes, namely, predispositions to create loosely coupled systems between headquarters and the field. The mixed case of part formal and part informal socialization avoids the unreality of an idealized view of the world (it has accuracy) and the unreality of one mentor's skewed view of the world (it has generality). In producing valid experience among likeminded peers, it might set the stage for tight coupling both with these peers and with other veterans who are actually doing what the socialization experiences portray them as doing. A mixture of formality and informality leads to tighter coupling than does either component when pursued by itself.

To change a loosely coupled system is to resocialize people away from provincial views adopted during the "second" socialization toward more comprehensive, more accurate views of different segments of the organization. This "third" socialization in effect suggests different practices adopted independently by similar loosely coupled systems elsewhere that might be of help to people who improvised their own current procedures without the benefit of much consultation. This third socialization also informs individual systems of the context within which their activities occur and of possible tacit interdependencies that exist among systems. Presumably, this information allows for more mutual adjustment and more coordination without a serious loss of adaptability.

To change a loosely coupled system is also to influence the original socialization processes so that their content is both more general and more accurate than is common when relatively pure socialization strategies are used. A mixture of indoctrination in key values plus training in the management of discretion and improvisation seems most appropriate to preserve the flexibility of a loosely coupled system but to stabilize that flexibility in terms of a handful of central values. To produce a blend of formality and flexibility seems to require that oppositions in socialization strategies, such as individual-collective or formal-informal, themselves be blended. The presence of relatively pure socialization strategies of the kind analyzed earlier should alert change agents that either generality (for example, informal practices) or accuracy (for example, formal practices) is being sacrificed in training. Either sacrifice loosens ties between people and ideology to such an extent that crucial functions may no longer be performed adequately when the newcomers are put in the field.

Centralized change seldom reaches the components of loosely coupled systems and routinely is undone when people are socialized, first, and then dispersed. The impact of change interventions addressed to loosely coupled systems increases when they are tailored to the realities that loosely coupled systems face (socialization content is accurate) and when they equip people to improvise in constructive, low-cost ways when these local realities change (socialization content is general).

Differential Participation. Equalization of participation has been a major tool in organizational change, but little attention has been paid to *differential* participation as a mechanism for change. Differential participation is more common in loosely coupled systems, less common in tightly coupled systems. As Pfeffer (1978, p. 31) notes, "organizations are loosely coupled, in part because few participants are constantly involved or care about every dimension of the organization's operation."

The mechanism for change implicit in differential participation is straightforward and has been analyzed most fully by Weiner (1976) in his discussion of the competence multiplier.

Change is possible in a loosely coupled system when one person becomes more closely coupled with issues and analysis and in doing so makes it harder for others to gain access to the decision-making process. Loose coupling among people in their rates of attendance and tight coupling among attendance, competence, and experience allow for differential amplification of individual efforts.

Participants who show up repeatedly at meetings produce an environment of sophisticated analyses that requires more participation from them, which makes them even more informed to deal with the issues that are presented. A vicious circle is created in which the regular participants of an advisory council enact the very set of sophisticated and subtle issues that their newfound competence enables only them to deal with. People who attend less often feel less informed, increasingly unable to catch up, and more reluctant to enter the conversation at the level of sophistication voiced by the persistent participants. The relatively less informed people select themselves out of the decision-making process, and this elevates the level of planning to an even more detailed and complicated level, where even fewer people can comprehend it. Over time the combination of high and low participation rates, a minor deviation in the beginning, changes the issues, plans, and environment that confront committees.

To change a loosely coupled system is to pay special attention to absentee members, latecomers, and regular attendees and then to alter attendance patterns, give thorough briefings to those who attend less frequently, change agendas without notice, thereby handicapping everyone equally, introduce topics on which infrequent participants have unique and visible expertise, change meeting times, or any other devices that introduce a new pattern of differential participation and a new pattern of concerns and expertise.

Constant Variables. Loose coupling may occur because variables in a system lose most of their variation and become constant. In Ashby's (1960, p. 169) words, "constancies can cut a system to pieces." To see this point, imagine a hammock that is narrow at the right and lefthand ends and broad in the middle. Imagine that there are two variables at the lefthand end labeled A_1 and A_2, three variables in the center of the hammock labeled $B_{1,2,3}$, and three variables at the righthand end labeled $C_{1,2,3}$. Imagine that A and C are connected by relationships that pass through B (see Figure 1).

Figure 1. Hypothetical System Vulnerable to Constant Variables.

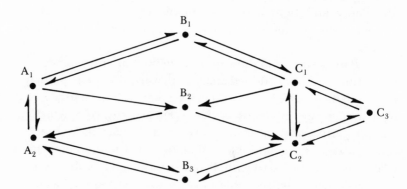

If the variables in B become constant, they construct a "wall of constancies" between subsystem A and subsystem C, and those two systems become severed and loosely coupled. If the constancies dissolve, the subsystems once again become fully jointed. As Ashby (1960, p. 169) notes, "if some variables or subsystems are constant for a time, then during that time the connexions through them are reduced functionally to zero, and the effect is as if the connexions had been severed in some material way during that time."

Secrets can sever systems. Jackson (1977) argues that educational administrators know more than they can say or use in their dealings with constituencies. They hear all kinds of secrets that they cannot pass along or invoke to rationalize and justify action. For our purposes, the administrator acts as a damper, as a constant variable, as a person who absorbs but does *not* pass along variation. A "quiet" administrator personifies the adverb "negligibly" in the statement, if A then B, negligibly. Superintendents are often praised as people who do not raise their voice (for example, McCleery, 1979), but what this means is that they are disconnecting portions of the system that are bound together by that voice. Administrators who make decisions by indecision effectively hold variables constant.

Bateson (1972, pp. 496–497) describes constant variables, although he prefers to call them uptight variables.

When, under stress, a variable must take the value close to its upper or lower limit of tolerance, we shall say, borrowing a phrase from the youth culture, that the system is "uptight" in respect to this variable, or lacks "flexibility" in this respect. But, because the variables are interlinked, to be uptight in respect to one variable commonly means that other variables cannot be changed without pushing the uptight variable. The loss of flexibility thus spreads throughout the system. In extreme cases, the system will only accept those changes which *change the tolerance limits* for the uptight variable. For example, an overpopulated society looks for those changes (increased food, new roads, more houses, etc.) which will make the pathological and pathogenic conditions of overpopulation more comfortable. But these *ad hoc* changes are precisely those which in longer time can lead to more fundamental ecological pathology. The pathologies of our time may broadly be said to be the accumulated results of this process—the eating up of flexibility in response to stresses of one sort or another (especially the stress of population pressure) and the refusal to bear with those byproducts of stress (e.g., epidemic and famine) which are the age old correctives for population excess.

Notice a crucial analytic subtlety that is associated with constant variables. In many organizational studies, the presence of variation and discretion is treated as an indicator of loose coupling. As discretion and variation decrease, the system is said to be more tightly coupled. Constant variables alter this reasoning. Evidence of low variation and low discretion can be interpreted to mean that variables are tightly coupled *or* that variables cannot move and may soon tear a system apart if they mediate crucial relationships. Variables with restricted variation do not tighten systems; they loosen them. Only when variation is restored do interactions increase and systems become more tightly coupled. To change a loosely coupled system is to restore variation to variables that have become constant and have frozen other variables that are dependent on them for variation. Variation can be restored by widening the tolerance limits of the constant variable, introducing lower standards of performance, circumventing the constant variable by introducing new linkages into the system, reversing the direction in which either the constant variable or related variables have been moving, institutionalizing and legitimatizing the separate severed systems while ignoring the original system, stressing the constant variable even more until the whole system explodes and forms new systems, and declaring a moratorium in the hope that relief from pressure will restore variation.

Change tactics that are useful for deescalation and conflict resolution often are effective because they restore variation to variables that have become unresponsive. Changes of this sort are especially important in loosely coupled systems.

Corruptions of Feedback. Conventional strategies for inducing change rely heavily on feedback (for example, Block, 1981). In loosely coupled systems, flawed feedback is often a major source of looseness. Consequently, feedback is often suspect when it is introduced, and sometimes people are not even clear how to use it. Loosely coupled systems often learn to make do with minimal feedback because feedback is unavailable, meaningless, or discredited. When feedback is offered by a change agent, people wonder why they should believe it and how they should use it.

Feedback becomes suspect in loosely coupled systems for a variety of reasons. For a tight coupling to form between actions and consequences, there must be swift, accurate feedback of those consequences to the action. As the speed and accuracy of feedback diminishes, there are looser couplings formed between actions and consequences and between actors. Loosely coupled systems show stability in the presence of environmental change. One way to understand this is to argue that organizations seldom benefit from trial-and-error learning because all they generate are trials. Data indicating errors are too noisy to coordinate with a specific action or too late for anyone to remember the precise trial that generated them.

When people in organizations take action and generate some consequences, these consequences may not inform subsequent actions because information about the consequences is (1) delayed, (2) neutralized (Millman, 1977), (3) confounded, (4) composed of lies, or (5) forgotten.

In each of these cases, it is predicted that the incidence of superstitious behavior will increase. Faced with imprecise information about what actions produce what outcomes, individuals on future occasions typically do more than is necessary to make specific outcomes happen. The individual overdetermines his or her own future responses when acting on the basis of ambiguous feedback. The important point is that action becomes even less finely tuned to the environment and to what other individuals are doing, and this is the prototypic situation for loose coupling.

Even though educational organizations produce feedback in large quantities, molecular analyses suggest that it is often not coupled to relevant actions. For example, professional norms among teachers often discourage offering assistance to faltering instructors unless it is asked for. Thus, faltering teachers get imprecise feedback about what they are doing wrong. As a result they are likely both to develop more elaborate teaching techniques and to find that these elaborated techniques are even more resistant to change because they are under the control of aperiodic reinforcement. In educational organizations, mistakes are often neutralized. As a result, actors in these systems are left with mere trials, an outcome that decouples action from environmental consequences and from the actions of other individuals.

Organizational actions are guided less often by their consequences fed back as an input than mechanistic metaphors would lead us to expect. Furthermore, despite abundant pronouncements about the value and importance of interpersonal feedback, organizational realities such as distance, diverse roles, infrequent inspection, professional norms respecting autonomy, limited vocabularies, and collective action the individual effects of which cannot be untangled, all blur feedback that people may try to give. As feedback becomes less credible and less frequent, actions become less tightly coupled to consequences and more difficult to coordinate. Continued neutralization of feedback can cut a system to pieces quite as handily as can constant variables.

To change a loosely coupled system requires either avoidance of feedback, at least initially, or "overkill" to avoid the discrediting of feedback that is given.

To change people without using feedback is to use modeling, role playing, case method, lectures, self-monitoring, guided imagery, audiovisual presentations, alone time, reading, projects, and field experiences (Walter and Marks, 1981). Each of these techniques is only moderately dependent on feedback for its impact or can be conducted so that feedback is incidental.

To change people by presenting convincing feedback is to be concerned with explicitness, immediacy, accuracy, and relevance and to have material presented by an expert source as an issue of fact rather than an issue of taste, dispassionately, and on an issue where the target person has no preconceptions (McGuire, 1968). These conditions make it harder to discredit and dismiss feedback, but they are also a harder set of conditions to create.

Loosely coupled systems can perceive their environments and themselves accurately because of their mediumlike quality noted earlier. As a result, feedback can be redundant and of little consequence as a vehicle for change. What a loosely coupled system often does not know is what other loosely coupled systems experience and how they cope with it. This ignorance is a result of minimal diffusion. Feedback may have more impact when it provides more information about *other* systems and less information about the target system.

Conclusion

A loosely coupled system is a problem in causal inference. For actors and observers alike, the prediction and activation of cause-effect relations is made more difficult because relations are intermittent, lagged, dampened, slow, abrupt, and mediated. Microchanges predominate in loosely coupled systems. The crucial links in a loosely coupled system occur among small groups of people, including dyads, triads, and small groups. That being the case, change models appropriate for small groups (for example, Herr and Weakland, 1979) seem most useful.

My own thinking about how to apply psychological findings to issues of change places a strong emphasis on language and communication. The main reason for this is that I use therapy as my model of application (Weick, 1981). My image is that of a conceptual therapist, a person who provides conceptual frameworks that individuals may not have previously imposed on their activities. A conceptual therapist articulates confusion and acts like a grammarian who gives people rules for tying together and labeling parts of their experiences. People provide a description in common language (Mandler and Kessen, 1959); the conceptual therapist consolidates, edits, and repunctuates the language and gives it back in somewhat different form. Having received back a somewhat novel version of what is going on, people may then monitor and do something different than before. Notice that the interventions of the person providing the gloss are innocuous. That person is directing attention, providing signals, asking questions, managing language, telling stories, and not much else. This way of acting is basically an elaboration of the following prototype: An individual says "I need a sounding board." Another individual says "I'll provide it." The two people meet regularly, and the sounding board provides feedback that is helpful to the degree that "(1) it provides information, (2) the learner is motivated to improve, (3) the learner has better response alternatives available" (McKeachie, 1976, p. 824).

Thus, one of the realities in loosely coupled systems is the reality that a person doing change can be no more or less effective than a therapist who builds conceptual frameworks and has only modest control over whether the feedback implicit in the communication provides information, induces motivation, and creates or elicits better response alternatives.

Actors in a loosely coupled system rely on trust and presumptions, persist, are often isolated, find social comparison difficult, have no one to borrow from, seldom imitate, suffer pluralistic ignorance, maintain discretion, improvise, and have less hubris because they know they cannot change the universe because it is not sufficiently connected to make this possible.

A loosely coupled system is not a flawed system. It is a social and cognitive solution to constant environmental change, to the impossibility of knowing another mind, and to limited information processing capacities. It is ethnocentrism writ small, and it is the ultimate neutralizer of managerial hubris. It is our recognition in our own language that delegation remains the primordial organizational act Selznick said it was and that it still remains the precarious venture he saw it to be. Loose coupling is to social systems as compartmentalization is to individuals, a means to achieve cognitive economy and a little peace.

References

Ashby, W. R. *Design for a Brain*. (2nd ed.) London: Chapman and Hall, 1960.

Bateson, G. *Steps to an Ecology of Mind*. New York: Ballantine, 1972.

Berger, M. A. "Coping with Anarchy in Organizations." In J. E. Jones and J. W. Pfeiffer (Eds.), *The 1981 Annual Handbook for Group Facilitators*. San Diego, Calif.: University Associates, 1981.

Block, P. *Flawless Consulting*. Austin, Tex.: Learning Concepts, 1981.

Bougon, M., Weick, K. E., and Binkhorst, D. "Cognition in Organizations: An Analysis of the Utrecht Jazz Orchestra." *Administrative Science Quarterly*, 1977, *22*, 606-639.

Campbell, D. T. "A Tribal Model of the Social System Vehicle Carrying Scientific Knowledge." *Knowledge: Creation, Diffusion, Utilization*, 1979, *1*, 141-201.

Cohen, M. D., and March, J. G. *Leadership and Ambiguity*. New York: McGraw-Hill, 1974.

Glassman, R. B. "Persistence and Loose Coupling in Living Systems." *Behavioral Science*, 1973, *18*, 83-98.

Heider, F. "Thing and Medium." *Psychological Issues*, 1959, *1*(3), 1-34.

Herr, H. H., and Weakland, J. H. *Counseling Elders and Their Families*. New York: Springer, 1979.

Jackson, P. W. "Lonely at the Top: Observations on the Genesis of Administrative Isolation." *School Review*, May 1977, pp. 425-432.

Jones, R. A. *Self-Fulfilling Prophecies*. Hillsdale, N.J.: Erlbaum, 1977.

Lawrence, P. R., and Lorsch, J. W. *Organization and Environment*. Homewood, Ill.: Irwin, 1969.

Lustick, I. "Explaining the Variable Utility of Disjointed Incrementalism: Four Propositions." *American Political Science Review*, 1980, *74*(2), 342-353.

McCleery, M. "Stranger in Paradise: Process and Product of a District Office." Unpublished manuscript, NIE, June 1979.

McGuire, W. J. "Personality and Susceptibility to Social Influence." In E. F. Borgatta and W. W. Lambert (Eds.), *Handbook of Personality Theory and Research.* Chicago: Rand McNally, 1968.

McKeachie, W. J. "Psychology in America's Bicentennial Year." *American Psychologist,* 1976, *31,* 819–833.

Mandler, G., and Kessen, W. *The Language of Psychology.* New York: Wiley, 1959.

March, J. G. "Footnotes to Organizational Change." *Administrative Science Quarterly,* 1981, *26,* 563–577.

Meyer, J. W., and Rowan, B. "Institutionalized Organizations: Formal Structure as Myth and Ceremony." *American Journal of Sociology,* 1977, *83,* 340–363.

Miller, J. G. *Living Systems.* New York: McGraw-Hill, 1978.

Millman, M. *The Unkindest Cut.* New York: Morrow, 1977.

Perrow, C. "Disintegrating Social Sciences." *New York University Education Quarterly,* 1981a, *12*(2), 2–9.

Perrow, C. "Normal Accident at Three Mile Island." *Society,* 1981b, *18*(5), 17–26.

Peters, T. J. "Structure as a Reorganizing Device: Shifting Attention and Altering the Flow of Biases." Unpublished manuscript, McKinsey & Co., 1979.

Peters, T. J. "Management Systems: The Language of Organizational Character and Competence." *Organizational Dynamics,* Summer 1980, pp. 3–26.

Pfeffer, J. "The Micropolitics of Organizations." In M. W. Meyer and Associates, *Environments and Organizations: Theoretical and Empirical Perspectives.* San Francisco: Jossey-Bass, 1978.

Scott, W. R. *Organizations: Rational, Natural, and Open Systems.* Englewood Cliffs, N.J.: Prentice-Hall, 1981.

Shapiro, D. H., Jr. *Precision Nirvana.* Englewood Cliffs, N.J.: Prentice-Hall, 1978.

Simon, H. A. "The Architecture of Complexity." *Proceedings of the American Philosophical Society,* 1962, *106*(6), 467–482.

Siu, R.G.K. *The Man of Many Qualities: A Legacy of the I Ching.* Cambridge, Mass.: M.I.T. Press, 1968.

Steinbruner, J. D. *The Cybernetic Theory of Decision.* Princeton, N.J.: Princeton University Press, 1974.

Thompson, J. D., and Tuden, A. "Strategies, Structures, and Processes of Organizational Decision." In J. D. Thompson, P. B. Hammond, R. W. Hawkes, B. H. Junker, and A. Tuden (Eds.), *Comparative Studies in Administration*. Pittsburgh: University of Pittsburgh Press, 1959.

Van Maanen, J. "People Processing: Strategies of Organizational Socialization." *Journal of Organizational Dynamics*, 1978, 7(1), 19–36.

Walter, G. A., and Marks, S. E. *Experiential Learning and Change*. New York: Wiley, 1981.

Weick, K. E. "Educational Organizations as Loosely Coupled Systems." *Administrative Science Quarterly*, 1976, *21*, 1–19.

Weick, K. E. "Organization Design: Organizations as Self-Designing Systems." *Organizational Dynamics*, 1977, *6*(2), 30–46.

Weick, K. E. "The Spines of Leaders." In M. W. McCall, Jr., and M. M. Lombardo (Eds.), *Leadership: Where Else Can We Go?* Durham, N.C.: Duke University Press, 1978.

Weick, K. E. *The Social Psychology of Organizing*. (2nd ed.) Reading, Mass.: Addison-Wesley, 1979.

Weick, K. E. "Psychology as Gloss." In R. A. Kasschau and C. N. Cofer (Eds.), *Psychology's Second Century*. New York: Praeger, 1981.

Weick, K. E., Gilfillan, D. P., and Keith, T. A. "The Effect of Composer Credibility on Orchestra Performance." *Sociometry*, 1973, *36*, 435–462.

Weiner, S. S. "Participation, Deadlines, and Choice." In J. G. March and J. P. Olsen (Eds.), *Ambiguity and Choice in Organizations*. Bergen, Norway: Universitetsforlaget, 1976.

Conclusion:
Critical Themes
in the Study
of Change

▣ ▣ ▣ ▣ ▣ ▣ ▣ ▣ ▣ ▣ ▣ ▣ ▣ ▣ ▣ ▣ ▣ ▣

Robert L. Kahn

If we take the nine preceding chapters as indicative of the emergent thinking of behavioral scientists about organizational change, as I believe we should, we are presented with an altered research agenda. The alterations include an enlarged conceptualization of change in human organizations, a reexamination of the obstacles to such change, and a new concern with its persistence and diffusion. Moreover, the discussion of these and the more familiar topics of intervention methods and interventionist roles is marked by a self-critical quality that is new and needed.

These assertions identify the several sections of this chapter. The extent to which they constitute an altered agenda for the study of organizational change depends on how one interprets past trends in that domain. I think most behavioral scientists have limited their theories to "planned change," by which they meant changes that *they* had planned in some state of collaboration with the formal leaders of an organization. The obstacles to such plans then consisted, predictably, of the varied forms of resistance and reluctance of people at lesser levels of hierarchy who were supposed to enact the planned changes.

As for the durability and diffusion of organizational change, little is known. Most research stops with the first icy crystals of Lewinian "refreezing." Seashore and Bowers's (1970) return to the Harwood-Weldon plant five years after their earlier measurement of change was thus exceptional, as was Miller's (1975) assessment of the Ahmedabad experiment seventeen years after the work of A. K. Rice. The concept of institutionalization has only recently been urged (Goodman, Bazerman, and Conlon, 1980) as a necessary component of theory and research on organizational change.

In this chapter I consider the implications of the preceding chapters for the conceptualization of organizational change itself, the identification of the obstacles to its accomplishment, and the factors that account for its durability and diffusion—or lack thereof. In the course of this discussion, I shall review the contributions of these chapters to two topics that have long been high on the agenda of change theorists—the goals of organizational change and the methods by which it can best be accomplished.

The Conceptualization of Organizational Change

Most research on organizations has been done on one organization at a time and for short periods. Theories of change reflect these facts and have been concerned with brief interventions in single organizations. Developmental changes in organizations have been neglected, as have changes at the species level, where populations of organizations would become the unit of analysis. Argyris, Weick, and Smith attempt, in different ways, a reconceptualization of organizational change in terms that comprehend species and life-cycle alterations as well as the more familiar planned interventions of behavioral scientists.

They share an emphasis on individual learning as the core process in organizational change, a preference for thinking about organizational change itself as learning at a different level, and a conviction that language is central to the induction of change. Argyris bases his theory of change on the distinction between two kinds of learning, single loop and double loop. Smith regards organizational change as knowledge acquisition attained only after an inevitable struggle with the "epistemological knots" that impede both organizational change itself and the development of more adequate theories of change. And Weick, who says that he uses therapy as his model for organizational change, does so in terms that emphasize learning. His conceptual therapist acts like a grammarian who gives people rules for tying together and labeling parts of their experiences. Let us consider more closely the conceptualization of organizational change proposed by each of these authors and the respects in which each is new.

Argyris's earlier work on organizational change emphasized interpersonal relationships, both as the targets of change and the means of change. The attainment of open, truth-telling, "authentic" relationships was an end in itself, and the guided enactment of such relations in T-groups or similar protected settings was the means to that end. The re-creation or adaptation of such relationships in organizational life then became the task of those men and women who had experienced the training.

The continuities between that work and Argyris's chapter in this book are substantial. The humanistic values are intact, and so is the emphasis on interpersonal transactions as the visible indicators of those values and as the prime targets in organizational change. The newer elements in Argyris's work grow out of the difficulties that he and the subjects of his research encountered as they attempted to change their mode of interpersonal behavior in organizational settings.

Patterns of behavior that reflected a striving for unilateral control, a win-or-lose orientation toward others, and a tactical concealment of feelings persisted even when they were in conflict with the actors' verbalized values and insights. Even the discovery that their behavior was not having the effects they intended failed to alter these patterns. People seemed unable to behave toward others in the ways they recommended and said they preferred.

The discontinuity between what people say and what they do is not new. It has led some theorists and practitioners of organizational change toward approaches that promise to mold behavior more directly—technostructural interventions and behavior modification, for example. Argyris and his colleague, Donald Schön, have moved instead toward a theory of organizational change that is both individual and developmental in its emphasis.

The theory is built around a series of dichotomies, beginning with the distinction between single-loop and double-loop learning—the former involving behavior changes that do not also require changes in values and other "governing variables" and the latter involving behavior changes that do require such value change. Almost without exception, people can accomplish the former and not the latter kind of change, a finding reminiscent of Rokeach's (1973) work on the stability of terminal values. Moreover, the inability to double-loop learn persists even when actions and verbalizations are inconsistent.

To take account of this gap between words and deeds, which people are alert to in others and unaware of in themselves, Argyris proposes a second dichotomy, between espoused theories and theories-in-use. Our theories-in-use, he hypothesizes, consist of values and premises about human behavior that are laid down early in life. They were among our earliest socializing experiences and they remain important and unquestioned. They continue to shape our behavior, but without awareness on our part of their continuing influence. Logically enough, we create organizations that maintain these "governing variables" intact, organizations that inhibit double-loop learning and maintain unawareness of the inhibition. Our organizations, like ourselves, avoid serious scrutiny of values and goals; they, too, are single-loop learners.

Up to this point, and it is a point very near the end of Argyris's chapter, we seem to have a theory of stability rather than change. Early socialization, values and cognitive premises buried beyond the reach of most learning experiences, and an unawareness of these facts that is reinforced by long practice and prevailing organizational norms and structures constitute a circular and change-resistant system. Argyris acknowledges the difficulties, but proposes a multistage approach to organizational change that he believes will take account of them.

It is an approach that includes individual, interpersonal, and organizational levels. Individual change is primary, however, although it is induced through training that relies mainly on interpersonal resources. Changes in the organization itself, of the kinds usually called structural, come later, as individuals bring into their organizational lives their new theories-in-use and their newly acquired ability to learn in ways that involve the examination of their own values. Two important concessions to organizational structures are built into the change process: It is to begin at the top of the organizational hierarchy, and it is to utilize groups of people who work together.

The importance of language in this approach to organizational change is paradoxical; both the problem and the solution are language-based. The problem manifests itself as an inconsistency between the kinds of interpersonal behavior people *say* they prefer and the kinds of *verbal* behavior that they are observed to use toward others. The mode of intervention involves the production of written case material by participants, a cooperative learning process in which they review and discuss such materials, and a gradual effort at acquiring the skills that express the new learning. The target of change is individual and internal, but the manifestation of change is in verbal interpersonal behavior.

Smith's thinking about organizational change has much in common with that of Argyris. Smith's core idea, that we need to change the organization of our thinking in order to think about how we change our organizing, could have served as a caption for Argyris's chapter. Smith, like Argyris, attaches great importance to distinguishing between two levels of change, one more profound than the other. He calls these morphostatic and morphogenetic, respectively, and is primarily concerned with ways of inducing the latter.

Smith's morphogenetic change, although it is not precisely defined, seems much the same as Argyris's double-loop learning— that is, change that involves the governing values of individuals or organizations. Smith recognizes this similarity but feels that Argyris's methods of change induction are morphostatic. I find the two authors to be similar in method as well as conceptualization. As evidence, consider the following elements in Smith's chapter, all of which are central to his exposition of change:

1. Although the behavior of two interacting parties can be observed, the meaning of the behavior, the relationship it represents, and the governing values it expresses must be inferred.
2. Change in such values (morphogenetic change) involves alteration from one logical type to another and is therefore not expressible as quantitative shifts on the same set of descriptive dimensions. Such change is notoriously difficult.
3. A crucial step in the creation of such change is bringing into discussion issues regarding governing values that were previously treated, by silent agreement, as undiscussable.
4. People are not aware of their own governing values.
5. The task of morphogenetic change thus involves the paradox of people discussing factors that influence their behavior but of which they are unaware.

Language has a unique significance in Smith's theory of change. As his own borrowing of the morphostatic/morphogenetic distinction from biology suggests, he believes that our choice of language and metaphor determines our view of organizations and the organizational actions of which we are capable. By implication, the social scientist who would attempt organizational change must provide a new language; the old language maintains the old ways.

Weick shares with Smith the tendency to regard organizations as quasi-biological systems. Weick calls them "natural," and, like Argyris, he emphasizes the distinction between verbalization and enactment—for example, in the anecdote about the corporate officer whose sermon on decentralization was interrupted by a teletype message from a plant manager in a distant city saying that he was going to lunch.

The newer elements in Weick's chapter are developed around the concept of loose coupling and its implications for organizational change. By a loosely coupled system, Weick means one in which change in one part does not generate necessary and predictable change in all others. Instead, the effects on other parts of the organization may be irregular, deferred, or otherwise moderated. Weick associates loose coupling with natural systems and tight coupling with rational systems, an association with which I do not agree. The important point, however, is that the degree of looseness or tightness among organizational parts is made a variable and the implications of that variable for organizational change are examined. Those implications are of two kinds.

First, the degree of looseness may itself become a target of organizational change. As Ashby (1960) points out, the difficulty of attaining equilibrium in a system is affected not only by the number of parts but by the degree of their interrelatedness (loose or tight coupling). For organizations that exist in a varied and changing environment, therefore, in which adaptability is important for continuing survival, loose coupling offers important advantages.

Second, to the extent that organizations are already loosely coupled, the nature of change and therefore the task of the behavioral scientist turned change agent are affected. It is in developing this point that Weick enlarges our conceptualization of organizational change.

For example, one cannot assume that action taken at the top of a loosely coupled organization will be rapidly emulated at other levels or that information about organizational functioning will be widely or uniformly distributed. The various organizational units are likely to be responsive to their own environments and to be linked by a limited set of shared norms, beliefs, and values. People may not be fully aware of these shared presumptions of logic, as Weick calls them, but in the absence of more mechanistic ties, they bind the organization together.

The strategy for an external change agent therefore is to respect such ties and to build on them. In doing so, he or she invites people to describe their own organizational experience in their own words and then consolidates, edits, and repunctuates the language and gives it back in somewhat different form. The change agent so described sounds like a therapist, a resemblance that Weick acknowledges. He believes that the role is particularly appropriate for the induction of change in loosely coupled systems, a hypothesis that is yet to be fully tested. In bringing the dimension of tight and loose coupling into the conceptualization of organization change, however, Weick has added an important and neglected variable.

Obstacles to Change

Four of the chapters in this book provide insight into and place emphasis on obstacles to change. Staw speaks of counterforces, Argyris of difficulties, Alderfer of problems, and Smith of knots. Obstacles and resistance to change are not new issues in organizational theory, but the emphasis is noew and represents a healthy contrast to a long period of overoptimistic claims and oversold packages.

In considering obstacles to change, we must keep in mind the deceptive nature of our concepts. When we want change, we speak of those who do not as presenting obstacles and resistance. When we want stability, we speak of perseverance and commitment among those who share our views. Behavior of people in the two situations might be identical; it is their stance relative to our own that dictates our choice of language. All this would be only semantic interest were it not for the human tendency to be influenced by our choice of language and often to be unaware that we are not influenced.

Neither opposition to change nor acceptance of it is an absolute virtue or even an organizational advantage. Every organization must have some resistance in its circuits; an organization that changed in response to every input for change would be no organization at all, for it would lack the day-to-day consistency of patterned behavior that is a defining characteristic of organization. An organization that refuses change under all circumstances is doomed.

What we require as organizational theorists is a set of criteria for assessing the appropriateness of persistence or change in organizational behavior. What we require as change agents are methods for increasing the quality of organizational decisions to alter or maintain a given course of action and for increasing the organizational ability to implement such decisions. The familiar concept of resistance would then have its place in a larger set of propositions about constancy and change in organizational life.

None of the chapters addresses these issues in their entirety. Argyris, Staw, and Alderfer postulate an inappropriate and persistent behavior pattern, search out explanations for its persistence, and propose ways of changing it. For Argyris, the persisting behavior is single-loop learning; for Staw, it is the continued investment of energy and resources in the face of sufficient evidence against doing so. For Alderfer, the change-resistant element is racism, which he defines as recurrent behavioral patterns with associated intellectual justifications.

These are very different kinds of behavior, and there are other differences as well. Argyris is more personality oriented than the others, and Staw is more concerned with immediate situational factors. Alderfer emphasizes the uniqueness of racist behavior; to the extent that he is willing to generalize, he does so at the level of group and intergroup relations. All three authors conclude, however, that the persisting behavior patterns with which they are concerned are sustained by deep-lying, individually held values, that the resistance of these behavior patterns to most attempts at change is explained in part by individual unawareness of the values that govern the behaviors, and that change through appropriate social-psychological intervention is nevertheless feasible. Let us examine these convergent themes as they appear in each chapter.

For Argyris, the persisting behaviors in question are interpersonal. He interprets them as reflecting a preference for unilateral control rather than joint decision making, for overcoming an apparent adversary rather than seeking mutually favorable outcome, for concealing one's feelings rather than acknowledging or expressing them directly, for "rational" (that is, emotion denying) solutions to problems, and for a face-saving etiquette of avoiding discussions that threaten these preferences. These value preferences and the beliefs associated with them are the variables that govern interpersonal behavior, at least in organizational settings. They do so universally, so far as Argyris's present evidence indicates.

All this is inferred from observations of interpersonal behavior. The governing variables are typically unacknowledged by the individuals themselves, not merely as part of a public presentation of self, but because people are genuinely unaware of them. People infer them in others, but not in themselves. This unawareness and denial, Argyris hypothesizes, means that such values and beliefs are laid down early in life, as part of the child's socialization into the world as it is.

To change them, therefore, requires nothing less than resocialization; didactic efforts and verbalized insights will not suffice. Indeed, the intensive combination of modeling, practice, and cooperative group interaction that Argyris describes fits the parameters of socialization well. Whether the process will diffuse through an organization without a comparably intensive effort with each interacting group remains to be determined.

Alderfer's treatment of racism among white men in organizations can be read as a special case of Argyris's assertions about interpersonal behavior, heightened by the visibility of group boundaries and by long historical usage. The persisting behaviors of whites, as Alderfer describes them, demean, subvert, or destroy the present condition or future potential of members of the subordinate racial group. Most white men would deny such behaviors and intentions. They would explain the disadvantaged position of blacks, if they acknowledged it, in terms of properties of blacks—physical, biological, social, or cultural—not in terms of behavior of whites. They are particularly unwilling to acknowledge that the differential status and rewards of the two races reflect differences in power or that their own material rewards result in part from their racial advantage.

These are contested assertions, and Alderfer would add that the unwillingness of whites to accept them is additional proof of their validity. This puts the (white male) researcher or critic in an untenable position, which is where Alderfer thinks he belongs. Organizational research continues to be a white male occupation and the authorship of these chapters illustrates that fact, as Alderfer points out. However one may feel about these matters, Alderfer's central points are beyond question: that interpersonal behaviors across racial lines are peculiarly difficult to modify, that white men tend to explain these difficulties and others in race relations in terms of black rather than white characteristics, and that many of the motives, values, and beliefs that underpin interracial behaviors are not readily accessible.

Like Argyris, Alderfer considers such values, beliefs, and behaviors modifiable nevertheless, and like Argyris, he describes an approach to modifying them that relies heavily on the direct production of the behaviors to be modified under special circumstances and on a process of cooperative learning. Alderfer's "microcosm group," like Argyris's natural organizational groups, is a device for resocialization.

The construction of microcosm groups is done in a way that represents the subpopulations whose relations are to be studied and, presumably, modified. Microcosm groups are necessary because subpopulations of potential interest (black-white, male-female, young-old, and the like) are very different in overall size and in organizational location. The underrepresentation of blacks and women in higher management, for example, is such that their substantial participation in the discussion of the phenomenon and the reasons for it requires the construction of "artificial" groups. More important, the significant presence in the microcosm group of the relevant minority population provides a setting in which most white men are not otherwise required to function. The experience of doing so is an important element in the resocialization experience.

Alderfer reminds us that these assertions come from work still ongoing. Quantitative data to support them are not offered in this chapter, and I therefore regard them as hypotheses—hypotheses well worth testing.

Staw discusses commitment to a given behavior pattern and escalation, which is a special case of commitment, as counterforces to change. Commitment is certainly antithetical to change; many investigators define it in those terms. Staw comes close to doing so; commitment is for him the set of psychological and situational forces that bind individuals to an action and therefore make change difficult. Staw's contribution consists of an insightful review of the experimental literature that deals with such forces, their integration into a comprehensive model that predicts commitment, and a number of interesting suggestions about ways to reduce inappropriately high levels of decisional commitment in organizational life.

The commonalities with Argyris and Alderfer are significant, although Staw gives much more importance than they to current situational factors. Let us consider first the commonalities and then the differences.

Staw assumes that in order to abandon a line of behavior to which one has been committed, a person must often alter the beliefs and cognitions about the world that led to the behavior in the first place and that supported its continuation. Such beliefs and the values that underpin them are highly resistant to change, as Alderfer and Argyris point out in other contexts. Staw's model of commitment also emphasizes the positive effects on the self of persisting in a line of action. Doing so reaffirms and justifies the original decision and therefore the wisdom and competence of the actor as decision maker. This aspect of Staw's model fits Argyris's emphasis on face-saving, winning through, and controlling as dominant elements in the theory-in-use of his managerial subjects. To the extent that these and the social norms of consistency and resoluteness against odds have been internalized, the task of increasing a person's flexibility (decreasing the commitment syndrome) requires the kind of adult resocialization that Argyris and Alderfer explore.

Staw is also interested in situational factors that affect commitments, however, and his review of the experimental literature suggests a number of them: the extent to which the person made the initial decision or shared in doing so, the extent to which the person will be judged responsible for a failure if the previous line of action is changed, and the extent to which the decision to persist or change is judged on the basis of past events ("sunk costs") rather than future cost/benefit prospects. Consideration of these factors leads Staw to propose such commitment-countering organizational measures as managerial rotation, attention to expert advice of people not involved in the original line of action, and reduced weighting of consistency as a criterion for promotion.

Commitment and perseverance are among the prime virtues in our culture, and it is difficult to think of them as dysfunctional under any circumstances. Designers of organizations typically attempt to increase commitment (by which they usually mean persistent performance of assigned tasks) at lower hierarchical levels. It is an important contribution on Staw's part to have illuminated the essential contradiction between leadership as commitment to an established course of action and leadership as the ability to initiate an alternative and more appropriate course. Where commitment is absolute, learning is absolutely excluded. In treating commitment as a counterforce to change, Staw has pointed up these paradoxical issues and has provided a number of testable hypotheses for moderating managerial overcommitment to more appropriate levels.

Durability and Diffusion in Organizational Change

Two chapters in this book, one by Goodman and Dean and the other by Cole, deal with the issues of durability and diffusion. They complement the chapters by Argyris, Smith, Alderfer, and Staw, all of which are concerned with unwanted or inappropriate persistencies in organizational life. The latter authors are searching for factors that account for what might be termed primary failures in organizational change, that is, the inability of an organization to induce a needed change in the first place. Goodman and Dean address a secondary form of failure, failure of organizations to maintain an induced change. Cole continues the analysis of factors in durability and diffusion at the cross-national level.

The maintenance of an organizational change is not an all-or-nothing phenomenon, and Goodman and Dean propose a model that incorporates this fact. They treat the institutionalization of change as a continuum defined by a hypothetical Guttman scale that begins with knowledge of the change and includes successively performance, preference, and incorporation in norms and values. Only when a change has been so incorporated do Goodman and Dean regard it as institutionalized. These successive criteria of institutionalization are predicted directly by five processes, which are in turn predicted by the structural properties of the organization and of the change itself.

Goodman and Dean explore the utility of the model by ordering nine instances of planned organizational change according to their observed degree of institutionalization and then examining their rank order on each of the processual and structural variables in the model. The result is a set of eighteen hypotheses (more or less, depending on how conservatively one reads the ranked data), all of them predictive of institutionalization. For example, the prospects for successful institutionalization of a planned change appear to be enhanced by the socialization of the new members, by opportunity for acts of explicit commitment at all hierarchical levels, by the provision of both intrinsic and extrinsic rewards for change, and by making such rewards clearly contingent on the maintenance of the changed behavior.

The importance of developing and testing such hypotheses is indicated by the apparent low success rate of planned change efforts when they are judged by the hard criteria of persistence over time. The Goodman-Dean sample is small, but it is the best we have and its conservative findings about the successful institutionalization of change fit the single-case experiences of other investigators. Behavioral science needs to study and understand the conditions that determine the persistence of organizational change or reversion to the status quo ante. Such work must ultimately include technological as well as social-psychological forms of change because the institutionalization of some technical innovations (the computer, for example) shows a pace and success rate unmatched by the organizational innovations of behavioral science itself. Cross-national comparisons are also needed because of the substantial differences between countries in their institutionalization and diffusion of similar organizational changes.

Cole extends the Goodman and Dean discussion in this and in several other ways. He adds cases; he provides information on diffusion between organizations as well as within them; and, most important, he compares the institutionalization of certain changes in work organizations in three countries—Japan, Sweden, and the United States. In bringing the discussion to the level of national differences, Cole necessarily makes qualitative and judgmental assessments. He concludes that in the United States the diffusion of participatory work structures has been very limited, with few companies involved and limited parts of them singled out for trial. In Japan, certain forms of worker participation have become very widespread, as part of a corporate strategy to mobilize all resources in the firm to overcome foreign and domestic competitive threats, rather than in service of larger social values. By contrast, in Sweden, participation in decisions at the shop floor level has been urged with some success in terms of a broad ideology of democratization and social justice.

Cole explores these national differences through a sequence of stages that ends with the widely diffused implementation of change: initial motivation, search, discovery, transmission, decision, and implementation. I find his identification of factors retarding the diffusion of participatory organizational changes in the United

States to be highly relevant to the analysis of obstacles and counterforces in the chapters already discussed. Cole's analysis implies that in the United States the organizational change agenda of behavioral science, if we can so describe a loosely aggregated array of proposals and activities, have simply had insufficient support from the larger society. Without such support, organizational changes do not take root.

Cole asserts that the initial motivation of chronic labor shortage, important in both Japan and Sweden, was lacking in the United States. So, in earlier years, was a sense of urgency with respect to international competition. The infrastructure of change-facilitating organizations—private and governmental, management and union —which was prominent and favorable to participatory change in Japan and Sweden, was neither well developed nor favorable in the United States. In short, Cole regards the diffusion of participatory work structures as a social movement, and he finds the conditions for such a movement lacking in the United States.

All this raises a number of questions that social scientists should ponder. One is an apparent process of diffusion that leaps national boundaries. The agenda of participatory organizational change that Japan and Sweden have adapted to their own national circumstances originated with American and British behavioral science. We must enlarge our theories of diffusion to explain simultaneously the failures near at hand and the successes at great distance; simple notions of spread through contiguous structures will not suffice.

Another question about the role of behavioral science and organizational change is raised by Cole and remains for us to answer. It is the paradoxical fact that behavioral scientists have been most active as organizational consultants and change agents in the United States, where the institutionalization and diffusion of such changes have been least successful. In Japan and Sweden, the responsibility for initiating and maintaining these changes has been more clearly with management and labor, relatively unassisted or undiluted by the efforts of behavioral scientists. This is a judgment that should be tested and, even if confirmed, may have only spurious associations with the lesser success of change efforts in this country.

The scrutiny of one's own discipline is often salutary, however, and this point invites such scrutiny.

The Exchange of Advice

Behavioral scientists do research, and behavioral scientists interested in the creation and diffusion of organizational change will continue to do research on that complex and intriguing phenomenon, in spite of its inherent difficulties. The chapters of this book, all of them by people active in such research, serve both to describe its present state and prescribe its future agenda. We can thus extract from these chapters the advice, explicit and implicit, that this group of behavioral scientists offered to each other and to their colleagues in research on organizational change.

Much of that advice is summarized in the second part of Lawler's chapter, and I will indicate the elements that it shares with chapters already discussed:

1. *Vision is critical.* This statement by Lawler, emphasizing the importance of shared goals and values in organizational change, has its counterparts in other chapters. Lawler argues that an explicit normative concept of the organization both energizes and directs the change efforts of participants. This is akin to Smith's emphasis on metaphor, Argyris's search for governing variables, and Cole's discussion of ideology as a factor in successful change. Goals are also explicit in the Goodman-Dean model.

2. *Planned change cannot be wholly planned.* Insistence on explicit goals does not imply rigidity of plan. On the contrary, Lawler says that changes seldom go as planned. Cole's description of participatory changes as social movements shows their variety in spite of common theoretical origins. Argyris has warned elsewhere of the unintended consequences of rigorous research. The creation of a participatory organization in detailed conformity with the prior plans of behavioral scientists is a contradiction of terms.

3. *Change is a process, not an event.* This statement by Lawler is a further warning against the application of conventional labora-

tory canons in organizational change. The brief manipulation of single variables, one for each experiment, is likely to produce a long sequence of unchanged organizations. This assertion fits with the emphasis on process and diffusion in the chapters of Goodman and Dean and others. A significant set of related changes, occurring throughout a well-bounded system or subsystem, is likely to be necessary for the attainment of a new stability. The low success rate cited by Goodman and Dean, and by Cole, is understandable in these terms.

4. *Our data are not their data.* This is perhaps the most difficult advice for behavioral scientists to absorb. Especially among those who rely on quantitative methods, large-scale surveys, and the like, the effort to change organizations has been built around a process of making such data "theirs." Weick and Smith, Argyris and Alderfer enter into the change process in ways more consistent with this dictum; they work the immediate data of interpersonal exchange, offering their own insights and "repunctuations" as commentary intrinsic to the process.

I am not prepared to judge quantitative measurement irrelevant to organizational change, nor does Lawler advocate doing so. I do concur with the idea that successful change requires attention to the criteria of judgment of those involved. Cole's reminder of the Japanese and Swedish experience is relevant; it shows substantial change toward participatory structures with modest amounts of measurement. We in the United States show something approximating the reverse pattern.

It is possible to include an increased understanding of measurement and data among the goals of organizational change. The Japanese appear to have done so successfully in the area of product quality. Nevertheless, change programs in participation must begin by taking into account the kinds of evidence on which participants act.

Conclusion

The title of this chapter refers to an altered agenda for research on organizational change. In this context, the word *agenda,* with its vague parliamentary associations, may overstate the case. The population of scholars who do research on organizational change is an aggregation of individuals. They influence each other, for the most part, by reading and writing—or rather, by writing and being read. The kind of direct influential exchange that produced this book is a rare event. To describe an agenda for research on organizational change, therefore, is an act of advocacy and an expression of personal preference rather than a statement of consensus and joint resolution. These, then, are my preferences for research on organizational change:

Study the processes of change. Mohr (1982) distinguishes between variance theories, in which the aim is to account for as much of the variability as possible in some criterion measure, and process theories, in which the aim is to describe how some outcome of interest occurs. Process theories incorporate a script, tell a story, and explain how something comes about.

We need process theories of organizational change, theories that tell us how such change comes about, what the characteristic sequence of events is, how the change becomes stabilized in its original locus, how it diffuses to others, how it is limited in time and space—and how the stability it then represents is in turn upset. To ask for such theories and the research that develops them is not antiquantitative; processes can be described in quantitative terms. They need not be, however. The Mendelian theory of genetic inheritance is not basically quantitative, nor is the double helix of Watson and Crick.

Study change over time. This is a corollary of the preceding point; processes take time. A process is a series of events, and to understand the process we must observe the series. In organizational change, the series may be long and the time period substantial.

It is easy to recommend the study of such series, but it is hard to act on the recommendation. Organizational hospitality has its limits, and so does the patience of investigators. The pressure to publish encourages short-cycle research, not extended observations of organizational life, and the observation of organizational change must often be abbreviated. My advice to the researcher would be, "Stay if you can. Return if you cannot stay. Use retrospective data if you must. But study the process of organizational change over time."

Study ongoing organizational changes. Organizations change by merger and acquisition, and by managerial succession. They change as they attempt to incorporate some new technology—word processors and computer terminals in the office, for example, or robotic machines on the shop floor. Moreover, organizations are "born" and they "die"—the two greatest of changes.

How quickly we can develop a general theory of organizational change that comprehends these phenotypically different sequences of events remains to be seen. I think that we must anticipate an extended period in which they will be treated separately in some respects, but I would hope for increasing convergence of concepts and explanations.

The emphasis on these kinds of change does not exclude experiments of investigator-initiated change in organizations, but it locates such change as one type in a large array—and not at the head of the list for the development of a process theory.

Study organizational change in relation to environmental events. Some organizational changes have their origins in the internal dynamics of organizational life. Most, I suspect, begin as responses to environmental constraints, demands, or opportunities. These may be actual or imagined, present or anticipated. They are, however, part of the change process; they are its context, and we understand change more profoundly when they are included in the research and in the process theory. The inclusion of such contextual factors is implied also by the conception of organizations as open systems. Most organizational scholars share this conception, but its implications are not apparent in most research on organizational change.

Study populations of organizations as well as single organizational units. Like individuals, organizations change in many ways. They grow, they develop (become more differentiated), they learn. To be more precise, let us say that organizations change by means of processes that appear to reflect learning; the processes include the acquisition of information, both through direct experience and symbolic means, the interpretation of such information, and the manifestation of subsequent behavior that incorporates the interpreted information in some fashion.

The limits of change, however, are different for individuals and organizations. Some characteristics of mature organisms—presence or absence of a prehensile tail, for example—do not change in the individual case. They do, however, change in populations of the organisms over succeeding generations. Theories of evolution address such changes; theories of learning and development deal with change of the individual sort.

The organizational case is interesting because such distinctions cannot be easily made. Human organizations may be evolving into ever larger and more differentiated forms, but individual organizations can also undergo gross changes in size and other structural characteristics. Units can be added or eliminated; whole organizations can divide, combine, or in other ways "re-organize."

We need to understand organizational change at the population level as well as in the individual case, and we can do so only through the study of populations of organizations. Processes of change occur at both levels.

Get out of the way. Textbooks are full of advice about the superiority of true experimental designs, their unique strengths for causal inference, and the importance of manipulating the experimental variable oneself while controlling all else. For some purposes this is good advice, and designs that incorporate it will continue to contribute to the march of science.

It is, however, a limited strategy for our purposes. The suns of organizational change do not revolve around the small domain of the researcher, nor are their large movements defined by the experimenter's small forces. And even if the researcher could manipulate a single variable and keep all else still, little might be learned. The processes of organizational change probably involve many driving forces, not one, and a succession of favorable modifications in context rather than immobility. One can imagine an enlarged experimental strategy that takes account of such issues. Meantime, I believe that we will learn most about the process of organizational change by studying full-scale manifestations of that process rather than by reducing it to the size of our experimental powers.

The six preceding points are idiosyncratic. They are not, however, the points that I would have urged on students of organizational change before attending the conference on which these chapters are based. They are an outcome of the Carnegie-Mellon Conference, but they are my outcome. Readers must construct their own. May they lead us to understand more deeply the ways of change in human organizations.

References

Ashby, W. R. *Design for a Brain*. (2nd ed.) New York: Wiley, 1960.

Goodman, P. S., Bazerman, M., and Conlon, E. "Institutionalization of Planned Organizational Change." In B. M. Staw and L. L. Cummings (Eds.), *Research in Organizational Behavior*. Greenwich, Conn.: JAI Press, 1980.

Miller, E. J. "Socio-Technical Systems in Weaving, 1953–1970: A Follow-Up Study." *Human Relations*, 1975, *28*, 349–386.

Mohr, L. B. *Explaining Organizational Behavior: The Limits and Possibilities of Theory and Research*. San Francisco: Jossey-Bass, 1982.

Rokeach, M. *The Nature of Human Values*. New York: Free Press, 1973.

Seashore, S. E., and Bowers, D. G. "The Durability of Organizational Change." *American Psychologist*, 1970, *25*(3), 227–233.

Name Index

■ ■ ■ ■ ■ ■ ■ ■ ■ ■ ■ ■ ■ ■ ■ ■ ■ ■

430

Subject Index